IN OUR TIME

IN OUR TIME

Edited by
Melvyn Bragg
A companion to the Radio 4 series

HODDER &
STOUGHTON

First published in Great Britain in 2009 by Hodder & Stoughton
An imprint of Hodder & Stoughton
An Hachette UK company

I

Copyright © Melvyn Bragg 2009

The right of Melvyn Bragg to be identified as the Author of the Work has been asserted
by him in accordance with the Copyright, Designs and Patents Act 1988.

By arrangement with the BBC.
The BBC logo is a trademark of the British Broadcasting Corporation and is used under licence.
BBC logo © BBC 1996

A CIP catalogue record for this title is available from the British Library

Hardback ISBN 978 0 340 97750 7
Trade Paperback ISBN 978 0 340 98053 8

Typeset in Garamond Three by Hewer Text UK Ltd

Printed and bound in the UK by CPI Mackays, Chatham ME5 8TD

Hodder & Stoughton policy is to use papers that are natural, renewable and recyclable products and
made from wood grown in sustainable forests. The logging and manufacturing processes are expected
to conform to the environmental regulations of the country of origin.

Hodder & Stoughton Ltd
338 Euston Road
London NW1 3BH

www.hodder.co.uk

To Alan Blaikley

CONTENTS

INTRODUCTION

In Our Time began with a sacking: mine. In 1998 I was appointed to the House of Lords and the BBC decided that *Start The Week* should be stripped of my presence to preserve its political integrity. As far as any of us on the programme could remember there had been no politics on *Start The Week* during my ten years in the chair, but I left with no complaints.

I'd been very lucky to broadcast on one of Radio 4's bedrock programmes. The producer, Marina Salandy Brown, and I introduced scientists, historians and philosophers on to that Monday morning slot, and changed the nature of the programme. A change which I am glad that my successor Jeremy Paxman and his successor Andrew Marr have kept.

Being fired turned out to be one of the best things that has happened to me in my broadcasting life. James Boyle, the then Controller of Radio 4, engineered a return to the air for what he called 'a ring-fenced programme' on what was then known as 'the death slot', Thursday mornings just after nine. I was grateful for his offer and the result was a programme I was able to build from scratch. Save for the weeks when the homework is too heavy or too obscure, I love doing it: a seminar without an exam at the end of it – though at times the seminar *is* the exam.

The idea was gradually to end the plugging of books, to focus on one subject only, to range over an eclectic and as intellectually demanding a spectrum as we could manage, to court unpredictability of subjects and, above all, to cast only scholars who were also teaching academics. It took a while to complete the jigsaw but these were the aims and eventually we got there. Olivia Seligman was the initial and enabling producer and away we went.

James Boyle supplied the wonderfully incongruous title. Helen Boaden, his successor as Controller of Radio 4, extended the programme from thirty minutes, which was just too tight, to forty-five, which gave it breath and made it possible to drive through a decent argument. Mark Damazer, the current Controller, has supported us in word, elliptical emails and deed. For instance, it was his idea to have the consecutive daily run for the four *Darwin In Our Time* programmes.

This book is a selection from the several hundred programmes broadcast over the last eleven years.

At first I thought that I would cut out choice pieces from scores of programmes and aim at a patchwork quilt. Or arrange gobbets from several programmes in disciplined sections: Physics, Philosophy, History, Biology, etc. Or simply pick out what seemed the juiciest bits and pitch them together rather as Ted Hughes and Seamus Heaney did in their *Rattle-Bag* collection. And there were other schemes, but none, I concluded, served the purpose.

This was to give to those interested the full benefit of the learning of the often outstandingly distinguished contributors. No matter they were asked to pour the accumulation of decades of scholarship into a half pint, at most a pint glass, they never wavered in the attempt to bring to the table the essence of their research so that the listeners got a taste of the best. And they do this with a lucid eloquence which is courteous even when they disagree.

I have kept the conversational nature of these discussion programmes intact. There are a few small cuts. About 95 per cent of the programmes are live and in the effort to press for concision there are often the manoeuvrings of 'sort of', 'actually', 'in a sense', like the minor adjustments ships make as they prepare to dock. Many of those have gone, as have the remarkably few repetitions.

Again, after several variations, I settled for the simplest form which was to lay out the discussions like a conversation and not for example turn it into a prose piece, which was one of many rejected ideas. You could say this discussion form had its origin in one of the oldest and most influential of all intellectual forms – the *Dialogues* of Plato. You could also bring less flattering examples to bear. But at this level it is, I think, an effective way to bring often complex ideas to an interested public without losing the complexity of the idea or, I hope, the interest of the public.

So here we go. From Socrates to the Fibonacci Sequence, from Plate Tectonics to the Calendar, Agincourt to Angels, the Peasants' Revolt to the Origins of Mathematics, Witchcraft to the Siege of Constantinople, Darwin to the Divine Right of Kings, the Field of the Cloth of Gold to Cryptography and more.

There were many contenders hard to leave out, especially, perhaps, the Alphabet. For some reason it became a toss-up between that and the Calendar. Yet it seems at the very least ungrateful to leave out what the Chambers Encyclopaedia calls 'a system of writing theoretically having a one-to-one relation between character (or letter) and phoneme'. And then there are the iconographic and ideographic writings of ancient man, cuneiform, hieroglyphics and our own alphabet begat by the Romans, heavily influenced by the Greeks. And the Cyrillic, Hebrew, Arabic . . .

Then I discovered that I had selected twenty-six 'chapters' and the way to pay a tribute to the apparently infinite power of these mere twenty-six letters was open.

a

—

The Calendar

T he calendar orders the lives of millions of people. It is an invention that gives meaning to the passing of time, it marks out our daily existence. It links us to the arcane movements of the heavens and the natural rhythms of the earth. It is both deeply practical and profoundly sacred.

But where does this strange and complex creation come from? Why does the week last seven days but the year twelve months? Who formed these concepts and through them shaped our lives? The answers involve Babylonian astronomers and Hebrew theologians, Roman emperors and English scholars. Isaac Newton, for instance, designed a calendar said to be mathematically flawless but no one could understand it. Gregory XIII seems to have got it right.

With me to discuss the calendar are Robert Poole, Reader in History at St Martin's College, Lancaster, and author of *Time's Alteration: Calendar Reformation in Early Modern England*; Kristen Lippincott, Deputy Director of the National Maritime Museum in Greenwich; and Peter Watson, Research Associate at the McDonald Institute for Archaeological Research at Cambridge University, and author of *A Terrible Beauty: A History of the People and Ideas that Shaped the Modern Mind*.

Kristen Lippincott, what were the first calendars based on?

KRISTEN LIPPINCOTT: The best way to think about the calendar is to put yourself back in the shoes of ancient man. You're sitting there in the middle of some field, watching the daily rhythms, and the first rhythm that you really notice, beyond day and night, is the waxing and waning of the moon. You notice that every twenty-eight days you get a full moon back, and almost all of the early calendars are lunar calendars. In fact we have lunar calendars dating back to 10,000 BC.

The next big cycle that you notice is the cycle of the year, and the first one is usually by the stars. When certain bright stars appear on the horizon, it marks the beginning of a new year. And then the third thing that you notice is that the sun is in the same place in the sky after 365 days. So those are the three basic kinds of calendars that you can have: a lunar calendar, a sidereal or star calendar, or a solar or sun calendar.

MELVYN BRAGG: Were these seen to be useful for diurnal existence from the very beginning?

KRISTEN LIPPINCOTT: Certainly we find that most early calendars, and most religious calendars, are lunar based, because it's something seen in the moon every night, waxing and waning, it's something that is ingrained very much in people's souls, if you like. Those of us who live in cities now don't really notice it. You can imagine, before electric lights, whether or not it was a full moon really mattered to people's lives, and so we find that most of the early religious calendars are lunar and are very deeply ingrained.

Beyond this, of course, the stars and the sun mark the seasons, so they tell you when to plant, when to reap, when to sow. Also things like navigation were based on calendars. There's a passage, I think in Homer, where it says: 'don't sail unless the Pleiades are rising on the horizon with the sun.'

MELVYN BRAGG: And then Hesiod talks about farming and agriculture with regard to the seasons.

KRISTEN LIPPINCOTT: All his *Works and Days* is saying is 'when the slug climbs the tree, that's the time when Orion is rising'. It really gives you a very good calendar that still works today.

MELVYN BRAGG: And that kind of country lore – 'when the slug climbs the tree' – lingered on in this country, in country areas, until quite recently.

KRISTEN LIPPINCOTT: Certainly the *Farmers' Almanac*, which you can still buy – not at any newsstand, but it is available – tells you that kind of folklore, which is true. It's based on observation.

MELVYN BRAGG: Peter Watson, as I understand it the first sophisticated calendar was developed by the Babylonians, who were mathematicians and astronomers. Could you tell us about that calendar?

PETER WATSON: As Kristen says, they noticed that there are twelve lunations, twelve months in a year, more or less. They had their twelve months, then they had an extra period. This has happened all over the world. A sort of thirteenth month of varying lengths, generally regarded as unlucky. But it was the Babylonians who devised this system based on sixty, sixty being the lowest common multiple of twelve and thirty, or roughly the number of days in a month. The Babylonians therefore gave us minutes and seconds, as well as weeks and years and days. The Latinisation of this is still based on sixty.

And the first division of this was called '*pars minuti prima*' in Latin, the 'first small division', and that phrase became corrupted to 'minute' and the second division was '*pars partes minutae seconde*', and that phrase in time became corrupted to 'second'. And then they also noticed that as the sun rises it passes through the stars and this idea comes down to us, via the Greeks, as the Zodiac – the Greek word 'zodion', meaning 'little animal'. Some of the stars in the sky were shapes. As the Babylonians saw it they looked like animals, and so this is how we arrive at both the Zodiac and the fact that it is a circle around a point, which we now divide into 360 degrees. It's all related to the same system.

MELVYN BRAGG: What did they do with the days that were left over?

PETER WATSON: This was called the intercollated month and it was regarded, not just in Babylon but in other early cultures around the world, as very bad luck. You were very careful about what you did on those days and some cultures don't even give this period a name. To name it was to make it even worse luck.

MELVYN BRAGG: Would you consider this to be a great legacy that the Babylonians passed on? Was this brought together for the first time in an extensive and coherent form by them?

PETER WATSON: Yes. The smaller parts of the calendar are the Babylonian legacy. As I say, everybody could notice the year and the months. The Babylonians regarded the seventh day, the fourteenth day, the twenty-first day and the twenty-eighth day as unlucky, and there were various taboos on what you could do on those days, and there you see the beginning of the week. They also regarded the twentieth day as very lucky, because the twentieth day of any one month was the forty-ninth day of the previous month. That's seven times seven, regarded as lucky. And the 'full moon day' was known as the 'shabatum', I think I've got that right. When the Jews then went into exile in Babylon, they appropriate the word as 'Shabbat', the Sabbath, the day on which you don't really do any work. That has come down to us from the Babylonians, and we still have the word and the concept of the Sabbath.

MELVYN BRAGG: Who did the Babylonians pass this calendar on to, who took it to the next stage?

PETER WATSON: I think both the Greeks took a lot of it on and, in time, the Romans. And the Romans eventually developed through the Julian reforms many new things. But the astrological influence that the Babylonians seemed to have started round about 500 BC has come down to us in the astrological week that we still essentially use.

MELVYN BRAGG: You mentioned the Romans – how did the early Roman calendar work?

PETER WATSON: According to legend the first king of Rome, Romulus, had a ten-month calendar.

MELVYN BRAGG: Why was that?

PETER WATSON: It began in March. To begin with they seem not to have had any words for what we now call January and February. People may have wondered why September, which is the ninth month, is based on a word that means seventh, and this is because originally the Roman year started after the spring equinox in March.

MELVYN BRAGG: So they just didn't bother with those? They had two fallow months there that they weren't even going to count?

PETER WATSON: Not to begin with, no.

MELVYN BRAGG: They didn't count them at all?

PETER WATSON: No. Then later on, the second king of Rome, I think it was, introduced February and January. And to begin with February came before January and later still this was changed and January started the year. But they also had, the same as the Babylonians, this overlap period, this intercollated thirteenth month, which they call 'Mercedonius', which is our word 'mercenary', meaning 'wages', because this was when all the people got paid. That eventually dropped out and we come to the Julian reforms.

MELVYN BRAGG: Let's talk about the Julian reforms with you, Robert Poole. What did Julius Caesar find wrong about the calendar that he thought needed reforming?

ROBERT POOLE: He found that the calendar, the Roman calendar, which had been more or less inherited wholesale from Egypt, had slipped out of sync with the year by very nearly a hundred days. This was partly because the Egyptian measurement of the year at 365 and a quarterish days was not quite right but partly also because these intercalary days and months had been manipulated for various political purposes to influence the dates of elections and the length of terms of office.

MELVYN BRAGG: You mean the days that didn't really count, the priests and politicians would just use to extend their stay in office?

ROBERT POOLE: That's right. And for some reason the balls had all rolled to one side of the snooker table. All the days had accumulated and the year was nearly three months out of sync. What should have been the time of the spring equinox was actually being counted in winter. So, in 45 BC there was a great year of confusion, which consisted of 445 days, which put everything back on line, and then Caesar got his astronomer, Sosigenes the Greek, to come up with a new calculation of the year, and they got it at 365 and a quarter days, and Caesar instituted the system of leap years – one day extra every four years – that kept the calendar more or less on track for many centuries to come. They were only eleven minutes out, on average, for each year, and it was centuries before anybody even noticed, so it was remarkably accurate.

MELVYN BRAGG: How successfully was this reform implemented? Did people begin to take the calendar more seriously because it was more accurate?

ROBERT POOLE: We don't have any records or information about that. The interesting thing is that you could actually put all these extra days in a year and it doesn't seem to have had any massive ill-effects in a slow agricultural society that didn't always calculate very precisely by days.

MELVYN BRAGG: Did it have any other uses, this calendar that Caesar implanted? We know him best in this country as a general, or whatever title he had, a warlord in some way. Did it help those administrative, military arrangements to have a more accurate calendar?

ROBERT POOLE: It certainly helped taxation. In fact the Roman cycle of taxation, the Indiction, remained in use in the Christian Church until the early modern period. The Romans were famous for being extremely well-organised people and the taxation system was helped no end by having accurate years.

PETER WATSON: Maybe we should point out that Julius Caesar was assassinated the year after the changes, and a lot of people thought that this was because he interfered with the calendar.

MELVYN BRAGG: He was assassinated under the old system, on the Ides of March, wasn't he?

PETER WATSON: That's right, yes.

MELVYN BRAGG: What about those Ides – was that the way the Roman calendar worked before Caesar got hold of it?

ROBERT POOLE: I'd have to pass that one over to Peter, the classicist.

PETER WATSON: Their month was divided into the Kalends, which started on the new moon – that's where our word 'calendar' comes from – into the Ides, which was on the full moon – Ides I think is derived from the word meaning 'to divide' – and the Nones, which was eight days before. They'd numbered the days and this was the system in use in Rome really until Christian times. And the astrological week that we use now caught on because astrology became very popular in Augustan Rome.

MELVYN BRAGG: Can we talk about the Christian calendar now, Kristen Lippincott? When did the Christians start to have a voice in the calendar?

KRISTEN LIPPINCOTT: The early Christians just kept on with the Roman calendar and didn't really change it at all, except probably with a man named Dionysius Exiguus or, as we often say, Denis the Short. He was the one that said why should we good Christians be keeping a Roman calendar, shouldn't we have a calendar based on the life of Christ? So he was the first one that really focused on the day of Easter, and that's when the problems started to arise with the calendar because Easter is, essentially, an inheritance from a lunar calendar and the Roman civil year is, essentially, a solar calendar, and one of the problems with the lunar cycles and the solar cycles is they don't match. That's to say they only line up once every nineteen years and this is why Easter's a moveable feast. It slides backwards and forwards in the civil calendar and this is when the problem began, because people said how are we going to start to fix our religious feasts, how are we even going to know when the religious feasts happen, when we've got this problem? And for about 500 years almost every educated monk was involved in calendar studies.

MELVYN BRAGG: And just to restate for people who may not be as up to date with early Christian history: the idea of dating Easter correctly was astoundingly important to early Christians, wasn't it? Crucial is a better word.

KRISTEN LIPPINCOTT: Yes. If your whole religion – that's perhaps putting it too broadly – but if you are a Christian one of the main reasons you are a Christian is because on a certain day, with a certain kind of celestial configuration, Christ was reborn. If you don't know what day that is, then this becomes really worrying.

One of the things that was established in the fourth century was that the Council of Nicaea said we must fix the date of Easter, we must know when this happens and they came up with a formula that's quite complex, and I probably won't remember it correctly, so please someone jump in and help me . . .

MELVYN BRAGG: Shall I push it over to Robert, he's worked it out. Can you tell us why it was so difficult a day, Easter, Robert Poole, and what factors were involved that made it difficult?

ROBERT POOLE: It's not just a matter of combining a lunar calendar with a solar calendar and the two not fitting. There are also political or religious considerations because Christ was crucified around about the time of the Jewish feast of the Passover, which is lunar, but the one thing the early Christians wanted to do was to distance themselves from the Jewish calendar, the Jewish religion and Jewish practice. So they had to find a method of having an Easter which on the one hand would track the Passover, so that Easter was happening at the right time of the year, but on the other hand it wouldn't actually reproduce it.

As a further complication, the Christian holiday was a Sunday whereas the Jewish one was a Saturday. The eventual result was the formula that Easter should be on the first Sunday on or after the first full moon after the vernal equinox, the spring equinox, which was defined as 21 March and not the actual natural equinox. And it was this fixing of Easter to a date and not to an actual natural event that caused it to drift out when the calendar drifted out over succeeding centuries.

MELVYN BRAGG: When did they actually get down to really fixing that?

PETER WATSON: Well, I think it's useful to say that for the first Christians time . . .

MELVYN BRAGG: We're talking about the first three centuries AD, three or four centuries?

PETER WATSON: Yes, time really wasn't very important because they all thought that Christ was coming again in their lifetime.

So they didn't actually pay too much attention to time to begin with. Then there's a really amazing coincidence that Kristen has mentioned, this nineteen-year cycle, which was pretty accurate but not quite accurate. This chap Victorius of Aquitaine found out that if you multiply it by twenty-eight it's even more accurate.

So, if you're still with me, we're on nineteen times twenty-eight, which gives you 532, and Denis the Small, he doesn't know it's year 532 at the time. If anything it's year 287 after the accession of Diocletian, the Roman emperor. So Denis does the calculations and by an astounding coincidence he finds that Christ was born exactly 532 years ago. In other words, the moon and the stars and the sun are in exactly the same position in the year he's doing this calculation as the year Christ was born, according to him. Therefore this is surely a sign from God that I'm in the right place at the right time and this idea of dating everything from the birth of Jesus is a sign from God saying yes, go ahead and do it.

MELVYN BRAGG: That was when the AD dating began?

ROBERT POOLE: Yes, and the previous reference point was the reign of Diocletian. Diocletian was famously a persecutor of Christians, so the birth of Christ was obviously a much, much better date for the Christian Church by then.

MELVYN BRAGG: Did Bede, the Venerable Bede, when he wrote his *Ecclesiastical History of the English Speaking Peoples*, did he bring dates to bear in there? Was he using the dating system that we've been talking about?

KRISTEN LIPPINCOTT: Most of the great, what we might call mathematicians, or you could call them religious men, of the Middle Ages were very interested in how the calendar worked. One of the things that Bede recognised, because there had been enough of a time difference from the early calendar, is that the equinox was slipping, the actual celestial equinox, was slipping backwards against the calendar. He was one of the first people to say we're going to have to do something about this calendar because we are slipping out of line with the stars.

MELVYN BRAGG: So there's the artificial and the natural, almost in competition all the time, certainly often in contradiction, aren't they? Did they realise that at the time?

ROBERT POOLE: It was realised by monks and astronomers and those who observed the sky, but it didn't really matter in everyday life. Plenty of civilisations, the entire Middle Eastern world, the entire Islamic world, work on lunar calendars that are very precise, the moon is very regular, but these calendars don't quite match the solar year, the new year. Every now and again there's an intercalary month.

It doesn't matter too much whether you're anything up to two or three weeks out in the seasons in an agricultural society. But of course it does matter when you're talking about calculating the date of Easter and it was a source of great embarrassment to the Christian Church that Islamic scholars would point out that their Easter, the Christians' famous Holy Day that was supposed to be on this first Sunday on or after the first full moon after the equinox, wasn't happening anywhere near the equinox at all. It was happening on completely the wrong date, and this appeared to undermine the claims of the Christian Church to be the true church.

PETER WATSON: Kristen is right. Easter is central to a Christian and to celebrate it in those days too early meant that you were guilty of hubris, you didn't need God for salvation. To celebrate it too late meant you didn't care. In both senses it was sacrilegious. The ancient kings in Egypt, when they came into office, had to swear that they would not change the calendar. Even today, I think, to change the Jewish calendar would need a meeting of the Great Sanhedrin, which is almost unthinkable. Yes, it was very, very important, and then a whole lore, in Christianity, developed around this, that the spring equinox was the day of maximum light because you had twelve hours of sunlight and twelve hours of moonlight. The moon had borrowed light from the sun, just as we 'borrow' our salvation from Christ. This is how the importance of Easter really grew and why so much time and energy went into settling the date, not just for the year you were in, but for future years.

MELVYN BRAGG: Was this the time when the sacred and the scientific became intensely intertwined?

KRISTEN LIPPINCOTT: They wouldn't have made those kinds of distinctions. They were scientists because they were looking for answers to religious problems and it's one of those things that waxes and wanes itself. Sometimes people will believe in dogma under the aegis of religion, sometimes they believe in dogma under the aegis of science, but just to add to what Peter was saying, there's another matter. In addition to both things that have been said, if Easter was moving backwards against the equinox, there's a possibility that you'd have Easter backing in hundreds of years, backing up against Christmas, and the horror of horrors would be that you'd sacrifice Christ before he was born. So anyone with any kind of sense of deep time realised that was on the cards.

MELVYN BRAGG: Can we move to 1582 when there was a major reform of the calendar under Pope Gregory XIII? Robert Poole, why was this necessary and what did he do? Was he worried about the problem that Kristen's been bringing up?

ROBERT POOLE: He was worried about the problem of Easter in particular, yes. The calendar reform of the Roman Catholic Church of 1582 has been a good subject for Catholic historians because there's a traditional story told about the Protestant rise of science, and yet here we have the Catholic reform of the calendar which appears to present a big scientific correction before the Protestant rise of science. But in fact if you look back the Catholic reform of the calendar was an act of the Counter-Reformation, an act of piety to do with the date of Easter.

From the late Middle Ages the Catholic Church had been aware, and very anxious, that the date of Easter was wrong. Copernicus was set on the job, and his book was eventually published. *De Revolutionibus* in 1543 was in fact meant to be a first draft of reform of the calendar, but he went a bit too far back to basics. And they didn't get around to the actual calendar reform until the Counter-Reformation Council of Trent. The Counter-Reformation Council of Trent was a failure in bringing the whole of Christendom, of western

Christendom, back together, but they could at least have a single reformed calendar, promulgated by the Roman Catholic Church under papal authority, and it would be obvious. It was generally accepted that the calculations were right, so at least that was one small thing that could become universal, a new calendar.

MELVYN BRAGG: What did this imply when they re-created it? Did the days change, the weeks, what happened?

ROBERT POOLE: They knocked ten days out of October 1582. It was promulgated by a papal bull, but very few countries, even Catholic countries, simply accepted the papal bull. They nearly all had some kind of law or civil decree that said they were reforming the calendar, not because the pope says so but because it's the right thing to do, and because we say so. Even one or two Protestant states picked up the reform, parts of the Netherlands, for example.

MELVYN BRAGG: As I understand it, it was more quickly accepted by Catholics than by Protestants, some of whom, including this country, resisted it for a very long time.

KRISTEN LIPPINCOTT: Well, they thought it was a papist plot. They were saying wait a minute, you're taking away ten of our days. What's this all about? And it's interesting because certainly when it was presented at the court of Elizabeth I, her best scientist, he's often called 'the Magus', her best scientist, John Dee, said of course it makes sense. But the politicians rallied round and elbowed Dee out of the way and said no, something sneaky's going on here and we must stick to our own calendar.

MELVYN BRAGG: Well, they were rightly anxious about what the pope said, as he'd put a price on the head of Elizabeth I. Not a man to be trusted in the courts of London. But Dee did his own calculation and came up with much the same as came out from the Council of Trent.

KRISTEN LIPPINCOTT: He was a brilliant mathematician. Unfortunately in later ages we see him as some sort of crazy astronomer and magician, but he had the right kind of ideas.

MELVYN BRAGG: What were the consequences of England and other Protestant countries resisting this Gregorian calendar, and how long did they resist for? What happened? One date in this part of Europe, another date in the other part of Europe?

PETER WATSON: Britain, I think, didn't go on to the new calendar until 1752, so there was nearly two hundred years when they were using a different calendar. It wasn't quite as important then as it is now. You know, you didn't get 'chariot-lag' or 'galleon-lag' like you get jet-lag.

KRISTEN LIPPINCOTT: But there were other problems. One of the things that we think about was the 'us' versus 'them'. If you think about it, the calendar, regardless of whether you were using a Julian calendar or a Gregorian calendar, from country to country and sometimes even from town to town, the date on which you started the year changed. There were six different days that people would begin the year on. So you could be in February and it could be February 1501 or February 1502. The day or the year wasn't something that was really solidified until much later.

MELVYN BRAGG: So the major difference with the Julian calendar was the difference of catching up on those days. Were there any other refinements on the Julian calendar?

ROBERT POOLE: Essentially the difference between Julian and Gregorian was the matter of the ten days that were different. There was a real patchwork of dates as Kristen says, particularly in Central Europe in all the German Protestant and Catholic princedoms. You could travel through several calendar zones in one day if you had a fast-enough coach. It created genuine difficulties with diplomatic correspondence and with the confusion of dates between diplomats.

KRISTEN LIPPINCOTT: And certainly for historians. The big health warning for any historian who thinks that if it says 15 February 1502 he knows what day it is, that's a complete misunderstanding of how the calendars worked in those days. We don't know what year it was unless they marked it 'old style', 'new style', 'German style', 'Italian style', 'Faroese style', 'Milanese style' . . .

MELVYN BRAGG: What effect did it have on the economy of these countries, their connecting economies?

KRISTEN LIPPINCOTT: I really don't think it had that much effect, because not only were the calendars different, weights and measures were different and distances were different, and it was just the kind of thing that you accepted. The same way that we cross the border and we realise that we have to give up our pounds for euros, they would give up their calendar, their time, their measurements and their distances, and that was just something that they accepted. It wasn't until travel became much more common that people started to realise that it was an inconvenience.

PETER WATSON: Yes, I think so. The other thing that happened around this time, the fifteenth and sixteenth centuries, is that the great voyages of discovery took place, and calendars around the world were discovered, in India, in Central America, in China, and found to be different. They were found to be very different in some ways and yet very similar in other ways. Most calendars end up with about 360 days in the year, twelve times thirty, and then something left over, and this was true in Central America, this was true in China, this was true in India, although India had six seasons, China had cycles of ten days, cycles of twelve days, all interlocking.

   The Jesuits thought that this is proof that these people were not saved and needed Christian help. They didn't have much success in changing that. As late as 1953, after Britain left India, Nehru, who was on a special commission to look at the Indian calendar, found that there were thirty calendars in use in 1953 in India. But again it was mainly, as Kristen says, an agricultural, fairly slow-moving society, and I think you can make too much of what we would think – that chaos would ensue. But we've only had the International Date Line since, what, 1886. So we've only been living with just over a century of what you might call 'jet time', where minutes matter rather than years.

MELVYN BRAGG: It was in the middle of the eighteenth century that England finally accepted the Gregorian calendar. Why did they think that they could unbend then?

KRISTEN LIPPINCOTT: I think it's a combination of things. The religious split between Catholicism and Protestantism wasn't quite as strong during that particular period and also it had to do with the increased trade in the continent – if you're bringing a lot of merchandise back and forth, you want to know what day it is.

MELVYN BRAGG: Robert Poole, did the calendar reform in England go smoothly? In 1750, it was done by Lord Chesterfield, as I understand it. What did he do?

ROBERT POOLE: The originator, if you like the guiding light, was Lord Chesterfield, who'd been ambassador in France and who'd had trouble writing to his mistress back in England, having to date the correspondence correctly. Chesterfield was well connected in the Royal Society and government and so was able to pilot a calendar reform bill through parliament. And what it did was to bring the English, or now British, Julian calendar in line with the continental calendar by removing eleven days from September 1752, so that Wednesday 2 September was followed by Thursday 14 September, and there were eleven days simply missing.

KRISTEN LIPPINCOTT: And it's wonderful if you look at diaries, like ladies' diaries or farmers' diaries of the period, because they just say 'this month is missing many days', and there's just a big blank in the middle of the calendar, usually with a little floral decoration.

ROBERT POOLE: Or sometimes with a very complicated explanation.

MELVYN BRAGG: What were the consequences?

ROBERT POOLE: Well, the consequences were quite mixed, because the calendar was only half reformed. The Act stated that anything, any human or Church date should simple move with the new calendar, so that for example Christmas Day, 25 December, would actually come eleven days sooner after the calendar reform. There were now eleven days fewer before Christmas, so Christmas was actually moved forward in the natural year, which may account for the fact that we don't have many white Christmases. Christmas used to be on our 5 or 6 January. That's when old Christmases were, more or less around Twelfth Night now.

However, there were two important exceptions made. One exception was for fairs. If you imagine a Michaelmas Fair on 29 September. Michaelmas is a time when apples ripen, you can bring your Michaelmas Fair forward eleven days in the natural year, but you can't make the apples ripen any sooner and your Michaelmas goose isn't going to be fat enough for the corporation feast. So fairs were to go with the old calendar. Your Michaelmas Fair was to happen, in the future, on 10 October, and if you think about it, this means that there are eleven days fewer between old Michaelmas and the new Christmas Day, so the relationship between the human year, the civil calendar, the Church calendar and the natural year was permanently disrupted. In the case of Chester you can see this. Chester had a mayor-making, a major celebration, on St Denis's Day, which was when the St Denis Day Fair was held in Chester. What happened was that the Act brought the mayor-making forward by eleven days but left the fair in the same natural position. The two were sundered and they had to bring in an amendment to the Calendar Reform Act which was hurriedly tacked on to an Act for preventing cattle distemper to bring the two back together again.

KRISTEN LIPPINCOTT: They say there were riots in the street, but I haven't seen any evidence that there were. You know, people waving banners saying 'Give us back our eleven days' seems to be a myth. But people were very concerned about taxes, because if you've lost eleven days of income, but you still have to pay tax for a year, did you have to pay that eleven days' worth of income? One of the things that did not change was the tax year. The old English year ended on 25 March, and one of the reasons why we still pay taxes beginning on 6 April is that it is eleven days after 25 March.

PETER WATSON: Because New Year's Day used to be in March and was changed at the same time.

ROBERT POOLE: Yes. That was purely a local convention, that was nothing to do with the Gregorian or Julian calendar. Pepys dated the New Year in his diary as 1 January, all the newspapers were 1 January, all the almanacs were then, but for certain legal purposes it was still 25 March, so the legal year started on 1 January too, but the tax year was left, in effect, where it is now.

MELVYN BRAGG: Is there an inference that somehow the natural year and the calendar year got out of sync, and we're still living with the consequences of this, which are not entirely happy?

ROBERT POOLE: We're still living with the tax year that starts on 6 April. The old tax year ends, in effect, on what is old Lady Day. But yes, in the upper echelons of society, amongst educated people, it was now normal to keep diaries and almanacs and to follow time day by day, but lower down in society people were still regulated much more roughly by feast days. They would date things according to so many weeks or so many Sundays after Michaelmas, and now that calculation, that relationship, was lost to people.

KRISTEN LIPPINCOTT: But then the question that's fundamental is, and perhaps what you're really asking is – does it really matter? I mean, does it matter if you have a certain fair when the apples ripen and it's called 10 October or it's called 21 October – does it really matter? And this is one of the things that I'm always surprised at when people talk about time or calendars, or they write to me at the museum. They think these things are real, that they're true. They forget that all of our timekeeping measurements are man-made. It's something we've created, so it's more or less making a rod for our own back. If things don't work, it's our fault.

MELVYN BRAGG: Peter Watson, has this now become the accepted calendar, the Gregorian calendar? Is it on the way to being a global calendar?

PETER WATSON: Oh, I think it's a global calendar now, yes. There are still remnants of other calendars. One, for example, is the Olympic cycle. There was a calendar, or a cycle, in ancient Greece called the octaeteris, which was another cycle which went out of kilter and was corrected every eight years, and so the Greeks held the Olympic Games – twice in an octaeteris – every four years, and we still have that four-year cycle. So there are remnants, I think, all over the world. And of course the Islamic calendar is different, the Jewish calendar is different, and . . .

KRISTEN LIPPINCOTT: The Chinese calendar.

PETER WATSON: Yes. You know, these people live quite happily. Jews in Britain live quite happily with both calendars, don't they, and so do the Indians. You can make too much of the difficulties. I think you don't have to be a master mathematician to live with the fact. We live with the fact that some months are thirty days, some are thirty-one. We manage, don't we?

ROBERT POOLE: The simple point about the calendar is that people always imagine that time should be mathematical and regular, that we should have something like an equivalent of the metric system and in the French Revolution they did try to metricate the calendar into ten days, ten-day weeks, but it just didn't work. It didn't, it just wasn't accepted.

PETER WATSON: Mainly because they only had a day off every ten days!

ROBERT POOLE: Yes, it was deeply unpopular. But what you have to accept is that the elements of the calendar simply don't divide into each other, they're incommensurable. It's like Alan Bennett's vicar and the sardine tin of life, whatever you do there's always a little bit left in the corner.

PETER WATSON: In the Russian Revolution they had a week of five days, with no time off, and you can imagine how popular that was. I did a couple of books out of Russia and there was a practice there, as well as this five-day week, in Communist Russia for people to work on Saturday mornings for the good of the state. They would work for nothing. This was after the weekend had been reintroduced in the Second World War, and if you did work on a Saturday morning you were known as a 'subotnik', and this is the same word as 'Shabbat', still surviving in Communist Russia. So the Babylonian idea is still there until very recently, the last ten years.

MELVYN BRAGG: How accurate is the present calendar?

ROBERT POOLE: Technically . . .

KRISTEN LIPPINCOTT: Good enough.

ROBERT POOLE: Good enough. Technically the standard of time is the number of how many millions of vibrations of a caesium atom – I don't know where they keep the actual atom ... but there is a theoretical standard. The interesting thing is that people have come up with all sorts of reform calendars. There's a sort of international standard calendar that was invented in Sweden which is much too boring to be popular. And whatever you do, in the end, all of these calendars, all these caesium atom vibrations, they all end up being adjusted back to the solar year. We get the extra pip now and again. The fundamental standard remains the solar year, and really if we want a different calendar we're going to have to go and colonise another planet.

PETER WATSON: It is getting shorter though, isn't it, by a few seconds every century?

KRISTEN LIPPINCOTT: That's why we add the pips. It's a nice sort of circle because what we're trying to do is bring it back almost to Homer and Hesiod, so that you know that when the Pleiades are rising on the horizon you shouldn't go sailing.

MELVYN BRAGG: That's what it's come to, has it?

ROBERT POOLE: If you want to know the time, ask an historian.

PETER WATSON: But to reinforce Kristen's point. There was an Easter Act in Britain in 1928 which said that we could celebrate Easter as on the first Sunday after the second Saturday in April, but we never bothered implementing it because we know what to do now and so the mystery's gone out of it. You just have to imagine that there are seven planets circling each other, so that the gravity is changing the configuration all the time, and this reinforces Robert's point that at any particular time the situation is untidy.

MELVYN BRAGG: Well, you said earlier, Kristen, that it's all artificial and I agree with you, intellectually you're right, it is artificial, but I would say now many people in the world are much more calendar-driven than they are natural-day driven.

KRISTEN LIPPINCOTT: The funny thing is that we as human beings have fallen so in love with our own structures that we think that they're true. People have this thing on their wrist and they think it controls their day. People have a calendar, therefore they use it to control their day. Try throwing away your wristwatch – you still live.

MELVYN BRAGG: But you don't control your day if you have to trade in Hong Kong.

KRISTEN LIPPINCOTT: Exactly.

MELVYN BRAGG: Or get to Frankfurt by such and such a time, or even get to Carlisle by such and such a time.

PETER WATSON: Who would want to do that?

MELVYN BRAGG: Too many people when I catch the train! And with that I'm off to Euston.

TRANSMITTED: 19.12.2002

b

The Field of the Cloth of Gold

In the spring of 1520, 6,000 Englishmen and their servants followed their king across the sea to France. They weren't part of an invasion force but were attendants to King Henry VIII travelling to take part in the greatest and most conspicuous display of wealth and culture and courtly sports that Europe had ever seen. They were met by Francis I, king of France, and 6,000 French noblemen, women and servants on English soil in northern France. The English erected a temporary palace; there were elaborate tents, jousting, pavilions and golden fountains spouting perpetual claret. For just over two weeks they created a temporary town the size of Norwich, then England's second most populous city, on the 'Camp du Drape d'Or', or Field of the Cloth of Gold.

What drove the French and the English to create such an extraordinary event? What did the two sides do when they got there, and what, if anything, was achieved?

With me to discuss the Field of the Cloth of Gold is John Guy, Fellow of Clare College, University of Cambridge; Steven Gunn, Fellow and Tutor in History at Merton College, Oxford University; and Penny Roberts, Senior Lecturer in History at the University of Warwick.

Steven Gunn, can we start with an outline of the European geopolitics of the time around 1520? Where are the main powers?

STEVEN GUNN: There were three leading powers in western Europe in the early sixteenth century, and of those three, England was the smallest. England had been quite an aggressive political power in the fourteenth and fifteenth centuries, had a well-established system of government, but its population was only about two and a half million. France, on the other hand, was a much larger population, something like sixteen million. It had expanded dramatically over the previous sixty, seventy years, with places like Brittany, Gascony, Normandy, Provence being taken under the control of the French crown. France had a tax system which was able to raise taxes without the consent of parliament, the parliament of the kind that English kings had to go to, and France had a standing army.

The most unpredictable of the European powers was the new multiple monarchy being put together by Charles of Hapsburg. Charles of Hapsburg had been ruler of the Netherlands since he was six. When he was sixteen he became king of the Spanish kingdoms, which he inherited from one of his grandfathers. When he was nineteen he inherited the Hapsburg hereditary lands in Austria, southern and western Germany from his other grandfather, and he was then elected Holy Roman Emperor, Emperor of Germany. So Charles of Hapsburg had put together the biggest empire in Europe for seven hundred years, and nobody knew quite what he was going to do with it. Clearly he was a rival of France, there were territorial disputes along the Pyrenees, in Italy, in the border between what is now Belgium and France, and one of the big questions at the Field of the Cloth of Gold was which side would England find itself on in that dispute.

MELVYN BRAGG: So we had tiny England, an expanding and powerful and confident France and this huge empire, as you say the biggest since Charlemagne for seven hundred years. But just to put it in perspective – although we needn't develop this for the moment or at all – lurking in the east were the Ottomans who, in 1529, nine years after the Cloth of Gold, were at the gates of Vienna. They were out there, bringing some sort of pressure from the east.

STEVEN GUNN: The Ottoman Empire had been expanding in a way like the French monarchy, very dramatically over the previous seventy years, taking Constantinople, overrunning Serbia, Bulgaria, and were about to overrun Hungary, and already by the 1490s you could see the fires lit by the Ottoman raiding parties if you went up to the top of the church towers in Venice. So Europe was well aware of the pressure from the Ottoman Empire from the south.

MELVYN BRAGG: In 1518 there was a Treaty of London – that was what we might call now an international treaty run mainly not by kings but by ambassadors. Can you tell us what happened there and how significant that was?

STEVEN GUNN: The idea of the Treaty of London was to make peace between all the European powers to enable them to resist the expansion of the Ottoman Empire. It started as a papal initiative but it was taken over by the king of England. That is why it becomes the Treaty of London. So it is outward-looking but it is also inward-looking amongst the European powers because it is a non-aggression pact. The idea is that none of the European powers will start a war against any other, and if one of them does the other powers who are signatories to the treaty will combine to back the person who is being attacked. But of course the problem with that is working out who is the aggressor and who is the offended party when things start to break down between any of those powers.

MELVYN BRAGG: Briefly before we move on. England is far and away the smallest force in all this and yet it keeps exercising its power. Was the fact that the Treaty was made in London indicative of the way in which Henry VIII and particularly Cardinal Wolsey seized the initiative? Let's concentrate on Cardinal Wolsey. John Guy.

JOHN GUY: Wolsey is a genuinely international figure. He is not just Henry VIII's chief minister he is a Renaissance cardinal and he is a special legate, a plenipotentiary legate, who has powers that almost make him, if you like, the pope of northern Europe. By the time of the Treaty of London he is riding high.

MELVYN BRAGG: Let's just get that clear. He is not only a representative of the pope, he can speak for the pope, he can make crucial decisions . . .

JOHN GUY: And he does. One of the complaints the pope has about the Field of the Cloth of Gold is that Wolsey doesn't tell him what is happening and just carries on and doesn't answer his letters, so he is exercising tremendous power here. At the Field of the Cloth of Gold he is not simply representing Henry VIII he is also representing Francis I in terms of organising it.

MELVYN BRAGG: Wolsey is immensely wealthy, he is a butcher's son from Ipswich but he has become an archbishop and then a cardinal – a great power with Henry VIII and a great power with Rome as well. *Alter rex* in Rome, *alter papa* in London. Where did that wealth and power come from? What was his grip on Henry VIII?

JOHN GUY: Well, his grip on Henry VIII is his charisma and of course he bolsters that by obtaining a series of wealthy bishoprics. He becomes Archbishop of York, he uses his position as papal legate to, if you like, extract money from the English Church. And quite a bit of that comes to him from things like the probate of wills. But the trick is really oratory. Wolsey is a master diplomat, he is a great personality, he is charismatic, but he is a master of rhetoric, persuasion. He is his own public relations consultant. It was said of him that he had a special gift of natural eloquence with a filed tongue so that he was able to persuade and allure all men to his purpose. He will sell you anything, he will talk you into anything.

MELVYN BRAGG: And Henry was beguiled by him, was he?

JOHN GUY: Henry was beguiled by him. Henry was by no means stupid and Henry was in control, but at this period he is very happy to license Wolsey to run most of domestic policy and much foreign policy on his behalf. He will chip in as and when. I think the key point is that by 1518 Wolsey is riding high and he is riding high on a policy of peace because England, as we said, is a small nation. It actually can't afford to be at war the whole time and what Wolsey does he taps into the wider Renaissance impulse of that time. Erasmus has written *The Complaint of Peace* in 1517. People think this is a special moment. Thomas More enters Henry VIII's service at this time and he does it because he thinks Wolsey is the man who is going to change not just England but the world, by which they mean Europe.

MELVYN BRAGG: It was the time of books changing you. Machiavelli has already written a book now but it isn't going to be published until the thirties, but there is a book called *De Cardinalatu*, published in Urbino in 1511. Wolsey seems to have followed its tenets very specifically.

JOHN GUY: This book *De Cardinalatu* is the A to Z of how to be a cardinal. It is the key text, if you like, of prescriptive literature. It is by Paolo Cortese, Bishop of Urbino. He has various jobs in the Vatican, he knows the Roman bureaucracy inside out. The book is in three parts and the most important are the first two.

The first says a cardinal will achieve greatness through first of all his moral virtue and justice, mercy, equity, peace – you know, these are stressed as the international values. But then the second book is how to do it. How to do it is first of all oratory, rhetoric, persuasion; the second is magnificence, your art collections, your palaces, you found a hospital, you found colleges, you found libraries, you are patron of music, because music is in their view part of health care. And what is interesting about this is all the parts that certainly in the English tradition have never been stressed about Wolsey or have been disliked – his palaces, his art collections, his colleges, the bits that don't seem to fit in – are central to the way he fashions his identity.

MELVYN BRAGG: Penny Roberts, did Wolsey instigate the Field of the Cloth of Gold?

PENNY ROBERTS: I think that would be a fair comment and, as John said, he clearly had influence or at least he had a good relation-ship with Francis I as well so he was able to act as a very effective broker between the French and the English kings. I think it would be fair to say that he is very much the architect of the Field of the Cloth of Gold.

MELVYN BRAGG: We have heard from Steven and John enough to know what the English were hoping to get out of it – prestige, being on equal terms, being a player. How did Wolsey persuade Francis I that there was something in it for France?

PENNY ROBERTS: It is very interesting, isn't it, to consider this idea of an alliance between England and France, the traditional enemies? France, of course, had traditionally also encouraged the Scots in their hostilities towards the English, so there was a great deal of latent suspicion between the English and the French. It is only some seventy years since the end of the Hundred Years War when English armies had come in waves devastating the French countryside in the name of upholding the claim of the English king to the French throne.

MELVYN BRAGG: Henry VIII still thought he had a claim to the French throne?

PENNY ROBERTS: Oh indeed. Henry himself had invaded France in 1513, won the Battle of the Spurs, taken the towns of Therouanne and Tournai and wanted to recreate the great days of Henry V. Henry V was very much his role model. Of course these weren't victories on the scale of Agincourt or anything of that type, but it did establish Henry's reputation as a military leader. For Francis, at the same time, he was establishing his prowess . . .

MELVYN BRAGG: They are both in their twenties, these young men?

PENNY ROBERTS: That's right. Francis comes to the throne about six years after Henry, but very early on his reign he establishes his military reputation in his Italian campaign, winning a famous battle at Marignano in 1515, after which the French actually capture the important city of Milan. This is a victory on a far greater scale than what Henry had achieved and I think both sides are aware of this. So France isn't concerned about England as the threatening force it had been in earlier centuries and, as Steven has said, France was a very much bigger and more powerful player by this time.

MELVYN BRAGG: What did Wolsey tell Francis I that made him think this is good for me to let the English force come to France, to let this man who had made claim to the French throne come to France, let as many English warriors and noblemen, who are a fighting force, a fighting machine, come to France? How did he persuade him?

PENNY ROBERTS: Well, Francis, like Henry, was very much influenced by these humanist ideals which John has already outlined. This idea of a universal peace. Kings, Renaissance princes, see themselves very much as peacemakers and so he is persuaded by this argument about creating an ideal of universal peace. It allows Francis, as it does Henry, to present themselves as great Renaissance princes, so on that level he is very much in line with the thinking about the ideal of universal peace. But there is also the wider political context of the aftermath of the imperial election where Charles V has become the leading power in Europe.

MELVYN BRAGG: In 1519, the year before?

PENNY ROBERTS: That's right, and indeed Francis had attempted to stop Charles becoming emperor at that time.

MELVYN BRAGG: But there is a narrower personal dimension as well, isn't there? Henry VIII was always asking, how tall is Francis, is he as tall as I am? Are his legs as strong as mine? I am not going to shave off my beard until I meet him. He saw this chap over there winning victories, the victories he wanted, but they both had imperial ambitions in terms of wanting to be Caesars. You got glory through war. I have got to meet this man and test myself and show that I am as big as he is.

PENNY ROBERTS: I think that is right. There are two parts to this: there is the wider political context which is clearly very important. England is able to act as a broker between the Empire and France and it is very nice for the English to feel they are being wooed by these two great powers but, as you say, there is this very personal element. This I think is very persuasive in terms of the actual meeting between the kings rather than the treaty itself which is obviously negotiated by ambassadors. Francis and Henry have a mutual curiosity about each other. They both have very similar reputations, tall, physically very strong, very athletic, they have great reputations in the jousts and those sort of military pursuits. They have a shared interest in hunting, in the ladies, they are very much men of their time. They like to surround themselves with the latest Renaissance fashions, humanists, and also to be great patrons of the arts. They have a lot in common and it is clear that this mutual curiosity is one of the driving forces behind them actually agreeing to this meeting.

MELVYN BRAGG: Just to end this introductory passage, John Guy, the man who wasn't there was the most powerful man in Europe by a long chalk, indeed as we said, the most powerful man for seven hundred years – a very young Charles V. But he made sure he had a little pincer movement on the encounter, didn't he?

JOHN GUY: Well, he is the absent presence because he meets Henry VIII the month before Henry VIII actually sets out for Calais on his way to the Cloth of Gold. Henry goes to meet Charles V and Henry crosses the border to Gravelines, he goes to the Netherlands, he brings Charles to Calais and entertains him there after the Field of the Cloth of Gold. So in a way the idea of this being bilateral is only achieved by looking narrowly at the Field of the Cloth of Gold. If you extend the context it is actually multilateral between these three great powers. But again Wolsey, I think, is the key figure behind the scenes, orchestrating the sequence of meetings.

MELVYN BRAGG: Must have been fun to be Wolsey, must have been great fun bringing them all together and playing around. OK, Steven Gunn, they are set and they go. How did they decide on a location? That must have been a lot of fuss: what are the distances and so on, English soil or French soil – can you get us to the Field of the Cloth of Gold?

STEVEN GUNN: As soon as they begin talking about where to meet it is obvious that they are going to meet somewhere around the edge of the English territory in France. The English have held Calais since 1347 and Calais is the main English military and trade base in France. But the question is how far will the English come away from Calais and how far in this calculation of royal honour will the French condescend to go into English territory, and so they end up meeting as near the edge of English territory as they can, but still inside English territory, because the English insist that because their king has had to come across the sea he has put more effort into the meeting and so he should be just inside his own territory.

MELVYN BRAGG: From what I have read, it seems as though Francis I was quite relaxed about all this?

STEVEN GUNN: I think he was. Where they end up meeting is in effect halfway between the last fortress of the English area in France, Guînes, and the first fortress of the French – or the last, coming from Paris – Ardres. So they have each got a small base from which they can move into this no-man's-land in the middle.

MELVYN BRAGG: As we have said, these are massive forces, 6,000. It is much the size of Henry V's army at Agincourt. Plus 6,000 on the French side, and they are there for a fortnight. Can you just give us some idea of the accommodation? They built a town as big as Norwich, the second most populous city in England, as I said in the introduction.

STEVEN GUNN: On the English side the English built a special palace, a temporary palace especially for the occasion, and what is really interesting about that is that it is on a classical design. It is an exact model, a replica of the sort of palace that you build as recommended in the *De Cardinalatu*. So we know Wolsey, who actually designed this, was the mastermind. There was a quadrant, each side over 300 feet long. At the entrance was a classical pillar. There were these fountains that you already mentioned that were spouting wine for much of the time.

MELVYN BRAGG: Perpetual claret. What a thought . . . !

STEVEN GUNN: Then you came in and the palace was eight feet high of brick and then the rest was temporary, timber, canvas – the canvas was painted to resemble brick. But you came into the court-yard and you were immediately struck because there was 5,000 feet of clear glass. It must have been stunning, with bay windows, and then the apartments laid out on a quadrant for Wolsey, for Henry VIII, for Catherine of Aragon and for Mary Tudor, the sister of Henry VIII, the former queen of France. Beyond that was a chapel and then there was a gallery which led to Guînes castle which was where a lot of the other English were staying.

So the English trumped the French in the accommodation. It was stunning. The French relied on tents, royal tents. Francis had a special tent built with a couple of almost ships' masts in the middle holding it together, wonderful decoration, astronomical symbols all over the roof. The English too needed tents. They said the French had 400 tents to back up the royal tents for this number of people. The English had what they said was 820 lodgings in tents and I think there must have been three or four people to each lodging.

MELVYN BRAGG: So the great palace built by Wolsey was a plantation of English greatness. It showed who was boss. I am sorry to be so vernacular in this, but it really did, didn't it? It surprised the French, who had a great show of men and were much richer and so on, and of course it survived a storm near the end. A lot of tents blew down but not the palace.

STEVEN GUNN: And also by building in this classical style the English were talking the international language of the Renaissance. This was not domestic architecture. So it seemed that England was somehow this great player on the European stage. After all, Wolsey is claiming here through art and diplomacy to be the arbiter of Europe. Interestingly that is exactly what Erasmus, the great humanist leader, had said in *The Complaint of Peace* – that since kings and princes will never agree on peace they will always tend to want to find glory in war. Therefore they will need some great leader of the Church, some great cardinal, to act as the arbitrator, and if you want to sum up Wolsey in a nutshell, he is an arbitrator in excelsis.

MELVYN BRAGG: What is really fascinating is that you seek peace through magnificence. That is the thing that took my imagination. I remember, when I read this stuff years ago, I hadn't got that. Can you give us some idea of what programme they had worked out? We hear of chivalric jousting – what else?

PENNY ROBERTS: It is very much about magnificence in forcing peace and, as I have said, the idea of monarchy as universal peacemaker is very important. But there is always this slight tension because at the same time they are supposed to be presenting themselves as very important military figures and this is where the jousting and the feats of arms come in. At the same time as they are making peace this is seen to be a sign of their strength. They are making peace because they wish to make peace, not because they are in a position of weakness, so they are also having these combats which demonstrate that they are very forceful and if they wanted to go to war they could do and they could cut a figure in that sense. So the actual occasion and all the events are very carefully planned because there is this need to have absolute balance between the two sides.

MELVYN BRAGG: So everywhere the two kings met they had to come precisely the same distance and all that. It must have been wonderful for the clerks working out those calculations.

PENNY ROBERTS: Absolutely. When they came to the actual meeting they had to elevate the two sides of the valley so that when they saw each other they were at exactly the same height so there wouldn't be any kind of sense of pre-eminence. A fanfare would sound so they would leave their entourages at exactly the same time and go down with their horses and meet at an appointed meeting place.

MELVYN BRAGG: Was this the one-to-one meeting?

PENNY ROBERTS: Yes, this was the one-to-one meeting that took place on 7 June and it was all very carefully mapped out. It was very interesting as well. They would ride towards each other as though they were going to actually have combat but just at the last moment they turn their horses and they embrace. So underlining each act of peace is a sense of rivalry, a sense that they could be in combat if they wished to be.

MELVYN BRAGG: Could you, John Guy, tell us a bit about the character of the kings? As we say, they are both in their twenties. Henry has been king for about eleven years, Francis has been king for about six years – and what sort of character? Were they similar in character? We know that Francis liked to think he was Caesar and Henry had imperial ambitions, but can you just give us more than that.

JOHN GUY: I think Francis and Henry are quite similar. I think actually Francis is more confident. He is more sure of himself. I think Henry always has this slight psychological sense of inferiority, the need to please, the need to go that extra mile. Charles V, I think, is on the sidelines. I think he is much cannier. I think he is much more practical than he is often made out to be. I think he is quite wily. He supposedly had a great theory of universal monarchy, which mostly came from his advisers, but I think in practice he is much more willing to broker deals. But Francis sees himself as Caesar, the most Christian King, like a Roman emperor, and Henry is chasing after that, he is coveting that. That is why Henry also runs when the post of Holy Roman Emperor is contested for in 1519.

MELVYN BRAGG: Splendour runs into gluttony at one stage, from my reading of it anyway. Steven, can you give us an idea of the amount drunk and eaten?

STEVEN GUNN: Well, keeping the fountains running with wine was obviously a major requirement, because the English had 40,000 gallons of wine with them, which works out about four pints per person per day. They also, being English, had 14,500 gallons of beer and ale, and they had the material with them to brew a lot more ale when they needed it. Obviously the French enjoying English hospitality may have been consuming some of that, but it is still an impressive scale of consumption.

MELVYN BRAGG: Did they take all of their own food? Or did they live off the land?

STEVEN GUNN: They took all their own food. This, as we have said, was something the size of an English army you might send to France, so in effect they move into army supply mode, except that because it is a grand display you don't only do quantity you also do variety. So, for example, we know from the royal household accounts their fish: they have got 9,100 plaice, 7,836 whiting, 5,554 soles, 2,800 crayfish, 700 conger eels, 3 porpoises and a dolphin. To have a proper banquet you have got to have a range of things like that.

JOHN GUY: And that was just the fish menu, because didn't they have 337 oxen and 2,000 sheep?

PENNY ROBERTS: 1,200 capons.

JOHN GUY: And I read someone was boiling beef for six weeks beforehand.

MELVYN BRAGG: What about their clothes? A Field of the Cloth of Gold – was that the dress code? Did everything have to be gold?

STEVEN GUNN: There is clearly a sense that you dress in the most spectacular fashion you can. One of the French memoirists who writes about it talks about seeing noblemen walking around with their estates on their backs because they have mortgaged their lands or sold off their woods in order to procure the best clothes they possibly can.

MELVYN BRAGG: And they took furniture as well. It is a big display. Can we just go into this? We are talking about display, aren't we?

JOHN GUY: The royal palaces, virtually all the standing palaces, were emptied and all the silver, gold, Westminster Abbey's copes and ornaments were taken, and of course the nobles took their own kit. I mean the displays of plate, the jewels, the imagery and the chapel. The chapel was very important in the royal palace too. These were just spectacular.

STEVEN GUNN: And you would take things like tapestries for hanging on the wall, carpets made in Turkey, the kind of things you see in Holbein portraits which are much too valuable to put on the floor, but you put them on tables. All those sorts of soft furnishings would be filling up these tents and the temporary palace to over-whelm people when they walk in and see them.

PENNY ROBERTS: Another example of the sort of extravagance and glamour as well is the ladies who come along in the finest Renaissance fashions. The French ladies in particular were asked by Francis to come and show off the latest Italian Renaissance fashions and were much criticised by the Italian ambassador in particular for wearing very provocative clothing. Polydor Virgil later on complains that the English ladies then adopt these, having seen these ladies at the Field of the Cloth of Gold in these magnificent costumes.

MELVYN BRAGG: Was there diplomacy going on round the edges?

PENNY ROBERTS: Absolutely. After the kings have their initial one-to-one meeting they then go into a tent with Cardinal Wolsey and Admiral Bonnivet, who were the two individuals who had mainly negotiated the Treaty of London, in order to sign a new Treaty. This agrees to the marriage of the Dauphin to the Princess Mary and to the handing over of monies as a royal pension to the English crown. So there are these various meetings but also all the time there are ambassadorial meetings and negotiations going on between the two sides.

MELVYN BRAGG: As I understand it, the days were organised around dinner – old-fashioned north country dinner between twelve and two o'clock – and they went to dinner and before and after that there were jousting. You have said jousting – what else? Can you go into a bit more detail, because the fun is in the detail of this, isn't it? So jousting every day, I presume – what else?

PENNY ROBERTS: Jousting every day except Sundays. On Sundays the kings go off and dine with each other's queens and Cardinal Wolsey dines with the Queen Mother of France, Louise of Savoy, so there are these very nice dining occasions on a Sunday. Obviously they are not allowed to fight on those days. Yes, most days there is jousting and there is what is termed feats of arms both on horseback and on foot and the . . .

MELVYN BRAGG: The English archers show how good they are, don't they, just to remind people about Agincourt? There are archery displays.

PENNY ROBERTS: That's right. There is also wrestling between the Bretons and the English. The Bretons are clearly seen as the best wrestlers in France and so there are various battles of that type, but there is also the fact that the two sides are organised into groups and they ensure that the two kings never meet each other directly within these combats.

MELVYN BRAGG: So imagine these people swirling around in that place – must have been extraordinary. We can't keep repeating it too often, because it is an extraordinary thing. Towards the end there was a great Mass, again engineered by and conducted by Cardinal Wolsey himself. It was Corpus Christi, which was a big event in the Catholic calendar and he must have known that when he set the dates. Can you just tell us the significance of that Mass, Steven Gunn, and how he conducted it?

STEVEN GUNN: Well, in some ways the Mass reproduces the kinds of competitive magnificence between the two courts that we have seen all the way through the meetings. The French king's chapel choir sings parts of the services, the English king's chapel choir sings other parts of the service and presumably there is a sense of competition between the two. But Wolsey demonstrates again a central role in the whole thing by the fact that he is the priest who sings Mass and he has attending on him, holding the bowls and towels, the highest English noblemen. These are people who certainly would have despised his father as a butcher from Ipswich and pretty clearly come close to despising him, and yet are having to be his servants for the purpose of singing Mass.

MELVYN BRAGG: And there is an unexpected – this is the worst prompt I have ever done in my life! – there is an unexpected interruption in the Mass, isn't there, Steven?

STEVEN GUNN: There was an unexpected interruption which remains rather obscure: something which must have been part of the entertainment appears flying over the crowd. No one is quite clear whether it is a firework or quite what it is. Some people report it as being something like a flying dragon. It may be like a flying salamander. There are particular heraldic problems here, because Francis I's personal badge is a salamander whereas the red dragon from the Welsh ancestry is part of the Tudor arms. It looks as though it may well have gone off early and was supposed to happen at some later point. It becomes untethered, or the fireworks go off unintentionally.

MELVYN BRAGG: But this is during the Mass and a lot of people think it was meant to be?

STEVEN GUNN: It was meant to be part of the spectacular display of the Mass, yes.

MELVYN BRAGG: Another of Wolsey's . . .

JOHN GUY: The Venetian ambassador says it is the Elevation of the Host, but he has got that completely wrong. There is one thing about the Mass though, to come back to the issue of peace, that I think is really important. Wolsey gets a man called Richard Pacey, who is the Dean of St Paul's and Henry's Secretary, to preach the sermon. Pacey is the same guy who is in fact giving the Latin oration on peace in the Treaty of London.

MELVYN BRAGG: What language did he preach in?

JOHN GUY: He would probably have preached in Latin. He is a great friend of Erasmus. He is one of the key figures in this humanist peace campaign, I think the other thing that the Mass did was something else that in a way was very comical. When they got to the Pax, where the kings were asked to kiss the special emblem of the Pax, in fact neither of them will go before the other, so they just look at each other and it is taken away and the queens do the same, but then they decide just to kiss each other.

PENNY ROBERTS: It is nice as well, isn't it, because the Mass is the ultimate ritual, it brings people together, it is seen as a uniting ritual, and so it is very important for the symbolism of peace and up to this point the kings mostly have been having their own Masses in their own chapels in their own pavilions and palaces. Except on one occasion when Francis bursts into Henry's bedchamber early one morning, hands him his sword and says, 'I am your prisoner' and accompanies him to Mass. I think it is a very nice breakdown of the etiquette, very much reinforcing the friendship and the unity and the wish for peace.

MELVYN BRAGG: Making himself completely vulnerable to him. There must have been hints, there had been assassinations before. Henry was being very bold going to meet his traditional, ferocious enemy – on English soil, but right on the edge of theirs. He was taking his life into his hands to a certain extent. Yet those two kept showing each other that they weren't enemies.

PENNY ROBERTS: Yes, and I think Francis was very disarming.

He was very magnanimous, allowing them to meet on English soil. He was quite prepared, he went along with the etiquette, but he was a very spontaneous kind of character and he often got himself into all kinds of scrapes and accidents and it is very characteristic of him to turn up in the bedchamber in this way. A performance which Henry repeated a few days later, so he wasn't offended. It demonstrated that he went along with it.

MELVYN BRAGG: Let's talk about the sources for a minute, because they might throw a lot out of joint. Was it thought at the time – by the chroniclers and the diarists – to be a great spectacular extraordinary event?

JOHN GUY: Oh absolutely. There were newsletters in France, that is one of the ways we know about this so much, the Venetian ambassador was enormously impressed with all this and wrote a very long account of it. It is true that the sources are actually contradictory. Take for example the fountains with the wine. One account says that one fountain was claret the other one was malmsey; another one says one was wine and the other was beer; one account says they were flowing all the time and everybody got sozzled, and another account says they were only actually switched on during the banquets when one of the kings was entertaining one of the queens. So the sources are rather confused.

STEVEN GUNN: There are also printed accounts. You can actually buy an account of the jousting and the meeting between the kings printed in a pamphlet on the streets of Paris. This is the first great age of European news printing, and clearly this is a big event that people wanted to read about.

PENNY ROBERTS: I think both sides are very much checking each other out as well. I mentioned about the fashions of the ladies, but the Venetian ambassador not only reports on the provocative fashions of the French ladies but also the excessive drinking of the English ladies. They are passing round cups and sharing it, which is seen, and these are reinforcing all kinds of stereotypes about one another. It is very much about matching up these forces and it makes an impression across Europe.

MELVYN BRAGG: Are there significant differences, Steven or John, significant differences in the accounts? Is there something there is a real clash on?

JOHN GUY: Well, there is a significant difference in terms of how we understand the meeting, because of the fact that the English administrative accounts survive much better than the French ones do because of various fires in archives and so on in the eighteenth and nineteenth centuries. So we really don't know much about what the French take with them. Whereas in France there is a much stronger tradition of memoir writing so we have people who were there later on writing in their memoirs of what happened in a way that people don't really do on the English side, so it gives a rather different quality to the two kinds of information.

MELVYN BRAGG: And this wrestling business, Penny, between Francis I and Henry VIII – it comes from a French source, doesn't it? Can you tell us about it?

PENNY ROBERTS: That's right. It comes from the memoir of the Sieur de l'Orange, who is a close childhood friend of Francis. He had grown up with him as one of his gentlemen of the chamber and he recounts this tale. After the kings have been watching some wrestling, as I have said, between the Bretons and the English . . .

MELVYN BRAGG: At which the English had won on that occasion?

PENNY ROBERTS: That's right.

STEVEN GUNN: Because the Bretons didn't turn up, I think that's right?

PENNY ROBERTS: I think that could well be the account, and . . .

STEVEN GUNN: They wrestled with non-Breton wrestlers.

PENNY ROBERTS: Yes, the Bretons were the best. The two kings were drinking together, bantering and exchanging comments, and Henry it is who challenges Francis – 'let's have a wrestle' – and grabs him by the shoulders. They are both very tall, as I mentioned, and physically strong, and I think Henry was hoping as rather the heavier figure that he would be able to outdo Francis, but Francis was rather more agile, a bit lighter, and was able to bring him down with what was termed a '*tour de Bretagne*', 'a Breton turn', which was clearly the best way to wrestle somebody to the ground, which is very humiliating for Henry of course.

It is only reported in one source and it is a great question about whether or not it is apocryphal and in fact never occurred. There is great silence from the other sources. May be good reasons for that, because obviously this is an occasion where there is supposed to be this equality and they are not supposed to have any direct combat. What is nice about it, I think, even if it is not true it signals how there is this intense rivalry which is bubbling under the surface at all times.

MELVYN BRAGG: And the source was Francis' best friend. An interesting and perhaps irrelevant point about the Brittany Throw is that Breton and Cornish wrestling and Cumberland wrestling are supposed to have come from the Celtic – he probably did the Buttock, as we call it in the north-west – but we can go into that in greater detail at another time. Probably a Cross-Buttock. If there was a competition in dazzle, Steven Gunn, who won?

STEVEN GUNN: I think they both won, because the economy of magnificence is something where if you have displayed in the right way then you have shown how kingly you both are. There is one sense in which it is a competition but there is another sense in which both the kings win because you have shown what magnificent kings you are. After all, you are talking to each other and to the international audience, but you are also talking to your own subjects and both kings can say, 'look how seriously I am taken, look at what a great ruler I am.'

MELVYN BRAGG: It seems like a magnificent folly because three years later they are at war again, these two, aren't they, and Henry's forces get very near Paris?

JOHN GUY: The thing breaks down because of what happens in Italy. Within months of the Field of the Cloth of Gold Charles and Francis are at war over Italy, over Milan and Naples which are key goals of Francis. It shows how fragile all of this was. On the other hand, if you look at it in their terms, you see this Renaissance spectacle, this dazzle. I disagree a little bit with Steven, I think both sides won, but I think England won more because England now seems to be right at the forefront of the Renaissance, of Renaissance diplomacy, of Renaissance ideas. England, the weaker state, the weakest of all these three great powers, is now able to tip the balance. So the question is when Charles and Francis fall out after the Field of the Cloth of Gold, what side England is going to back and probably at that moment Henry and Wolsey have never been more powerful.

MELVYN BRAGG: Henry VIII and Wolsey by force of personality, we must remember again how tiny England was, less than a fifth of the size of France, the king had no standing army, which the French had, very low tax base and nothing like the size of Charles V, and yet they came on and said, 'we are equal to you, we hold the balance.' And it was personality, it was personality politics.

JOHN GUY: It was personality and magnificence, because the trick is this PR through magnificence. And another thing, the Mass – at the end of the Mass, Cardinal Wolsey pronounced a plenary indulgence, a general indulgence, dispensation, forgiving everybody all their sins. Now very few people could do that. Only the pope could do that, but Wolsey could do it because of his special plenipotentiary powers. That is charismatic, you know, that religious element which marks out Henry VIII and Wolsey. Of course Henry sees what can be done through this method and within ten years he is claiming himself and not the pope to be Supreme Head of the Church in England.

MELVYN BRAGG: Penny Roberts, do you think it was an expensive waste of time for the French, then?

PENNY ROBERTS: No, I don't. They are establishing their reputation as a very magnificent court. It is a fantastically glamorous event which everybody in Europe recognises and the fact is we still see it as an exemplar of what Renaissance princes do. It still has that resonance and I think from that point of view it wasn't a waste of time for them. Francis was spending quite a lot of money on all kinds of things during this period of his rule. He had been spending on the imperial election, his Italian campaigns and so on, so it was just part of his sense of extravagance. I don't think the French feel that they lost out.

STEVEN GUNN: I think it is striking also that it is clearly something that contemporaries could read in two different ways. Some people can say what a magnificent occasion it had been. Then you have someone like Bishop John Fisher who preaches a sermon not long afterwards and uses it as an illustration of how the joys of heaven are much more solid than the joys of earth, because the joys of earth are transient like the Field of the Cloth of Gold, where they were having a war again afterwards. No one could even see the cloth of gold when the wind blew and the dust got in the clothes. So it is something that contemporaries could use as a sign of how passing things are.

MELVYN BRAGG: Did it do anything about the perception of kingship at the time, John Guy?

JOHN GUY: I think the focus now is very much on this side of imperial kingship. What is the difference between a Roman emperor as Francis sees himself, and a king? Of course the answer is that imperial kings are sovereign and increasingly they look not just to the great Roman emperors like Constantine, Justinian and so on, they also look to the priest kings of the Old Testament, who have sacerdotal powers. Francis was the Most Christian King. Henry coveted a similar title . . .

MELVYN BRAGG: Henry was thought to be the Most Christian King at that time, wasn't he? The pope thought better of Henry than he thought of Francis, there were more rumblings in France than there were in England at the time.

PENNY ROBERTS: The traditional French title is of Most Christian King. First Son of the Church is always cited and Francis had had an agreement with the pope whereby he had increased his powers over the Church at this time.

STEVEN GUNN: And that is why Henry wants to get the title of

Defender of the Faith, which he then does within a couple of years afterwards.

JOHN GUY: And then it moves on, because within ten years Henry has failed to get his divorce because Wolsey's plenipotentiary powers are not strong enough to beat Charles V in Italy. And so when Wolsey falls, Henry, as it were, subsumes Wolsey's powers as well as his own and ousts the Pope and then declares that England is an empire and he is Priest King.

PENNY ROBERTS: And Henry needs to get Francis back on side at that point as well because he wants the support of the Parlement of Paris for his divorce and he gets Francis to assist him in this way, and Anne Boleyn is very keen on nurturing Anglo–French relations.

STEVEN GUNN: They meet again, they meet again in Boulogne in 1532, as part of those negotiations.

MELVYN BRAGG: But never again to be such a single spectacular event.

TRANSMITTED: 6.10.2005

c

The Origins of Mathematics

Galileo Galilei wrote: 'The Universe cannot be read until we have learnt the language and become familiar with the characters in which it was written. It is written in mathematical language, and the letters are triangles, circles and other geometrical figures, without which means it is humanly impossible to comprehend a single word.'

But is he right that mathematics is the script in which the universe was written, or is it really just one of many possible systems that humankind has invented to interpret our world?

With me to discuss whether mathematics is a process of invention or a voyage of discovery is Ian Stewart, Professor of Mathematics and Gresham Professor of Geometry at the University of Warwick, author of many books including *Nature's Numbers*. Also with us is the science writer and journalist Margaret Wertheim, author of *Pythagoras' Trousers*; and John D. Barrow, Professor of Applied Mathematics and Theoretical Physics at the University of Cambridge, and the author of *The Universe That Discovered Itself*.

Ian Stewart, if people remember anything from maths at school it is Pythagoras' theorem. Pythagoras in the sixth century BC is credited with being the leading force in the origins of mathematics in the West. What was his philosophy of mathematics and what would you say he is supposed to have given to it?

IAN STEWART: The interesting thing about Pythagoras is his name has come down to us but it is really the cult that he was heavily associated with that we know most about. We know amazingly little about Pythagoras himself. In fact, we don't know for certain he existed. The cult was an interesting mixture of number mysticism and what would now be considered serious mathematics, so the number 2 is the male principle, the number 3 is the female principle, 5 is 2 plus 3, so that represents marriage. All that kind of thing. This is one of the things that Pythagoreans did and that in a sense is not very interesting mathematically.

But they also discovered lots of interesting patterns in numbers, general patterns, things like triangular numbers: 1 + 2 + 3 + 4 makes 10 and so on, that kind of thing. They found patterns in triangular numbers and they discovered the five regular solids, the cube and its more exotic relatives, and Pythagoras' theorem which is the one everyone remembers. Flanders and Swann fans will all know the square on the hypotenuse of a right-angled triangle is equal to the sum of squares on the two adjacent sides. They may have trouble in remembering what a hypotenuse is but it is the long side of a triangle.

Anyway the Pythagoreans and their mystical founder discovered this amazing fact about right-angled triangles which is, if you know what two of the sides are then the third one can be calculated and a huge amount of maths comes from that one fact.

MELVYN BRAGG: Would you like to add to that, John Barrow? Would you like to talk a bit about the place that Pythagoras' idea of numbers has in his version of the universe.

JOHN BARROW: One of the most important differences between Pythagoras' sect and what they thought about numbers and what mathematicians today might think is the difference between numerology and mathematics. Pythagoras in many situations thought that there were some intrinsic meanings to the numbers themselves. So if he found that if there were seven of one thing somewhere in nature it should be related to everything else that had a seven-ness about it.

But nowadays mathematicians don't think there is anything magical or mystical about the numbers themselves but are interested in the relations between numbers so mathematics is really the study of all possible patterns – that is the way I see it. This is probably something that Pythagoras would have liked. He liked to see analogies and relationships between things, so when he could strike gongs and make sounds he noticed how the tones would change with the length of the gong that he was striking.

MELVYN BRAGG: Margaret Wertheim, do you think that Pythagoras, whether he existed or not, according to Ian Stewart, do you think that time in sixth century BC in the West could be considered the beginning of the driving force of mathematics?

MARGARET WERTHEIM: I think that is true. Pythagoras did something that is really incredibly important for the world. He is not the first person who started to explore mathematics seriously and in fact it was the Babylonians who discovered the Pythagorean Theorem that we know. Pythagoras picked it up from them but what he did was he gave the world something else. Pythagoras is the first person that we know of who came up with the idea that mathematics could be the language of the physical world. Other cultures had developed mathematics but no other culture beforehand had had the idea that mathematics would be the ultimate language to describe physical reality and it really is to Pythagoras that we owe this.

So not only do we see the huge inspiration for getting serious mathematics going in the West but more importantly, I think, he is the philosophical inspiration for the idea that we could find mathematical patterns in the physical world. And it is interesting that for most of the ancient western world, including the Greeks and the Romans, and for the first 1,500 years of Christianity that idea was rejected because the alternative scientific tradition in the ancient world was the Aristotelian one and Aristotle very specifically rejected the idea that mathematics could describe the physical.

That I think is one of the ways you can interpret the scientific revolution. The scientific revolution is the time in western history and indeed world history when that transition was made, when our culture as a whole effectively took on the Pythagorean idea that mathematics is the language through which we can study the physical world.

MELVYN BRAGG: You threw away the idea that Pythagoras got his theorem from the Babylonians – you mean the theory about the hypotenuse?

MARGARET WERTHEIM: That's right. Yes, it is well and truly known that the Babylonians had this long before Pythagoras and it is believed that Pythagoras went to Babylon though, as Ian says, his life is clouded in shadow. He lived at that time before there were concrete historical records but it is well and truly believed that he got it from the Babylonians, and incidentally the Chinese discovered the theory independently, but the Babylonians knew it long before Pythagoras and it is believed that is where he ultimately got it. But there is no question that he himself made mathematical discoveries, particularly the patterns and the numbers like the triangular and the square numbers.

JOHN BARROW: There are some very interesting Indian parallels at just about the same time.

MELVYN BRAGG: Yes, in the sixth century BC, and are the Chinese discoveries about the same time, sixth century BC?

MARGARET WERTHEIM: I am not actually sure when the Chinese discovered it.

JOHN BARROW: The Indians wanted it for religious reasons. They liked to have family and village altars that might be just as large as this table in front of us.

MELVYN BRAGG: This table is a normal size dining table. Could seat six.

JOHN BARROW: But for religious reasons, the altars were made in shapes of strange creatures like falcons and birds which have an unusual angular shape and they would be made of lots of small bricks of triangular and rectangular and square shapes. Now if things went badly for you you had to appease the gods in some way and you did this by doubling the area of your altar. This is a non-trivial problem if your altar is not just a simple square or even if it is a simple square. So there was a great book of recipes of geometry as to how you change the area of your altar. It is called *The Silver Sutra*, 'The Book of the Cord', and this really contains lots of geometry about Pythagorean thought. There was a great tradition that Pythagoras sacrificed an ox to the gods when he found his theorem. This couldn't possibly be true because he didn't eat animals. It is not something that his sect would have done but the suspicion was that this came with the tradition from the Indian culture, that Pythagoras and triangles and theorems of this sort were about altars and sacrifice.

MARGARET WERTHEIM: One of the interesting things is that the link between mathematics and religion is very strong in many cultures and as Ian rightly points out the Pythagorean cult was as much a religious community as it was a proto-scientific community. Indeed in the Pythagorean community to be inducted in the mystery of numbers, to learn mathematical theorems, one had to go through rituals of purification.

Pythagoras associated numbers with the gods. In fact he literally associated the numbers one through ten with the major gods, with the Greek pantheon. For him Apollo was the primary god and he associated him with number one. In Pythagoras' mind the number one was the ultimate god and so Pythagoras believed that studying the relationships between numbers was actually understanding the properties of divine beings.

MELVYN BRAGG: Can we move on to Plato? Ian, Plato believed that mathematics was the finest training of the mind. Above his Academy he wrote 'Let no one unversed in geometry enter here' and that Academy lasted for about 900 years. It was perhaps the most influential mathematical university in western history. Can you explain why he thought it was the finest training for the mind first of all and, secondly, what would you say was his theory of mathematical form?

IAN STEWART: The Greeks developed mathematics and more and more they turned it into a very logically rigorous way of thinking. You would start from very simple statements that nobody could reasonably disagree with or at least everyone knew what those statements were and then you could build upon those. You could prove Pythagoras' theorem not just discover it experimentally or have hand-waving arguments that said it ought to be true.

And Plato is looking at this tradition and formalising in his own philosophical way what is going on and there is this feeling that somehow mathematical arguments in that form are crystal clear. There is less room for disagreement about what you are saying than in almost any other area of human activity. Even today you have mathematicians who disagree about something. They will fight, they will argue, they will spend six months fighting and arguing about some obscure fact and one day one of them will turn to the other and say, whoops, sorry, I have been completely wrong, I have just seen what you have been trying to tell me – you are absolutely right. I have see a this happen and in fact I have been involved in this kind of thing myself.

And Plato, looking at this, is saying if you want a model for being pretty sure you know what you are talking about, then this is the model. In that sense he sees it as the highest form of intellectual activity. Then the question arises of just what is it you are really doing here and what are these things. Plato gets very involved in trying to find a kind of mental image and a description of what mathematicians are doing when they do mathematics.

MELVYN BRAGG: And what do we come up with, John Barrow? What is his notion of mathematical forms? Plato's notion.

JOHN BARROW: He is interested in the unchanging aspects of the universe. These are the things he thinks are most fundamental, most important, most worthy of study. So although the Greeks moved to the study of mathematics for its own sake it appears they are not just counting and using their fingers but they had the idea, as Ian said, of laying down axioms, rules for the game, and then exploring what sorts of games could follow from that. Plato was persuaded that there existed behind reality perfect blueprints of everything that we see around us and the things that we see, like this cup here, are just poor versions, poor copies of the eternal blueprints.

MELVYN BRAGG: There is a perfect line that has no breadth which is a line that we can perhaps imagine but never reproduce.

JOHN BARROW: Yes. It never seemed a terribly persuasive philosophy to me because if I see a wavy line on the page, do I regard this as a perfect reproduction of the eternal form for a slightly wavy line or as the imperfect reproduction of the perfect form for a completely straight line? So this philosophy enabled you to take a very hard-nosed realist view of things that you really were discovering, properties of cubes and triangles, because they really existed somewhere. You couldn't get your hands on the place where they really existed but nonetheless you were discovering things that were true somewhere and somehow.

This view has all sorts of subtle aspects to it. If you work in cosmology, as I do, you are very used to the whole argument of was the universe created out of nothing or not. For a Platonist this idea doesn't really make very much sense. The idea of nothing is inconceivable. Even if there isn't a material universe with all the chairs and people in it, there are still the ideas, the blueprints, they still exist. And so the idea of creating a universe out of nothing is not an idea you are going to latch on to if you are a Platonist.

MELVYN BRAGG: Margaret Wertheim, therefore do you think Platonic mathematical reality can be seen as a rival to the idea of an omnipotent God?

MARGARET WERTHEIM: It is a rival to the Christian one in one way, but in fact the Christian tradition picks up the Platonic tradition so the two have had a very lovely history of being entwined. Effectively, the idea of Platonic eternal forms is an extension of the Pythagorean idea. Pythagoras did something very interesting. What he said was that if you can arrange numbers into patterns, like Ian pointed out before – ten dots can be arranged into a triangle – what Pythagoras said then that all numbers have form therefore number is the ultimate archetype of form.

Plato extended this idea to make a more universal concept of it that all physical forms on earth have archetypal transcendent forms in some idealised realm. In a sense these Platonic forms become like gods themselves and that idea has met very well with Christianity because God in the Christian tradition is the transcendent, the ultimate transcendent form. Christianity therefore picked up the Platonic idea and has a very long history of that even before the seventeenth century and the development of modern science. That Platonic idea was picked up in the Renaissance and even before that in the Middle Ages.

MELVYN BRAGG: Ian Stewart, both Plato and Pythagoras appear to have believed in an ordered universe. Do you think this was an act of faith or a positive deduction?

IAN STEWART: I think it is both. It depends on what spectacles you are wearing when you are looking at the universe. You can look at the universe and say look how amazingly ordered it is and as we understand more of it we uncover more and more order. You look at the sky and it all seems this random mass of little lights that go round and round and then you start to see various patterns. On the other hand you can wake up the next morning and say look at the total mess out there, it is all unpredictable, I don't know what is going to happen next. I can walk out the door and something dreadful will happen to me and I just have no idea what is coming.

It is really not until about the eighteenth century onwards that you get some sort of synthesis that says well, those are two different aspects of basically the same thing. I think that even back in Plato and Pythagoras' time they did have that feeling that there are these two aspects to the universe and in some sense they must be related. One way certain cultures would explain this is that order is when the gods decide to set the thing up, set up the machinery and let the machinery run and disorder is when the gods come along and meddle with it.

It is very puzzling and I think we are still puzzling about it today, this clear source of order in the world around us and apparently deep and important structures and patterns and laws, laws of nature as some people say.

MELVYN BRAGG: Can I just bring it slightly more up to date by going to the second century with Ptolemy who discovered, made a breakthrough, predicted the cycle of the planets? It was used for navigation successfully for many years and indeed for many centuries. Yet these great discoveries of Ptolomaic thought are based on wrong mathematics because they were based on the idea that the sun and the planets revolved around the earth. What does that tell you about mathematics? It doesn't have to be true to be effective – is that what you would draw from that, John Barrow?

JOHN BARROW: Mathematics is the only thing related to science that we do that is really infinite, there is no limit to the number of mathematical structures and patterns which could be invented and there is no reason to expect that all of them are actually manifested in nature. Some are. And this is really one of the messages of how modern mathematics is very different from the mathematics of Plato and Pythagoras.

If you take something like geometry, the Greeks discovered the rules and regulations of what we now call Euclidian geometry, geometry on a flat, plain surface where the interior angles of triangles add up to 180 degrees. Right until the beginning of the nineteenth century it was believed that this was the one and only possible geometry and this was how the world actually was. The discovery of Euclidean geometry, this rule, had a deep philosophical and religious significance for many people because it showed that human thinking could get at part of the ultimate truth of reality. If a theologian was to start pontificating about the nature of God or something, someone might object and say how can you possibly know anything about ultimate things? He could point at Euclidean geometry and say this is part of the ultimate truth of how things were.

And so there was a major shock to the system when in the early nineteenth century mathematicians discovered that you could invent other geometries which were logically self-consistent but they were not Euclidean. They were geometries that applied on curved surfaces. If you looked at a Euclidean triangle in a curved mirror you would see a rather bent triangle. All of a sudden mathematics was about the free invention of rules and regulations which just had to be logically consistent and they didn't actually have to have examples in the real world that you could point at.

People started writing peculiar books and pamphlets with titles like *Non-Euclidean Forms of Government* or *Non-Euclidean Economics*. Non-Euclidean became a byword that was relativist and anti-establishment and so forth. This is one of the messages of modem mathematics that it works jolly well as a description of nature but you can invent any structures you want. Mathematical existence just means it is logically self-consistent.

MELVYN BRAGG: Margaret Wertheim, can I come to the point
of the nature of mathematics: whether it is a process of discovery,
whether the mathematics is there, whether the calculus is there,
whether Newton and Leibnitz discovered it or whether mathematics is somehow out there. Can you give us your views on
that?

MARGARET WERTHEIM: The question is generally put in those
terms: is it discovered or is it invented? And I think that is actually
a wrong way of characterising the problem. I agree with what John
has said. I have always believed that mathematics is the language
of pattern. It is the formal language in which we can discuss the
properties of patterns and the relationships between various patterns
and, as John said, because the world is structured, because it is not
complete chaos there must be patterns in it so it is not surprising
that we find mathematical patterns in nature.

I don't think that necessarily means that those patterns are
invented however. What I reject is the notion that those patterns had
some kind of archetypal transcendent existence without conscious
human beings there to find them.

MELVYN BRAGG: So on other planets there are not mathematics.
Other planets without human beings do not have mathematics.

MARGARET WERTHEIM: Well it doesn't have to be human beings
but I think some subconscious . . .

MELVYN BRAGG: Intelligent life, whatever that is . . .

MARGARET WERTHEIM: Conscious intelligent life. Absolutely. I
would argue that in the absence of conscious intelligent beings there
are no such things as numbers, that numbers don't have a Platonic
or Pythagorean transcendent existence.

MELVYN BRAGG: But how can you believe both that the universe
is ordered, as you said a few sentences ago, and that it doesn't exist
without an observer?

MARGARET WERTHEIM: The universe has an existence but then
the question is . . .

MELVYN BRAGG: But isn't its existence to a great extent dependent on its mathematics? As the three of you have been arguing.

MARGARET WERTHEIM: I don't think the existence of the universe is dependent on mathematics at all. I think that mathematics is a language that we have found which is an extremely powerful language because it is a language that can discuss the formal properties of patterns.

MELVYN BRAGG: But don't you think that part of the order is due to the working of mathematics? I'll ask Ian Stewart to come in here.

IAN STEWART: I am going to sit on the fence here but there are two possibilities. One is that human mathematics is our understanding of something that is genuinely there as a basic ingredient of the universe. That God was a mathematician and we are picking up bits and pieces of it. The other extreme is to say no, no. Mathematics is like it is because that is the way our minds work, that's the way we have evolved to structure the universe around us.

I think there is a middle ground which says a lot of these patterns must be real in some sense but we haven't got the ultimate understanding of what they are. The whole history of science shows that what we thought a hundred years ago as the ultimate pattern of gravitation or something turns out to be pretty good, but something else comes along that seems to be better.

MELVYN BRAGG: But it is still a workable version of how the universe works. Ptolemy's was, Newton's was, Einstein and so on.

IAN STEWART: I agree with Margaret and I think most mathematicians if you pin them into a corner will agree that what we call mathematics on this planet, and it is the only one we know, is really a kind of shared experience of human minds. It's a mental construct but it is not one that we have just made up for its own sake, we have made it up because we see a lot of things in the world around us.

MARGARET WERTHEIM: That's why I think the problem is this dichotomy. Is it discovered or invented? I think those words are problematic particularly.

MELVYN BRAGG: They are difficult to answer, I think. I am sorry, I am trying to maintain the integrity of the question. I don't think it is problematic. I think you are finding it quite difficult to answer because it seems to me that you have all been saying that we take from Pythagoras and Plato a fundamental place of mathematics in the formation and ordering of the universe. I am saying, well, is that in the universe, in itself, or is that in the universe because we see it and I think that is interesting ... if you don't think it is interesting, let's move on . . .

MARGARET WERTHEIM: No, no it is a fascinating question.

MELVYN BRAGG: John Barrow wants to come in.

JOHN BARROW: There's a couple of things to say. First I think it is a mistake to lump all mathematics into one bag and say is mathematics discovered or is it invented? Suppose that Plato was correct and mathematics lived out there, a great body of it, and we discovered it by some extrasensory perception. Imagine we did but, having discovered it, we would be free to use what we discovered to invent other generalisations and things that flowed from it.

So I think it is clear that we do invent some bits of mathematics for the purposes of generalisation. But it is well to remember that our minds which, you know, do this generalisation, which do this studying are the result of the process of natural selection in which selection acts in a real environment and selects against something which really exists. The fact that we have ears, which have all sorts of interesting properties as acoustic detectors which evolved before we were conscious, is witness to the fact that there really is something called sound that has very definite properties.

You know that an evolutionary process can select and optimise reception. So when we end up with minds that can process information in logical ways and have intuitions about geometry and counting, I think this is a reflection of the fact that embedded in the world, the world around us, there are aspects of what we would call a mathematical sword which are true. They are part of reality.

MELVYN BRAGG: Margaret?

MARGARET WERTHEIM: I think that is a very important point, that the mathematical patterns that we find in nature are absolutely parts of reality and they are very powerful parts of reality because they allow us to make very concrete predictions. For instance, the mathematics of quantum physics has given us microchips. Nature does exhibit these very complex mathematical structures that we can then turn into practical applications. But the question whether mathematics is discovered or invented can be looked at as a question that has been asked by the mathematician and philosopher Brian Rotman which is – where do the numbers come from? The Platonist answer to this, or the Pythagorean answer, is they have some transcendent existence above and beyond the physical world.

MELVYN BRAGG: There will always be numbers . . .

MARGARET WERTHEIM: If there is no physical world or if something is prior to the existence of the physical world, numbers had an existence out there, as John said, in some sort of disembodied realm. But Brian Rotman suggests this idea. He says numbers come from the process of counting. So if I can go one cup, two cups, three cups, four cups, there are four cups here and in some sense four has an existence. But if there weren't any conscious beings who could count, do numbers have an existence? And his answer is no and I think that is a very valid point. If there are no beings who can do the counting in what sense can you say the numbers exists?

MELVYN BRAGG: That implies that in the end nothing can exist without an observer.

JOHN BARROW: Brian Rotman's point, I think, is an invalid point.

MELVYN BRAGG: Can you explain why?

JOHN BARROW: In astronomy you have a nice way of getting at this because when you look out into space, enormous distances, you are also looking back in time. When you receive light from distant quasars that light left with all its bar codings telling you what atoms produced the light billions of years ago, billions of years before there was any life on earth. And so we can tell that there really was an ordered structure, there were things like counting, there were interrelationships between frequencies, the sort that we understand today, long before there were anything like people, long before there were anything like stars.

I think in a curious way we have direct observational evidence that there were patterns of a numerical sort certainly before there were people to do the counting. But again we are just getting at this point that maths is about patterns and the universe is about patterns. The mystery, I think, which has now shifted somewhere else is the fact that the patterns are often extraordinarily simple. The universe is much easier to understand in many respects than we might have suspected.

The human brain is proving a much more challenging thing to understand than many aspects of the early structure of the whole universe, or the nature of elementary particles. That just because things are ultimate and cosmic does not necessarily mean they are harder to understand than a piece of wood that is sitting on the table in front of you. I think that the mystery is that often simple mathematics, mathematics that we are able to understand, that we are able to write down, is so powerful and enables us to make such astonishingly accurate predictions.

This is the type of prediction that people in the social sciences would give their eye teeth for. To be able to predict things correctly to sixteen decimal places. It then becomes really unconvincing when a sociologist or scientist says, 'well, you know, you really are just inventing this, it is just a way of looking at it. I can nearly predict how people are going to behave in one hour's time but I may be wrong.' There is clearly something going on here that is of much deeper significance.

IAN STEWART: I just wanted to throw in a quick yes-but. I have this image in my mind of creatures that live in a world, some alien world, not even a planet necessarily, it is a gas cloud, and these are creatures of flows, or flux, they don't have things, they don't have cups, they can't count things because there aren't any things, they can't do the geometry of triangles because as soon as they put a point down it moves. Now we started from numbers which we think are basic and worked our way, we say up, to things like fluid flow patterns and vortices and things like this. These creatures might well start with an intuition for vorticity and discover much later, if ever, there are these wonderful discreet things called numbers which come out of the topology of the flow.

These are really terrible esoteric things that you don't do until you are a PhD at these creatures' universities. I have described that in terms of their maths that overlaps us but they have followed a different route through it. I think it certainly possible once you start thinking that way that there might be almost completely independent ways of carving up these patterns and structures. In other words, there is something in the universe that we pull numbers out from and say numbers are very fundamental. The fundamental nature of numbers might be an illusion but the thing we are trying to capture is a lot more real.

In that sense I agree with Melvyn in that I think there is something there and we are pulling it out and it is very basic. On the other hand, although I am a mathematician, I am not particularly committed to numbers as the basis of this. This could be something that we like. We live in a world of discreet objects and we are possessive creatures, we like to count how many sheep we have got, count how many cups we own, that kind of thing. Other creatures might not do that at all.

MELVYN BRAGG: Margaret Wertheim, did mathematics change fundamentally in its application to the real world after Galileo, Descartes, Newton, those advances?

MARGARET WERTHEIM: Yes. I think the seventeenth century was a very critical time because what those physicists really demonstrated was the Pythagorean point that mathematics can indeed be extremely useful for actually describing the world. Now Pythagoras had believed that it was but, as I said, the Aristotelian tradition had rejected that and I think that what people like Galileo, Descartes and Newton demonstrated was that in some sense Pythagoras was right.

Mathematics is an incredibly powerful language for describing the properties and qualities and patterns in the physical world and a particularly critical part of this was the discovery of calculus because that demonstrated that mathematics could in some sense talk about changing patterns. Prior to that mathematics had really only been useful for describing the relationships between the heavenly bodies, the stars and the planets, which as far as the ancients could tell was eternal and static and timeless.

Calculus opened up the whole possibility that mathematics could be used for describing processes that changed. That knocked down Aristotle's major argument that mathematics was OK for describing eternal things like the stars but it could tell us nothing about the nature of change. In the seventeenth century we came to see that we could in fact describe change with mathematics.

MELVYN BRAGG: Talking about application, John Barrow, Kepler studied the six-sidedness of snowflakes and from that there is a line towards atomic physics. Is there something about mathematics that is the law of unintended consequences, as it were?

JOHN BARROW: Yes. The period that Margaret picked on then with Galileo and Newton and Kepler before gives us a good illustration of this. Back with the early Greeks, Apollonius, who came after Euclid and was their next greatest mathematician, studied all the properties of ellipses and hyperbole and so forth and there is a great book of rather pure mathematics, all very elegant and possibly not terribly useful.

Then suddenly if you want to be Kepler and Newton and you want to study the shapes of the orbits of planets around the sun or the paths that comets take as they pass by you have got this off-the-shelf mathematics which is precisely what you require to explain something.

MELVYN BRAGG: From about 1,500 years earlier?

JOHN BARROW: Yes. This happens on many occasions. In the development of the general theory of relativity Einstein was fortunate that people like Riemann before him had developed the detailed geometry of these non-Euclidean surfaces that we talked about earlier and other mathematical formulas that he could take off the shelf. Now these formulisms are often developed for almost aesthetic reasons, mathematicians just exploring the patterns for their own sake.

In modem elementary particle physics it is particular types of patterns and symmetries catalogued by an area of maths called group theory which are really the key to unlocking how elementary particles behave. It is mysterious that mathematics developed for other purposes, or perhaps no purpose whatsoever, turn out to be miraculously appropriate as a description of what is going on in a problem of physics or chemistry.

MELVYN BRAGG: Ian Stewart, is Platonism still alive in mathematics? Are mathematicians still looking for what is transcendent? I would like to throw a little spoke into the works and it seems to me – and this is very personal and possibly completely irrelevant – that music is the best evidence for the perfection of mathematics, and it is interesting that Pythagoras talked about the harmony of the spheres and Mozart was a great mathematician as a boy.

IAN STEWART: This is a long-running undercurrent and there is something to it if you talk to professional mathematicians. On the one hand they know that what they do is a collective human activity and on the other hand they are all closet Platonists. I am.

MELVYN BRAGG: What is a closet Platonist? Let's have it out!

IAN STEWART: OK. While you are trying to do creative mathematics, what you are trying to do – is it invent, is it discover? I don't know but I am trying to do it – something new, you are trying to solve a problem that has not been solved before. You have the very strong feeling that there is only one answer and it is sitting there and your job is to try and find what it is. You can't make it up as you go along, you can make up your exploratory route towards finding it. We all do but you have this mental image of moving through some sort of landscape or some sort of world looking for things and in order to carry out that process it makes it much more possible to do it if, while you are doing it, you have this illusion that these things exist. How can I look for something that isn't there?

I think that what really goes on here is not so much music, it is a narrative, we are telling ourselves a story, a mathematical proof is a story. We are acting out a narrative in our minds and this is the way mathematicians discover or invent new things. If you then say now that is what it feels like when you are doing it but is it really that? Some of them will say yes it is really that and get very aggressive about it but most will say no this is just a convenient way of thinking about it and it is a very effective way of thinking about it.

So Platonism is alive and well in the operative working philosophy of mathematicians but they wouldn't formalise it into something in the sense that a hardcore philosopher would formalise it and say this is what is really going on.

MELVYN BRAGG: John Barrow, what is your comment on that?

JOHN BARROW: I think if you did a poll of mathematicians and you were to ask mathematicians what their subject was you would get a strangely ambiguous answer. If you went round universities asking historians what their subject was or chemists they would probably be able to tell you without any difficulty but most mathematicians probably couldn't tell you.

MELVYN BRAGG: Why is that?

JOHN BARROW: Because they have this dichotomy about invention and discovery and whereas Monday to Friday, as Ian said, they might act as though they were Platonists, if you caught them at the weekend in the armchair and asked them they would be more philosophical and circumspect about it. So it is a curious ambiguity and puzzle that you can have different sectors of this huge subject having quite different views about what its nature is. For some people it is just a game, it is like chess. You lay down rules and regulations and you simply explore the finite steps and consequences of that. You catalogue all the possible moves, all the possible positions that the possible games can have. Other people, notably Roger Penrose, regard mathematics as very much existing in the Platonic realm and we pick out these counterintuitive ideas from that realm.

MELVYN BRAGG: Margaret Wertheim.

MARGARET WERTHEIM: I think that Platonism is still alive and well among mathematicians and perhaps even more so among physicists that I have spoken to. I think it raises a very interesting question that if the mathematics is in the world then what is doing the calculating, and apparently the physicist Richard Feynman became a bit obsessed with this idea. Are the atoms out there actually calculating these very complex mathematical structures or are the structures somehow there and we are the ones who somehow reflect the calculating on to them?

TRANSMITTED: 11.1.2001

d

Witchcraft

In 1486 a book was published in Latin, it was called *Malleus Maleficarum: The Hammer of Witches*, and it very soon outsold every publication in Europe but the Bible. It was written by Heinrich Kramer, a German Dominican priest and a witch-finder. He wrote:

> Magicians, who are commonly called witches, are thus termed on account of the magnitude of their evil deeds. These are they who by the permission of God disturb the elements, who drive to distraction the minds of men, such as have lost their trust in God, and by the terrible power of their evil spells, without any actual draught or poison, kill human beings.

'Thou shalt not suffer a witch to live,' says *Exodus*, and in the period of the Reformation and after, it is estimated that over a hundred thousand men and women in Europe met their death after being convicted of witchcraft. Why did practices that had been tolerated for centuries suddenly become such a threat? What brought the prosecution of witchcraft to an end, and was there anyone ever in Europe who could truly be termed a witch?

With me to discuss witchcraft in Europe is Alison Rowlands, Senior Lecturer in European History at the University of Essex; Lyndal Roper, Fellow and Tutor in History at Balliol College, University of Oxford and author of *Witch Craze*; and Malcolm Gaskill, Fellow and Director of Studies in History at Churchill College, Cambridge.

Alison Rowlands, before we discuss the witchcraft trials and how they started, what is behind them? Can we tease out the ideas of what witches were and what ideas magicians or so called 'cunning folk' had before, let us say, the fifteenth century? What was going on?

ALISON ROWLANDS: The late medieval period is one where the possibility and power of magic permeates the whole of society from the elite down to the lowest orders. I think we can distinguish three ideas about magical witchcraft. One is the belief that people could work black magic or *maleficium* or harmful magic against other people. Conversely, there are also ideas about individuals who could work good through magic, the so-called white witches or cunning folk, who could heal disease and protect against witchcraft and so on.

So we have a very longstanding set of beliefs around the idea of the possibility of sorcery or black magic and also white magic. What really changes, and what I would see as an essential precondition of the period of the trials, is a sort of third layer of belief in witchcraft as demonic or diabolic.

MELVYN BRAGG: Before we come to the witchcraft trials, before we come to the Reformation, in the centuries before that, there were people who, at a folk level or at a court level, could be called magicians or sorcerers. You have talked about white magic and black magic, so what were they dealing in? How did they trade, as it were, in their occupation?

ALISON ROWLANDS: Well, white witches, or cunning folk, those who were deemed to be able to work good magic, would very often have another occupation, perhaps one linked to working with livestock, like shepherds or blacksmiths. Their working in white magic was a kind of sideline, if you like, often to protect livestock which was extremely valuable at this period So they literally did trade in white magic, they offered cures to the population.

MELVYN BRAGG: What sort of cures did they offer? Are we going back to pagan times? Are we going back to old folk recipes? I would just like some details.

ALISON ROWLANDS: It varies enormously. One of the problems is actually tracing the origins. We have a very longstanding process whereby pre-Christian beliefs get Christian ideas superimposed on them. So for example one thing that cunning folk might do is speak blessings over animals to try and protect them, so they are appropriating the magic of the Church by using quasi-Christian ritual. They are very eclectic. They take whatever they feel might be useful. It could be the use of herbs, it could be sort of blessings, it could be use of rituals and so on. So it is an eclectic mix of the pre-Christian and Christian as well.

MELVYN BRAGG: This may be regarded as shamanistic and rather mysterious but on the other hand another way of looking at it was as a search for knowledge in a world where exact knowledge was far from available, wasn't it? They were looking at ways to find how the world worked.

ALISON ROWLANDS: How the world worked and also how to cope with the daily misfortunes and hardships of life – disease death, dearth and so on. But I don't think we should make it seem too shamanistic and mysterious. These are people who live in their communities, they are known and used by their neighbours, so I don't think we should try and see them as something too mysterious necessarily.

MELVYN BRAGG: Lyndal Roper, did the witch craze start before the Reformation? Had the magicians, the sorcerers, the cunning folk become persons open to persecution before the Reformation?

LYNDAL ROPER: Yes, they had, and there are a series of witch panics. There are some in the early fifteenth century and then you get occasional ones throughout and up to the late fifteenth century. One of the interesting things about the *Malleus* is that it was written out of that inquisitor's experience of a failed witch panic in 1485. What prompts the persecution before the Reformation are fears that the Devil is at work in the world and that it is a new kind of heresy that has to be attacked. What is absolutely fascinating is that once you get to the Reformation itself, witch-hunting seems to stop, so there is a period when there is not really much of it going on. Then it is a new generation of people who have been formed by the Reformation and by the experience of the Counter-Reformation who are the ones who get interested in witch-hunting.

MELVYN BRAGG: So what date are we talking about?

LYNDAL ROPER: It starts in the 1560s but it really gets going in the 1580s.

MELVYN BRAGG: And are we talking about the Catholics and Protestants being equally zealous?

LYNDAL ROPER: We are talking about both of them being zealous witch-hunters, although we are also discovering the places where there are most victims turn out to be areas ruled by Catholic prince-bishops.

MELVYN BRAGG: And mostly in Germany.

LYNDAL ROPER: Mostly in Germany. Just to give you a sense of that, we think that in Germany there are something like 20,000 executions, that is about half the total that we know for western Europe.

MELVYN BRAGG: I will come back to that in a second, because why should it be Germany and why so heavily is a very interesting point. But why, given that Catholics and Protestants were so opposed to each other in so many ways, why did they both go for witches in much the same way, with much the same venom?

LYNDAL ROPER: You are absolutely right, it is very puzzling. You would think Catholics and Protestants, they hate each other, and if you think about their views of women, for example, it's an issue on which these two are completely polarised. Catholics venerate Mary; Protestants are saying Mary is just an example for all Christians, she is not someone to be venerated. Catholics are insisting on the importance of the convent and the spiritual role for women. Protestants are closing down convents. So you would think that on the issue of women they would take very different standpoints and yet they both hunt witches. It is very puzzling.

MELVYN BRAGG: Let's just note at this point about 20 to 25 per cent of the witches hunted were men. So it isn't just women.

LYNDAL ROPER: No, it is not just women.

MELVYN BRAGG: It is to do with the idea of the release of the Devil, isn't it, Malcolm Gaskill? However imperfect (and we hear very little except how imperfect the Catholic Church was in the Middle Ages) however imperfect it was it was one thing, it was a canopy, and then it is riven, and that must have been – if we can try and re-imagine ourselves back there, which is very difficult – it must have been terrifying for many people, that there was not just one truth, there were two ways at least and maybe there were several ways and they were at odds with each other. So what had caused this? One cause could be the Devil had got loose.

MALCOLM GASKILL: Yes, that is absolutely right. Before the Reformation the apparatus of the ideology of witchcraft was already being quite well formed, and so what we see from the later Middle Ages into the early modern period is the way that trials for heresy and a more centralised idea for the Catholic Church shades into witchcraft, mostly because of the inclusion of the idea of the Devil.

We see this in the western Christian tradition in Thomas Aquinas and in St Augustine. There is an idea of the demonic coming into Christianity, deviance and the idea particularly that ordinary human beings can actually form pacts with Satan. So I think the idea of the Devil is coming to the fore before the Reformation, but in the Reformation period this monopoly over Christian truth is really being divided into more of a free market of ideas between Protestantism and Catholicism which opens up a fault line in society from the top to the bottom in popular tradition and in the learning tradition.

MELVYN BRAGG: So before this eruption there is quite a lot of preparation, as it were, going on inside the culture. It's what Alison was talking about, ideas of magic which had gone on for centuries and cunning folk, sometimes black and sometimes white. The idea of persecution before the Reformation and the idea of the Devil being named and thought to be the cause of disruption developed inside the Catholic Church before the Reformation.

MALCOLM GASKILL: Yes, that is a lot to do with it. One of the ideas about witchcraft, which I think we need to grasp, is that it never means just one thing, it is always in itself a contested definition right from the earliest days. So it is always an area in which other ideas about society and culture and religion can be thrashed out. It is a kind of symbolic vehicle, certainly by the period of the Reformation. The Protestant reformers, for example, sometimes argue that the Devil has actually been rather idle in the pre-Reformation period and that by exposing the pope as Antichrist the Devil is reactivated and is furious and goes charging through the world trying to corrupt ordinary Christians to lead them to their own damnation. So the clock is ticking for the last days of man for many of these radical Protestant thinkers.

MELVYN BRAGG: Before we come to the horrible and sometimes comically strange details of these terrible trials, just one more piece of contextualisation. We have talked about what is happening in the Catholic Church, we have talked about what is happening in the area of magic. But there are also the meteorological conditions of the time, which all three of you have written about, that played a very important part.

MALCOLM GASKILL: This period, the early modern period, roughly 1500 to 1700, is sometimes called the Little Ice Age. There is an overall dip in temperatures across Europe which affects crop yields and this is sometimes linked to the fact that it does coincide with the witch craze. It is sometimes seen as being one of the causal factors. It is undeniably the case that there are a series of bad harvests. In England, for example, in the 1590s, this is both the period when witch-hunting and witchcraft prosecutions escalate and also a period of great hardship and failed harvests. Now I think part of the connection here is that this reduces the quality of life for most people, raises competition within communities, causing tension between neighbours that might be expressed as a witchcraft accusation, rather than something that directly leads to witch-hunting.

MELVYN BRAGG: Because we are talking about a period where just getting through the winter for a great number of people in let's call it loosely Europe was enormously difficult.

ALISON ROWLANDS: We are looking at a very subsistent society where people are permanently teetering on the edge of survival and potentially not surviving. For many centuries people believed that one of the types of evil magic that witches could work was weather magic, that they could manipulate the weather and did that to damage harvests, destroy harvests.

So for early modern peasants, if their harvest is destroyed, perhaps by a severe hailstorm, this happens in Germany in the 1580s, it is one of the triggers for the persecutions around the city of Trier. It's not just being able to explain something strange and unfortunate, it's actually being able to take action. You can petition your overlord to bring prosecutions against the witches who you fear have caused this catastrophe to your local subsistence.

MELVYN BRAGG: OK. Well, let's go into much more detail now. Lyndal Roper, let's look at this book, *Malleus Maleficarum: The Hammer of the Witches*, written by Heinrich Kramer, a German Dominican. Can you give us one or two instances from this book which was tremendously influential, the first of the demonologies. What was his drive? What was he essentially saying?

LYNDAL ROPER: He thinks that there is a conspiracy of witches who are out to attack Christendom and he thinks that those witches are primarily women and he has these extraordinary passages in the work which are incredibly misogynistic which talk about women's slippery tongues, which talk about how they meet and hold assemblies and how they take children and how they kill them and eat them in horrible banquets. It is a very gruesome book, it is a very strange book. It is set up as a scholastic treatise with a series of questions and answers, and it is an intellectual *tour de force* which has all kinds of authorities that it appeals to, but it also has the most extraordinary stories within it.

MELVYN BRAGG: The stories are those he collected while he was going round being a witch-finder, and they are sometimes comical, sometimes odd. Witches, for example, could make the male member disappear and they could also produce a bowl of male members from which you could choose the male member most suited to your purposes and get on with it. So what is all that about? Are these reported tales?

LYNDAL ROPER: It is a strange mixture. It is tales that he has come across during interrogation but I think there are also tales that have come out of popular culture, like the extraordinary one you mentioned. These are male members in a nest who are seen to eat wheat and corn and when a man looks at these he says, 'Oh, I will have that one' – pointing to the biggest, and he is told, 'Oh no you can't, because that one belongs to the parish priest.' Here Kramer is taking up a whole series of popular tales which are directed against clergy and often written by monks who are in competition with secular clergy.

MELVYN BRAGG: So the whole thing becomes a complete mix of settling scores, heavy theology, folk misogyny and trying to find a way to turn the sorcerers and magicians and people in these tightly connected communities into something else. Can you give us a map of Europe at this time? You have said already that it was in Germany that this happened most ferociously and most extensively. How did other countries, just briefly, compare? Obviously England and Scotland, but Italy and so on.

LYNDAL ROPER: Well, Spain and Italy seem to have had comparatively little witch-hunting and that is very strange because they are the areas where the Inquisition is important in witch-hunting. We all have this negative view of the Inquisition and we think that the Inquisition was really hot on witches, but in fact, because the Inquisition is concerned to convert people and bring them back to true belief, witch-hunting in Spain and Italy doesn't result in as many executions.

MELVYN BRAGG: Why was it as ferocious as it was in Germany?

LYNDAL ROPER: I think that that is to do with the very particular moral climate that you get in the wake of the Reformation and Counter-Reformation, when people are absolutely convinced that the Devil is about, that he is someone who might appear to you, who might talk to you and tempt you and where people are very concerned that the last days are coming, as Malcolm said, and where their religious identity has to be proved in competition with another faith.

MELVYN BRAGG: Briefly, England and Scotland, how do they compare?

ALISON ROWLANDS: England and Scotland have what one might call milder intensities of persecution. For example, in England it has been estimated that there are around 500 executions throughout the early modern period, as opposed to the 20,000 that Lyndal mentioned for Germany. In Scotland the number is somewhat higher, it is around 1,000, although the population in Scotland is much smaller, so I guess when we are talking about intensity of persecution we always need to bear in mind the ratio of persecutions to population.

One little note of caution I would just add is that we are talking about nations as though they were whole units, whereas there are areas of Germany which experienced virtually no executions for witchcraft, various southern imperial cities, for example, or the Rhineland Palatinate. We need to take things down to a regional level because it is a very patchy phenomenon. There are places, as Lyndal has rightly said, which are very, very severely affected by witch persecution, but others which aren't. One thing to think about is, given the beliefs are there and given that there are laws in place to persecute witches, why doesn't it happen at the same rate everywhere?

MELVYN BRAGG: Coming back to the texts, there's the drive of misogyny and the basic idea that women had uncontrollable sexual desires. This according to many of the demonologists was the root cause, because this put women in contact with the Devil. The Devil could seduce them and the seduction was very unsatisfactory because of his ice cold member, by which they knew he was the Devil. Nevertheless, women's unlimited sexual desire was the cause of the problem, according to some of these writers.

ALISON ROWLANDS: Again, I think we need to be careful not to generalise too much from the *Malleus*. Lyndal has already said it is a particularly misogynistic text. It stands out even amongst the demonologies, which are generally misogynistic, as being peculiarly misogynistic and also peculiarly obsessed with that sexual aspect of the pact with the Devil. But certainly that is the essential idea, that women are irrational, weaker in faith, more governed by their carnal lusts and therefore they are more likely to be liable to the seduction of the Devil.

MALCOLM GASKILL: Yes, that's right. One thing we need also to remember is that misogyny wasn't something that was unusual in society. This is a patriarchal society and patriarchy is about political authority and it is about the way that all early modern society is structured. To that extent there is not an equation between women and evil or between women and witches. There is an association based on the fact that women are seen through biblical authority and through tradition to be morally weak and therefore more vulnerable to diabolical temptation, which is why we find only 20 per cent of witches being men. It is a tendency, it is not an exact correlation between women and witches.

LYNDAL ROPER: I think it is not just that women are very sexual and therefore open to the seductive wiles of the Devil, it is partly that, but I think that beneath that is the idea that sex with the Devil can lead to no issue. I think it is the idea that the evil is out to attack fertility in the human as well as the natural world. And that is why the stuff about weather and the crops comes together with fears which are very often to do with the deaths and diseases suffered by individual babies and children in particular. That is why these fears really grab hold of people.

MALCOLM GASKILL: Which after all must be at the root of magic because they are the oldest human anxieties going back to fifty thousand or a hundred thousand years ago.

MELVYN BRAGG: Fertility?

MALCOLM GASKILL: The life cycle and looking forward in winter to getting to spring.

MELVYN BRAGG: Malcolm Gaskill, to continue with the demonologists and to bring it literally closer to home in this country, Britain. James VI of Scotland before he became James I of England wrote a famous demonology. What drove him to write that?

MALCOLM GASKILL: Well, he was a rather bookish precocious teenager who absorbed these texts and his demonology is very derivative, but again this really returns us to the question of politics and to a sort of constitutional insecurity. James is interested in witches and obviously his demonology is a book about witchcraft, but again behind that, if we dig a bit deeper, it is actually about the state, it is actually about the divine right of kingship and the anxiety that centralising monarchies would be feeling in the sixteenth century.

MELVYN BRAGG: Can you develop that a bit more? It's useful to particularise James's case. What triggered him to write a demonology? Precocious, bookish, he could have written all sorts of things. He wrote a demonology. Why did he do that?

MALCOLM GASKILL: One of the things that particularly triggers his interest is that there is a marriage between himself and a Danish princess and, as I recall, there are witches in North Berwick in Scotland who try and sink the ship that he is on. This is reported back to him and James takes a very personal interest in the examination of these witches and is actually there himself and it is claimed that one of the witches whispers into his ear the words that he said to his bride on their marriage night. This little bit of pillow talk is said to ultimately persuade him. Now whether this is true or not we don't really know, but it is certainly seen to be the trigger in the established version.

MELVYN BRAGG: So this culture is not just a culture of going round talking to ordinary folk but something else, kings are taking this very seriously too. Can we move on now to specific trials, because I wouldn't mind talking about one or two in a bit more detail. Lyndal Roper, there is the trial of Ursula Hider, tried as a witch in 1589 – let's talk about that.

LYNDAL ROPER: Ursula Hider is a kind of childminder, and she has two children in her care, and the first one dies. When the second one dies the parents start being a bit alarmed about her and they start to suspect her of witchcraft and when she approaches the body of the child who has died the corpse starts to bleed and that is the classic sign that witchcraft is at work and she has caused the child to die. So she is interrogated and gradually she starts to confess to having met the Devil.

MELVYN BRAGG: Is it under torture that she starts to confess?

LYNDAL ROPER: Yes.

MELVYN BRAGG: And torture starts with thumbscrews and then it is strapado? What is that?

LYNDAL ROPER: Stretching on the rack and it can involve a variety of techniques.

MELVYN BRAGG: So she is being tortured and under torture she confesses.

LYNDAL ROPER: And then the story changes and she starts telling stories about meetings under the cellars in the town where a whole series of prominent townswomen have met with her and they have had these diabolic banquets.

MELVYN BRAGG: So what we are seeing here is the beginning of a body of evidence about witches which comes from women – and men, but let's keep to women – who are accused of being witches under torture. And the only evidence we have, which is the basic evidence of there being witchcraft, comes from the distressed confessions of tortured people?

LYNDAL ROPER: Yes, and the town council, interestingly enough, when it gets these confessions it doesn't just say, well, fine, they are all witches, it says, these women say that they are having these banquets where they are consuming the flesh of babies that have been dug up from the churchyard, so let's check. So they go to the churchyard and they check to see whether the graves have been disturbed. The graves have not been disturbed, so you would think they would conclude that this is just all delusion, but they don't, because the Devil is the master of illusion. So if one can't actually see the evidence that just proves that the Devil is more cunning.

MELVYN BRAGG: And this puts everybody at risk in the community, doesn't it, Alison Rowlands? Especially older women. Older
women have to earn their keep by being very useful – looking after
younger children and superintending lying in, as childbirth was
a very protracted business at that time. So they are looking after
babies, they are looking after young children, they are baking, they
are feeding families, and this puts them at risk because any illness
can be traced back to these older women who looked after everything. Is there something in that?

ALISON ROWLANDS: I think there is. One thing that we should
probably backtrack on is this idea of the Witches' Sabbath, which
comes from a late medieval context of changing beliefs that
witchcraft is a heresy, witchcraft is a pact with the Devil. The
momentum for the prosecutions of the type that Lyndal was
talking about is that you don't just ask one individual to confess
to being a witch herself. You then say, 'who else did you see at the
witches' gathering? Who else did you see at the Sabbath?' And that
creates a snowballing effect. Again, if we are thinking about why
the early modern period sees these large witch trials, this idea of the
gathering, the collective, the scale of this demonic threat has to be
taken into account.

   I certainly think that older women, because of the sorts of jobs
that they may be doing, as you rightly said, are potentially more
vulnerable. There are other factors as well. For example, if they are
very poor they are more likely to be doing those sorts of poorly paid,
potentially vulnerable jobs. They may also be widowed and not
have the protection of a husband who could perhaps help them if
they were accused. Yet we do have to bear in mind, however, that
many individuals can be reputed as witches for years and years, even
decades. I have got one case of a woman who is finally prosecuted
in 1671 at the age of fifty-six, and as far as I can trace back through
court records she had actually been reputed a witch since the age of
eleven. So we need to be careful about the issue of reputation, how a
reputation for being a witch is built up before an actual accusation is
made. The point of accusation is very important but we also need to
trace back the roots of that reputation.

MELVYN BRAGG: Are what you started this programme talking about, the cunning folk, the magicians, are they now called witches for doing exactly what they were doing before?

ALISON ROWLANDS: You would expect that. The expectation is that these white witches, these helpful witches, would be demonised in the context of these anxieties about the Devil, but what is surprising is that it doesn't happen that much. For example, research that has been done on the Duchy of Lorraine, which had a very large number of witch trials, has suggested that only about 10 per cent of those prosecuted were in fact cunning folk.

So I think what we are actually seeing are early modern peasants who were very wily. They keep the white and the black witch conceptually distinct because it is in their interest. The white witch is still their main way of fighting disease and of fighting bewitchment and of fighting misfortune, so it doesn't really do them much good to hoick them off to court and get them executed because they are left without that very useful service.

MELVYN BRAGG: Malcolm Gaskill, did English and Scottish witch trials differ from those, say, in Germany?

MALCOLM GASKILL: Yes, they did. There are two different types of legal systems essentially and we really do have to think about what the mechanics of prosecution are. How people actually convert a suspicion into a prosecution and into a conviction and execution. The Roman law tradition is much more prevalent in central and western Europe. England has developed differently and England has what is called an accusatory system, which basically means trial by jury. It means putting the responsibility for prosecution on the individual accuser. In Europe that is similar, to the extent that probably most cases do come to the attention of the authorities from below, but once the case gets into that official inquisition then the process is much more professionalised.

And the torture which is used is actually forbidden under English common law, so this idea where you torture women and then they name others and you get a craze exploding can't happen in England because of all the checks and balances from within the centralisation of the state, except for one two-year period during the Civil War where, once those brakes are taken off, England has its own witch craze.

MELVYN BRAGG: Lyndal Roper, what attributes and abilities was a witch assumed to have? How did you suspect a witch was a witch? There is an accusation and there is a lot of spite going on and settling of scores, but when they try to nail the witch as being a witch, how do they do it?

LYNDAL ROPER: The witch is someone with whom you have a connection and that is what is so awful about so many of these cases. What is clear is that there is an established relationship with that person and she (or he) is often in the role of helper, as in helping or being involved, for instance, in caring for a child, like the case I mentioned earlier. It is often the woman who looks after the new mother, who cooks the soups for her during that period of lying in and who helps care for the baby, who, when the baby sickens and dies, is the one you suspect.

MELVYN BRAGG: What about the witch's cat? It represented two or three things, didn't it?

LYNDAL ROPER: The cat, I think, is connected with sexuality.

MELVYN BRAGG: In what ways?

LYNDAL ROPER: Well, cats are very ambiguous, ambivalent creatures. The witch is also connected with the goat and the goat is strongly connected with sexuality and witches ride on goats to the Sabbath. I know of one witch whose goat very obligingly bleats outside her door when it is time to head off to the Sabbath.

MELVYN BRAGG: And what about the miaow woman?

LYNDAL ROPER: There is one case I have come across where it's a woman who is known as the miaow woman. She was an old woman and she was also accused of having sexual relations with a lot of younger men and she is seen naked at a window with her hair flying loose. She is someone who people connected with inappropriate sexuality, sexuality in an old woman, and that is seen as deeply frightening.

MELVYN BRAGG: But again connected to the cat?

LYNDAL ROPER: Yes, she has a cat.

ALISON ROWLANDS: I think the association that we have nowadays between a witch and a cat probably stems mainly from the English context where this idea of a pact with the Devil becomes better developed in the seventeenth century. But before then there is a far stronger idea of a supposed witch making a contract with a familiar, which was some sort of demonic imp in the shape of a small animal, which could be a cat or a ferret or a frog.

MALCOLM GASKILL: Yes, the cat has come down to us through the folklore of witchcraft but in fact if one looks particularly at the English witchcraft of the seventeenth century then the diabolical familiar was a whole range of creatures.

MELVYN BRAGG: Were they looking for any physical markings, Lyndal?

LYNDAL ROPER: Yes, they absolutely are looking for physical markings. In the case of the English ones it is the teats where the diabolical familiar sucks. In the German cases what they do as part of the interrogation is have the witch shaved completely and they inspect her body in case the devil has secreted some kind of powerful charm in her hair. But it is also a terrible sexual humiliation and when that is done before interrogation what often happens is that you find that women will confess without even any torture being applied because of the degradation involved. This is partly because the executioner who does the shaving and who is in charge of torture is a dishonourable person and if you are touched by him you yourself become dishonourable and that means that you are excluded from relationships with other people.

MELVYN BRAGG: At the same time as this terrible thing is going on we have the person of the Magus, working magic, like John Dee, who is the most famous example in the court of Elizabeth I, and later to some extent, with alchemy, Sir Isaac Newton. But these people are not being persecuted and tortured. Are they exempt because they are rich and well protected? Are they too rich to be confined?

MALCOLM GASKILL: To an extent, yes. But certainly in England most prosecutions do take place for *maleficia* – that is to say, causing harm through witchcraft. So you really need somebody who is going to go to the authorities and prosecute. There certainly could be suspicions. For example, what happens to John Dee is his house in Mortlake is sacked by a mob who suspect he is a witch.

MELVYN BRAGG: His library is burnt.

MALCOLM GASKILL: And his books are scattered in the street, yes. But there is always a kind of calculus of social relationships which witchcraft fits into. As Alison said, the reputation could build up over a great deal of time and it is always an accumulation of factors that come together to cause a prosecution. So Newton alone, practising numerology or alchemy or conjuring spirits, wouldn't be enough to have him prosecuted as a witch.

MELVYN BRAGG: But we are talking about an atmosphere in village after village and in town and city where the fear of who is a witch, will they get me for being a witch, am I going to call him or her a witch, this is the temperature of the time?

MALCOLM GASKILL: It certainly is, but it is not hysteria except perhaps at very fixed points at certain places, at certain times, when certain factors absolutely come together.

ALISON ROWLANDS: I was just going to come in on that. I think one of the real ironies and tragedies of the whole affair is large persecution, where you get caught up in this atmosphere of anxiety and you see lots and lots of people being executed. I think that helps increase anxiety about witches. The authorities probably think they are eradicating witchcraft, they are solving the problem, but actually by promoting large scale persecution they are instead stoking the fires.

We have to be very wary of assuming this happens everywhere, however. There are quite large parts of Europe where this level of anxiety, for reasons we are not necessarily clear on yet, is kept relatively low. We need to bear in mind that the whole of early modern Europe isn't caught up in a massive panic for hundreds of years. It is a patchy phenomenon.

MELVYN BRAGG: But other things feed into it, don't they? We have talked about the Reformation being fed by what was already happening pre-Reformation and feeding forwards into the Counter-Reformation. Then there is the example of an external disruption, a political disruption, as in the English Civil War. When that erupts you have massive witch-hunting, in one region particularly. Matthew Hopkins in East Anglia became known as the Witchfinder General. Malcolm Gaskill, can you tell us a bit about him?

MALCOLM GASKILL: Matthew Hopkins is an opportunist, he is not in any way an official authority. He just takes advantage of the fact that there are certain polarised political and religious conditions in East Anglian communities. The fact is that the professionals in the English legal system, the judges, who typically ride out on circuit and make sure the law is followed through in proper procedure in trials, are taken out of the equation because of the dangers of the Civil War.

So there is a lot more local justice, as you see in, for example, some German Catholic states, or in Scotland where on the local level it means that witchcraft can get out of hand. That is really what is happening then in East Anglia. The story of the Witchfinder General is an aberration in England, it is not normal political and administrative circumstances.

MELVYN BRAGG: We are talking about the middle of the seventeenth century and about here the movement against it. Were you fearful to talk against witchcraft before then?

ALISON ROWLANDS: I think it depended where you were. I certainly think that in Germany, perhaps in the sixteenth century, you could be at risk of being accused of witchcraft. There is a physician who published a sceptical tract in 1563 and he was certainly — the suspicion was voiced that he was in league with witches, otherwise why would he have written that? So I think in certain parts of Germany you could be at risk of being associated with the Devil and with witches if you wrote against them.

MELVYN BRAGG: We can talk about the Enlightenment, but in your view, Lyndal, when did opinion begin to turn against witch-hunting? When did this persecution of witches really begin to fall away and people no longer follow it?

LYNDAL ROPER: It falls away in a very interesting manner. The great age of the witch craze is really over by about the 1640s, but then witch-hunting doesn't die out completely. And one of the things that I found most surprising and most disturbing was the witch cases I looked at from the middle of the eighteenth century, which is ages after I expected.

MELVYN BRAGG: Whereabouts are these?

LYNDAL ROPER: These are in south Germany, and in one village that I looked at in particular, a tiny village which hunts witches in the 1580s, then again in the 1620s, and then in 1747 and even 1756.

MELVYN BRAGG: But that is exceptional, isn't it?

LYNDAL ROPER: It is exceptional, but what it has made me rethink is the way I think about the Enlightenment. I had seen it as being about stopping the belief in witch-hunting and having a completely different attitude towards the world. Yet at the same time in this village there is an early Enlightenment poet who is transcribing the local dialect and he is very interested in language. And I think what it has made me see is that at the heart of the Enlightenment is also an interest in human evil.

ALISON ROWLANDS: I think what happens when there are very large panics where we got lots of executions and very severe torture and basically the legal rulebook thrown out of the window, is that people tend to lose confidence in their legal procedures. So I think what we see in the later seventeenth century in Germany is that people still believe in witches but they no longer have the confidence in their legal procedures to identify them very effectively and that is why the trials stop long before the belief dies away.

TRANSMITTED: 21.10.2004

e
—

Socrates

As a philosopher, Socrates is the most intriguing one of all. Born in 469 BC into the Golden Age of the city of Athens, his impact is so profound that all the thinkers who went before are simply known as pre-Socratic. In person Socrates seems to have been inquisitive, even irritating – he was funny, he was rude and he was relentless.

He didn't like democracy and he spent a lot of time in the market-place accosting citizens with questions such as, 'what is courage, or virtue, or knowledge?' He claimed he was on a mission from God to educate his fellow humans.

But he's left us nothing in his own hand because he refused to write anything down. Plato, his pupil, wrote about and for him and in doing so provided the pillar – some say the spring – of western philosophy.

With me to discuss the elusive and mercurial Socrates are David Sedley, Laurence Professor of Ancient Philosophy at Cambridge University; Angie Hobbs, Associate Professor of Philosophy at Warwick University; and Paul Millet, Senior Lecturer in Classics at the University of Cambridge.

Angie Hobbs, Socrates didn't write anything down. Why didn't he write anything down?

ANGIE HOBBS: I think a clue comes from a dialogue written by Plato, a late dialogue called the *Phaedrus*. Plato knew Socrates well and in the *Phaedrus* they discuss the dangers of the art of writing. Because you can't discuss with a book, it can't answer you back, it can't really deal with your questions. We know that Socrates thought that the ideal way to do philosophy was to have a one-to-one conversation. However, of course, a lot of his followers were extremely keen that his legacy should continue in some way. So they wrote a lot down and wrote dialogues, with Socrates as one of the major characters.

MELVYN BRAGG: It shows a commendable indifference to posterity, doesn't it?

ANGIE HOBBS: It does, but I think maybe he knew that Plato and Xenophon and others of his followers were going to write things down, so maybe he wasn't quite as indifferent as we might think.

MELVYN BRAGG: But basically he thought that once it was written down it wasn't malleable, it wasn't plastic, it was set in a stone that no idea should be set in.

ANGIE HOBBS: Possibly, and possibly this is why a lot of his followers chose to write in these fictional dialogue forms. Maybe the idea is that reading a dialogue we become characters in the dialogue ourselves almost, so we're part of the conversation.

MELVYN BRAGG: What do we know about him?

ANGIE HOBBS: We know from some of his followers who knew him well, who did write, particularly Plato and Xenophon, who was a retired military commander who'd known Socrates well in his youth. These are our two main sources from the lifetime of Socrates.

All the sources agree, and there are many others, that Socrates was compelling, he was charismatic, he was self-controlled, he was self-contained, he was provocative and above all he was utterly unique. Absolutely nobody else like him. They all say that. Then things get interesting because though they all agree on those points, there are also some significant differences, particularly between Plato's and Xenophon's portrayals.

MELVYN BRAGG: They're precise contemporaries, those two, aren't they?

ANGIE HOBBS: Yes. For Plato, Socrates is more ironic, teasing, more elusive, more provocative, whereas Xenophon's Socrates is more conventional, he's more didactic, he's more approachable, he's chattier.

MELVYN BRAGG: He could have been both.

ANGIE HOBBS: He could have been both, yes. It could be that historically Socrates was even more complex than even in Plato's portrayal. He was very adept at projecting different aspects of himself to different people. Or it could be that each author saw what they wanted to see in Socrates, and focused on their own particular concerns, which, of course, would have been facilitated by the fact that the historical Socrates was so elusive. However, it does seem that many of the brightest people in the Athens of Socrates' day were fascinated by him. It seems to me that Plato's portrait would probably be closer to the truth because it's Plato's Socrates who would have exerted the greater magnetism. And also I think Plato would have had the philosophical gifts to appreciate Socrates a little more than Xenophon.

MELVYN BRAGG: So he was iconic in his own lifetime. David Sedley, we know that he didn't write anything down. I want to pursue this because I'm sure it intrigues everybody. Can you tell us about his attitude to philosophy and can you go a bit further into that?

DAVID SEDLEY: Yes. One can add another reason as to why he didn't write anything down. It was conventional in his day to write a book setting out the wisdom that you had discovered. Socrates claimed that he didn't know anything – he didn't have any understanding, he was still working on it. And therefore he wasn't really in a position to write a book. His activity, his philosophical activity, was essentially an oral, interpersonal, interacted one. His method has come to be known as the *elenchus*, which means cross-examination or interrogation of quizzing. Plato regarded him as the founder of dialectic, which is really the science of working towards truth through question and answer.

What Socrates would do, typically, was to buttonhole somebody for a conversation in the streets in Athens. He would get into a casual conversation and then it would turn out that the person he was talking to had pretensions at understanding some important concept, probably some moral value. And then Socrates would put himself in the weaker position, using his characteristic irony. 'Well, I don't understand this but perhaps you could help me to understand it since you know so much more.' Then he would ask the person to define the concept, but Socrates would say, 'But just a minute, don't you also think so and so, and if so, isn't that in conflict with your definition, or doesn't the definition have the following inconsistencies?'

That would lead to the interlocutor withdrawing the definition, maybe coming up with a better one. That's the way progress could occur. Socrates' own explanation of how this came about is a story he tells. A friend of his called Chaerephon went to the Oracle at Delphi and said, 'Is there anybody wiser than Socrates?' and the Oracle said no. Socrates, when he heard this, was baffled, so he claims, because he said, 'I don't understand anything, so how could there be nobody wiser than me?' And he set out to test what the Oracle meant by going round questioning people who really did have pretensions to understanding. And every time he questioned them it turned out that their pretensions were actually based on some kind of misapprehension, so he said, 'actually, it turned out the Oracle was right, I am the wisest of all the people, or at least I'm a paradigm of what it is to be a wise human being' because really human wisdom consist of nothing more than recognising the limits of your own understanding. And that's contrasted with divine wisdom.

MELVYN BRAGG: He was on this mission to educate the people of Athens, wasn't he?

DAVID SEDLEY: Yes.

MELVYN BRAGG: And that's what he pursued, and the priority of definition seems to be something that is attributed to Socrates as having if not invented than certainly established as a commanding position in philosophy. Can you develop that?

DAVID SEDLEY: Indeed. Aristotle in fact tells us that in his view the importance of definition is one of Socrates' two contributions to the development of philosophical method. It is a methodological point. Socrates takes the view that the most fundamental question you could ask people about anything is – what is it? If you don't even know what the thing is you couldn't possibly ask any further questions.

MELVYN BRAGG: Courage is an example.

DAVID SEDLEY: Yes. Courage is a good one. But let's just take the examples of the question that Socrates gets engaged in. Does justice benefit the person who possesses it? Or another one – is virtue teachable?

Now what Socrates says when those questions come up is: 'Well, obviously I couldn't answer the question whether virtue is teachable until we first of all know what virtue is. Because, for example, if virtue is some kind of knowledge, then there's a good case for saying it's teachable. If it's something other than knowledge then there's a very good case for saying it's not teachable.' So you always come back to the primary question – what is the thing – before you can actually move on to any of those other questions.

MELVYN BRAGG: Paul Millet, there's the Agora or marketplace in Athens, can you tell us in fifth-century Athens, the Golden Age, a miraculous time – can you tell us about this marketplace and why it was so important for Socrates?

PAUL MILLET: Yes. It's still there today. In the centre of Athens there is this area of about twenty acres or so, you can walk through it in ten minutes, which is the Agora. You called it the marketplace – it certainly was that. It was much more than that, though, it was the focal point of public life in the city. We have there the public buildings. It's the nodal point of activity for religion and shrines. There's the Temple of Hephaestus, still there at the northern end of the Agora. It's also a centre for justice, the law courts – many of them are there, including the court where Socrates himself was tried. It's also where civilians gather together to interact. They'll go there to talk, argue, gossip, get the news, get hired as casual labourers, find out the time from the water clock and, of course, do all their shopping.

MELVYN BRAGG: So was it unusual for somebody to approach somebody else and question them? Socrates wouldn't be the only person – he isn't a lone figure in the Agora?

PAUL MILLET: No, there are lots of places where people would gather and have discussions like this. We hear of Socrates, for example, at the bankers' tables, looking for people to talk to, and finding them as well. And also Socrates visiting various shops where people would gather as a matter of habit to meet and talk.

And then there were the various porticoes, colonnades around the Agora where people would gather and chat and discuss. So he's not the only person doing this. I think just one point I would make is that it's not just citizens. The Agora is full of all sorts of different people, non-citizens, slaves as well. Women too, non-citizen women and also women from poorer families who would have to go out to work.

MELVYN BRAGG: There's such a glow around fifth-century Athens. You think of philosophers being at the centre of it. Everyone walking around in stately stone-washed togas and the philosophers being the unacknowledged kings of the Agora. Was it like that?

PAUL MILLET: No, I'm sure not. This idea of people wafting around in bed sheets around marble pillars – I'm sure the Agora was a noisy, vibrant, lively, smelly, dirty kind of place.

MELVYN BRAGG: But is it possible from the evidence that you have to give us some idea of the status and place of philosophers in Athens at that time?

PAUL MILLET: I think there's one good piece of evidence that Socrates and other philosophers were in the public eye. I'm thinking of this famous play by Aristophanes, a comedy called *The Clouds*, where Socrates is a main figure and is caricatured in that comedy.

MELVYN BRAGG: Socrates was quite a young man at that time, wasn't he?

PAUL MILLET: Yes, he would have been – what? – in his forties.

MELVYN BRAGG: So he's sent up by the greatest comic writer of the day in a way that was understood by the mass audiences who gathered for the Comedy Olympics?

PAUL MILLET: I'm sure that's right. It's not just a one-off because there are other comedians who also brought Socrates into their plays.

MELVYN BRAGG: David Sedley, all the thinkers who went before Socrates, and there are many, were collectively referred to as 'pre-Socratic'. What were the pre-Socratics doing?

DAVID SEDLEY: They were asking the big questions about the nature of reality, the structure of the universe. Many of them were experts on astronomy, for example, because they thought that you couldn't possibly understand how the cosmos works unless you started with the laws underlying your heavens. So they were enormously diverse. They were a rather brilliant collection of thinkers, all extremely independent.

MELVYN BRAGG: So we come to Socrates. What was radical and new about him? What did he bring that made him such a significant figure to other significant figures like Plato and then from Plato to Aristotle and down to the present day? What was new?

ANGIE HOBBS: I think Cicero put it really well in his *Tusculan Disputations*. He says that Socrates was the first to bring philosophy down from the heavens and into the towns and into people's homes. Socrates' passion is for ethics. He starts off with what he believes is the fundamental question of life – how should it be lived? That's the question he asks again and again. And the answer he gives, which he assumes, perhaps wrongly, that everybody would assent to, is that life should be lived flourishingly, or less accurately, happiness is all we want. Now his next move is a much more controversial one, because he then says that the flourishing life is, in fact, the virtuous life – which, of course, not all people would assent to. Various characters in Plato do not assent to that. The reason Socrates gives for saying this, or one of the reasons, is that he thinks that the soul is far more precious than the body or than external goods. Indeed, that nothing else, neither an external such as wealth or even physical health, can do you any good unless you exercise it virtuously. So your soul is absolutely all-important. Therefore the virtuous life must be flourishing life. The Greek word is *eudaimonia* and there is an element of subjective happiness and feeling good in it, but it's also a more objective concept than the one that we would have today. It's connected perhaps with actualising your potential as a human being – with being a successful human being. So if you act viciously, if you hurt other people, you are in fact hurting yourself.

MELVYN BRAGG: It's completely entwined with virtue, isn't it?

ANGIE HOBBS: For Socrates it is. For Socrates this is his big move. He wants to say we all agree that we want happiness, the flourishing life, and what I'm telling you is that you're not going to get the flourishing life unless you live virtuously. Because otherwise you're going to be harming yourself more than the people you hurt because you will harm your own soul. You can only hurt other people's bodies or their possessions. Only the agent can harm his or her own soul. That was the controversial claim. That was a radical claim.

DAVID SEDLEY: What Angie's talking about there brings us on to one of Socrates' most distinctive doctrines. He didn't have many doctrines. In fact, that was one of the puzzles about him, he asked questions but it wasn't always clear what he thought himself. But one doctrine that he's very emphatic about is that it's never in any circumstances right to harm another person. You should not return wrong for wrong, you should not return harm for harm. This rejection of retaliation, he makes it quite clear, is a rejection of a whole amoral tradition.

MELVYN BRAGG: So this is radical in a time when the way to behave was to kill your enemies and the way to succeed was to massacre those who stood in your way?

DAVID SEDLEY: Exactly. There's an obvious parallel to the Sermon on the Mount. You know – the rejection of Old Testament retributive morality in favour of turn the other cheek. It's a very strong parallel. Socrates is standing against an existing tradition.

PAUL MILLET: In fact, Xenophon's Socrates does speak in favour of retaliation.

DAVID SEDLEY: The evidence comes from Plato. And there are often discrepancies like this. Xenophon's portrayal of Socrates is very much more as a conventional moralist. It's hard not to think that Xenophon portrays Socrates to some extent in his own image. Xenophon being himself a rather conservative thinker.

The evidence in Plato is so striking in the way that Socrates just for once says this is actually my position, my circle and I have always agreed on it. It sets us apart. This makes it, I think, pretty clear that this was actually historical fact.

PAUL MILLET: It's not just Plato projecting himself back on Socrates?

DAVID SEDLEY: Not at all, no.

MELVYN BRAGG: Can we rummage around a bit more with this idea of radical. I don't know whether it's a useful word for that time, but I want to establish now what was so distinctive and so influential. Paul Millet, can you put in your two penn'orth?

PAUL MILLET: That is a tricky one. I think Angie's put it exactly right – it's a different way of looking at things philosophically, this idea of bringing philosophy into the streets. I must confess, David, I find the pre-Socratics pretty incomprehensible.

DAVID SEDLEY: I think Socrates did too. That was one of his points. Actually, he said that all this talk about what makes the heavens move and the underlying structure of the world, he didn't understand it. It was completely unprovable and anyway he said it was a diversion from the question that actually matters to us, which is how we are to lead our lives.

PAUL MILLET: So these are issues he could discuss with ordinary people on the streets?

DAVID SEDLEY: Yes.

ANGIE HOBBS: Socrates has only just begun his radical quest when he says that the happy life, the flourishing life, is the virtuous life. He charges on from there. Because now we have to ask ourselves what he thinks virtue is. And this is where he really branches off. Because his answer is that virtue is knowledge. It is in some sense, which we'll come on to in a moment, knowledge of the human good.

As we've seen, if you don't have knowledge of the human good then no other apparent goods that you possess such as health or wealth can do you any good. Then he says: 'each individual virtue such as temperance or justice or courage is, in fact, united as one as knowledge of the human good.'

And there's a very keen philosophical debate that still goes on about exactly what Socrates meant by this thesis of the unity of virtue. Does he simply mean that all the individual virtues are interdependent, you can't have one without them all? Or does he mean something stronger, that all the virtues, all the individual virtues, are in fact one thing. This one thing that's knowledge. Now, of course, the counter to that is that if virtue is knowledge then we get to possibly his most radical claim of all, which is that vice is ignorance. It is simply ignorance. And he says that no one does wrong willingly, which I think will still surprise some people. And the weakness of the will is impossible. There can be no such thing as conflict of desires. All you need to do is find out what the best thing for you as a human being is and then if you know what that is you couldn't fail to do it.

MELVYN BRAGG: What if you think the best thing for you as a human being is to go and kill a lot of people?

ANGIE HOBBS: That shows that you've not understood, Socrates would say, how precious your soul is to you. He's not actually anti-war.

MELVYN BRAGG: He served in wars, with distinction?

ANGIE HOBBS: He did. He fights at Delium and Potidaea and at other battles. And, according to reports, very courageously. But you don't do it for revenge, that's the point.

DAVID SEDLEY: That's exactly right. Socrates' insistence that if you knew enough you would always do the right thing in itself sounds terribly implausible. There's so many obvious counterexamples to it. Knowing you shouldn't smoke the cigarette but you give in, weakness of will prevails.

I think the reason why Socrates had such a powerful case was that the way he lived his own life seemed to prove it true. Socrates was quite extraordinary for his power of mind over matter. There were legendary tales of his courage, his fortitude, going barefoot in winter, putting up with all kinds of dangers. And there's his total calm in the face of his impending death. It really seemed to people that Socrates had a level of understanding which did enable him always to do the right thing without any kind of conflict from his emotions.

MELVYN BRAGG: The fifth century BC is a Golden Age, but towards the end of it, it was very turbulent for Athenian democracy, the wars, the great one with Sparta, the crushing of the Athenian fleet and the plague that came to Athens. Can you flesh that out and then say how that affected the Athens that we're talking about?

PAUL MILLET: As you say, they make it a rather tarnished Golden Age, the last thirty years of the fifth century. There was this great war with Sparta which dragged on and on. Plague, battle losses. When the war is completely lost the Spartans impose on Athens this brutal junta of thirty pro-Spartan oligarchs, the so-called Thirty Tyrants.

They ruled over Athens for a year or so. And then by a remarkable series of events democracy was restored in 403. Four years later Socrates was brought to trial. I find it hard to believe that those awful events didn't have some impact on what happened in the court.

MELVYN BRAGG: In the sense that he was very anti-democratic and therefore could be seen to be pro-oligarch and therefore pro the Thirty Tyrants and therefore, when the democracy came back, he wasn't with the movement.

DAVID SEDLEY: We've talked about the differences between Plato's and Xenophon's Socrates. In fact, one area, one of the few areas, where they do converge and agree is over Socrates' dislike, if not of democracy itself, of certain key aspects of Athens democracy, such as public pay for people to hold office and selection of people to hold office by drawing lots. Both Plato and Xenophon made it quite clear that this did not meet with Socrates' approval. And because politics in Athens was very much polarised between oligarchs and democrats, if you weren't for one group then you must be for the other.

MELVYN BRAGG: It is interesting how much he was mixed up in war, he was deeply mixed up in politics, he was deeply mixed up in philosophy. He was in all those things. But let's move to the trial. David Sedley, shortly after the end of this war and the resumption of democracy in Athens he was put on trial. Do we know precisely why?

DAVID SEDLEY: Well, we know what the charges were. They were: corrupting the young and denying the gods of the city while introducing new gods. Those were the official charges.

MELVYN BRAGG: Corrupting there has often been taken to mean encouraging homosexuality?

DAVID SEDLEY: Not really. Homosexuality was a normal relationship in the male society that Socrates moved in. Actually the idea was rather that by questioning basic moral values he had undermined the moral fibre of the young.

MELVYN BRAGG: As I understand it, charges were brought against people by individuals?

DAVID SEDLEY: Yes.

MELVYN BRAGG: So, therefore, this could have been an act of personal revenge?

DAVID SEDLEY: Yes. Socrates says in Plato's reconstruction of his defence speech that he's made a huge number of enemies. And you can absolutely see why in the papers of Plato. Lots of people loathed him because of the way he undermined their public standing by the way he questioned them in front of their peers and their juniors.

MELVYN BRAGG: Because it revealed ignorance time after time – their ignorance.

DAVID SEDLEY: Their ignorance, that's exactly right. So it's completely understandable that the three individuals who brought the charges should have done so out of personal motivation.

MELVYN BRAGG: Do you know anything more, Paul Millet, about these people?

PAUL MILLET: We know a bit about one of the three accusers, a man called Anytus who acted as a democratic politician. He had been exiled when the Tyrants were in control in Athens. We also know that around the time of the trial of Socrates there were a number of other political trials held, where people who had been on the oligarchic side, in the time of the Thirty Tyrants – well, life was made rather difficult for them, shall we say. I would see Socrates' trial as part of that sequence of trials.

MELVYN BRAGG: Angie Hobbs, we have this trial. The court at one end of the market place, the Agora. Five hundred citizens of Athens are the jury. It lasts for one day and lawyers had at the most an hour each as measured by the water-clock – something we could reintroduce into this country with great effect. How did Socrates acquit himself at that trial?

ANGIE HOBBS: It depends which source you put your faith in. If you go with Plato's account, Socrates gives a magnificent – some might say a rather high-handed – defence of philosophy and his life in Athens. He refuses to beg. He refuses to supplicate or ask for pity. He says in fact, 'I think I have served Athens well, so you should be paying me money.' He absolutely will not grovel, which of course would have got some people's backs up. Some of his friends thought he'd decided that he'd lived his life. He was seventy, he didn't want to sink into decrepitude and he wasn't too upset at the thought of dying. And certainly he ends the speech that Plato puts into his mouth magnificently, he says at the end: 'So I go to die and you to live. Which of us goes to the better lot? Only God can know.' Very moving, but also you can see a certain imperiousness about it which might have rather annoyed some of the jurors.

MELVYN BRAGG: When they said, 'you will be sentenced to death', he could have said, 'Why not send me into voluntary exile?'

ANGIE HOBBS: He could have put in a counter-plea.

MELVYN BRAGG: But he didn't do that?

ANGIE HOBBS: He didn't. He could have done. Paul will know more about this, the factual details here, than I do.

PAUL MILLET: It was the kind of trial where the two opposing parties put forward proposals for punishment. And Socrates' first punishment was being maintained at public expense for the rest of his life, which was for Olympic heroes and the like. And then he offered a very modest fine. But he did not propose exile. In Xenophon's account he refused to make any proposal at all.

MELVYN BRAGG: Which account, David Sedley, do you come down on the side of? Do you think there's one coherent trustworthy account, or are we forever stuck with five?

DAVID SEDLEY: Socratic literature was burgeoning in the early fourth century BC, and it was basically a branch of fiction. But these people were writing as apologists for Socrates, so extracting the historical facts about the trial is probably a hopeless task. What we really have to say is that, for better or worse, we live with Plato's account, because Plato's account is the one that carries conviction.

MELVYN BRAGG: He was there?

DAVID SEDLEY: He was there.

MELVYN BRAGG: And about twenty-five years old?

DAVID SEDLEY: That's right. And one of the only occasions when Plato mentions himself in his work is when Socrates mentions his presence at the trial, in his defence speech. So because Plato has fixed the later tradition about Socrates we tend to go with it. But do we really know that was right? No, we don't.

ANGIE HOBBS: Well, I have a question for Paul. Because there's a tradition from antiquity, which you'll know more about than I do, that Socrates said nothing at his trial, isn't there? There was silence. And it was Plato and Xenophon who desperately tried to put into his mouth the words they felt he should or would have said.

PAUL MILLET: Yes. And of course there are discrepancies between

Xenophon and Plato about whether he had supporting speakers as well, who spoke on his behalf. But can I just talk about the site of the trial? That is interesting. There are these stone benches at the end of the Agora. There were, we think, five originally and they could seat 500 people. It could be where the trial took place. If so, it's right in the public domain. You're sat there looking out over all the noise and bustle, the arguing, the bargaining. Behind them on the hill there were the bronze-founders' workshops. You know, this is justice in the community. And the jurors would be thinking all the time my decision will affect all that's going on around me here. I think silence in court was not a concept the Athenians would have understood.

MELVYN BRAGG: Shall we just briefly refer to the actual death and then move on to the influence. David Sedley, could you steer us through the death of Socrates? Curiously he wasn't crucified, because people were then.

DAVID SEDLEY: That would have been an option. He was lucky he got hemlock instead. The description in Plato is of a very calm Socrates drinking the hemlock – all his friends fall about weeping but he's completely calm throughout. And the effect of the hemlock, as Plato describes it, is gradual paralysis from the feet up. There has been some modern dispute about whether this is actually medically correct or not, and it turns out it all depends which variety of hemlock was used. And there is a variety which would have produced these effects.

MELVYN BRAGG: So Plato could have been right?

DAVID SEDLEY: Yes.

MELVYN BRAGG: Let's try to discuss his influence. Angie – you want to get a word in?

ANGIE HOBBS: Yes. It does seem to me from Plato's *Phaedo*, where we get this account of Socrates' death that you also get a more unattractive side of Socrates coming in here. There's a chilliness, it seems to me. He banishes even his wife from his death scene and all the other womenfolk because they were weeping and wailing and he wanted everything calm. It is significant that all the women are banished from the prison cell. He was not, I don't think, a particularly good husband.

DAVID SEDLEY: But there's no reason to think he was untypical of his male contemporaries.

ANGIE HOBBS: No. And he says, 'well, I'm going to die but that's OK, if there is an afterlife I'll find people there to discuss other things with.' My friends are replaceable, is basically what he says. And I find that rather chilling.

MELVYN BRAGG: Paul, you're nodding, do you find it chilling too?

PAUL MILLET: Yes, I do. If I may go back to the poison by hemlock, I think even this sort of nice kind poison sounds pretty horrible. You die through suffocation. You know, I find it hard to believe it would have been quite as calm as Plato suggests.

DAVID SEDLEY: That is true, but Socrates was notable for. his control over his own body. For example, he could drink gallons of alcohol and remain sober.

PAUL MILLET: Well, so Plato tells us.

DAVID SEDLEY: Part of the same portrayal.

MELVYN BRAGG: You keep saying 'so Plato tells us'. Plato was writing to people who'd known Socrates and – this is *en passant* – there's not much reason for him to lie. If he had lied, wouldn't somebody say, 'look, you're telling untruths, because I knew him as well and, for example, he didn't drink at all.' I think you have to begin to believe some of the stuff.

PAUL MILLET: Well, yes and no. I mean my knowledge here is from Thucydides who was an early contemporary of Plato and a historian. Thucydides can invent speeches which he puts in people's mouths. Now a historian can do that; I have no problem with a philosopher doing the same sort of thing.

MELVYN BRAGG: Yes, speeches are one thing, but there are the things he did and that people would know about. They would know that Socrates was a brave soldier. They would know that he went to the Agora.

PAUL MILLET: Sure.

MELVYN BRAGG: And they might well know that he could drink a lot or did drink a lot. They'd know that he went around barefoot – but there you go ... Can we talk, David Sedley, about his influence, first of all on the classical world, the influence of Socrates' philosophy through the dialogues of Plato. Plato wrote dialogues, to imitate the style in which Socrates had conducted his philosophy, as I understand it.

DAVID SEDLEY: Exactly, yes. Socrates' philosophical influence ... well, first of all it was ubiquitous, but it was different on Plato from his influence on other thinkers. Plato clearly takes the view that Socrates represents stage one of the process of enlightenment. Socrates had to come first before Plato in order to clear away all the misconceptions and all the pretensions to knowledge that were actually ill-founded. Then that left a vacuum that Plato with his own philosophy was able to go on to fill. There were other thinkers and many, many philosophers who called themselves Socratics and claimed to be followers of Socrates, particularly in the fourth century BC, but carrying on to the Stoics from 300 BC onwards. For them Socrates had already achieved full enlightenment because that was the only way of explaining why he led the perfect philosophical life. Therefore the project for all these Socratic philosophers in his wake was to find out what it was that Socrates understood that enabled him to live that life. Then there were competing views about it.

The usual view was one that comes back to something that Angie talked about, which is that the only important good is wisdom. And that if you know enough then not only does nothing else matter – what happens to your body or possessions doesn't matter – but also you will always do the right thing. So that was a recurrent theme in schools that called themselves Socratics and became indeed one of the main bases of Stoicism. But there were other views, there were many other views, about what the secret of Socrates' life had been and other philosophical schools developed.

Just to give you one example, from the third century BC onwards the school founded by Plato, the Academy, became a Sceptical school. It was devoted to showing that knowledge claims can never be firmly established. All philosophical questions must admit to opposed points of view, they can never be closed down. And that they regarded as being the real message of Socrates. Socrates was the person who showed you that you can never rest content with your beliefs, the beliefs you currently hold. Every question much be constantly re-opened and re-examined. But that was invariably the message of Socrates and that was what made Socrates' life an exemplary life.

MELVYN BRAGG: Do you see, Angie Hobbs, the influence of Socrates through Plato beaming light through philosophy and western thought and setting the pattern for western thought not only in philosophy but in other areas of knowledge for a couple of thousand years?

ANGIE HOBBS: Absolutely. I mean there's masses more we could say about Plato, who does move on from some of Socrates' views and complicates the psychology and the theory of action and so on. Yes, if we take for instance the Renaissance from Montaigne. To the Sceptical humanist Montaigne Socrates was a hero. And Montaigne, paraphrasing the quote from Cicero that we looked at earlier about Socrates bringing philosophy down from the heavens and into people's homes, Montaigne says that Socrates has done humanity a great favour because he's shown how we can try to work out how to live the good life for ourselves without relying on gods or religion or tradition. We can have a bash at this ourselves. And Montaigne is hugely impressed by that. And then you've got Hegel in his History. He sees Socrates as making this huge turn from cosmology and physics into ethics. Socrates is a hero of Kierkegaard's *Concept of Irony*, which is subtitled in reference to Socrates.

But for me the most interesting character is Nietzsche, because Nietzsche is hostile to Socrates right from the very early *Birth of Tragedy,* which I think is 1872, right up to *Twilight of the Idols,* which he writes a year or two before he allegedly goes mad. For Nietzsche Socrates is this chilly, life-denying rationalist who is anti-tragedy, he's anti-music, he's anti-the instincts, he's anti all the things that Nietzsche thinks affirms life. However, Nietzsche always admits that Socrates holds a fascination and, of course, he shows how fascinated he is by the fact that he keeps returning to him. And what Nietzsche and Socrates have in common is turning philosophy into a personal life quest.

MELVYN BRAGG: Paul Millet, do you think that Socrates is as important as an icon as he is as a thinker? The man who pursued philosophy all his life. He did it without gain, he did it above anything else and he did it for the moment, for the present, with people he met and he could talk to.

PAUL MILLET: I speak as an historian when I agree with that. I think so large is our hinterland of ignorance about Socrates that he can be appropriated for all sorts of purposes.

DAVID SEDLEY: I think that's right. Everybody can create, recreate Socrates in their own image or to suit their own agenda. But it does seem to me that there are many ways in which he is uniquely inspiring and influential in the history of philosophy. I think the most important single thing is that he is the person who put on the map the idea that philosophy needn't be just an academic discipline. It can actually be about how you lead your life. In fact, perhaps his most inspiring saying on this, as recorded by Plato, is that taking time out of every day to discuss questions of basic values, the ones that shape your life, is the best way – thing you can do to improve your own life. And as he puts it, 'the unexamined life is not worth living.'

MELVYN BRAGG: Angie Hobbs, do you think there's any conflict between Socrates as an icon which overtakes Socrates as a philosophical influence?

ANGIE HOBBS: As an icon he can be a bit dangerous. I think he absolutely stands up as a philosopher in his own right.

MELVYN BRAGG: Why do you think he's a bit dangerous as an icon?

ANGIE HOBBS: Because people can make him into such a perfect human being that in a sense he loses his influence and we stop thinking that we could really learn anything from him for ourselves. And I think that would be to do him a great disservice. He uses very simple non-jargon language, he uses very simple metaphors. He wants us, every day, to think how can I best live my life? What sort of person should I be? And as David said, the unexamined life is not worth living.

TRANSMITTED: 27.09.2007

f

_____

Cryptography

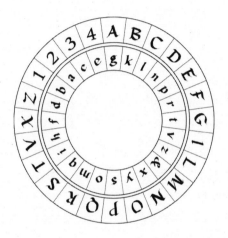

In October 1586, in the forbidding hall of Fotheringhay Castle, Mary Queen of Scots was on trial for her life. Accused of treason and denied legal representation, she sat alone in the shadow of a vast and empty throne belonging to her absent cousin and arch rival Elizabeth I of England. Walsingham, Elizabeth's Principal Secretary, had already arrested and executed Mary's fellow conspirators. Her only hope lay in the code she had used in all her letters concerning the plot. If her cipher remained unbroken she might yet be saved. Not for the first time the life of an individual and the course of history depended on the arcane art of cryptography.

What are the origins of this secretive science? And what links the 'Caesar Cipher' with the complex algorithms which underpin so much of our modern age?

With me to discuss the history of cryptography are Simon Singh, science writer and author of *The Code Book: The Secret History of Codes and Code-Breaking*; Lisa Jardine, Professor of Renaissance Studies at Queen Mary College; and Professor Fred Piper, Director of the Department of Information Security at Royal Holloway College, University of London.

Simon Singh, can you tell us how secret messages were communicated before the inventions of the first forms of cryptography? What were the examples of what we call 'steganography' – and what is that?

SIMON SINGH: Steganography is something that people don't talk about much nowadays. Today you hide the message by scrambling it up so nobody can read it. It is there in front of you, staring you in the face, but nobody knows what it means. With steganography you hide the existence of the message itself. So what the Chinese did was write on silk, wrap the silk into a wax ball, swallow the ball and then the messenger goes on his way, any guard would check the messenger but no find any paper or anything to see. Another nice example, which I think the Greeks used, was to shave the messenger's head, tattoo the message on the scalp, wait for the hair to regrow, send the messenger on his way and at the other end you shave the head and reveal the message. So it is use of invisible inks, all of these techniques where you cannot see the message.

MELVYN BRAGG: We are talking about the Babylonians, the Egyptians, the Greeks all using these techniques?

SIMON SINGH: Yes, and everyone has their own, and people are continually being inventive. So one example again is instead of writing on a wax tablet you scrape off the wax, write on the wooden board, put the wax back and it looks like a blank or innocent letter, but at the other end you scrape off the wax and you find the message. So you are continually trying to innovate in case somebody discovers your steganographic technique.

MELVYN BRAGG: Another way was to kill the messenger, wasn't it, so he couldn't give the message to anyone else – you had this disposable messenger system?

SIMON SINGH: Yes, I think that is the equivalent of chopping somebody's telephone line today, just chop the messenger.

MELVYN BRAGG: And that obtained for a very long time. That was *the* method. How did it change from hiding the message literally to hiding the message in language? We are talking about an increase in literacy for one thing, but are we talking about increased sophistication? Can you just take us from that big switch from steganography to cryptography?

SIMON SINGH: I think one of the interesting things is that the Chinese work with steganography a lot because, with Chinese characters, there is not much you can do to them. If the whole word is a character, a whole concept is a character and you can't jumble it up. But once you have a Roman alphabet or a more conventional alphabet then it is much easier to either take the letters and jumble them round to make a kind of anagram, that is transposition, or to substitute the letters for different letters or symbols, and so that is where the transition happened between steganography, where you are hiding the existence of a message, and cryptography where you are hiding the meaning by jumbling the letters or substituting them.

MELVYN BRAGG: That is fascinating. Coding goes hand in hand with the alphabet. We decode speech one way and we encode it with the same methods.

SIMON SINGH: Yes, absolutely.

MELVYN BRAGG: Can you tell us, have you any idea when cryptography came in?

SIMON SINGH: I think it is as soon as people start writing down information. People immediately start writing down secrets, whether it is personal diaries or political or military strategies or messages. As soon as people write down secrets they need to think of mechanisms for hiding those secrets.

I think there is an example of a Babylonian potter who comes up with the recipe of a glaze and wants to protect that recipe and so it has been encrypted. The remarkable thing about that is that somebody had to decipher cuneiform, which to us seems like a code because we didn't know what it meant, and once you have unravelled the true meaning of how cuneiform works, you then have to unravel a code that somebody has encoded in cuneiform. There are remarkable achievements in decoding codes.

MELVYN BRAGG: Yes. Reading up on this, one of the things that impressed me is the intensity of the intelligence that went into the whole operation. Fred Piper, one of the earliest substitution ciphers that we know about was Caesar's, who did two ciphers. Can you tell us first of all about the Caesar Cipher and of the dramatic occasion where it comes to our attention, and then we can talk about the Caesar Shift Cipher.

FRED PIPER: The first Caesar Cipher is basically used in the Gallic Wars in the mid-first century BC. And the first idea that Caesar had was just change the alphabet. Instead of writing in Roman letters, just substitute for each Roman letter a Greek letter, send it in Greek letters but in Roman meaning. People won't understand it and you have got your secret message and all you need to know to decode it is exactly what has happened. People were just unaware that this type of thing was going on.

MELVYN BRAGG: And he did this rather dramatically as he describes in the Gallic Wars to raise a siege which was being held by Cicero.

FRED PIPER: The courier was a little nervous about crossing the line so he threw the message on a spear to tell Cicero that help was coming but the spear got stuck in a tree and for a couple of days the troops were just waiting, not knowing what was happening. The message telling them they were saved was above them, and I think it was the third day that they realised it was there and read it.

   Now the Caesar Shift Cipher is rather different. Here what you are doing is replacing letters of the alphabet by other letters and the Caesar Shift Cipher simply explained is – shift every letter three letters to the right in the alphabet, so *a* becomes *d*, *b* becomes *e* and then at the end *x* goes round to the front and becomes *a*, *y* becomes *b*, and *z* becomes *c*, and so now what you see is not what the message says. It is a coded version or cryptogram.

MELVYN BRAGG: That seems to be quite simple but it held for an amazing amount of time, didn't it – about 900 years? Why is that?

FRED PIPER: They extended it a little to what is called a substitution cipher so instead of just shifting, because then there are only twenty-six shifts you can do, they then just made arbitrary substitutions, so we could say let *a* become *q*, *b* become *t*, we could choose what the shift was. So instead of having twenty-six keys you have got millions and millions of keys.

MELVYN BRAGG: Sorry, I missed that stage out, my fault. Once you start the substitution, but still using the basic Caesar method you go from having a very few possibilities to having – the figure I have here is once you start the shifting you have been talking about, our key will be *a* will become *x*, you are talking about something in the nature of four hundred million billion billion ways. That's true, isn't it? Four hundred million billion billion ways.

FRED PIPER: Four and twenty-six noughts at the end, yes.

MELVYN BRAGG: To actually play with those twenty-six letters?

FRED PIPER: Yes, that is right.

MELVYN BRAGG: Stunning.

FRED PIPER: Yes, it is a heck of a lot. Nobody is going to guess what you have done. They would have to work it out.

MELVYN BRAGG: So no wonder it held for 900 years.

FRED PIPER: Yes, that held for a long time.

MELVYN BRAGG: Then it was over to the Arabs. Can you describe this, Lisa Jardine? When the Arabs took up various Greek through Roman forms of learning, they heightened interest in linguistics and mathematics and statistics, often for religious purposes. So we are talking about a fine example of the law of unexpected consequences. What did they do?

LISA JARDINE: Well, they are studying the Koran, as indeed they still would, in meticulous detail and the Jews are studying Hebrew scripture in the same way. You then begin to see if you are looking for God's word . . .

MELVYN BRAGG: Just to be accurate here – it is the Arabs we are talking about. Al-Kindi, the Arab philosopher, was the man who did what we are about to talk about.

LISA JARDINE: Absolutely. I am suggesting that they might have done it elsewhere as well. But what al-Kindi recognised was the frequency. They are looking for patterns and they identify that various letters occur with greater frequency than other letters in any written text, so in English it would be *e* is the most frequent letter used.

MELVYN BRAGG: Let's just go back one step because it is important to understand how this came about. It came about because of a wonderful accident of history. They are not looking to crack codes. Simon, please come in on this, because it is important to get this clear. These things can go by indirections. They are looking, as I understand it, to find the accuracy of the time scale of the Revelations of Mohammed, when he said certain things in which order and what time, therefore what weight they have. Are we right so far? And they are trying to place in time when these different Revelations came, so they are analysing the text to do with time. And out of that comes this frequency analysis, crypto-analysis.

SIMON SINGH: Yes. It is very sophisticated analysis of text in the same way we might look at a text now and say, well, did Shakespeare really write this? Is this the way Shakespeare structured his language? People would look at these texts and say, well, is this really the way the Prophet Mohammed wrote things down? And they would look at the length of the words he was using, complication of sentences and clauses and so on, and by studying that for the first time they began to realise subtleties like vowels are incredibly common when you write things down.

LISA JARDINE: You are quite right, it is about trying to identify authenticity and it is done right across written language, but it is in this strictly Islamic context that it first recognised. Whilst you are trying to identify authenticity you note repetitions and repeated uses and that then gives you an actual grid of the occurrence of letters. This suddenly makes it clear that if you have got a straight substitution code, however you scramble the letters, you substitute a single letter for another single letter. Then by looking at a piece of writing of any length, if it were in English you would see that there were *x*'s everywhere and that would be an *e*.

MELVYN BRAGG: Can we just go even further into that, Fred Piper? So we are talking about these scholars working in Basra and Baghdad in the ninth century and we haven't time to go into why they got so advanced in mathematics and linguistics and statistics but they did. Lisa has described it. I wonder if it can be described again because it is so important, I think. Al-Kindi set it out very plainly. He said you take a text and then what did he say?

FRED PIPER: OK. Well, can we translate it into English?

MELVYN BRAGG: Yes.

FRED PIPER: If you take a text in English, a page of writing just with no particular bias, no particular words, then *e* will represent roughly 12 per cent of that page, and *t* will represent another 9 per cent and the *a* and *o* and these frequencies are well documented. Now, if all you do is encode by making a letter for letter substitution then if *e* represents 12 per cent of the – let's call it the plain text, the clear message – then whatever represents *e* will represent 12 per cent of the cryptogram or the coded message. And so all you need to do is a frequency analysis of the coded message and with different letters it will agree with the frequency analysis of the real message and so you have worked out what the substitution was.

MELVYN BRAGG: And al-Kindi did this with Arabic first and he used the words, the most frequent letter we will call the first and then we will call the second and then call the third, and they will make mistakes with the *p*'s and the *q*'s and that because they are not used all the time.

FRED PIPER: And also the statistics are never totally reliable. I mean sometimes *a* will be more popular than *t* for people's style, but given this frequency analysis it is now possible. I do a lot of teaching to thirteen-year-olds and you give them a text and they can break it by giving them a table of frequencies in English. Let them count and they do it.

MELVYN BRAGG: So we have cryptography, the doing, and crypto-analysis, the undoing of it. And we are in the ninth century and the stage is set for the battle of the codes. Have we done enough now to move on to the next bit?

LISA JARDINE: I would like to say one thing, because you picked up about the growth of literacy. Actually it isn't so much growth of literacy – well, it is growth of literacy – but when messages are passed illiterate interceptors are on many occasions quite capable of passing it to a literate person, but what I think is important is the empire, because it is the reach of empire that requires a communication to the furthest regions. You might not be able to get one messenger all the way and in fact the boundaries of an empire are generally defined, with the Roman Empire or the Ottoman Empire or with the Hapsburg Empire, by how far you can get provisions, armaments and messages and communications.

So cryptography escalates and I think that is what we are watching as we move from the ninth century. You see an absolute point where, unlike the Greeks, we have this reach and therefore the need for communication to reach the edges. Now as we move forward into the Renaissance with competing empires we will get this sense that you have to write it down. Ideally you wouldn't write a message down but if the empire is big enough you have to write it down.

SIMON SINGH: The frequency analysis that has been described was very simple and straightforward. You look at the text, look at the most common letter, that must be *e*, second most common letter must be *t* and so on, but there are some lovely subtleties about frequency analysis. Other properties of language, such as that vowels are very sociable letters, the letter *o* will be next to *b* as in bottom or next to *c* as in cog or *d* as in dog so the vowel will sit next to all the other letters very happily. Whereas with consonants you don't find *d* coming after *b* or *d* coming after *g* or *d* coming after *h*, so the consonants cluster around vowels but the vowels cluster around everything. So if I have got a coded message and I see a letter there which is very sociable and is always sprinkled amongst all the other letters I can say, well, I know its frequency and I know it is a vowel.

MELVYN BRAGG: Thank you. I have to move on. The example I started with at the beginning of the programme was Mary Queen of Scots, the trial in 1586, Queen Elizabeth's cousin, nevertheless a threat because of Catholic assassination plots against Queen Elizabeth. Very worrying for Queen Elizabeth. Mary had been caught up in a plot and ciphers had been used. Now then, Simon, can you briefly tell us how that case is said to have turned on ciphers. We are persuaded it was turned, she was convicted because the cipher was broken, it was a very difficult cipher, the cipher was broken by Walsingham and his men and she was convicted on the basis of that.

SIMON SINGH: Right. The details are slightly murky because you are never quite sure what really happened and what was set up for historians to discover later, but one version of events is that Mary is communicating with plotters who are trying to release Mary from prison and assassinate Elizabeth.

MELVYN BRAGG: Babington.

SIMON SINGH: Babington, exactly. And they use a code because these are clearly treacherous attempts on the life of a queen and the code they use is not very different from the one we have just described. They are going to swap *a* for a diamond, they are going to swap *b* for a square, *c* for a cross. They throw in some nice details. They throw in some red herrings, some spurious characters which just pepper the cipher, which would confuse a potential code-breaker, they throw in a character which doubles the previous one, so if you are doing 'bottle' you put something after the *t* to double the *t*. These messages are sent to and fro. Mary replies back and says, 'yes, let's go for it, I am on board for this plot.' Unfortunately, the person delivering the messages is a double agent.

MELVYN BRAGG: Gifford.

SIMON SINGH: That's it. So whenever Gifford gets a message he takes it to Elizabeth's spymaster, Walsingham. Walsingham makes a duplicate and hands it to the code-breaker and, despite all these little embroideries around the code, you count the letters, you see which ones are most common, you reckon that is *e*, and you break the code and there in front of you, Elizabeth's spymaster sees a letter which proves undoubtedly that Mary is involved in a plot to assassinate Elizabeth.

MELVYN BRAGG: And as you said at the beginning, with the proper caution of a historian, that is perhaps what was laid down for us to believe later. There are doubters. Lisa Jardine.

LISA JARDINE: The first thing to recognise with that is that it wouldn't be Mary who encoded her own message, so that you are not talking about someone's handwriting and indeed, since you are using symbols, you couldn't. So it is the person called a 'secretorie', who is a secret, a maker of secrets. In this period it is spelt secret-o-r-i-e, so it is your man who puts your stuff into secret form. The secretorie puts it into code.

MELVYN BRAGG: Hasn't changed much.

LISA JARDINE: Elizabeth needed concrete proof. She was so reluctant to execute her cousin. You needed a bit of paper. What we don't know is whether these are the codes that were supposedly put into the bungs of barrels and the barrels were smuggled into Fotheringhay Castle and then somebody took the bung.

MELVYN BRAGG: Is that where 'taking a bung' comes from?

LISA JARDINE: I don't know!
Simon? We'd better look it up. You will tell people next week ... So now of course we don't know whether this was a set-up or if it was real. The fact was she had been in prison for eighteen years, eighteen years she had been in prison! She had been exchanging ciphered letters all the time because the next thing from history you have to understand is that if the post is leaky, as between a castle and the outside world, you will use simple ciphers even if you are just asking for a laundry list.

MELVYN BRAGG: Fred Piper, where are we with ciphers at this time in the Elizabethan age? The great intellectuals are extremely interested in it. Francis Bacon is a supreme scholar and he is fascinated by ciphers, he constructs ciphers. How was it developing? Lisa said and Simon said it wasn't unlike the Caesar Shift Cipher. Is it developing, can you bring us up to speed on that?

FRED PIPER: Yes. Whether Mary Queen of Scots' cipher was broken or not I wouldn't dream of arguing with historians. The fact is that it could have been broken. It did rely on the frequency analysis.

MELVYN BRAGG: Still the same ninth-century stuff?

FRED PIPER: For this particular cipher, yes, with a few additions that Simon has spoken about. The truth however is that if you wanted to have a code in those days what you had to realise was that you had to break those frequencies and there were various techniques for doing this. One was putting in spurious characters that Simon spoke about. If you have a character that has no meaning anybody doing the frequency analysis for the text will have that as a frequency somewhere and that throws off their calculation.

The other option was to have two letters representing one and that throws them as well. But over a hundred years before this Leon Alberti had had the idea to use two substitution ciphers for one message and for the first letter use one of the ciphers, for the second use the second, then for the third one use the first one again, so suggesting using two in rotation and this does have the effect of changing the statistics because now in your cipher text or in your cryptogram there will be two letters representing *e* and two letters representing *t* and so on.

MELVYN BRAGG: So it will be a lower frequency. Instead of 12 per cent it will be 6 per cent, like lots of other *t*'s and *s*'s etcetera.

FRED PIPER: That's right. Whatever happens, the frequency changes and this idea was what mid-fifteenth-century England did. In that particular case there were lots of people doing this. Even the Mary Queen of Scots cipher cottoned on to the idea of trying to destroy the statistics by adding spurious characters, but this concept of using more than one cipher in the same message appears to have started with Alberti. Now this didn't really push in until another hundred years later, when there came the Vigenère Cipher, and the Vigenère Cipher then takes the very simple Caesar Cipher . . .

MELVYN BRAGG: Can I just hold on to the Vigenère Cipher for one moment? I want to go that way and it is very important because in a sense it takes us to the Enigma but I just want to talk about the Civil War, how ciphers worked then. Maybe there was just more of them, populations were getting bigger, literacy is growing, but you do get the intellectuals involved. I have talked about Bacon, but there's Wilkins and there is Wallis and there's Hooke. Newton is using cipher for alchemy, Pepys is using cipher in his diary, and codes, and away they are going. The seventeenth century is like a rush of ciphers to the head.

LISA JARDINE: I think, as you were saying to Fred, that there's this big gap. The fact is that difficulty in encryption responds to need. If you can get by with simple encryption a lot of code is just about deterring the casual reader. When you have a lot of mail being passed around for all kinds of purposes, some of which are confidential, what you need is that the casual glance doesn't tell you what it means. Now you can use the Caesar code for that quite happily, you can use very simple codes, and the harder, the more complicated the encryption the harder it is to decode, even if you yourself have the key.

In periods of danger we move to more complicated ciphers. In the English Civil War we suddenly get barrages of mathematicians working on cipher because you now have life or death, as it was for Mary Queen of Scots actually, life and death. Imagine if Charles I is sending his instructions to his army. He is sending it across his own country in his own language, through hostile territory. The code has to hold. In fact Charles I's code was seized in an ambush. A whole lot of letters were seized, enough to be decoded by John Wallis, who remained one of the greatest mathematicians of the Civil War and Restoration period.

When King Charles II came back, John Wallis became master cryptographer for Charles II. Great mathematicians become the people who make code more difficult but as they make it more difficult ordinary people like us can't decode. I can decode a Caesar code and a simple double substitution code but after that I put my hands up and say no, somebody more expert has to do it.

MELVYN BRAGG: Simon, can you just develop what Lisa said?

SIMON SINGH: I think it is a case of is this just my personal diary which I want to keep for my own and I just don't want my servants to read what I am writing, so it's a nice simple code. Or is this a matter of state? Could this lead to a calamity if this code is broken? So at the other end of the scale you have got people like Caldano creating a piece of card with little holes poked in it and so I send my letter, but if you put the card over the letter you can only see maybe seven or eight key letters which might spell out the location of where an attack might happen.

LISA JARDINE: Is that still steganography?

SIMON SINGH: Yes, it is a form of steganography, and what it involves is having to make this card, cut out the holes, make sure it fits, write the text, make sure it works, make a copy of that card, get that card to the other end so they can decode it, and that's hard work. It is complicated but it is worth it if you have got a valuable message.

MELVYN BRAGG: Fred, now can you take us to the Vigenère Code? When it came in and how much of an advance it was.

FRED PIPER: Well, there is the simple substitution, the Caesar Cipher, which came back, which we can all break. The Vigenère idea is based on – there are twenty-six different keys. You shift by 1, 2, 3, 4, up to 26, and then shifting by 26 is the same as shifting by 0, because you have gone right round.

MELVYN BRAGG: Now you had better explain this further. I haven't got it with me, it is down here in those notes somewhere, but maybe I can remember it. You have a square and the top line says A to Z and down the left hand side it says A to Z, and down the right hand side it says Z to A and at the bottom line it says Z to A. And inside there are 26 versions across and down it so you have that square of a multiple, the alphabet, and so A to Z first column, B to A second column, C to X and away it goes.

FRED PIPER: So the first row is the Caesar Cipher with shift 0, the second row is the Caesar Cipher with shift 1, the third row is Caesar Cipher with shift 2 and so on, and the bottom row is Caesar Cipher with shift 25.

MELVYN BRAGG: So you now have billions of options?

FRED PIPER: And now with the Vigenère Cipher you just agree on a sequence of numbers – let's say 1, 3, 7 – and you use the first row first, the third row second, seventh row third, then you come back and use the first row again. So now you are using three ciphers, and if you choose the sequence of four numbers you will be using four ciphers and if you choose a sequence of five numbers you will be using five different ciphers, and you keep cycling round and round and round until you get to the end of the message.

MELVYN BRAGG: Right. Now what does this give that nothing else has given so far?

FRED PIPER: Well, it breaks the frequency analysis.

MELVYN BRAGG: It was invented at the end of the sixteenth century, but it wasn't really taken up until the eighteenth century. Was this because it was too hard?

FRED PIPER: No. It is very unfortunate for Mary Queen of Scots because the publication of the Vigenère Cipher was the year after she was executed. It was very close. The effect it has is just breaking the letter frequency and the longer your sequence the more letters in the cipher text will represent the same letter *e* and so the frequency statistics get flatter and flatter and flatter. In theory if you use the sequence that is as long as the message, then there will be no information there at all. And the breaking of the Vigenère Cipher was because they used short sequences and so you kept repeating and it was the repetition that was then exploited to break it.

MELVYN BRAGG: Do you want to say more about the Vigenère Cipher, Simon?

SIMON SINGH: It is a really hard one to explain, but the key thing . . .

MELVYN BRAGG: You can start again, we have got bags of time. You have a square of paper and we all know the alphabet.

SIMON SINGH: Here's one way to explain it. If I want to encrypt the word 'dog', using simple Caesar, I am going to shift every letter by one, so *d* becomes *e*, *o* becomes *p* and *g* becomes *h* – so *eph*. If you want to crack that code you think – well, it's a Caesar cipher, maybe I will shift it by eight places, no, it doesn't work; shift it by seven places, doesn't work; twenty-three, doesn't work – and eventually once you have checked all twenty-five you think – oh it's just a simple shift of one place. So all you have to do is try twenty-five different shifts and you will get it.

With the Vigenère Cipher you are saying – OK, the first letter I am going to shift by eight places, the second letter I am going to shift by nine places, the third letter I am going to shift by two places, the fourth letter I am going to shift back to whatever the first number I thought of was. So suddenly there are twenty-six cubed different ways. What you are trying to do is break up the patterns.

Language has rich, rich patterns which is how we started when we said there are word lengths, vowel relationships and so on. What you are trying to do is get from a very rich patterned message to something that looks completely random, that has no patterns in it, which has no structure. Code-breakers really do devour structure and patterns in order to get back to the original message, so you are always trying to break up that pattern and that is what the Vigenère Cipher does.

MELVYN BRAGG: So we can leave the Vigenère Cipher, do you think, Fred?

FRED PIPER: It will keep coming back, it will keep coming back.

MELVYN BRAGG: It does, it persists, but we will leave it for the moment. That is the template for encoding, for cryptography ever since.

LISA JARDINE: And as the historian rather than the person who is an expert in codes, I would say it is ever so much easier if you have the grid in front of you, which is on the website where you can look at it. It is not nearly as difficult to understand as it sounds when you try and spell it out. But it is beautiful, it has a beauty and elegance about it because it does involve a simple grid of letters.

SIMON SINGH: I think it comes to what Fred said earlier. Fred could teach code-breaking to thirteen-year-olds and this was something that geniuses of the tenth century wrestled with. Now you can teach the Vigenère Cipher to a ten-year-old, but it took somebody with the brilliance of Alberti and Vigenère to work this out. So concepts which are incredibly difficult 500 years ago to us seem trivial, but they were huge leaps of intuition to make these breakthroughs in codes and code-breaking.

MELVYN BRAGG: Another one, Simon, was at the end of the First World War. There was a new method of code writing called the One Time Pad and as I understand this is still used today as the code system for the London to Washington hotline. What is the basic idea of this One Time Pad?

SIMON SINGH: The One Time Pad is absolutely unbreakable. I can guarantee rock solid if I encrypted a message with the One Time Pad and I sent it to Fred and MI5 tapped our phone line they would never, ever, ever be able to break it, and that is why it is so important, so wonderful. And what you do is, you take every single letter of your message, you write out your message so you have got this sequence of a hundred letters and you are going to shift every letter. Now we are always talking about these shifts, but the shift for each letter inside the alphabet is going to be completely random.

So before I encrypt a message I might say I have got a twenty-six-sided dice, I roll the dice a hundred times so I get a sequence of a hundred random shifts and the first letter is going to be shifted by maybe ten places, the second by four, the third one by eighteen and so on, and because every shift is completely random, the output is completely random and the code-breaker has absolutely no pattern. The definition of randomness is something without any pattern or structure and that is why he cannot break it.

MELVYN BRAGG: But the shortcomings are, Fred?

FRED PIPER: Well, let's suppose you are in Australia and I am here. I have done this, I send you the cryptogram – what can you do with it? Absolutely nothing until you know those random numbers I added so you can take them off.

MELVYN BRAGG: So we have still got the problem of the messenger.

FRED PIPER: That's right, so we have still got the problem of getting what we call the key of this random sequence to you. Now in certain scenarios that is not too difficult and the London to Washington hotline is probably one of them. They can send them in advance and I just tell you which one I am using so you will have for example a thousand random sequences that I have sent you earlier by some very secure means.

MELVYN BRAGG: They actually do put people in airplanes with armed guards?

FRED PIPER: Presumably, yes.

MELVYN BRAGG: That is what we were told.

FRED PIPER: Yes, that is right. So the problem is that the extra material you send to protect your messages is as much material as the messages themselves.

MELVYN BRAGG: And it is called the One Time Pad because it used once and then destroyed.

LISA JARDINE: And that is because of this beauty that both our mathematicians take absolutely for granted, which is as soon as you repeat anything in a cipher you run the risk of being decoded. Repetition is the bugbear of any pattern, they are so good at patterns that if you use a One Time Pad twice someone will notice.

SIMON SINGH: And this undermined some of the Soviet codes. When you have got to generate randomness I talked about rolling a dice with twenty-six sides. The way the Russians did it was they randomly typed on a keyboard, but it is actually very hard to randomly type on a keyboard because typically you do one letter with your right hand and one with your left, one with your right and one with your left, and so that is not random. It might look random, but it is not. The odd ones may contain an *e* but the even ones probably won't because the *e* is on the left-hand side of the keyboard. It is not random. And because it is hard work to generate these random ciphers, the temptation is we will make fewer of them and we will reuse them and once you reuse them that is when you get caught and people like the atom spies were captured because the Soviet codes were decoded because they were lazy and used non-random One Time Pads and then reused them.

FRED PIPER: It is very difficult for humans to generate random things.

MELVYN BRAGG: Why is that?

FRED PIPER: Well, I will give you an example, say the banking ATM network where you have a pin number. The bank lets you choose your pin. If you go up to the ATM, not knowing what you are going to do, and they say now put in a randomly chosen four-digit pin, if you really do it randomly, without thought, you will put in and you will have forgotten what you put in and you have locked yourself out of the system. So you will have your own favourite what you might call random numbers. And it is very difficult for humans to generate a random sequence.

SIMON SINGH: You can catch children at school, maths teachers do this all the time. They say – this is your homework, go home, toss a coin a hundred times and write down the sequence of heads and tails that you have got. And the children say I am not going to bother doing that, and they just write down a random sequence – heads, tails, tails, heads, heads, heads, tails, tails – and they try and make it random to fool the teacher. But in fact what they fail to realise is that in randomness you will get long strings of heads and long strings of tails, and the children won't do that and then they will get caught out.

MELVYN BRAGG: I have to assume that people know a great deal about Enigma. Can we just bounce through it and come to the present day? It is my fault we have spent too much time in the Middle Ages and the Renaissance. Simon, tell us why Enigma was such an extraordinary thing, both the making of the code and the cracking of it by Turing at Bletchley. If you can do it briefly we can come on to what is happening now.

SIMON SINGH: Right. I think the key technological device is radio. People are sending radio messages all over the battlefields, all over Europe into the Atlantic. That's great for communication but it is great for people who are eavesdropping because it is easy, people are listening to radio waves now and listening to us. It is very easy to pick up radio messages. So if everything can be intercepted, everything has to be encoded and that is what Enigma is great for.

It is a kind of mechanised typewriter for encoding and it takes an *e* and it might encrypt an e as a w the first time, the next time it comes to an e it might encrypt it as z, so you can't tell really what represents e because sometimes it is w, sometimes it is z and so on, and it has got this huge key space as well. The Enigma has lots and lots of different settings so the British not only had to capture Enigma they had to capture the setting for that particular message on that particular day.

LISA JARDINE: So following on from what Simon said, that we are not good at randomness, it electrically and mechanically generates multiple patterns of randomness, so it lays randomness on randomness but in ways that can be undone, literally reversed at the other end. So somebody has a machine at the other end and this machine has the capacity of reversing immediately all that complexity that you put in randomly when you encoded the message.

SIMON SINGH: The phrase is 'pseudo-randomness'.

MELVYN BRAGG: Anything to add, Fred, before we move on to Mr Cox at Cheltenham?

FRED PIPER: No, that's fine. Let's get on to where you're going.

MELVYN BRAGG: All right. Mr Cox of Cheltenham in the 1970s was unknown until recently because of the Information Act. What did Mr Cox of Cheltenham do that was so important?

FRED PIPER: Well, basically he did two or three things that are quite important, but I think the thing that you are getting at is if you look at all the cryptography we have looked at so far, it is done between two people who have to share a secret. Like the One Time Pad is difficult to operate because we need to share a secret, and the introduction of something that is called Public Hyptography, which was the idea of Cox and Ellis at CSG and later Diffie-Hellman publicly, is that there is no need. You can communicate secretly without sharing a secret, but it is possible for you to be able to decrypt something, for me to be able to encrypt it to send it to you but we don't need to share a secret.

MELVYN BRAGG: So I don't need – let's just spend the time that's necessary to get that right because this is very important. So in other words we don't need a key in that sense?

FRED PIPER: We don't need a key . . .

MELVYN BRAGG: And we don't need a messenger?

FRED PIPER: . . . to encrypt. We don't need a key to encrypt the information because it is public. Everybody has it. Think of a mortice lock. With a mortice lock you need a key to lock. I need a key to unlock. It is the same key. If you take a Yale lock, anybody can lock the door. You just shut it. You only need a key to unlock it. So in the first case the mortice lock is rather symmetric cryptography because we need to share the same key or copies, but the Yale lock is the equivalent to public key cryptography in the sense that anybody can lock the information up but only you can unlock it, and this is a concept that Cox, Ellis and Diffie-Hellman came up with.

MELVYN BRAGG: So just say once more why this was so original. Simon?

SIMON SINGH: If I want to send you a message I scramble it up according to a recipe. The only way you can unscramble it is if you know the recipe as well. And for 2,000 years everybody said the sender has a recipe, the receiver has got to have the same recipe, otherwise it doesn't work. So that means if I want to buy something online from somewhere in America, I want to buy the latest Britney Spears album, I type in my credit card details, I hit send, I scramble it up. I have to run all the way to America to give them the scrambling routine so they can unscramble it, and it doesn't really make e-commerce work. So the wonderful thing about this idea that Fred has described that Cox invented is that I can scramble up a message using a recipe. I have never communicated with the receiver ever before and yet they can still unscramble it. It sounds impossible.

The analogy that cryptographers often use is: I want to send you a message. I put it in a box, I lock the box and I send it to you, and you say, look, I can't open it, I don't have the key. So what I do is, I put the message in the box, I lock the box, I padlock it and I send it to you. You still can't open it. What you do is you put your padlock on it and send it back to me. I have now got a box with two padlocks on. I take my padlock off, so the box with one padlock left is sent back to you. It is your padlock, you can open it, you can open the box and read the message.

No key was ever transferred between us, the box was always locked and at the end of the day you could open the message and read the message. So this proves you do not need to share your recipe necessarily and that is how e-commerce, pay-TV, mobile phones, all work on this technology.

MELVYN BRAGG: It is fairly characteristic that this seems to have been found here in England but patented and money made out of it by two people who took it up in America.

SIMON SINGH: Yes. The Vigenère Cipher was broken by Babbage in the nineteenth century. Nobody knew about that for a hundred years. Enigma was broken here in Britain, nobody knew about that for thirty years. Nobody knew about Cox's work for twenty years. It is a secret business.

MELVYN BRAGG: Oh dear, well, never mind.

TRANSMITTED: 29.1.2004

g

Antimatter

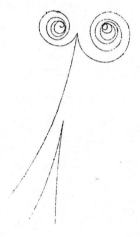

The Nobel Prize-winning British physicist, Paul Dirac, declared that 'the laws of nature should be expressed in beautiful equations'. True to his word, he is responsible for one of the most beautiful. Formulated in 1928, it describes the behaviour of electrons and is called the Dirac Equation.

But the Dirac Equation is strange. To every question it gives two answers – one positive and one negative. From this its author concluded that for every electron there is an equal and opposite twin. He called this twin the anti-electron and so the concept of antimatter was born.

Since then physicists have created antimatter in the laboratory and we even use it in our hospitals, but antimatter remains fundamentally mysterious. There should be much more of it around, but there isn't. To understand why may bring us closer to understanding events at the origin of the universe.

With me to discuss antimatter are Ruth Gregory, Professor of Mathematics and Physics at the University of Durham; Frank Close, Professor of Physics at Exeter College, University of Oxford; and Val Gibson, Reader in High Energy Physics at the University of Cambridge.

Val Gibson, let's establish some basic definitions. Before we talk about antimatter, can you outline for us the picture of matter and explain how that breaks down?

VAL GIBSON: Matter is the stuff that we and everything around us is made of. So if you had the most powerful microscope in the world you could look inside yourself and you would see you are made of atoms. In the atoms you have a nucleus and surrounding the nucleus there is a cloud of electrons. The nucleus is made of what we call protons and neutrons and then if you could see a thousand times deeper inside the nucleus you would discover that the protons and neutrons were made of quarks and these are the limits of our resolution.

They are the smallest particles that we know about and that is why, along with the electrons, we call the quarks the most fundamental particles. Now in ordinary matter you will find that there are two sorts of quarks – there are up and down quarks, and each of them has a different charge. The up quark has plus two-thirds of the electron charge and the down quark has minus one-third of the electron charge and the three combine together – the two up quarks and the down quark – to give us the proton. The two down quarks and the up quark combine to give us the neutron and that is what matter is.

MELVYN BRAGG: And that is everything?

VAL GIBSON: Everything you see around you, yes.

MELVYN BRAGG: Can you give us some idea of the sizes involved here? Let's start with the atom because after that it gets to be an issue of the imagination as far as I am concerned.

VAL GIBSON: The atom is of the order of what we call one angstrom, so it is one over one and ten zeros metres.

MELVYN BRAGG: I am sorry to reduce this to the nursery, please forgive me, but I read in the notes that one million atoms would go across one strand of hair.

VAL GIBSON: Yes.

MELVYN BRAGG: I can't imagine that either but it gets us a bit nearer. So we are going to be talking about the most fundamental thing in nature based on the most minute things that we know about.

VAL GIBSON: Absolutely.

MELVYN BRAGG: So you've given the picture of matter which you have been very clear about down to the building blocks, the quarks – a wonderful word. What is antimatter?

VAL GIBSON: Well, antimatter, although it is beloved of science fiction, is not extraordinary in any way. For every matter particle has a partner, which we call an antimatter particle, and in most respects they are identical. If you could see it, it would look the same as matter.

MELVYN BRAGG: But you can't see it?

VAL GIBSON: But you can't see it. It would look the same. It has the same mass, it has the same size, it has the same amount of electric charge – but in one respect they are very different. The electron has minus electric charge. The antimatter equivalent of the electron, which we call the positive electron or positron, has plus electric charge. That's the main difference between them. There is another subtle symmetry between them and that is as an electron travels through matter it likes to spin and it spins with a left-handed corkscrew, whereas the positron when it travels through matter spins with a right-handed corkscrew. There seems to be a perfect symmetry between the two.

MELVYN BRAGG: You are talking about this in rather a cosy way. From my reading, antimatter is something that you find most mysterious and that is what we are going to try to get towards in this programme, the most mysterious entity or non-entity.

VAL GIBSON: Well, it is mysterious in the sense that we don't know where it is, but it is not mysterious in the sense that there is lots of antimatter being made all the time. When for example high energy cosmic rays travel through the atmosphere it produces lots of antimatter. We can make antimatter in particle accelerators, but the mystery is why there is more matter than antimatter.

MELVYN BRAGG: Frank Close, I mentioned in the introduction that antimatter was first conceived by Paul Dirac in what is now known as the Dirac Equation. Can you explain in more detail what that equation is?

FRANK CLOSE: It was back in 1928. Dirac was a mathematician working at Cambridge and quantum mechanics had just been created. And Dirac came up with the idea of trying to combine quantum mechanics with the other great pillar of twentieth-century physics, which was Einstein's Theory of Relativity, and to apply it to the simplest thing then known which was the electron. And the surprise was that he found that he couldn't do it, at least not just by writing a single equation. He set out to write a single equation to describe the energy of the electron and the equation insisted on splitting into four parts.

In mathematical jargon he had to use matrices, but for our purpose there were four equations, whereas he only wanted one and they all had to mean something, and the question was what. Now he quickly realised what two of them meant. As Val has said, the electron is a sort of corkscrew. Think of it as a spinning top going clockwise or anticlockwise and that spin had been recognised. People knew that atoms behaved that way. When electrons were in magnetic fields they would spin one way or another. For the first time Dirac's Equation was saying there is doubling up of these two spin possibilities, but what about the other two?

That was the great puzzle because as he looked at the equations they seemed to be saying the electron can exist with negative energy. At this point I imagine Dirac's thoughts were probably: what is going on here? Negative with respect to what? What on earth does this mean? Clearly it is a nonsense phrased that way. Then he had what to me was a great insight, which was there was another way of interpreting this doubling up and it was that the negatively charged electron with negative energy seemed to be saying the equations wanted a positively charged electron with positive energy. So now at least one had got something sensible, positive energy had appeared which makes sense. But a positively charged electron? There was no such thing. No one knew of any such thing, the only positively charged particle that was then known was the proton and there has been a lot of debate about whether Dirac had actually thought he had explained the proton.

The fact that it is 2,000 times heavier, he thought, might just be an incidental problem to be solved later, but within four years the positron was discovered in cosmic rays by Carl Anderson in the States. The way that he detected these things is just like aircraft flying across the sky leave a vapour trail behind them. Charged particles passing through what was called a cloud chamber would leave a little trail of drops where they had gone through and with a magnetic field around the chamber you could make the trails bend left or right depending upon whether their charge was negative or positive.

Anderson discovered a trail in his cloud chamber with all the characteristics of an electron except it bent the wrong way. A positively charged electron. So that is four ways, after Dirac had written his equation. To me it is remarkable. I find it in a strange way quite uncomfortable that Dirac is writing, scribbling things on a piece of paper, and the equations say, you can't just have an electron, old boy, you have got to have a positive version as well. And the equations know about nature and then we go out and do an experiment and discover that is how it is. It is a very profound and in some ways a disturbing thing.

MELVYN BRAGG: And how significant was this? I have read Dirac mentioned in the same sort of paragraph as Newton in terms of his grasp and impact as a mathematician.

FRANK CLOSE: In your introduction you quote him saying that mathematics has to be beautiful. There is a sense of beauty in mathematics just like there is a sense of beauty in poetry and so forth. The problem with science is that if you write beautiful poetry and nature doesn't respect it, bad luck. But in Dirac's case he had the gift of producing beautiful mathematics in the way that the mathematicians would understand which seems to talk about nature as it really is and it is that special genius he really is unique for.

MELVYN BRAGG: Ruth Gregory, what does it signify, this theory of Dirac's, how did it take the argument forward?

RUTH GREGORY: I think that first of all, as Frank has just said, one major impact was the bringing together of mathematicians and physicists, so I think this is a strength that has continued. Dirac, was one of the pioneers of taking quite a sophisticated mathematical equation yet also extracting physics from it. It has begun a dialogue between mathematicians and physicists that continues to this day, where people trying to find out the very fundamental theories of nature do turn to mathematics to try and get tools to help them.

It is not just a one-way street. People working on fundamental theories of physics have come up with mathematical advances which then the mathematicians have gone off and taken and worked out and found out to have very interesting and deep mathematical worth as well. So I think this was, if you like, a start of a beautiful friendship between mathematicians and physicists which has led to a lot of interesting new ideas.

MELVYN BRAGG: What antimatter is and how it was arrived at I think has been very well described. One of the big points for myself is what happens when matter and antimatter meet. Can you describe that?

RUTH GREGORY: I think you have now got to the reason why antimatter is so beloved of science-fiction writers and of course the reason it is used for the propulsion system of the Enterprise. What we have found out is that matter and antimatter appear the same from afar, but once you get in closer you see that what matter does, antimatter does the opposite. Electron spins left, positron spins right. Electron is negative, positron is positive. It is as if the two are mirror images of one another. But the only thing they have in common is they both have a positive mass, so what happens when an electron and a positron destroy each other in a burst of energy, of radiation? When matter and antimatter meet, the simplest way of putting it is that they totally wipe each other out.

If you think now of a nuclear bomb, say the original Trinity test, in that explosion – and you know that nuclear bombs are roughly the most powerful explosion you can create – only about a gram of matter there is annihilated. Now going back to Einstein, Einstein has his famous equation $e = mc^2$, which I think is known beyond the scientific community, and what this tells you is that matter and energy are related. They are not two totally different concepts. You can in fact turn one into the other and Einstein tells us how to do this. He tells us how much energy is created by a particular amount of mass and you multiply by the c which is the speed of light. Now the speed of light is huge, the speed of light is 186,000 miles per second, so you multiply a very small mass by this huge number twice, because it is c^2, that means multiply by c and then c again. You get an enormous number. So one gram of matter or annihilation in a nuclear test is what gives you that huge mushroom cloud. Imagine what a kilogram of antimatter meeting with a kilogram of matter would do. It would be like having a thousand nuclear bombs going off all at once. That's pretty dramatic, if you can do it.

FRANK CLOSE: The good news and the bad news. The good news is do not worry about the idea of an antimatter bomb – that's the good news. The great paradox which is confronting us all is that antimatter doesn't exist out there. You don't just dig it up, you can't dig up antimatter and make your antimatter bomb, you have to make anti-atoms one at a time and the fastest we can do that today to make even a gram would take you as long as the universe. So that is the good news – don't worry about antimatter bombs. Of course the bad news is – don't think very much about antimatter being a source of power. It costs you more to make it than you get back at the end.

MELVYN BRAGG: Let's come to this question now, Frank Close, why there isn't more antimatter in the universe. There is plenty of matter and, as pointed out by Val at the beginning of the programme, very little antimatter. This is an asymmetry. Can you develop that?

FRANK CLOSE: Well, the experiments we have done at CERN by using positrons and annihilating them with electrons at very . . .

MELVYN BRAGG: Remind us what CERN is because we are going to be coming back to CERN several times.

FRANK CLOSE: Right. CERN is the particle physics laboratory in Geneva and for many years at the end of the twentieth century they were able to accelerate positrons and electrons around a twenty-seven-kilometre ring, to almost the speed of light, smashing them into one another head on, and from the annihilation energy for a brief moment in a very small region of space you were recreating the sort of conditions that the universe itself had about a billionth of a second after the original Big Bang.

So at the individual particle level we can see what was going on then and what we find is that particles of matter and antimatter, electrons and positrons, quarks and antiquarks, protons and antiprotons, emerge from this in perfect balance which is what the understanding of the symmetries between matter and antimatter that were buried in Dirac's Equation and every experiment done since says should be the case; which is fine up to a point. We understand in pretty good ways how the particles of matter ended up making atoms and stars and galaxies and you and me and pretty well everything we see out there today. The remnant of the original radiation is still out there in the microwave, background radiation, but the antimatter we don't find any at all in any bulk.

MELVYN BRAGG: Val Gibson, can I come back to you, can we just dig into this because this seems to me to be the core of it. What evidence is there for thinking there was an equal amount of matter and antimatter a billionth of a second after the Big Bang?

VAL GIBSON: If you take yourself back towards the Big Bang you may ask yourself what was there. The common belief on the cosmology side of things is that there was just energy there. And when you have got matter and antimatter you bring them together to produce energy. Then you can go in the reverse process and you have energy to start with and that will give you matter and antimatter in equal amounts. So at the beginning of the universe all that energy turns into matter and antimatter and at that point then the matter and antimatter can annihilate and become energy. But we found that there must be some flaw in the laws of nature . . .

MELVYN BRAGG: Can I jump in for a second here? We have been told categorically that they annihilate each other, so why didn't they annihilate each other before the universe got going?

VAL GIBSON: True. Good question. I don't know.

RUTH GREGORY: You can imagine this as a two-way street, just as Val was saying. You know if something can go one way it can go back the other way and you know if there is one thing we know in nature – if it can happen then it will. I think the whole point is that if they can annihilate and produce energy they can also go back the other way, at least if the temperature is high enough, so if we are in the very early universe when conditions are very different from today in some sense, we can't just say, oh, it will all annihilate. It will all go back to having energy, there is a lot of jostling, a lot of going one way and going the other way, so it is where that takes you that is the real question.

VAL GIBSON: There is an analogy that you can do at the beginning of the universe. You have got all this matter and antimatter around and you can consider them, if you like, as two armies that meet. As in an army in Napoleonic times where the ranks are firing muskets at each other and have to reload and fire, reload and fire, so you get waves through the matter and antimatter armies. You just find that the matter army is slightly quicker than the antimatter army and the net effect of that is that it soon annihilates all the antimatter and you are left with matter and that happens in the minutest fraction of a second.

MELVYN BRAGG: This is the theory?

VAL GIBSON: Yes, that is right. There is some flaw there which we can describe in our current theories of particle physics which actually would give you the imbalance of matter and antimatter at the beginning of the universe.

RUTH GREGORY: And also it is actually quite incredible the fine balance that there is because of this flaw. We can actually see it, we can measure it, in terms of parameters that we can look at in the early universe, and for every ten billion atoms, if you like, or units of matter and antimatter, there is one extra unit of matter. It is that finely balanced.

MELVYN BRAGG: So is that what you are working on?

RUTH GREGORY: I am actually working even earlier trying to get to that point, so I work on even higher energy physics.

FRANK CLOSE: What it shows is that the stuff that we are made of, the whole universe as we perceive it, is but one billionth part of a grander creation. We are the little bit left over after that huge anni-hilation took place.

MELVYN BRAGG: So are you saying that antimatter might be somewhere else? It might have parked itself, it might have gone away and be in another universe that we don't know about?

FRANK CLOSE: That's one possibility. I mean there are well-known examples that we are all familiar with. Take a magnet. If you heat it up enough it loses the magnetism. If you cool it back down again it doesn't necessarily have the North Pole ending up the same way it was before. A metal that is very hot cools down and you will start finding that in one part of the magnet it will be North Poles pointing to the right, if you like, and over the other side the North Poles are pointing to the left, so you will get a big domain of magnetism of one type in one area and the other type in the other area and a wall between them where the two boundaries meet.

Now it is possible that the hot very early universe was like that hot lump of metal and when it cooled down matter went out in some regions where we happen to live and antimatter went out in other regions where maybe anti-we are living but there will be presumably a region, a boundary between those two and that is of course where the problems arise, because at that boundary particles of matter and particles of antimatter, electrons and positrons in particular, will be meeting and annihilating and from the energy that they produce it will be very easy for the astronomers to detect such things.

The bottom line is there is no evidence for that. So although that is the simplest idea it is one for which there is no experimental support. We suspect that there is something subtly different between matter and antimatter and exactly what it is is what we are trying to find out.

VAL GIBSON: Can I just come in? We are talking here about the early universe and the biggest observation we can have is the one that we are made of matter and not antimatter. But we can create the conditions of the early universe in the particle physics experiments that we have done and we can recreate this matter-antimatter asymmetry in the experiments themselves and in fact one of the greatest breakthroughs of recent times was the discovery of the matter-antimatter asymmetry in the 1960s. That showed us that we could explain this flaw in the symmetries of nature. Unfortunately the flaw is not big enough to explain the universe completely made of matter, so there is something missing there.

MELVYN BRAGG: Can you say that again? I didn't get it.

VAL GIBSON: Well, we can recreate the conditions of the early universe in our particle physics experiments. So we can recreate all the debris that was around at the beginning of the universe and one nice particle that was around then was something called a kayon, which is itself made of matter and antimatter, so it is really trying to annihilate itself all the time. And the kayon is made of ordinary matter that we know about, but also made of some matter which is not of this world. It is called strange, anti-strange quark. For the kayon there is an antikayon, and they dance together in the quantum world, they have a quantum dance, and it was just looking at the decays of the different frequencies of this dance, different modes of this dance, that led to the discovery of matter-antimatter asymmetries in the laboratory.

MELVYN BRAGG: Ruth Gregory, can we talk about the process of baryogenesis?

RUTH GREGORY: Oh yes. That is what lies at the heart of this.

MELVYN BRAGG: Can you tell us what a baryon is first and then baryogenesis and why this fits in to the process we are going through now?

RUTH GREGORY: I suppose if you put it simply, baryons are the stuff that nuclei are made of and so in a sense you can think when cosmologists use baryons we are often using it as a short cut to saying matter. In the context of this discussion when we talk about baryogenesis we are talking about the generation of matter, using genesis in its actual biblical form. I don't know why but cosmologists often tend to get quite biblical. Baryogenesis is the word we use for saying how do we create the matter-antimatter asymmetry, how do we create the matter that we are made of? And I think it is perhaps worth pointing out that we have so many interesting questions in cosmology that one thing that we should remember is the matter that we are made of is actually a small component of the universe that we live in. There is an awful lot more out there.

MELVYN BRAGG: What more, Frank Close?

FRANK CLOSE: Well, a thing called dark matter because it doesn't shine but we know, it tugs on the galaxies. We get these beautiful spiral galaxies that are like Catherine wheels that you can see with your own eyes. They are emitting spectral light at us and the frequency, the colour of that light shifts, depending on whether it is coming towards you or away from you. It's a bit like an ambulance siren going neowwww as it approaches and then as it goes past. Similarly the frequency of light, the colour of light shifts so you can tell whether the stars are coming at you or going away from you. From that you can work out how fast some of these galaxies are spinning around. And the rate that they are spinning is so fast that you would think they should be falling apart and yet they manage to hold themselves together, which says there must be a much more powerful gravitational tug on those outer stars than would be the case if the only source of gravity were the stars that we actually saw.

From this we can say there must be some dark stuff out there. Dark because it doesn't shine and show through our telescopes but stuff because it has got a gravitational pull to it. When you do the sums, and Ruth will be much better at it than I am, I am sure, you find that the stuff that we see and we are made of is only a percentage or so of everything. There is far more of this mysterious dark matter and we are now discovering things about dark energy and exactly what that is. If I knew that I would be off to Stockholm but we are in fact the flotsam on a sea that has got far more mysterious things in it than the stuff we have met so far.

MELVYN BRAGG: Val Gibson, can I just come back before we go on to the final third of the programme, just to ask where you are in finding out about this vital asymmetry? There must have been an asymmetry one in ten millionth seconds. In the Napoleonic wars those who fired first could theoretically have mown down those who fired just a second after if they stood against each other. Where is that now?

VAL GIBSON: The first discovery of this asymmetry in the laboratory was in 1964 and that was, as I mentioned, something with the kayon, with this very strange quark. We now know from the experiments that we did at the end of the last century that we have what we call three families, three generations of quarks, we have the up and down quarks that all matter is made of. We have the second generation, which includes this strange quark, and we have a third generation which has what we call the top and bottom quark. I apologise for the naming schemes of these quarks.

MELVYN BRAGG: When you say 'strange' do you mean strange as we understand it or strange using it in a particular way?

VAL GIBSON: Strange as in using it in a particular way. It is a label. It was something that we didn't understand at the time when it was discovered, so it got the label 'strange'.

FRANK CLOSE: To put your mind at rest, it was called 'strange' because it was strange when first discovered.

VAL GIBSON: So we now know we have three generations of quarks and nothing more. There are no other quarks around, so we have these six quarks, three generations at the beginning.

MELVYN BRAGG: And these are the building blocks?

VAL GIBSON: These are the building blocks of all matter that we know. So we have seen the matter-antimatter asymmetry with the second family of quarks and we now know that we would expect a bigger effect in the third generation of quarks and indeed we have done experiments at the end of the last century which have shown that we get bigger matter-antimatter asymmetry. It is a factor of ten bigger than the second generation using this bottom quark. That has now been discovered.

We have seen it in two places in the laboratory. Unfortunately in both of those places the amount of matter-antimatter we have observed is still not enough to describe the overall matter-antimatter asymmetry in the universe so we need some new phenomena which are going to produce a bigger effect. And that is what we need to look for.

MELVYN BRAGG: You need more evidence?

VAL GIBSON: We need a clue, we need a clue. There has got to be some new physics out there. It may have a label of super symmetry, extra dimensions, multi Higgs models – you name it. There are lots of theories.

MELVYN BRAGG: It reminds me of Bertrand Russell saying, 'if I woke up dead and met God I would say sir – yes, I would call him sir – you should have given me more evidence.'

FRANK CLOSE: Actually what Val has just described, going back to Dirac, it is another example of how mathematics starts telling you things. As Val said, the matter that we know – there are at least three different copies, three generations, and mathematicians of twenty or so years ago were trying to build a theory of how you describe the particles if there are indeed three generations. The maths that they found was forcing them to the conclusion that actually a symmetry between matter and antimatter is almost likely to be not an exact symmetry and from the fact, as Val said, that we had already, at that stage, seen a small asymmetry in the world of the strange particles, their maths then told them there should be a very big asymmetry in the world of the bottom particles. One of the exciting discoveries in the last ten years has been that there has been that big asymmetry in the world of bottom particles. So another beautiful example of how maths and nature somehow talk to each other, but again as Val said, it turns out that this of itself is not the answer to the asymmetry in the matter that we are made of here and now.

MELVYN BRAGG: Ruth Gregory, can we come back up in a slightly different direction? Can you give us any sense of the challenge involved in trying to understand the behaviour of matter at high temperatures?

RUTH GREGORY: Gosh. Yes. Val has said that in the colliders, the conditions of the early universe are recreated. This was in a highly specialised and a very small sense. I think that when we study high-energy physics we often tend to take for granted these, as you said, all the zeros. I am not sure if we truly understand it or if we've just become used to it. If you wind the clock back our universe we know is expanding now. Rewind the clock back, it contracts to the very early universe which was a very compact small dense and extremely hot place. As you squash things together they tend to heat up and one of the things that we know about matter in general and certainly about the theories of physics that Val and Frank have been describing is that as you heat things up they tend to change in nature.

So we have ice, we warm it up and get water, warm that up, it boils and we have a gas, steam. If you had someone coming from outside with no means of measuring the temperature they may think those were three different states, three different things, three different compounds, but in the early universe the same sort of thing happens. As you heat it up our whole idea of physics changes so the matter that we see and are made up of now is not necessarily the same. We wouldn't see the same things as we go up to high temperatures. And I think the real difference between the early universe and the colliders where we try and recreate those conditions is the fact that it is not just at some single point in the tunnel under Geneva but it is everywhere and this idea of having something where everywhere is at that temperature is at least one possibility for accessing new phenomena.

We believe that there isn't a way of creating the asymmetry of matter with the physics that we know but of course there is always the possibility of someone coming in with a brand-new idea. But it is a very strange place. It is very hard to extrapolate ourselves to somewhere where the temperature is ten to all these zeros, where physics is not as we know it and everything gets extremely strange. These are the challenges that we all in our way work on.

MELVYN BRAGG: Can we come back to antimatter in this way, Val? You said, I think, at the beginning and it has been picked up by others, that you can create antimatter and it is in use now. What we have been calling antimatter is actually being used in some ways now? Can you just tell us what those ways are?

VAL GIBSON: There are, if you like, useful ways that antimatter can be used. I will just give you one as a spin-off of all these studies really. If we go back to our beloved positron, it is being used in hospitals all over the country in PET scanners, positron emission tomography scanners. That is a pure use of antimatter.

MELVYN BRAGG: What does it do?

VAL GIBSON: Well, for a PET scanner you have to inject the patient with a small radio isotope that emits positrons and you can detect the positrons, for example, in the brain. When they collide with the matter in the brain, you get two photons, some light coming out and it comes out back to back 180 degrees apart, and you can just . . .

MELVYN BRAGG: But isn't annihilation going on there then?

VAL GIBSON: Yes, that's right. It's not harmful, it's not harmful.

MELVYN BRAGG: You can put things in your brain and it annihilates things and this is not harmful?

FRANK CLOSE: You have got a million, million, million, million of these things in there and you don't mind if you lose a few.

MELVYN BRAGG: It depends who you are.

VAL GIBSON: I would say one of the best uses of antimatter is when we just do it for the pure research of trying to understand what nature is. In order to do that we can make anti-atoms at CERN. We can't contain them very well, we don't have huge bottles sitting in a laboratory somewhere. We have a few thousand maximum.

MELVYN BRAGG: If they went in bottles, the antimatter, they would bomb the bottles, wouldn't they?

VAL GIBSON: Absolutely, yes, you have got to try and keep it away from matter, so that is very, very difficult.

MELVYN BRAGG: So what do you confine it in?

VAL GIBSON: In what we call a magnetic bottle.

MELVYN BRAGG: So there is antimatter round the place now but it is in magnetic bottles and if we let it out . . .

VAL GIBSON: The problem is that it always collides with the matter and then you lose it. Also if you have two things which have opposite energy charges they like to attract each other and annihilate each other.

FRANK CLOSE: Twenty years ago they were flying these bottles with antimatter in across the Atlantic to do experiments on the east coast of the States. Whether you could do that now I have no idea.

Whether people knew they were doing that then but it was remarkably perfectly safe.

MELVYN BRAGG: I think you mentioned the phrase earlier – when
you were talking about going into this for the sake of going into it
and hoping that the law of unexpected consequences kicks in.

VAL GIBSON: Yes, this is the reason. I think the thing that drives
myself and I hope my colleagues is that we do it really just to try
and understand the laws of nature. I am just coming on to what the
biggest project is that is going to happen. It is going to start next
year and that is the Large Hedron Collider. Thousands of physicists,
engineers, students all over the world have been working on this for
fifteen years, building this thing for fifteen years, and now it is going
to come to fruition next year. As Frank mentioned earlier, we had
a twenty-seven-kilometre tunnel which we collided electrons and
positrons in at the end of the last century. We have now replaced
all the magnets and things in there to enable us to collide protons
on protons. And that means we can go to the highest energy ever
achievable in order to understand, to look for the new phenomena
out there.

The energies that we are talking about, as if, say, you had one
proton of energy just like having a little elastic band and a piece of
paper and you flick it across the room. It does nothing. It just falls
to the floor. But when you put a hundred thousand million protons
in bunches and you accelerate them to the speed of light and you
collide them together and it is in such a small area, a hundredth of
a tenth of a millimetre of an area, then you have got such a concentrated energy that all that energy you can turn $e=mc^2$ into mass.
And you know experiments at CERN will be looking next year for
new forms of mass, new forms of matter which will hopefully give us
some indication of the new phenomena around.

RUTH GREGORY: I think from the point of view of trying to
describe the universe we see around us, I think cosmologists accept
that we really do need to have some input from these experiments
and I think everybody is just sitting and waiting and hoping something new will be seen. Because Frank was describing the fraction of

the universe that we really feel that we know about is very small, we are hoping that we will find some clues as to the other components of the universe. At least, at the very least, of this dark matter. Of course, whether we do or not, we hope, but . . .

MELVYN BRAGG: Is this a sense in which evidence has overtaken theory? Dirac had a theory, he didn't have a collider and later this has proved to be true in observation in a very advanced laboratory as it was then in the 1930s in the US. So is there a sense in which you are saying we have come to the end of theory, we have got to have some more evidence before we can construct any more theories?

FRANK CLOSE: No. If you go through history you find that sometimes theory leads the way, as in the case of Dirac writing equations which predict the things you then find, and on other occasions you have experiments that lead the way and the best example of that was the origins of quantum mechanics. It was the fact that experimental phenomena seen at the end of the Victorian era in the way that atoms emitted light could not be understood in the theory of the time which led to the invention of quantum mechanics.

Sometimes it is an experimental discovery which demands explanation that points us to the way to go and that is in part where the LHC comes in on both sides. On the other hand there are fundamental ideas in theory which say there are phenomena which we expect to manifest themselves under the sort of conditions that the LHC will access – for example discovering the Higgs Boson the elusive fundamental particle. The Large Hedron Collider should be able to discover the Higgs Boson or whatever nature does to play that trick. But the thing that I am sure of is only nature knows what is really going on. The answer is out there somewhere and the LHC is the only way we know that we can go and answer such things within the technology that we currently have.

RUTH GREGORY: I hope I haven't given the impression that experiment is leading the way. I think the problem is that theorists are getting too clever. We have several very good ideas about what may lie beyond the problem but we as theorists have no way of discriminating between them at the current time and this is what we are waiting for.

MELVYN BRAGG: Well, for three theorists you have enlightened me massively and I hope that I can remember it long enough.

TRANSMITTED: 4.10.2007

h

Darwin: Programme 1

These programmes on Darwin differ from the others. There are four of them and they were not live but all recorded on location.

It's been called the most important idea in human history – Charles Darwin's argument that human life, indeed all life, can be explained as the result of evolution by means of natural selection. Darwin suggested that the great array and complexity of life on earth was not created by God fully formed but evolved incrementally at the hands of unremitting, often violent and wasteful, yet relentless, meticulous forces. It's an idea that has changed our understanding of ourselves radically, an idea that created the science of biology and that more than anything else provided evidence for a case against God.

Darwin's been feted as an intellectual revolutionary, an iconoclast of the highest order. But when you look at the biography of Charles Darwin and how he came to this profound insight you find a story that's subtler, more complex and more conflicted that that. Which is why I'm standing here in the pulpit of Great St Mary's in Cambridge, the university where in 1828 Darwin came to train to become a priest. That he left Cambridge a naturalist is one of the great turning points in the intellectual history of this country and indeed the world.

I'm here with a biographer of Darwin – Jim Moore. It's tempting to think because of the ideas that came out of it at that time, when Darwin came up here, that this was a hotbed of revolutionary thought. But as I understand it the Church was still dominating and central to the intellectual life of the university?

JIM MOORE: Yes. Cambridge was a gentle police state, you might say. You would have to go some place else in the world today, perhaps Tehran, to discover the clergy similarly in power, both religiously and in the civil realm. The university dominated the town, there were only 2,000 collegians, but there were also the college servants and others in the orbit. The town had about 16,000 inhabitants. These 2,000 collegians were the wealth, the life blood, of all local business and the university stood as judge and jury over the locals. The university had two members of parliament, the town had no members of parliament. You had to sign the Thirty-Nine Articles of the Church of England to graduate from this university. Half of the students here were intended to become priests of the Church of England. This was an ecclesiastical powerhouse.

MELVYN BRAGG: And this particular church that we're in now, Great St Mary's, had a special significance?

JIM MOORE: This is an amazing space. Let me see if I can answer that question by describing how it worked. The pews we see in front of us came after Darwin. The galleries on the left and the right, the north and south aisle, were present then. In the north and south galleries above sat the undergraduates – that's where Darwin would have sat – on long benches without backs on them. And beneath them sat the MAs of the university, the graduates, all of them sitting parallel to the nave and looking right or left to see the chancel which is behind us here. The centre, the nave today, was vacant. They called it the pit, and in the centre of the pit was a three-decker pulpit with a door at the bottom. And the clergymen would enter that door and go up the steps and appear almost miraculously at the top like a jack-in-the-box and from there preach the sermon.

MELVYN BRAGG: What view of Creation would he have received in this great church?

JIM MOORE: Cambridge priests, theologians, naturalists, all believed that everything held together in this universe by the word of His power, by the word of God. If God took His hand off this world it would all fly apart. Things were kept stable and fixed and that included the forms of life. Right above our heads here there was an enormous and grotesque oak box called the Doctors' Gallery, with a throne in the centre where the Vice-Chancellor sat and where royalty sat when they were visiting the university. And on either side of the Vice-Chancellor sat the heads of houses, all of them clergymen. So this is an auditorium, an arena, it's a real theatre of power. Churchly power and civil power. Here the best sermons in Cambridge were preached, here also trials took place, presided over by the Vice-Chancellor.

MELVYN BRAGG: In what sense was Darwin engaged in this? Was he – let's put it simply – was he a true believer? He came to the place here full of clergy and would-be clergy, you've described it very dramatically, you've compared it with Tehran – when he came up to Cambridge did he go along with all that?

JIM MOORE: Becoming a clergyman of the Church of England was a fairly easygoing thing in the age of Jane Austen. It was a respectable occupation, perhaps second in respect to being a physician. So he came here with professional ambitions – to train as a gentleman first of all. He had no difficulty convincing himself that he could sign the Thirty-Nine Articles by the time he finished here in 1831.

MELVYN BRAGG: And that meant he believed in the Trinity and all the rest of it?

JIM MOORE: Yes, Darwin, I think, saw no good reason to dissent from that at that time.

MELVYN BRAGG: Still, to probe a bit, do you know from what you've discovered about him in writing about him, any personal or private qualms, difficulties, agonising he might have had at that time?

JIM MOORE: There is a second-hand remark recorded after his first year at Cambridge – that he didn't feel moved by the spirit of God and to the Church, that he didn't see it as a calling. That didn't prevent other people from entering the Church of England, but Darwin was prepared to admit that.

MELVYN BRAGG: But in this place, in this church, we're talking about a powerhouse – black-gowned men, different varieties of gowns, but all black-gowned men – God was the Father, the Church was the authority.

JIM MOORE: The doctors, the theologians, the heads of colleges assembled here, up in this great Doctors' Gallery, they were all men. College fellows had to renounce marriage to retain their fellowship. And the young women were kept at a distance officially. Of course they were the college servants, but there was a massive maldistribution of power in Cambridge – testosterone-fuelled men on the one hand and young women, very anxious just to make a living, on the other.

MELVYN BRAGG: And in this sort of gathering Darwin came to participate in the unchallenged fact of his university existence.

JIM MOORE: Later in life he would refer to the fabric that falls if one species, one instinct be acquired, one species change. This is the fabric in this church, this structure of medieval power represented by Cambridge University, God in His world controlling His creation, holding things stable and fixed. Darwin didn't know that quite at the time but this is where he absorbed that vision of the fabric that would have to fall and be transformed.

MELVYN BRAGG: Jim Moore and I have come out of the church now and we're going to move around Cambridge. You have a map of Darwin's Cambridge which you're nobly unfurling in a high wind.

JIM MOORE: Yes. This map was actually on sale here in the shops at the beginning of Darwin's last year in 1830. It's a highly accurate map. In the centre – it's really quite a large map – you can see Cambridge town. It's immersed in a sea of fenland. And right at the centre, we're right at the centre now, at Great St Mary's church, it's ground zero, the prime meridian.

The streets going north to Huntingdon and south down to London are all marked with milestones from the west door of St Mary's church, that's the centre of power, here where we are. We can see the Senate House, the Old Schools, the Library.

And Darwin had only to go half a mile or less in any direction to get to the Fens. In fact, the footpath went from the back of Darwin's college out towards what was called Maids' Causeway, because that was the way the maids came in across the Fens from Barnwell along the river, where the gasworks were. And the young men, Darwin included, at Christ's were not to go beyond the end of the path at St Radigund's which led on to Maids' Causeway and the girls. The proctors here at Cambridge were – part of the job was as a vice squad to keep single women from what was called 'street-walking' – the anti-vice squad.

MELVYN BRAGG: So he's surrounded in the Fens by what we call without being too fanciful his first laboratory?

JIM MOORE: It was his first great outdoor collecting site. It was not a highly diverse area, he had to go further into the Fens with some of his professors and students to get to those places which were particularly watery, but quite enough. Darwin knew every square inch of this map.

MELVYN BRAGG: The Mill Pond in Cambridge still runs to the rhythms of university life. On warmer days than this students sit out on the Green drinking and talking and perhaps occasionally discussing evolutionary theory. But the Mill Pond is important for another reason, it is, or at least was 180 years ago, extremely good beetle-hunting country.

DARWIN: No pursuit at Cambridge was followed with nearly so much eagerness or gave me so much pleasure as collecting beetles. One day on tearing off some old bark I saw two rare beetles and seized one in each hand. Then I saw a third – a new kind – which I could not bear to lose. So that I popped the one which held in my right hand into my mouth. Alas, it ejected some intensely acrid fluid which burnt my tongue so that I was forced to spit the beetle out which was lost, as was the third one.

MELVYN BRAGG: I've been joined by Professor Steve Jones from University College, London. Steve Jones, what was it about beetles that attracted Darwin so much?

STEVE JONES: At that time biology was still a kind of advanced stamp collecting, and if you're interested in stamp collecting what you're most keen on are tiny and apparently meaningless differences among apparently identical specimens. And beetles are famous then and now for being vastly diverse. It's the well-known comment by J.B.S. Haldane, the great Darwinian, when asked what he could work out of the nature of God from the Creation. 'God has an inordinate fondness for beetles,' he replied. Darwin would have loved that statement.

MELVYN BRAGG: So we're talking about serious classification. This young man, who has often been written about as someone who wasted his time at Cambridge, was in fact laying the foundation about what he'd do for the rest of his life.

STEVE JONES: Yes, that's certainly true.

MELVYN BRAGG: He wasn't doing it through the work on his degree though.

STEVE JONES: No. Well, like most students, he took no account whatsoever what was going on in the lecture theatre and he was probably very wise to do so.

MELVYN BRAGG: Jim Moore, why was this Mill Pond such a fertile place for beetle-hunting?

JIM MOORE: We have to understand that the Mill Pond stood at the junction of the River Granta on one side here and the River Cam on the left. This was an industrial artery, a hub of activity in Darwin's Cambridge. This was the furthest navigable point inland for barges. And the payoff for him was that these barges, at least the ones that transported reeds from the Fens, were loaded with wild-life. And once the reeds had been emptied out to thatch houses, the beetles were left.

DARWIN: I was very successful in collecting and invented two new methods. I employed a labourer to scrape during the winter, moss of old trees and place it in a large bag. And like-wise to collect the rubbish at the bottom of the barges in which reeds are brought from the Fens. And thus I got some very rare species. No poet ever felt more delighted at seeing his first poem published than I did at seeing in Stephens's *Illustrations of British Insects* the magic words – Captured by C. Darwin Esq.

MELVYN BRAGG: Would this seem to be a sort of truancy, what he was doing?

STEVE JONES: I don't think so. I mean they weren't really training to be priests, they were training to be gents – that's the most important thing.

MELVYN BRAGG: Gents in priests' clothing.

STEVE JONES: Exactly. For Darwin, who was pretty much a natural gentleman and pretty wealthy, this was really a bit of a finishing school from that point of view. And I think many of the people who were studying to be priests perhaps didn't take their ecclesiastical studies all that seriously. They knew they would pass, nobody ever fails at the University of Cambridge, it's well known, still true. Their hobbies actually, for many of them, became their life's work, not just for Darwin.

MELVYN BRAGG: Was there any sense, Jim Moore, that in pursuing these investigations with beetles, for instance, as intensively as he did, that he was relating it to or required to relate it to the theological structure with which he was surrounded?

JIM MOORE: I think the theological interpretation of beetles went without saying for Darwin, it was part of the air he breathed. These were God's creatures, God had made these creatures in their infinite diversity at the Creation somehow, we know not how, and so they have remained since then. Darwin got a lot of practice in identifying habitats, remember this is a competitive field sport, so he wants to be the first to find something and he knows where to go to get it.

MELVYN BRAGG: You say 'competitive' – were there others on the track as well?

JIM MOORE: Oh yes, even some of the local clergymen, perhaps one or two of the professors, undergraduates like Albert Way who drew a wonderful cartoon of Darwin sitting on the back of a beetle, and it says 'Go it, Charlie' underneath. Darwin was notorious for his vigour. He discovered, on one occasion, that his servant had been secretly supplying a competitor named Babbington, who was later known as Beetles Babbington, he was the botany professor here, but Darwin nearly threw him down the stairs over at Christ's College, saying, 'you won't do that again, you belong to me.'

MELVYN BRAGG: To summarise then, from this place. Could this be called in any way a starting point, Steve Jones? Is this where Darwin began to pull together an interest which he had pursued since childhood and just gave it more body, more weight of his attention? Are we standing here on an historic spot, here at the Mill Pond in Cambridge?

STEVE JONES: Yes. I think here is really where Darwin became a professional. Most biologists, myself included, have a guilty secret – they started as birdwatchers – and Darwin started as a beetle-watcher. He liked shooting birds. And there's a big difference between being a birdwatcher and being an ornithologist – somebody who under- stands and studies and has theories about birds. And I think here, now, was the beginning of the turning point for Darwin. He wasn't just a beetle collector, he started becoming an entomologist, an expert on insects. And from there it's a simple step to trying to make theories as to where insects had emerged from. He saw differences between species, differences between places which must have begun to implant the idea of change. I think the fact that he worked on beetles was priming the fuse which finally exploded two or three decades later. And I think those theories probably found the begin- ning of their genesis just about on this spot.

MELVYN BRAGG: And when he had his specimens he'd wander up the road to his rooms here in Christ's College, where we are now. He would later describe them as 'in an old court, middle staircase, on right hand on going into court, up one flight, right-hand door and capital rooms they were'. And they are. Jim Moore and Steve Jones are still with me and we've been joined by David Norman, Reader in Vertebrate Paleobiology and Fellow of this College – Christ's College – in which we now find ourselves. So these rooms, David Norman, are very much, you would say, as Darwin knew them?

DAVID NORMAN: They are again now. We've got a lot of college records which show us what Darwin brought and how he furnished the room, because that was one of the obligations of undergraduates when they came to take up residence in college. So we are going to reinstate the room as it approximately would have looked when Charles Darwin was an undergraduate here.

MELVYN BRAGG: Jim Moore, the image we have of Darwin is of Darwin the old man – the grey hair, the jutting eyebrows, the Godlike beard, the simian features ridiculed by his opponents – it's hard to remember that he was also a young man. What sort of a young man was he?

JIM MOORE: I think Darwin was very much like his contemporaries. I've lived with him in my imagination for a very long time. He came up here to enjoy himself. He was with genial fellows, he paid his way – his father paid his way – he was what's called a pensioner. And he ran up bills, so he was always having to tap his father for more money. He brought a horse up one year and had it stabled nearby and would ride out into the country. Eventually he brought a gun up with him and he used to take aim and fire, but it wasn't loaded, at the candles in his room.

DARWIN: And if the aim was accurate a little puff of air would blow out the candle. I do not believe that anyone could have shown more zeal for the most holy cause than I did for shooting birds. How well I remember killing my first snipe and my excitement was so great that I had much difficulty in reloading my gun from the trembling of my hands. This taste long continued.

MELVYN BRAGG: Let's go back towards the beginning of his life, Jim Moore. He was born on 12 February in 1809 in Shrewsbury. He was educated locally. What sort of childhood did he have?

JIM MOORE: Darwin was the second youngest in the family; he had an older brother and he had three older sisters. His mother died when he was nine years old. And he had a difficult childhood in many ways. He remembers times of being angry, he remembers times of being locked in rooms. He doesn't remember anything about his mother except the scene after she was gone, everything was kept bottled up.

DARWIN: My mother died in July 1817, and it is odd that I can remember hardly anything about her, except her deathbed, her black velvet gown and her curiously constructed worktable. In the spring of this same year I was sent to a day school in Shrewsbury where I stayed a year. I've been told that I was much slower in learning than my younger sister Catherine and I believe that I was in many ways a naughty boy.

STEVE JONES: His father was by no means pleased with him when he was a young man, he accused him of being no good for anything apart from rat-catching and chasing dogs and hunting. He was accused by his headmaster of being a boy unable to pay attention to anything. So the schooling wasn't particularly happy.

JIM MOORE: His father became domineering, his sisters pestered him to behave properly, he went on long solitary walks about which he didn't remember very much. He did enjoy collecting things.

DARWIN: I tried to make out the names of plants and collected all sorts of things – shells, seals, franks, coins and minerals. The passion for collecting which leads a man to be a systematic naturalist, a virtuoso or a miser was very strong in me.

MELVYN BRAGG: Can we talk a little about his mother's side of the family, which was rather more radical that his father's, wasn't it, Steve Jones?

STEVE JONES: Yes. They were a very inbred family and had been for many generations, as indeed were aristocratic families in general in those days. His mother's family were linked to the Wedgwoods who, as well as being of course important in the history of British industry in terms of pottery, were passionate anti-slavery activists and really very forward-looking in their attitudes. And for a rich, a very rich family, they were remarkably, as we'd say today I suppose, left-wing.

MELVYN BRAGG: On his father's side there was the great Erasmus Darwin in the background. Was he made aware of that intellectual heritage?

DAVID NORMAN: He was undoubtedly aware of it. He knew of the writings of Erasmus Darwin, both the poetry and the sort of quasi-scientific work that he'd done. He was undoubtedly aware of the intellectual power of the Lunar Men and the way they had powered the Industrial Revolution.

MELVYN BRAGG: The Lunar Men were a group of intellectuals around the west Midlands, who met at each other's houses, supposedly every month. They contained in their number some people who achieved great things and great fame.

DAVID NORMAN: Absolutely, and Erasmus was one of the leading lights of that particular society at the time.

JIM MOORE: What they believe in, above all, these two families, was freedom. The most important four-letter word to those families throughout the nineteenth century was 'free'. That meant free trade, free enterprise, free religion, the freedom to think and to choose – democracy with limits. These were people who supported the French Revolution and the American Revolution and the freedom of the slaves. It all comes together in an ideological package in Darwin's upbringing. So that by the time he gets to Cambridge his natural friends are Whig reformers.

MELVYN BRAGG: Before he came here to Cambridge he was enrolled in a medical school at Edinburgh. He didn't last very long there. What did he get out of it and why did he get out of it?

STEVE JONES: I think he was horrified by the reality of medicine. That was part of the problem. You've got to remember we're talking very early in modern medicine's time. Doctors stopped killing more people than they cured only in about 1910 and we're talking about almost a century earlier. And Darwin saw some awful operations, one of which was upon a child, and he just ran from the room, he couldn't stand it. And he was extraordinarily badly taught. I mean, Edinburgh is an experiment in geology, Edinburgh is the Galapagos of North Britain, how can you not believe in volcanism – in volcanoes – and look at Arthur's Seat. But his teachers ignored that. And the following year he came down to Cambridge where I think he felt immediately at home.

MELVYN BRAGG: The last key to this is, David Norman, did he ask to leave Edinburgh to come to Cambridge or did somebody say it isn't working for you here, we'll send you to Cambridge?

DAVID NORMAN: Not quite as simple as that. Word got to his father, probably through his sisters, that he was no longer regularly attending lectures at Edinburgh. That, I think, resulted in, to some extent, a family showdown between Charles and his father where his future was discussed. Between them, in a very civilised way, they decided that the most appropriate direction would be to get a BA degree in Cambridge and with that BA degree then read for holy orders and become a cleric. That seemed very appealing to Charles Darwin at the time. He thought, that's for me, that's a worthwhile career, I can enjoy myself, spend a considerable amount of time watching nature, observing the miracle of nature, I can be well paid, I'll be comfortable. That would appeal to his father for the ne'er-do-well son, obviously. And therefore a career in Cambridge as an undergraduate beckoned.

MELVYN BRAGG: We're being led into the Old Library at Christ's College where Darwin must have studied sometimes when he could tear himself away from the Fens.

You can find traces of Darwin all over Cambridge and all over Christ's College, but you can particularly find them here in the Christ's College Library where they keep many of his letters and the books he was known to have read, including William Herschel's astronomical writings, the poetry of Milton – another Christ's College man – and the early novel *Clarissa* by Samuel Richardson. Colin Higgins is the Assistant College Librarian, and again I'm with Darwin's biographer Jim Moore. Colin Higgins, can you take us through some of the things you've got on the table?

COLIN HIGGINS: Perhaps the first thing to look at would be the admission of Darwin to the college. When he came here, like every other student, he'd sign an admissions book and we actually have three different books that record his entry into the college. Next to that we have some newly discovered college accounts which show what Darwin, alongside the other students and the fellows of the college, was paying for their meals, paying for coal, paying for their shoes to be shined, that kind of thing.

MELVYN BRAGG: How do you find out what he'd read at the time? How do we know about the poetry of John Milton, for instance?

COLIN HIGGINS: The Milton one we know about because he says it was the only book that he never left behind on his land journeys throughout South America. We've recently purchased a miniature edition of *Paradise Lost*, the kind of thing that he would have taken with him.

MELVYN BRAGG: It's the size of a palm of the hand.

COLIN HIGGINS: It's absolutely tiny and it's remarkable that . . .

MELVYN BRAGG: . . . anybody could read it.

COLIN HIGGINS: The text is so small. What's also interesting about this copy is that none of the pages are cut, so whoever owned this one never read it.

MELVYN BRAGG: These drawings are his, aren't they?

COLIN HIGGINS: This is from a volume of entomology published by Michael Stevens.

MELVYN BRAGG: We're looking at six beautifully drawn beetles.

COLIN HIGGINS: Darwin was the first one to discover those in the United Kingdom. So this is essentially the first place where Darwin gets published beside pictures of beetles because he's the first to find them. Above it you see letters written by Darwin to his cousin William Darwin Fox, we've two of those out on display, illustrated with beetles, which he was known to be collecting at that time.

DARWIN: My dear Fox, I am dying by inches from not having anybody to talk to about insects. My sister has made rough drawings of three of them. One is, I'm nearly sure, the same insect as Hawe of Queen's took in a willow tree and which

Garland did not know. I think this is an admirable prize. The second is an extremely common insect, the third a most beautiful leptura, very like the quadrifasciata, only the body is of the same size throughout. I tell you all these particulars as I'm anxious to know something about these. I'm constantly saying I do wish Fox was here.

COLIN HIGGINS: His cousin, William Darwin Fox, was here for six months, they overlapped, and during that six months they became friends and their friendship lasted their entire lives. The core of our collection is a 150 or so letters that he's written to this cousin.

MELVYN BRAGG: Which Jim Moore is devouring as we speak. If I can tease him away – Jim, if you can come over and join us and stop being quite as immersed in things you must have read a thousand times already! Colin mentioned Darwin's cousin, William Darwin Fox. Can you talk about his relationship with him, was he rather a mentor to him at that time?

JIM MOORE: Darwin was sent here to Christ's College to be under the example of his cousin. William Darwin Fox wasn't a first cousin, slightly more distant, came from Derbyshire, a country gentleman's son, raised in a menagerie of animals in the countryside and loved God's creation. He was a safe conservative evangelically influenced young man who was certainly destined for the Church of England. There was a tremendous male camaraderie – collecting beetles, sometimes going out into the countryside with horses and chasing things. Fox ended up having an extremely large family once he married.

Fox and Darwin began corresponding from the time that they were undergraduates, separated during the summer. This correspondence continued for the rest of his life until Fox died in 1880. Almost all the letters are here at Christ's College and they are absolutely indispensable for understanding the fine texture of Darwin's private personal life and his family life, his health, his emotional swings, his intentions to publish or not publish, his fears and his hopes.

MELVYN BRAGG: We've heard about his development almost under his own steam with the beetles, collecting beetles and going for walks in the meadows and collecting and collecting and collecting. What about his intellectual developments – now we're in his room, this is presumably where he did a great deal of his reading – what books would he be reading at the time, do we know that? I mean according to college tradition, for instance, Darwin's rooms were once occupied by William Paley. Did he fit into Darwin's reading and how does he fit in anyway?

STEVE JONES: He certainly read Paley's *Evidences of Creation*. He mentioned this. And in some ways Paley was a fascinating figure because he was a more than competent biologist. He was a wonderful describer of the world, he described plants and animals, he described intestinal systems often in painful detail and his descriptions were all to one end – wasn't this amazing, the way you digest a lump of meat – well, it is amazing but then he took the next step – wasn't this amazing, it must have been done by God. And if you have that mindset it makes perfect sense. It doesn't take you anywhere because it doesn't ask any questions but it rationalises the accumulation of yet more facts. And I think that at that time Darwin, as everybody else was, was a Paleyite – what he saw around him was the work of God. And by doing natural history he was in his own mind doing theology – the two things were really inseparable.

JIM MOORE: From Paley Darwin received first and foremost an ability to reason empirically and deductively. He said later in life that he could almost have repeated Paley's argument by heart. Later on he was so impressed with Paley that he chose to read as his extra-curricular entertainment Paley's *Natural Theology*, in which Paley established the principle that the design of living things proved the existence of a wise and beneficent Creator.

MELVYN BRAGG: Did the word 'evolution' ever come up while he was an undergraduate?

JIM MOORE: The word 'evolution' at this time was used habitu-ally for a series of numbers or a curve evolving, it wasn't about species evolving. His grandfather had talked about the generation of species, not even the transmutation, the generation of new species from existing organic species. The word 'transmutation' was in use thanks to John Ray, a Cambridge clergyman and naturalist, who talked about the heresies of transmutation and spontaneous generation of life. Darwin would undoubtedly have picked up the notions of generation from his grandfather's book *Zoonomia*, and the notion of transmutation from the experience in Edinburgh where his zoology instructor, Robert Grant, was a follower of Lamarck.

MELVYN BRAGG: Is there any sense of him being rather a racy character, because we see this great man of granite in the representations we have of him and certainly in his work. But here we have him hunting, we have him bringing horses up – not up to this room, we hope, but still up to Cambridge – what else can we say about him that will enliven that period of his life?

STEVE JONES: Well, he admitted going to the pub now and again, or at least drinking now and again, something which he didn't do much later in life, although occasionally he used to like a bit of brandy. I think in terms of the behaviour of the average modern undergraduate he was probably rather restrained. People who were training for the priesthood would be expected to be somewhat restrained. So he was a generally educated rather well-off young man of liberal tendency. I don't think anybody, when he came to Cambridge, could possibly have imagined for a moment what he would become.

DAVID NORMAN: Christ's was fairly lax, an easy-going sort of college compared to the discipline imposed by some other colleges. So I think the young Charles would have had plenty of opportunities to enjoy himself. He became a member of what's called the Glutton Club because he enjoyed food and drink, albeit for a short period of time. So he was a warm-blooded, hot-blooded maybe, young undergraduate and enjoyed himself.

MELVYN BRAGG: Darwin found the lectures on offer uninspiring much of the time. He spent time in the pub. He loved shooting and enjoying himself with a circle of friends. He didn't seem at all marked for greatness. But there's one place and one person from whom he learned a great deal and, typical of the man, it wasn't cloistered in the library but out here where I'm standing on Coe Fen, just a few hundred yards from the Mill Pond. This was Darwin's classroom and his teacher was a man called John Stevens Henslow. So much so that Darwin became known as 'the man who walked with Henslow'.

And I'm on Coe Fen as the man who walks with Jim Moore and Steve Jones. Can you tell us about John Stevens Henslow, Jim?

JIM MOORE: Henslow was thirteen years older than Darwin, he wanted to do natural history, he obtained the Chair of Mineralogy at Cambridge and then he went into holy orders.

DARWIN: He was deeply religious. And so orthodox that he told me one day he should be grieved if a single word of the Thirty-Nine Articles were altered. His moral qualities were in every way admirable. He was free from every tinge of vanity or other petty feelings. And I never saw a man who thought so little about himself or his own concerns. His temper was imperturbably good with the most winning and courteous manners. Yet as I have seen he could be roused by any bad action to the warmest indignation and prompt action.

JIM MOORE: He was a model for Darwin, a real paradigm of what an Anglican priest could be. The man was warm, he was highly moral, he was open to new ideas, he belonged to a network of fellow clergymen that would do Darwin's career a great deal of good. He was a Cambridge don, Darwin could begin to see himself like all of those things.

DARWIN: His knowledge was great in botany, entomology, chemistry, mineralogy and geology. His strongest taste was to draw conclusions from long-continued minute observations. His judgement was excellent and his whole mind well balanced. But I do not suppose that anyone would say that he possessed much original genius.

MELVYN BRAGG: Steve Jones, can you give us some idea of the sort of information that Henslow imparted to Darwin and why it's considered to be such a very important part of Darwin's education at this stage?

STEVE JONES: Henslow introduced him to plants and plant biology plays quite a large part in Darwin's work, particularly his later work. Henslow also introduced him to a science whose name hadn't been invented then, which is ecology, the notion that there's more to life than stamp collecting or plant collecting: you need to know where there are, how they're related to each other, why some grow in certain places, why there are so many different kinds. And this field we're in was then common grazing, as it's called, which is famous for having vast numbers of different plants upon it because heavily grazed landscapes tend to be very diverse. I mean, looking around, even on this rather chill day, you can see – I can see – at least half a dozen species of grass and on that wall over there probably eight to ten obvious different species of plant. And I think Darwin began to look for patterns. And that's what Henslow began to do, to suggest that there might be patterns in nature. This rather unprepossessing piece of green was an important part of Darwin's education.

JIM MOORE: Henslow was, in his own time, quite progressive for introducing plants really as living organisms not just as dried specimens to classify. He had students dissect plants and look how they reproduce. He believed that plants had a considerable scope for variation, they could change within limits, with the limits of the species, and Darwin learnt that from him too.

STEVE JONES: Darwin calls the nature of species 'the mystery of mysteries'. And as usual he was uncannily right. It's still possible to go to week-long conferences where distinguished biologists tear each other's throats out about what is the nature of species, what is a species. I often think of them as being, as it were, republics of genes – within a species individuals can mate and exchange genes, between species they can't. But that doesn't always work, there are transitional forms. That's one of the things that brought Darwin's idea of change to the fore – the intermediates between species. And speciation is today's word really for the origin of species.

MELVYN BRAGG: What was the intellectual context to Henslow and Darwin at the time, would there be ideas behind the looking at plants, collecting plants, classifying of plants – what would they be?

STEVE JONES: Well, I think it was true for all scientists – and that word hadn't been invented either – really what they were doing, explicitly or implicitly, was just checking out what God had done. Newton really had that idea, the universe was a gigantic clock that had been put together by God, and Newton, as somebody profoundly religious, much more so that Darwin ever was I think, saw it as his duty to disentangle how that clock was made. And really the logic behind all the natural history, all the human anatomy, everything – the whole of biology – was the logic of Paley, who had been a predecessor of Darwin, who saw in the beauties of nature God's work.

MELVYN BRAGG: Can you tell us, Steve, and before we come to an end or rush for cover as the Cambridge rain comes down very cold, can you briskly tell us, do you think that in walking with Henslow and the tutorials he was thereby getting, there was a reaching out to what would be his great idea?

STEVE JONES: Well, hindsight's a wonderful thing and there's a whole community of scholars that spend their entire lives picking the lint out of Darwin's navel and no doubt many of them will have seen this work on this patch of green as a direct predecessor of the *Origin of Species*. I'm not quite sure that that's right. I mean, Darwin famously some years later said, 'At last I have a theory to work with.' When he was at Cambridge he had no theory to work with. And what use are facts without theory, he also suggested. So here he was really becoming technically adept and that's a very important part for any biologist – to know and understand and classify the plants and animals around them. And there's a lot of technology in that, he was learning that. I think it took some years before the penny dropped and that technology turned it into genius.

MELVYN BRAGG: We've come to the end of this first programme. It's time to take stock of Darwin. We're in front of the portrait they have of Darwin here in Christ's College, Cambridge. In later life Darwin said this portrait made him look like a very venerable, acute, melancholy old dog. We're used to that image of him as an old man but what about the young Darwin who left Christ's in 1831, Jim Moore?

JIM MOORE: Darwin was educated here as a gentleman. He would be an adornment to society. In a country parish he would hunt knowledgeably with the squire. He would share a parson's interest in the beetles and the birds in the local neighbourhood. He might even write a book about God's creatures. He could speak about geology because he'd rubbed shoulders with clerical geologists. He could speak about geometry because he read Euclid. He could quote Horace because he could read Greek and studied the classics. He had it all. He was not destined to become a great scientist, he was destined to become a parish naturalist. He was off to Wales to learn some geology and then he would come back and take his ordination examination and enter the Church of England. That's what he knew when he left Cambridge.

MELVYN BRAGG: David Norman, this trip to Wales, what did that add to his knowledge?

DAVID NORMAN: It added practical geology. He'd learned quite a lot of theory about how geology works by attending Adam Sedgwick's lectures and he'd realised that he was deficient in field skills – how to observe, how to note down, how to do basic geolog- ical observation in the field. He needed a practitioner to show him how to do it. John Henslow intervened and suggested that Charles Darwin accompany Adam Sedgwick on a field trip to North Wales. And that field trip was of a simple intent in a way because George Greenough had published a geological map of that part of the world and Adam Sedgwick didn't believe it. Adam Sedgwick wanted to go to the rocky outcrops, look at the types of rocks that were exposed and prove that Greenough was right or wrong. It was as simple as that.

STEVE JONES: The walk across North Wales was, I think, a central moment in his life, central moment in any scientist's life. The moment when you make your first, what you can define as your own discovery, which nobody else knows. You could see that in Darwin's work. He realised, looking at the Greenough map, that actually it was wrong and he, Darwin, had shown it to be wrong. I think that was a most important moment. When he got back to his grand house at Shrewsbury, there was a letter on the mat and opening that letter was the first step to proving that most of biology, until then, had been wrong.

MELVYN BRAGG: The letter was from John Stevens Henslow, pulling strings for his favourite pupil. Henslow had recommended Darwin to become a gentleman's companion to one Captain Robert Fitzroy. Fitzroy was planning to survey the coastline of South America in a small ship that would become synonymous with the Darwin legend. It was called the *Beagle*.

The voyage of the *Beagle* would make Darwin as a scientist and establish him in scientific society. In the next programme we embark with Darwin on that voyage and look at the extraordinary array of fossils, rocks and animals that he sent home, a collection that laid the foundations for the theory of evolution by natural selection.

TRANSMITTED: 5.1.2009

Darwin: Programme 2

I n programme one, we left the twenty-two-year-old Darwin on the cusp of a grand adventure. A voyage on a ship called the *Beagle* to map the coast of South America. It would take five years, at that stage a quarter of the twenty-two-year-old Darwin's life, and would radically change his ambitions, his understanding of the world and his status as a naturalist.

We're in Darwin's rooms in Christ's College, Cambridge, panelled, windows overlooking a small quad, and I'm joined by David Norman, Reader in Vertebrate Paleobiology and Fellow of this college; Steve Jones, Professor of Genetics at UCL; and Jim Moore, a biographer of Darwin.

Jim Moore, what kind of a boat was the *Beagle*? How big was it and who was Darwin sailing with?

JIM MOORE: HMS *Beagle* was a Royal Naval 10-gun brig, thirty metres long and about eight or nine metres wide. A member of the coffin class of brigs because of their instability. Not particularly successful as a warship, it had been adapted purposefully to sail on this voyage and it was immensely crowded with seventy-odd people.

STEVE JONES: Charles Darwin had to share a cabin with the captain of the boat. All his specimens were jammed in there. I think the level of claustrophobia must have been absolutely terrifying. And of course they were all men, that didn't make life any easier.

DARWIN: After having been twice driven back by heavy south western gales, Her Majesty's ship *Beagle*, a 10-gun brig, under the command of Captain Fitzroy, sailed from Devonport on the 27th December 1831. The object of the expedition was to complete the survey of Patagonia and Tierra del Fuego, to survey the shores of Chile, Peru and some of the islands in the Pacific and to carry a chain of chronometrical measurements round the world.

DAVID NORMAN: Charles Darwin was seasick and he was to discover this on the voyage of the *Beagle*. I think any excuse that he found to spend time on land and do his adventures and collecting on land was gratefully received as far as he was concerned because you can't imagine the misery he went through for persistent periods of time being seasick. It must have been awful.

DARWIN: On the 6th January we reached Tenerife but were prevented landing by fears of our bringing the cholera. The next morning we saw the sun rise behind the rugged outline of the Grand Canary Island.

MELVYN BRAGG: The *Beagle* voyage was a *Boys' Own* adventure. Darwin was twenty-two years old, Captain Fitzroy was only twenty-six, and most of the crew were late teenagers or in their early twenties. You can see then why Fitzroy needed a companion like Darwin, a gentleman like himself, even though the two of them were chalk and cheese politically. Extraordinary responsibility to take a boat that size all around the world.

DARWIN: Among the scenes which are deeply impressed on my mind none exceed in sublimity the primeval forest untouched by the hand of man, temples filled with the varied productions of the god of nature. No one can stand in these solitudes unmoved and not feel that there is more in man than the mere breath of his body.

MELVYN BRAGG: Fitzroy really didn't realise what he had taken on board.

DAVID NORMAN: There was actually a raw intellect here that would be asking questions and probing questions about the earth and the process of life. And as the voyage progressed, as he began to question what he was seeing with the variety and variation of nature, then the more he began to question some of the cardinal values of people like Fitzroy.

STEVE JONES: And they had some extremely unpleasant disagreements, although as gentlemen they did actually in the end make up. I think there must have been moments during the voyage when Fitzroy quite wondered what he'd taken on, so it wasn't all fun and games, I'm sure there were quite a lot of personal quarrels that went on.

MELVYN BRAGG: Can you tell us, Jim Moore, the principal reading matter that Darwin took with him?

JIM MOORE: The most important books Darwin took were Charles Lyell's *Principles of Geology*. The first volume was given to Darwin as they left by Fitzroy himself. This was the latest textbook on how to reason in the earth sciences. It established principles which Darwin took on board, quite literally, and applied to what he saw. Darwin was interested in geodynamics, he was interested in what made the earth's crust the way it is.

DAVID NORMAN: Some of the most important influences on him must have been in South America because he witnessed an earthquake in Concepcion.

DARWIN: A bad earthquake at once destroys our oldest associations – the earth, the very emblem of solidity, has moved beneath our feet like a thin crust over a fluid. One second of time has created in the mind a strange idea of insecurity which hours of reflection would not have produced.

DAVID NORMAN: After the earthquake he noticed that the sea level in the area on the seashore had been lifted up and marine animals were just stranded on this raised seashore. He also realised that earthquakes were linked to volcanic eruption, he tied these two together within the dynamic earth. So he realised there was a huge interlinked set of phenomena – volcanoes, earthquakes and elevation of the land.

MELVYN BRAGG: He was also studying people, wasn't he, Jim Moore?

JIM MOORE: He was. When Darwin got to South America he was tuned to understand racial differences because his family had brought him up in anti-slavery and here he found slavery in the raw. This shocked him.

DARWIN: I may mention one very trifling anecdote which at the time struck me more forcibly than any other story of cruelty. I was crossing a ferry with a negro who was uncommonly stupid. In endeavouring to make him understand I talked loud and made signs. In doing which I passed my hand near his face. He, I suppose, thought I was in a passion and was going to strike him, for instantly, with a frightened look and half shut eyes, he dropped his hands. I shall never forget my feelings of surprise, disgust and shame at seeing a great powerful man afraid even to ward off a blow directed, as he thought, at his face. This man had been trained to a degradation lower than the slavery of the most helpless animal.

JIM MOORE: That made Darwin wonder how humans could be created so high and so low. Could the same God have created Cambridge dons and these savages who lay upon the ground and lived hand to mouth? This, I think, was the most disturbing intellectual experience in Darwin's entire life. It shook him to the core to see naked people his own age surviving in a hostile environment. And of course he was seeing them not only as people but as living organisms.

MELVYN BRAGG: Can we try to imagine or speculate – what did the Charles Darwin who stepped off the *Beagle* know that the Charles Darwin who stepped on to the *Beagle* from Cambridge not know?

STEVE JONES: I guess what he saw on his journey was the transforming power of time. The realisation that very, very slight and trivial effects, very slow events, can have enormous effects, given enough years. He says somewhere that the maxim '*de minima non curat lex'* does not apply to biology – the maxim that the law takes no account of trifles does not apply to biology. So the tiny and apparently unimportant changes can have grotesquely huge effects, given a long enough time. And I think that's what really struck him on the *Beagle*.

JIM MOORE: I suppose if there's one word it's 'patterns'. There was a method in his collecting. He didn't just pick up pebbles on the seashore. He wanted to know why certain things were where they were and not in other places. That is to say he was a philosophical naturalist, he was interested in causes. Why are similar things in different environments? Why are different things in the same kind of environments? Why does the fauna change from one side of the Andes to the other? Why do the ostriches in South America change from north to south? Why do you find different races of people in different places? These were all part of the same problematic. All of these things come together in the most extraordinary synthesis in this young man's mind.

STEVE JONES: When he came back from the *Beagle* voyage he was a collector but a much better collector than he had been before. He was trembling on the edge of having what he called a theory to work with.

JIM MOORE: Remember he's still in his twenties.

DARWIN: In conclusion it appears to me that nothing can be more improving to a young naturalist than a journey in distant countries. The excitement from the novelty of objects and the chance of success stimulate him to increased activity. Moreover, as a number of isolated facts soon become uninteresting, the habit of comparison leads to generalisation.

MELVYN BRAGG: The *Beagle* returned to Plymouth in October 1836 and the Charles Darwin that stepped off it had no doubt about the direction of his future life. From this point on Darwin, the would-be priest and avid collector and occasional dissolute, was gone. He saw himself as a geologist. Darwin had collected hundreds of samples of rocks, animals, fossils, far more than could ever be held on board. He shipped them all back to Cambridge and to his mentor John Stevens Henslow. When Darwin returned they both had a small measure of scientific fame for his collection which was waiting for him at Cambridge, and some of the objects are still here where I am in the Sedgwick Museum in Cambridge. I'm joined by David Norman, the Director of the Sedgwick Museum, and Jim Moore.

People talk about Darwin and Galapagos and one of the first things that comes to mind is finches. It's nearly always animals. But the rocks he brought back are very important indeed and the number he brought back. What can we read into this about Darwin's interests?

DAVID NORMAN: As a very simple numerical observation of what he thought when he was on the voyage of the *Beagle*, he put together about 360 pages worth of zoological notes and about 140 pages of geological notes. So clearly while he was on the *Beagle*, while he was doing his interpretative work, there was a large emphasis on rocks and geology.

MELVYN BRAGG: Geology was very important and very disturbing for people at the time. Ruskin, for instance, thought that geologists themselves were destroying his idea of God with 'the clinking of hammers' that he talked about. Can you bring us into the picture of why geology so excited the minds of these intelligent young people?

DAVID NORMAN: It was at a time of equipoise about how you did science and how you made observations on the world about you. And it was a time where you could either sit in an armchair and come up with very grandiose schemes that explained the structure and history of the earth or, as the Geological Society tried to demonstrate, you actually had to go out and do fieldwork, you had to make observations in the field and only after you'd brought material and made observations and began to integrate those observations could you really genuinely come up with a proper credible theory.

MELVYN BRAGG: And in the rocks, Jim Moore, he was looking for fossils of course and finding them, we have them here all around us.

JIM MOORE:　For all geologists, no one just looked at rocks, they wanted to know whether there were beings in those rocks. Darwin was collecting rock samples from different places to figure out how the continent itself, America particularly, was formed and he was collecting the adjacent fossils, where he could find them, as a further clue to how life was correlated with the geological changes.

DAVID NORMAN:　What Darwin was trying to do was generate a theory of the earth. It was a very common aim amongst natural philosophers, not scientists, natural philosophers. They were trying to come up with a theory of how the earth worked. In making observations, as he was doing on this global trip round the world, one hope was that he would see in a practical way the earth working.

JIM MOORE:　And as the voyage passed Darwin realised that there was a missing element in Lyell's system – it was where life came from.

MELVYN BRAGG:　Despite the abundance of rocks and fossils, many of the most famous items in Darwin's collection were animals, and in the university Museum of Zoology at Cambridge, which is where I am at the moment, they house some of the things that Darwin had to kill before he sent them home. They would help him answer one of the great questions on his mind – the problem of speciation, or how species developed and what the relationships were between them. The museum houses octopuses from Cape Verde, marine sponges, bottled fish, but most famously Galapagos finches.

So at last we're standing beside the Darwin finches, Steve Jones, here in the Museum of Geology in Cambridge. What sort of finches are they, first of all?

STEVE JONES:　Well, they're finches, insect-eating birds, most of them, some of them crack open seeds, some of them actually use tools in order to hook out insect larvae from rotten fruits. They are often painted as the sort of eureka moment – the finch moment – in evolution.

MELVYN BRAGG:　These finches in the glass case before us, when they had life it was in the Galapagos?

STEVE JONES: Exactly. And Darwin, without doubt, did collect them, there's no question of that. But it wasn't that magic moment. In fact he jumbled all his finches together and he didn't even know which islands they came from initially. He was actually much more interested and struck by things like the giant tortoises. He landed on one island and he stayed there for several days camping, and as people did in those days, killing off and eating the tortoises, which is unthinkable nowadays. And he noted that on this particular island the tortoises were blacker and had a sweeter taste than those on a different island. And that's a very unusual sort of conjunction of taxonomy and gastronomy. And it really was a statement – hang on, why aren't all the tortoises the same? If they were made by God why do we have different tortoises on different islands? Now since then the same notion has emerged with these finches and a huge amount of absolutely brilliant research has been done on these finches – but not by Darwin.

MELVYN BRAGG: Are Darwin's finches the key because of what happened post-Darwin?

STEVE JONES: I think so, yes. And they are a beautiful exemplar of something which Darwin never imagined would be possible, an exemplar of seeing evolution happening in front of your eyes . . .

MELVYN BRAGG: Can you just spell that out for us on that – how is evolution happening before your eyes with the finches? Because it has captured the public imagination.

STEVE JONES: Yes. People know about El Niño, this change in climate that takes place every few years in the Galapagos, everything goes green and then everything burns up. And a very heroic British couple, the Grants, have been following these birds for thirty or forty years. They now see that after an El Niño what happens is that only a tiny proportion of them survive and the ones that survived in one particular species are those with big heavy, exceptionally heavy, beaks which are able to crack open the dry seeds. The heavy hard seeds, that's all that's left to eat. As the weather gets better again the small beaks creep back in once more. So you see evolution happening, which would have been unthinkable to Darwin. So maybe these finches are more iconic than I make out.

MELVYN BRAGG: You think the mockingbird has been undeservedly neglected?

STEVE JONES: Yes, the poor old mockingbird. It is the mockingbird that Darwin actually commented on as being different on different islands. We see that they were different but related species and that you could see how Darwin on the Galapagos couldn't fail to notice the fact that there were unique forms of life there, that were somewhat similar but rather different from the forms of life in South America. And this is one of them.

> DARWIN: My attention was first thoroughly aroused by comparing together the numerous specimens shot by myself and several other parties onboard, of the mocking thrushes. When to my astonishment I discovered that all those from Charles Island belonged to one species, all from Albemarle Island to another and all from James and Chatham Islands, between which two other islands are situated as connecting links, belong to a third. These two latter species are closely allied and would by some ornithologists be considered as only well-marked races or varieties. But the first species is very distinct.

STEVE JONES: Now what we've got along here is an octopus collected by Charles Darwin himself, looking like so many other things I've spent my life looking at, something disgusting in a glass vessel with all kinds of suckers and so on. He collected this one on the Cape Verde Islands at the very beginning of the *Beagle* voyage. And he noticed that as they dart from side to side of the pond, they can change colour. He's being a natural historian. And soon he began to realise that octopuses, squids and the like are all related, that they've all changed over time, they've evolved.

JIM MOORE: Darwin was fascinated by the great diversity and the intricate beauty of many of these organisms. Once he threw his dredging bucket out behind the *Beagle* and hauled in a huge array of marine invertebrates. And he wrote in his diary: 'it makes me wonder why God created so much beauty out here where there's no one to observe it.' That's an interesting problem. He put his finger on any number of things that called for a solution that wasn't God directly creating things in places but laws. Darwin is on a quest for the laws of nature, the laws of life he says, when he gets back in London from the *Beagle* voyage.

MELVYN BRAGG: We've come backstage in the museum, into the bird store, where there's a gallery of stuffed birds all around us and in front of us is a duck. A significant duck. Steve Jones, can you explain why this duck is significant?

STEVE JONES: Well, this duck did not die in vain, although it probably felt that it did. It was hit smartly on the back of the head with a geological hammer and at the other end of the hammer was Charles Darwin himself. And you tend to forget that actually being a collector can be rather a bloody business and Darwin went out and shot – he was a very good shot – he shot, he strangled, he beat, he garrotted, poisoned, and of course he was a biologist, so he had to do it. At least he didn't eat this one. He's famous for having discovered one species of bird in South America, Darwin's rhea, which is a flightless bird, which he had for his dinner one night by mistake, but fortunately he could reassemble the remains from his plate.

MELVYN BRAGG: To continue that for a moment, Jim Moore, we're still in Cambridge, although we do seem in another world in the bowels of this extraordinary museum, and he is a young gentleman of means and he rides to hounds and he hunts, and to pursue what Steve said, to take it further, there's little compunction about the slaughter of the animals he was to treasure.

JIM MOORE: Darwin's a bit of a paradox here because he had an aversion to blood and he believed he'd inherited that from his father. He did not approve of cruelty, he never did in his life, nor did his family. He was brought up on anti-cruelty. At the same time he had an ambition to be praised for his ability to collect. And he believed that he had a collecting instinct, so he was giving vent to that, all around the world, and slaughtering animals.

MELVYN BRAGG: Just to pin this down with both of you, it is from the collecting, from the assiduous collecting year in, year out, beetles and on to ducks, dead ducks, that he builds up his theory?

STEVE JONES: Yes, I think in the end he can't do science without facts. Many philosophers and theoreticians picked up Darwin's theories, they still do, and didn't bother with fact. One Herbert Spencer was a famous one, and it was said of Herbert Spencer that his definition of a tragedy was a beautiful theory killed by an ugly fact. What Darwin specialised in was ugly facts and he got all those ugly facts together and he formed of them a beautiful theory.

MELVYN BRAGG: Still in this extraordinary museum we're standing in front of a collection of the barnacles he brought back. I'm joined by Jenny Clack, who's Professor and Curator of Vertebrate Paleontology here at the Zoology Museum in Cambridge. Can you talk about these barnacles?

JENNY CLACK: His barnacle work started stimulated by a curious barnacle he found on the *Beagle* expedition in South America. He started by describing this particular peculiar one that he found but he also wanted to understand how you do classification and the barnacles are a particularly puzzling group at that point. And he thought, I'll just describe this one, the peculiar one, and that mushroomed into an eight-year study, starting a few years after he'd got back from the *Beagle* expedition. He went on to investigate the relationships between barnacles, finding that, for example, in some barnacles the males were absolutely minute and actually lived inside the females. And by looking at the differences between the males and the females and between different species, which have got different shapes, he tried to think about what a species was and how you differentiated from other species.

STEVE JONES: Darwin spent eight years working on barnacles, wrote four stunningly boring books on them, which are still the standard work on the taxonomy of barnacles. He dissected thousands of specimens, he described them in eye-watering detail, he analysed their fossils, he made a family tree of barnacles and once you begin to make a family tree almost by definition you have in your mind the notion of shared descent form a common ancestor and once you have that, you have it — you have evolution.

MELVYN BRAGG: If we walk over here, Steve, we're at the other end of the scale from a barnacle, we're in front of a megatherium, not the one that Darwin brought back but very like. Can you tell us about it?

STEVE JONES: Well, a megatherium is indeed at the other end of the scale from a barnacle. It's an enormous extinct sloth. This is twelve, fifteen feet high, and it's being very slothful at the moment because its bones have been pieced together. This is the remnant we now know of an extraordinary gang of mammals that lived in South America when South America was still separate from North America, giant creatures of many kinds, all of which were driven to extinction by aggressive invaders from the north. Darwin found an example of this in Chile, collected most of it and brought it back. The sloth is arranged in this museum in rather the way that many extinct mammals were supposed to be. Its nose is up in the air. Why? Because it's trying to escape from Noah's flood which has washed it off the surface of the earth. It didn't take long though for Darwin to see the faults in that argument.

MELVYN BRAGG: We're joined by Jim Moore.

JIM MOORE: When he got back, Darwin realised that there were pint-sized versions of this enormous mammal still existing in South America and it made him wonder why did God go on creating smaller versions of the same thing. Maybe there was some kind of rule that governed the way sloths are introduced into an unchanging environment. In other words, a law. It was part of what got Darwin started by developing a theory.

MELVYN BRAGG: Was the Victorian public aware of this massive and meticulous collecting, and if so how did they react?

STEVE JONES: I think the scientific public was very much aware of it.

JIM MOORE: Professor Henslow and Professor Sedgwick, both of whom taught him at Cambridge, sang his praises and everyone admired what this young man out in South America was capable of. When Darwin heard that his name was on everyone's tongue, his hammer, his geological hammer, made the rocks ring in the Falkland Islands, where he was. It spurred him on in science.

STEVE JONES: And it was immediately clear when Darwin came back that here we had a collector extraordinaire, with the ability to collect and to classify and to understand an astounding diversity of creatures, from barnacles to birds. And I think that this made his reputation. Darwin won the Gold Medal of the Royal Society when he was still a young man. He was by no means a shrinking violet.

MELVYN BRAGG: Charles Darwin was twenty-eight and his star was rising, he was developing his ideas and upping his standing. He became a Fellow of the Geological Society of London and had presented a paper to the Zoological Society in London. Darwin was increasingly pulled towards London, feted by the scientific institutions there. It was becoming the centre of his intellectual world and on 6 March 1837 he moved there.

STEVE JONES: The notion of change was in the air in London, not only in the world of biology but also in the world of politics and religion. In what had seemed to be static, the plates were shifting, although we knew nothing about continental plates at the time. And that's the milieu which Darwin joined.

JIM MOORE: Science was political, particularly the life sciences. They could threaten social stability if they were taught the wrong way.

MELVYN BRAGG: Are we talking about the great reform movements getting under way, about Chartism getting under way, still the reverberations of the French Revolution becoming anglicised once more?

JIM MOORE: Already geology had threatened to a certain extent. Because of its extended timescale, perhaps it indicated the Book of Genesis, the Bible, wasn't reliable but, more importantly, to believe in transmutation, that is the natural evolution of new species, was believed to culminate necessarily in the bestialisation of human beings. And if humans were only beasts it meant the overthrow of the established religion of Christianity and therefore social stability. All Darwin's friends accepted that political connection.

MELVYN BRAGG: We're in the Grant Zoological Museum at University College, London. What was Darwin's relationship with Dr Robert Grant and why is it important? This goes right back to his medical student days, doesn't it, where Grant set him off on a more congenial course.

STEVE JONES: Grant was his teacher in Edinburgh. And he took Darwin on no doubt chilly field trips to the Firth of Forth where they collected various kinds of animals. Darwin wrote his first scientific note about some obscure marine creature in the Firth of Forth with the encouragement of Grant. Darwin belonged to a rather exclusive student society called the Plinian Society in Edinburgh. It was the student biological society, which was very taxonomic and descriptive in its nature, and if you look at their records there are some rather odd crossings out in Darwin's time and there seems to be some hint of evolution creeping into them and they take them out. Grant really was important in introducing Darwin to the world of animal biology.

JIM MOORE: When Darwin returned to London Grant had to go to him to ask whether he could describe the coral specimens Darwin had brought back from the *Beagle*. And he didn't get the job. He was the only person we know who actually applied to Darwin to work for him and Darwin apparently snubbed him. It all really came to a head at a meeting of the Zoological Society where the old guard assembled to almost ritually humiliate Grant because of his attempts to reform this old gentlemen's club – the Zoological Society – and as a result Grant was pushed to the margin of London science, where he remained.

MELVYN BRAGG: But it's quite a fall, isn't it, and from the way you tell it, Jim Moore, Grant seems to have been rather badly treated?

JIM MOORE: You could say that, yes, but he was an oddball, he was always an oddball.

MELVYN BRAGG: You can be an oddball without meriting being badly treated, lots of oddballs don't deserve to be badly treated.

JIM MOORE: He was tall, he was satirical, sarcastic even, he was a Scot.

MELVYN BRAGG: They got him, didn't they? Why did they get him?

STEVE JONES: There is a rumour, it's not much more than that, but it descends from professor of zoology to professor of zoology in UCL, that actually one of the reasons was that Grant was a homosexual and this was of course almost unthinkable but almost certainly do-able in the area of UCL. There were a number of famous homosexual male brothels nearby. And there is this undercurrent that there may have been – the break with Darwin and the others which was really almost complete – may have had something to do with that.

JIM MOORE: Grant was also a radical democrat, he wanted the disestablishment of the Church, he used the evidence in this museum to establish a view of life's history on earth and development naturally which came out of revolutionary France and from Lamarck. This was considered to be bad science, bad politics and abominable religion.

MELVYN BRAGG: Can we just describe in rather more detail why we are in this particular museum, Steve, and as your office is just above it, perhaps you can describe it?

STEVE JONES: This is the Grant Museum and it's a beautiful Victorian museum which, to use Dylan Thomas's famous phrase, 'is a museum that should have been in a museum'. Thousands and thousands of waves and waves of bones jammed into Victorian cases, a lot of it not on show because it's so big. We have basically the whole of life, now somewhat jumbled together, but in Darwin's day far from that. And these are some of his actual specimens. There's an eye, the tusk of a mammoth, some dolphins looking rather sad, we have sea urchins, sea stars, we have starfish, a specimen here which would have been familiar to Darwin and this is a marine iguana, now permanently in liquid. I often think it is impossible to have too many moles and what we've got down there is maybe thirty or forty moles all pickled together in some great moleish holocaust. Here we have a very eclectic collection of rather disgusting things in glass jars filled with liquid – the foetus of a fin whale – Darwin would have liked that because of course the fact that a foetus of a fin whale looks quite like a human foetus was really an important path in his argument for common descent. A jar of assorted reptiles, the brains of various apes and monkeys and that of course was of great interest to comparative anatomy because it might tell us something about the human brain. If you'd seen this in its original form there would have been a great chain of being, you'd have started with the lowest form of life, which would seamlessly have gone through until you got to Robert Grant himself. And that's really his mistake – the idea that it was progress. So here we've got a microcosm of biology just before it made sense.

MELVYN BRAGG: As Queen Victoria settled on the British throne, Charles Darwin sat down in July 1837, four months after coming to London, and made a small sketch of an idea that would come to dominate the scientific, intellectual and religious agenda of Queen Victoria's age. It was a single line dividing and dividing again into many lines. It looked like a tree and it was of sorts – an evolutionary tree that represented the idea that all the various creatures Darwin had studied, all the myriad of life itself, came from a single origin, a single line that had diverged and diverged again into all the creatures on God's earth. Can you characterise the sketch, Steve Jones?

STEVE JONES: Well, the sketch is indeed a family tree. It's very preliminary. It's got one long branch and then a series of sub-branches which split into twigs and next to it there's a sentence which begins with two pregnant words: 'I think'. And clearly they're important words. He's begun to think about the meaning of what he'd found. And what he discovered was really what I think of as the grammar of biology – you can't speak a language without understanding the grammar. Darwin realised that biology is a language, it has a structure, it all hangs together, it makes sense. And that sketch has really haunted biology ever since. I'm at the moment trying to get it appliquéd on to the front of this building as an enormous gold object. It probably won't happen but it is the most important diagram in biology, without question. And from that everything else follows.

JIM MOORE: To understand Darwin in his day we have to see that that tree was heretical because it grew by itself, God didn't create the species out on the twigs separately and miraculously. That whole tree of life grew up through time. It's worth a thousand words, that picture, two thousand, ten thousand. He shows the branches that have failed, he draws a line through them, he says – that's a line that went extinct, these are the ones that are left – and he labels the twigs A, B, C, D – he's got the whole apparatus up and running.

STEVE JONES: He was really almost the first biologist to think deeply about the whole of biology, and that's the beginning of the theory, the theory that everything is interconnected. He was a polymath of biology. Most people are specialists on one group or another and it was almost a matter of egotism to assume that your own group was unique and separate from all the others. He knew so much that he saw the big picture.

JIM MOORE: Darwin believed that life fitted on one tree, why did he choose a family tree as his image for life's history on earth? The answer is that he believed all human varieties belonged to one family, all the races were one in their source of life. There was a human background to this.

STEVE JONES: Yes, that's true. I think this is one of the cases – rare cases – where Darwin's intellectual and scientific life was clearly influenced by his political background because it was the general belief then and the belief came back and is still around to some degree, that races of humankind were very, very different from each other and indeed sprang from different stocks. And if you believe that, it's an extremely convenient alibi for all kinds of nasty politics. Slave owners certainly believed that. And I think that this unity of life, which is summarised in this tree, clearly had implicit in it the unity of human life too. But I always feel – I think most scientists feel – that one has to separate the science from the scientist. In the end what's wonderful about that diagram is that it's right about biology.

MELVYN BRAGG: Darwin seemed to be poised over a profound new idea but success was no guarantee of health and in September 1837 Darwin suffered palpitations of the heart, which would plague him throughout his life. Recuperating in his home town of Shrewsbury he was introduced to his cousin – Emma Wedgwood – who mended his heart and then won it. Charles Darwin and Emma Wedgwood fell in love but, ever a man of method, he drew up two lists, one called 'marry', one called 'not marry', and he worked through the pros and cons. He concluded that 'a constant companion and a friend in old age' outweighed 'less money for books and the terrible loss of time'.

Steve Jones, we're in the Darwin Lecture Theatre. One lecture is just breaking up and some of them are staying for the next lecture and some are not, so that's the background noise. Why are we in this particular room?

STEVE JONES: When I teach in here, as I often do, I say I'm speaking to you from Charles Darwin's bunker and that's literally true, because this is the site of Charles Darwin's house in Gower Street, which he moved to just as he was married. They called it McCaw Cottage because of the garish decorations, so not much has changed as you can see. There was a dead dog in the back garden they had to get rid of before his wife would agree to move in.

MELVYN BRAGG: They came here from Wales, Charles and Emma, a married couple. Jim Moore, have you any idea what it was like for them to settle in here?

JIM MOORE: It was a great relief. Darwin was dying to get married, he'd been biting the bullet for years. Emma wanted to take her time. They rushed into the wedding, it was the end of January 1839. He'd sorted out the house, he'd furnished it and he'd organised a cook and housekeeper and installed Emma with the fires glowing bright. And then the walls began to move in and the shutters close and Darwin found a protective cocoon, he had a guardian angel in his house who knew him intimately. They began having children almost immediately and Darwin's withdrawal from the world continued.

MELVYN BRAGG: When he made those lists about whether to have a wife or not to have a wife he was convincing himself in his lists but his choice worked out very well for him as a professional working man.

STEVE JONES: I think his marriage in the end was extraordinarily happy. He had many children, he notes at some moment that his wife had been very lazy recently because they hadn't had a baby for more than a year. So it was obviously a sexually quite contented marriage too.

MELVYN BRAGG: Finally in this place, as the lecture room fills up for the next lecture, Jim Moore, what about Darwin's own thoughts at this time, around these two or three years? He's still reading massively, can you give us some idea of that reading?

JIM MOORE: Darwin's reading everything for his notebooks. By now he has a series of five or six transmutation notebooks. These are kept entirely private. He's filling them with information from books on theology, on economics, on what we would call sociology, as well as every branch of natural history. He was reaching out in all directions in a most scientifically disreputable manner. 1839 was his year. In that year he published his *Beagle* journal, that year he became a Fellow of the Royal Society, that year he got married, that year he finished his last transmutation notebook.

MELVYN BRAGG: We'd better leave now. The next lecture is about to start.

We've gone up in the lift from the basement of the Darwin Building, from the lecture theatre, into Steve Jones' office – Steve, Jim Moore and myself. We are at the beginning of the time of the long wait in which he did not publish ideas that he seemed to be poised to publish. Why, in your view did he not publish around 1842?

STEVE JONES: I think he felt he wasn't ready. He was a good scientist, he wanted evidence. Ideas were not enough, he wanted facts.

And he set out to find those facts from a rather unlikely field, which is working on barnacles. And for eight years he studied barnacles and became a great expert. He would happily have spent the rest of his life accumulating facts, probably, and not publishing his theory perhaps until after he died.

JIM MOORE: Darwin's scientific reasons for not publishing were also political and religious. The scientists, so called, the naturalists that he looked up to and who'd sponsored his career, believed in their hearts that his programme of evolution was wrong and immoral if published. He had his respectability to defend, he had his family to defend, he could not go public with something that wasn't well thought through. It was huge, he understood its ramifications, he also understood the problems he would get into if he did publish. Those would first of all be because of its religious and political implications. The naturalists he looked up to most of all were clergymen and devout men of science. He could not publish something that would be seen to subvert the foundations of religion and social order.

MELVYN BRAGG: Had he talked to anyone about the true nature or what we might call the ultimate nature of his thinking?

JIM MOORE: No one. He had talked to no one except possibly members of his family. His father knew, we can be sure his father knew. His father's advice about this was kept in two notebooks with 'private' written on the front. He kept all his notebooks private, all of his speculations private. He probably told his brother, his brother was a freethinker, nothing shocked him. He told his wife and this became a sore point in their relationship.

MELVYN BRAGG: Can I just develop this business of his wife's upset. What do we know about that and how germane was it to this particular period in his life, Steve Jones?

STEVE JONES: Certainly as the model became more overt and as his wife was drawn into his private world she was deeply shocked. It was a deeply shocking idea. And I think it did cause quite a family problem, which was a microcosm of the much larger problem which it caused to society.

MELVYN BRAGG: Darwin didn't publish his ideas for another seventeen years and only then because his hand was forced by Alfred Russel Wallace who had hit upon a similar idea. Darwin rushed to print and in 1859 one of the most important scientific books ever written rolled off the presses of John Murray – *On The Origin of Species* by Charles Darwin. In the next programme we will learn about that book, the ideas within it and the storm they created, one that would roll out from Darwin's mind through the societies, the Linnaean Society, the Geological Society, into a voracious Victorian public and then controversially into the world. One that's still rolling today.

TRANSMITTED: 6.1.2009

j

Darwin: Programme 3

We ended the previous programme with a question – in May 1842 Darwin wrote an outline of what would later become his theory of evolution by natural selection, but he waited another seventeen years, until November 1859, before publishing his theory in book form. Why did he wait so long? Part of the answer to that question is here, at Burlington House on London's Piccadilly. By the mid-nineteenth century, Burlington House had become the hub of British science. The Royal Society had offices here, where we are now, so did the Linnaean Society, the Chemical Society, the Geological Society and the Royal Astronomical Society. This was a world that Darwin wanted to be part of.

Darwin had moved from Bloomsbury as insanitary and not fit for purpose. He wanted air, space, a large house to hold a study and the domestic appurtenances of a gentleman's home and – above all – a large garden and land which could serve as his laboratory. He found Down House near Bromley in Kent, isolated but within easy distance of London.

I have with me Jim Moore, Darwin biographer; Jim Secord, Director of the Darwin Correspondence Project; and Sandy Knapp, a botanist at the Natural History Museum and Botanical Secretary of the Linnaean Society.

Jim Secord, I mentioned some of the societies that had premises here, can you tell us a little more about them and which of them Darwin belonged to?

JIM SECORD: When Darwin went on his great voyage around the world in the *Beagle* he came back to London and in London he really wanted to be associated with the best men of science of the time. Science in this period was a gentlemanly activity, so effectively the societies that we see around us were extensions of that gentlemanly world. They were gentlemen's clubs for science. And so almost immediately he joined the various societies that were relevant to his interest, particularly the Geological Society in 1836. He became a Fellow of the Zoological Society in 1837 and then he was elected a Fellow of the Royal Society a couple of years after that.

MELVYN BRAGG: Jim Moore, in this part of London it wasn't just the learned societies that had offices here. Jim Secord mentioned the word 'gentleman' – this was a gentleman's part of London. Could you develop that?

JIM MOORE: Well, today's West End was a bit like a large fashionable village in relationship to the City of London back in Darwin's day. And here in this upper-class village were the gentlemen's clubs, and Darwin was elected to a proper gentlemen's club – the Athenaeum. He could stay there overnight, he could eat there, he could meet his friends there, this gave him a connection with what was later called the intellectual aristocracy. Another thing, just around the corner here in Albemarle Street, was a major science publisher, John Murray's, and it was there that Darwin would eventually publish *The Origin of Species* and most of his other later books.

MELVYN BRAGG: I think it's worth emphasising to those who don't know this part of London that when Jim Moore says around the corner he means around the corner, round the corner is Albemarle Street, and Darwin joined the Athenaeum Club which is across the road and down a street and there's the Athenaeum Club, in which were not just scientists but there were bishops, there were scholars from Oxford and Cambridge. This part of London at that time was an intellectual hub, a centre, it was the sort of Silicon Valley of science of its time. Can I ask you, Sandy Knapp, you're Botanical Secretary of the Linnaean Society which has offices here, why was it so important for him to be part of this scientific community?

SANDY KNAPP: I think being part of a community, as a scientist, is actually as important now as it was then. Being part of a community meant you met people who had ideas and I think being a member of the Linnaean Society was particularly important because it was the one society that combined all of natural history – it combines zoology, botany, geology – it was a little bit of everything, the whole natural philosophy which was lacking in the other more specialist societies.

MELVYN BRAGG: He would come up to London to attend these learned societies after he moved to Down House, Jim Moore, and we've got to realise that there was this double life. There was Down House, working away on his classification, and coming up here to meet like-minded men.

JIM MOORE: Absolutely, he didn't have to be here all the time, he could go away from it all and control access to himself in that way. He could borrow books here and take them away with him, he could borrow specimens in London and take them away with him and return them. He had a trusted relationship with these people because the most important thing about a gentleman of science is that you were trustworthy, that you were a moral and upright person, that was the defining *sine qua non*.

MELVYN BRAGG: Then Darwin got a shock. In November 1844, eight years after he'd come back from the voyage of the *Beagle*, an anonymous book called *Vestiges of the Natural History of Creation* was published, and we'll go into the Linnaean Society to talk about it.

SANDY KNAPP: So here we go – come in – come into my lair.

MELVYN BRAGG: We're in this very small room, about twelve by twelve, panelled by rows of leather-bound books and wonderfully carpentered sliding drawers holding all the specimens. Is this the heart of the Linnaean Society?

SANDY KNAPP: It is, it's the heart of the Linnaean Society, it's the strong room that's built to house Linnaeus' own library and collections when Linnaeus died. And this is where we keep very important things.

MELVYN BRAGG: When you say 'strong room' you mean it! We came through a door that would do credit to Fort Knox.

SANDY KNAPP: It is a strong room and I can never quite remember how to use the key.

MELVYN BRAGG: Jim Secord, why did this book, *Vestiges of the Natural History of Creation*, published anonymously, come as such a shock to Darwin?

JIM SECORD: Darwin had been working on an evolutionary theory, really from the time he got back from the *Beagle* voyage, and he'd actually written up a draft of it in the spring of 1844. In other words, his ideas were pretty well formed. And so when *Vestiges* was published towards the end of the year suddenly you had a book which was arguing for, effectively, a broad-scale evolutionary cosmology and it was doing it in a very accessible kind of way.

MELVYN BRAGG: And what impact did it have at the time on the reading public?

JIM SECORD: The impact was really pretty gigantic because evolutionary theories and theories of the natural creation of species had been quite common currency during the Enlightenment. But with the French Revolution these had tended to go underground. *Vestiges* really brought this kind of question back on to the intellectual map of Victorian Britain. It meant that people were talking about it everywhere from pubs to places like the Linnaean Society. It was a huge sensation, something like 20,000 copies sold during its first two decades of publication.

MELVYN BRAGG: I used the word 'shock'. It gave Darwin a shock. Can you describe the extent and the effect of this shock?

JIM SECORD: Well, in some sense it was muddying the waters for him. He was worried that people were actually going to see his theories in something like *Vestiges*, that he was going to be identified as one of the anonymous authors, that he was Mr Vestiges. In another way, though, the book was actually quite useful for him. On one level it was like a lightning rod, it drew controversy, it made a place where people could debate these questions in really quite a vehement sort of way. I think that also for Darwin it was an object lesson in things to avoid when he was working on his own theory. He was much more reticent about stressing the relationship between his theory and a general theory of progress, for example. His book was much more toned down when he started to think about how to deal with this. So it was an object lesson for him.

MELVYN BRAGG: Jim Moore, can you take that argument forward?

JIM MOORE: *Vestiges* was a perfect example to Darwin of what not to do when he got around to publishing his theory. He avoided its grandiose claims. Darwin avoided the origin of the universe, he avoided the origin of life, he avoided the origin of man, he made his theory ideologically more acceptable by not committing the anonymous *Vestiges'* errors. In 1844, the same year *Vestiges* came out, but earlier, he had completed a publishable draft of his theory. That draft now got set aside and he got to work on barnacles, comprehensively revising the classification of all the barnacles, living and extinct, in the entire world at that time.

Why barnacles, somebody challenged him. You can't talk about the origin of species unless you can describe many species and show how they differ ever so slightly from one another. Now barnacles are very important to study in a seafaring nation, any expert on barnacles is obviously promoting British trade, ships can go faster if you understand how these things behave and how to get them off your hulls. So it's not surprising that in 1853 Darwin was awarded the Royal Medal of the Royal Society of London, a great gold medal.

MELVYN BRAGG: Before we go on with that, Jim, an event in his own life affected him considerably. In April 1851, Darwin's favourite daughter Annie died. It was a terrible blow to him and to the whole family, but what impact do you think it had on his studies, on the way he was thinking about what he was doing?

JIM MOORE: While he was working on barnacles Darwin, without realising it, reached a watershed in his personal life. In 1848 his father died, not unexpectedly, but Darwin was deeply moved and plunged into a state of depression. A couple of years after that, just when he was starting to recover, his eldest daughter, his favourite daughter, Anne Elizabeth, became ill with what Darwin believed was a hereditary ailment, and he of course put her under his own doctor who had helped get him back on his feet. But she deteriorated, his wife was pregnant with her eighth child, and over Easter weekend 1851 this little girl died in Darwin's presence. And you would think maybe he would get over this.

He wrote a beautiful threnody about her a week after the death. You might think that would put an end to it. But if you read *The Origin of Species* carefully, in the third chapter, in the struggle for existence, we see an evocation of this child in the face of 'nature bright with gladness', into which Darwin says selection like the force of a hundred thousand wedges is being driven, adapting species to their environment. And at the end of the chapter Darwin talks about consoling ourselves. And the question is in a scientific book, like *The Origin of Species* – why should someone console themselves at the struggle for existence? In this period, when he's working on barnacles, leading up to the great work he would embark upon in 1856, Darwin was struck by the tragedy of life and how all life must die that other life might succeed it. And that became part of his emotional reaction to nature and all of his subsequent work.

MELVYN BRAGG: Jim Secord, throughout this period we have a sense of the pace of scientific enquiry into evolution hotting up. First there was *Vestiges*, and then in 1855 Alfred Russell Wallace published *On The Law on Which is Regulated the Introduction of New Species*. I think, Jim Secord, that Darwin had to take this publication much more seriously than the previous one?

JIM SECORD: During the late 1840s and particularly in the 1850s it was clear that the species problem was really coming on to the scientific agenda. Wallace was working half a world away, and writing these very fascinating papers about geographical distribution. I think above all it showed that potentially a climate for Darwin's work was starting to appear. So that, combined with the completion of his barnacle monographs, really meant that he could start to be more open about this question. One of the most interesting things, I think, is that this is the first time that Darwin starts to tell some of his real scientific colleagues and friends about the specifics of his views – and it is in relationship to this paper from Wallace.

MELVYN BRAGG: Hadn't Darwin received information on specimens from Wallace, who was in Borneo? Hadn't they corresponded as well?

JIM MOORE: It's important to understand Darwin and Wallace's relationship. Wallace was not, strictly speaking, a gentleman. He was a self-employed specimen collector working in the Far East, supporting himself by sending back collections. Darwin was one of his clients, or you could say that Wallace was employed by Darwin to send certain bird specimens back. Darwin complained about how much it cost. But he used these specimens as some of his evidence for the varieties of domestic races that were so important for his theory of natural selection.

MELVYN BRAGG: As I understand it, Jim Moore, three years later Wallace finally forced Darwin's hand, in February 1858, when he sent Darwin another paper called *On The Tendencies of Varieties to Depart Indefinitely From the Original Type*. The argument Wallace put forward was very close to Darwin's own thinking about evolution at this time and Darwin perhaps saw that as a threat.

JIM MOORE: Wallace's paper arrived at Down – Darwin's house – in June 1858. Darwin was in a state of crisis, the children were ill, disease was rampant in the village, and on 1 July 1858 he was standing in the graveyard burying his infant son Charles. This paper he read as an anticipation of his own theory. He read it quickly and he decided that this man had scooped him. He couldn't deal with it himself, he was in an emotional mess, and he turned the entire matter over to his friends – Charles Lyell and Joseph Hooker. He had to claim somehow his own priority.

MELVYN BRAGG: And then we had a famous meeting, Sandy Knapp, here where we are, in this building, in the Linnaean Society. Can you tell us what happened? Joint papers were presented but neither Darwin nor Wallace was present?

SANDY KNAPP: Darwin received the manuscript version – the paper arrived with him from Wallace. It wasn't published. Wallace sent him the draft paper to have his comments on it. And when this was all resolved, his friends Lyell and Hooker basically said, 'well, we think the best thing to do here is to have your paper and Wallace's paper both read at the Linnaean Society.' This was common practice at the time, scientists were often not present when their papers we read.

And so a meeting was arranged for 1 July 1858, at which Darwin's and Wallace's papers were specially put on the agenda and read – first Darwin's and then Wallace's.

MELVYN BRAGG: And the President of the Linnaean Society in May 1859 said of that year that the year hadn't been marked by any revolutionary discoveries, so the presentations hadn't stirred up much controversy.

SANDY KNAPP: I think it stirred up things in conversation. His actual words are here, I'll read them: 'The year which has passed since I last had the pleasure of meeting you on our anniversary has not been unproductive in contributions of interest and value ... it has not indeed been marked by any of those striking discoveries which at once revolutionise.' So he acknowledged that there were things of interest and value but what he didn't see is the fact that these two papers, this idea, would actually revolutionise science. And I think no one really saw how it would revolutionise science so completely, except perhaps Darwin himself.

MELVYN BRAGG: We've moved from the small, studious, intimate rooms of the Linnaean Society to the booming large open spaces of the Natural History Museum in Kensington, early in the morning to have some peace before it opens. In the first programme we began Darwin's story in the church of Great St Mary's in Cambridge, and this building where I am now has the same reverberating acoustic. In a sense that shouldn't be surprising. Strongly influenced by religious architecture, this museum was conceived as a place where God could be worshipped through nature.

It has all the architectural trappings of a Romanesque cathedral – rounded arches, carved capitals, stained glass and side chapels. But unlike Great St Mary's in Cambridge there's no pulpit or altar or backless hard benches. Instead this central nave where I'm standing is filled with a vast skeleton of a diplodocus, twenty-six metres from head to tail. And sitting at the top of a flight of stairs, looking down on it, relaxed with legs crossed, is Charles Darwin.

Sixteen months after that meeting at the Linnaean Society, Darwin had completed a substantial book that would guarantee his own immortality. On 22 November 1859, John Murray published *On The Origin of Species by Means of Natural Selection, or the Preservation of Favoured Races in the Struggle for Life.*

We're now in the Darwin exhibition in the museum. *The Origin of Species* is one of the few books that have revolutionised the way we understand the world. Despite Darwin's publisher, John Murray, having reservations about the book's appeal, the entire stock of 1,250 copies was sold on the first day. A second edition was quickly prepared and the book was back in the bookshops by January 1860. So why was it so popular? What impact did its ideas have? I'm joined by Johannes Vogel and Sandy Knapp again, both from the Natural History Museum. Also by the biologist Steve Jones. Steve Jones, how important is *The Origin of Species* as a piece of sustained argument in support of evolution by natural selection, and what did Darwin understand by that phrase?

STEVE JONES: He invented the term and I think he understood it pretty clearly. Natural selection is simply inherited differences in the chances of reproduction. So that if a certain individual bears a variant, which makes it more likely that he or she will survive, find a mate and reproduce, whereas others have different versions of the same thing which make it less likely, one will prevail and the others will disappear. And as this goes on there will be more and more change until at last new forms of life appear, and that's what evolution under natural selection is. But you're persuaded in chapter one that life is flexible, it can change, look at all the different pigeons we've got around us here, how did that happen? And then we go step by step, very logically, inexorably, from the familiar to the less familiar to the unknown – to embryology and instinct – and then a sort of killer summary at the end. The word 'evolution' never appears in the whole book, the only time the word 'evolved' appears is in the very last word of the book. And the whole book almost leads up to that last word. And you put it down with a sense of relief but you can't fail to have a sense of conviction that this argument is logical, it's straightforward, it's supported, it's right.

SANDY KNAPP: I think *The Origin of Species* is a beautifully constructed book. I hadn't read *The Origin of Species* for twenty years

and in preparation for 2009 I thought I ought to read this great
book again. And I was completely struck by how beautifully it was
put together and how each chapter develops the argument, summa-
rises the argument, sets you up for the next chapter. You start with
pigeons and that's all quite familiar because you see them all around
you and by the time you get to embryology you feel as though you
understand where this is going and how it's working and you feel
surrounded by a set of things that you – any reader – can understand.
And I think it's that construction of the book, it's very plain, simple
and in straightforward language. It has its Victorian idiosyncrasies
of course, but it's really the construction of the book and the way it
leads you from one step into another that's so wonderful.

JOHANNES VOGEL: What is so powerful about Charles Darwin in
this book is that he starts this way of developing things and he takes
the reader with him and the type of observations and experiments is
something that can actually be not just understood but potentially
also repeated by ordinary members of science. Any pigeon breeder
has the power to inflict artificial selection under domestication on his
animals and so on and so forth. So it's really something that relates
very well to the ordinary person and in a way also a bit demystifies
science as something that has only to be done by anointed men in
white coats.

MELVYN BRAGG: This is an aspect, isn't it, Steve Jones? Darwin
loved being with pigeon men, he became the pigeon fanciers' pigeon
fancier, and the idea of saying to people 'what you're doing is part of
the essential scheme of things' was very important to him.

STEVE JONES: Yes, he has a phrase somewhere: '*de minimus curat
lex*' – the law does not concern itself with trifles – does not apply to
science. And that's a brilliant, brilliant statement, because what it
means is however trivial your interest might be – breeding a pigeon
with a bigger tail – actually it makes a noticeable addition to science.
Many people then and now open *The Origin of Species*, chapter one,
and say this is going to be like reading Nietzsche or Kant, it's going
to change my philosophy of life. It's not, it's going to tell you about
the banal birds that poo all over the pavement. But it's that ability to

take the simple, to take the apparently trivial, and join these trifles into a magnificent whole which makes the book.

JOHANNES VOGEL: In a way I feel that is also one of the arguments that still rage today. We have a lot of arguments that concern citizens and science today, technology is advancing but this book, gives people the choice to say you actually have the power with your observations, with your interests, to be scientific in your everyday life, and so you have a stake in the development of the world. And that is, for me, also one of the lasting legacies of this book and Charles Darwin's work.

SANDY KNAPP: Another thing that Darwin does very well in *The Origin of Species* is he opens a wide door for people to participate in but he also opens a door by saying there are many things that we do not know. And I think that's an important thing that science says this. That means there's plenty of scope for people to contribute to science. You know, in his obsession with the marshalling of facts, I always think of him as a sort of pack rat who marshalled facts in a kind of corner somewhere and he must have a huge pile of them which he selectively used. Imagine if he actually put all the facts in *The Origin of Species* – it would be so big we couldn't carry it around. But the realisation that every fact or every piece of evidence can be brought to bear to support an idea is actually the central tenet of science.

STEVE JONES: Darwin in his autobiography, which he wrote when he was an old man, said: 'my mind is like a machine, grinding general laws out of collections of facts.' That would make a wonderful obituary for any scientist.

MELVYN BRAGG: Do you think the central idea is sufficiently supported by facts in the book? Johannes Vogel.

JOHANNES VOGEL: Probably not. A lot of developments have come along since – the incorporation of the Mendelian laws, the discovery of chromosomes, the discovery of DNA as a mechanism, the sequencing of DNA – there's lots and lots of evidence that has come since that has allowed us to examine these ideas in more detail, but fortunately they all support this original idea, so that's the enduring power.

STEVE JONES: Yes, I think that's right. The great strength of the book is its framework. The strength of this museum is its framework, its contents have changed enormously over the years and what goes on behind the doors of the museum would not be recognised in many ways by nineteenth-century biology. But what the book in some ways did was to invent the science of biology. There was no single science of biology before that. There were people who studied islands or fossils or domestic animals, but nobody realised they were doing the same thing. And suddenly you have this crystalline argument that points out to these unlikely individuals, many of whom hated each other's guts, that actually this was the unifying theory and what you're doing is what your worst enemy is also doing, and that must have been a very refreshing experience.

MELVYN BRAGG: What sort of criticisms did the book face at the time?

SANDY KNAPP: Darwin is of course very nervous about publishing his book, partly because he was pushed into it by circumstances beyond his control but also because I think he was concerned about what his ideas would engender. And one of the things – he says in the book – is that many naturalists may believe that all life is interconnected by descent with modification but that actually what he's doing in the book is providing the mechanism by which that happens. And I think it was the joining of those two ideas which probably frightened him a bit. There was a certain amount of furore and there were reviews that were written that were very negative, a lot of that negative reaction at the very publication of the book was the knee-jerk reaction of some people.

MELVYN BRAGG: Were there people at the time criticising the evidence, were they saying there isn't enough of this, he has not convinced us about that? I'm talking about 1859, 1860.

STEVE JONES: There were many people who bitterly disputed the book. First of all they disputed the evidence. One of them went so far as to say, 'when I read this book I laughed out loud.' That must have been difficult, I've never laughed out loud and I've read it several times. Yes, they disputed the evidence. They disputed the age of the earth, the nature of the fossils, the fact that there were intermediate forms. All this people fought against. But of course that's a natural method of scientists. I mean scientists are professional pessimists, their job is to dispute the evidence. And there are certainly holes in Darwin's argument, there's no question, but most of those holes have been filled.

It's ironic that in this museum here, Richard Owen, who founded it, loathed Darwin. Darwin wrote about Owen in respect of his review of *The Origin* that it was 'spiteful, extremely malignant and clever'. And then he wrote: 'it is painful to be hated in the intense degree with which Owen hates me.' That gives you a flavour of the times. This museum here, this was the temple of anti-evolutionism when it was built and now ironically we've torn down the temple and we've rebuilt it in the form of Darwinism.

MELVYN BRAGG: There's almost no mention of man in *The Origin of Species*. This seems rather a strange omission, can you explain it?

STEVE JONES: People have speculated about it. 'Light may be cast upon man and his origins' is all it really says. I think the reason was twofold. First of all, almost nothing was known about the origin of man, the first human fossil had not really been recognised as such. There was perhaps one that was clearly humanlike. And secondly he was concerned – he was already turning over the apple cart and overturning the idols by talking about evolution itself. To suggest that it would apply to humans might have been a step too far. It took him another twelve years before he wrote a book on that. And thirdly, and probably the simplest explanation, is he wrote it in such a rush that he felt do I need to open this can of worms, so to speak, by talking about man? And I think he just nodded: 'I'm going to come back to this.'

JOHANNES VOGEL: But doesn't he also in a way do the clever thing by saying, 'I will present you with a very powerful argument and then you, the intelligent reader, if you extrapolate from that, if you think the argument through to the end, you can come to your own conclusions.' Again sort of deflecting any controversy but he leaves it to the reader and the audience to actually come up with the answer themselves.

SANDY KNAPP: I think that's right and I think one of the things that's clever about *The Origin of Species* is it develops the argument without the specifics. I mean it is full of facts and it could have been full of lots more facts, but in a way it develops an overarching framework argument into which any specific piece of evidence can be put. And in a way by introducing man into *The Origin of Species* what would have happened, I think, is that we would have had an argument about man's origins instead of about what is really important about the book.

MELVYN BRAGG: I'm now in the Library of the Natural History Museum with Judith Magee, Librarian. We've a number of editions of *On The Origin of Species* helpfully displayed on the table here. Judith, could you tell us something about them?

JUDITH MAGEE: The Darwin collection in the Library of the Natural History Museum is the foremost library internationally. We have a splendid collection of just under 2,000 items of Darwin published material in many languages, and here we have a wonderful example of a first edition of *On The Origin of Species*. This volume is particularly interesting because it was sent to a gentleman called William Tegetmeier, who was a pigeon fancier amongst other things, and Darwin corresponded with him on selection of features and characteristics of pigeons because he was interested in selection. Darwin wrote to Tegetmeier, and here is the letter, just before *On The Origin of Species* was published, telling Tegetmeier that he was going to send him a first edition copy. Tegetmeier had the good sense to tape it into his book so that this book is of great value – not only is it a first edition but there's a letter as well.

MELVYN BRAGG: Can you tell us about some of the other editions you've laid out?

JUDITH MAGEE: Yes. These are different language editions of *The Origin of Species*. We have twenty-nine different languages in total, the most recent is an Icelandic translation. But here in front of us we have an Arabic edition, which is quite unusual I think, Armenian, Turkish as you see, Chinese, we also have Japanese, and here is a Catalan edition.

MELVYN BRAGG: Do you have any idea how many editions there are?

JUDITH MAGEE: We hold just under 500 editions but there are many more.

MELVYN BRAGG: From the range of stuff here, you're talking about Hebrew, Arabic, Japanese, Chinese, all the European languages and so on, it doesn't seem that religious and cultural differences around the world have stopped people reading Darwin?

JUDITH MAGEE: No, that's what's so wonderful about the collection, that no matter where you go you'll find it being translated, because the theory of natural selection is so important and science isn't alien to any culture or nation, I think.

MELVYN BRAGG: Back in the main museum in the Darwin exhibition. In a few moments the museum door will open, the public will come streaming in and many of them will make their way to this special exhibition about Charles Darwin called 'Darwin's Big Idea'. One of the most eye-catching parts of the exhibition is the animals – some stuffed, some living. They're all specimens that Darwin would have seen and in many cases eaten on the *Beagle* voyage we talked about. It's a richly exotic world of iguanas, armadillos, giant tortoises and horned frogs. Jim Secord, there's clearly a public appetite for these sort of displays today. In Darwin's day, were people just as excited by them?

JIM SECORD: People in the nineteenth century were absolutely fascinated by the kinds of objects we see around us – in fact, many of them date from the nineteenth century and many of them came from Darwin's own collections. The British Museum, Natural History, as it was called then, was a place where the Victorians flocked to see all sorts of animals from around the world, from the growing British Empire.

MELVYN BRAGG: Would you say that there was already a natural audience, if I can use the word 'natural' in this place, waiting for Darwin, that people were already greatly interested in stuff we see around us now?

JIM SECORD: Absolutely. In fact, Darwin had helped to create this audience through the *Journal of the Beagle* that he had written. This became a bestseller, especially during the 1840s when it was published in the Colonial and Home Library by John Murray. In that book he describes all sorts of creatures from around the world.

MELVYN BRAGG: We're now sitting in the middle of the Darwin exhibition, so can you give us some idea of what is surrounding us?

JIM SECORD: Well, there's a range of animals, and next to us there's an exhibition of birds which were one of the Victorians' favourite creatures, but I think the most interesting one that we can see behind us is the toxodon. This was one of the great mammals, ancient mammals, that Darwin found when he was on the *Beagle* voyage. For the Victorians the toxodon was just one of a number of creatures that allowed the imagination to extend into the deep past, not only just into these mammals but back into dinosaurs, to early reptiles, to amphibians and ultimately to the very origins of life itself. This was an incredibly new vision for the Victorians from the 1820s and '30s onwards, and it's one that Darwin was able to appeal to very directly in *The Origin*.

MELVYN BRAGG: What impact did the book's success have on Darwin himself?

JIM MOORE: The obvious impact on Darwin is he was extremely busy preparing new editions. He spent a very large percentage of time for the next twelve or thirteen years answering his critics by changing sentence after sentence after sentence. The book became about 25 per cent larger as a result. That's one effect. The other effect is that he got quite a lot of income. This was a real bread and butter book for John Murray, the publisher. The book sold for fifteen shillings, which was about a week's wages for an average paid labourer. And if you just take fifteen shillings, Darwin got about 10 per cent of that and multiply it by thousands upon thousands upon thousands of copies and you can see why Darwin died a multimillionaire in our money. The other effect that this book had on Darwin was to make him famous across Europe and across the world.

MELVYN BRAGG: Can you tell us how the book was received at the time, let's say a few months afterwards, we'll stay in that period at the moment, Jim Moore, by Darwin's academic peers?

JIM MOORE: *The Origin of Species* was received with a great deal of serious consideration. The fears that the book would be burnt in public and a great battle royal breaking out are simply not true. Darwin was pleased to discover that most of the academics that he respected were polite, even when they disagreed with him. So the book was taken seriously, Darwin became famous and he made a lot of money.

MELVYN BRAGG: Nevertheless a great debate broke out. A debate between the different factions which came to a head in June 1860 with what's become known as the Oxford Evolutionary Debate. Perhaps you could give us some idea of who is involved and what the main lines of the debate were.

JIM MOORE: An extraordinary thing, we talk about the Oxford Debate, 30 June 1860, as if it's an event like Waterloo. Well, it really wasn't. This is the story of a fifty-five-year-old bishop getting mugged in his own diocese by a thirty-five-year-old zoologist. Bishop Wilberforce had just published a review of *The Origin of Species* which was fairly negative, condescending, old plum-in-the-mouth Wilberforce in his own diocese and young Huxley is lying in wait for him. Wilberforce gives him an opportunity to attack and Huxley goes for the jugular.

It was not a premeditated set piece debate, it was an opportunistic attack. Huxley says to Wilberforce: 'you will respect us, we rising young men of science, you cannot use your authority to crush us.' Huxley was ineffective, he was too angry to project his voice, it was young Hooker – Darwin's closest friend in science – who got up and really put the bishop in his place. I think the bishop did deserve to be put in his place, it would be outrageous if something like that happened today, it was even more outrageous that it happened at that time. But it's come to symbolise a whole series of events because the victors – the Darwinians – have used this contretemps as paradigmatic for the whole discussion of evolution, and that's a mistake.

MELVYN BRAGG: Well, can I ask you then, is this just part of the Darwin legend or did it happen that Wilberforce, the Bishop of Oxford, when he enquired whether Huxley, who was known as 'Darwin's bulldog', whether he was descended from monkeys on his grandfather's side or his grandmother's side, Huxley replied that he would 'rather be descended from an ape than from a cultivated man who uses gifts of culture and eloquence in the service of prejudice and falsehood' – was that said?

JIM MOORE: Something like that was probably said. Notice that the issue is apes. *The Origin of Species* is not supposed to be about humans, but everyone knew, including Charles Darwin and Huxley and the bishop, that this was a book about people and our origins. So was it on your mum's side or your dad's side that you have your ape ancestors – there's a frisson there of 'could women be descended from apes, could your mother be?' It was a witty jibe, typical Wilberforce, ecclesiastical politician, and he got hammered by a young scientific puritan.

MELVYN BRAGG: So, Jim Secord, are we talking about battle lines being drawn up? Is this a split between younger scientists and cultured men, is there a religious divide breaking there already? By the sound of Bishop Wilberforce there is. Can you go into the deeper nature of the fissure, of the factionalism?

JIM SECORD: Well, in some ways I think the Oxford Debate just wasn't very typical of the disputes that were happening during this period. There weren't two camps forming in this early period. What we've got here is in some sense a bishop who was seen by many to be out of control and a young man who was actually going beyond his remit in terms of what the British Association was about. There certainly are groups which find what Darwin is doing abhorrent but they tend to be rather marginalised. There are other groups that find what Darwin is doing is fantastic and is going to lead ultimately to the victory of atheism over religion but those people are in the minority. If you're looking at the general Victorian debate, it's much more about people, in some sense, broadly coming to accept that Darwinism combines the best science with the idea of progress in a kind of way that shows, well, maybe we have come from the apes but it's a divinely inspired process. And that's what we can really see.

MELVYN BRAGG: Can I ask both of you – when people think of the publication of *On The Origin of Species* one of the things that a lot of people say is – it was an attack on religion. The religiously minded people, of whom there are a great number, rose up against it and it began an argument which fuses through to this day. How far is that true?

JIM MOORE: *The Origin of Species* was quite a conservative and temperate book. It referred to God or the Creator a fair number of times. This was a personal book, it was a vision of creation by law. It's been put this way: *The Origin of Species* addressed a debate that had been going on amongst theologians in an area called natural theology, about whether God works in the world by miracles or by laws of nature. Laws of nature had come out on top in field after field, astronomy, chemistry and so forth. Now Darwin was extending the rule of God's law to the origin of species. And Darwin helped resolve that debate within natural theology, which was all part of science at that time, in favour of law. It was a law book.

MELVYN BRAGG: On the other hand, I don't think that, accurate as I'm absolutely certain you are, I don't think it gets to the question that I'm asking. Did this, at the time, seem to spark off a debate with the religiously minded people who thought that they were now being attacked and they had to defend themselves against and continue to do so? Jim Secord.

JIM SECORD: I think that *The Origin of Species* created a focal point for debate about the relationship between God and science. That doesn't mean that it immediately was a weapon for one group or another group. One of Darwin's best friends at Harvard – Asa

Gray – wrote very movingly about the way in which you could understand both natural selection and also God and those two things could come together. And that's something I think that Darwin himself was perfectly willing to have read into the book. He didn't think that the natural meaning of the book was atheism, in fact he generally sent anybody who was a freethinker packing from Down House. But it certainly did provide a real kind of sparking point for a variety of debates.

JIM MOORE: Atheists love *The Origin of Species*. Freethinkers, secularists, Francophiles – this was a book that could be used as a weapon to liberate British society from the thraldom of religion, the state church, the monarchy – these were republicans as well as atheists. That's not Darwin's responsibility. The book was extremely useful to that irreligious sector. The book was not liked by Anglicans as a whole. Politely they disagreed, even Darwin's colleagues. Many thoughtful dissenters, we're talking about people outside of the Church of England, thought that the book was devout and useful because he had established God's law rather than his whim as the principle by which the universe is governed. So there was a mixed response.

MELVYN BRAGG: If we take a broad view, Jim Secord, in the balance between science and religion was this book, the publication of this book, a tipping point where the intellectual energies and the sense of intellectual rightness began to flow towards science?

JIM SECORD: I think that is probably the case. If you look at it in a very long timespan, certainly in the last 150 years, then I think that there's something to be said for that view. Of course that wasn't necessarily Darwin's own meaning and I think one of the fascinating things about *The Origin of Species* is what a generous text it is in the kind of ways in which it opens up so many possibilities for different forms of reading. And in many ways when we see that kind of division between science and religion what we're seeing is not so much something that Darwin necessarily even intended to start, but something that has much broader causes within our society, in terms of the way our institutions are organised. It has effectively to do with the way that we read *The Origin of Species* in a different way now than it was read in the 1860s and '70s.

MELVYN BRAGG: However popular and influential *On The Origin of Species* has become, Darwin himself was always critical of the book, especially the lack of a factual basis for many of its assertions. In his introduction he wrote: 'no one can feel more sensible than I do of the necessity of hereafter publishing in detail all the facts with references on which my conclusions have been grounded. And I hope in a future work to do this.'

Darwin fulfilled his pledge, which is why he sits here at the top of the steps in the museum's main hall, calmly surveying the throng of people who come each day to enjoy natural history and absorb the significance of evolution by natural selection.

In the next and final programme we'll discuss how Darwin spent the last twenty-two years of his life providing those facts and references in support of his theory with a series of books, including books about flowers, worms and humanity itself.

TRANSMITTED: 7.1.2009

k
———

Darwin: Programme 4

The publication of *On The Origin of Species* in November 1859, written here where I am in Darwin's study, caused quite a stir. The first print run of 1,250 copies was oversubscribed and the printers had to organise a second run, this time of 3,000 copies. As Darwin's arguments became more generally known, two factions began to form – those for and those against an evolutionary principle that was able to explain the development of living things without divine intervention.

While his friends and enemies battled it out, Darwin characteristically kept his distance. When Thomas Huxley and Bishop Wilberforce clashed at the Oxford Union in June 1860, Darwin was in Richmond in a hydrotherapy pool receiving treatment for his various ailments which included nausea, palpitation and fainting fits. But he was kept in the picture. Both Huxley and Darwin's friend Joseph Hooker sent him letters describing the debate in great detail. Darwin read and reread the accounts from his watery sickbed.

As soon as he returned to the family home here in Kent, Down House, Darwin went back to work. He was an early riser and would usually go for a walk before breakfast. But the centre of his world was this room – his study – where he would begin work at eight o'clock every morning, surrounded by letters, bottles of chemicals and family portraits on the wall over the fireplace. There's a keen sense of a personal space in this study. This was Darwin's room, his sanctuary. It is calm, shady, cluttered. His high-backed armchair and footrest are pulled up to the table. His privy is conveniently nearby behind the screen. It's the study of a learned collector and a scholar.

Jim Moore, you're the biographer of Darwin – why do you think he needed Down House?

JIM MOORE: Darwin came to live here at Down House in 1842 at a
time when London was racked with turmoil. Down House represented
the fulfilment of a vision that he had for years. All of his professors at
Cambridge enjoyed comfortable studies like this one. This is where he
could work out and finally publish a theory that he knew was something very, very big. It was a place of safety, it was, as you said, his
sanctuary. It was also a place to bring up a family with his first cousin
Emma Wedgwood. They had both grown up near the country or in the
country, in houses rather like Down House here and with studies rather
like this study. So this was home in a very deep sense for Darwin.

MELVYN BRAGG: How did he get hold of this house? Steve Jones,
you're a geneticist and biologist but you've also written extensively
about Darwin. How did he afford it, it's a very roomy house – dining
room, extensive gardens, surrounding land?

STEVE JONES: Yes. Only a banker could afford a house like this
today. And people often tend to think of Darwin as this indigent
daring young man who went on the *Beagle* and was paid a pitiful
salary to do so. But that wasn't true at all. In those days to be
a scientist – and the word scientist had just been invented – to be a
scientist one needed a decent private income and he certainly had
a decent private income. And as soon as he could he moved out
from that terrible dank dirty dangerous part of London known as
Bloomsbury, and began to look at houses around the countryside and
it didn't take him long to find this. He didn't like the house at first
sight, he called it dark and gloomy, but with the help of the healing
power of cash he turned it into a most delightful place to live and
this study, a most delightful place in which to work.

MELVYN BRAGG: The word 'sanctuary' has been mentioned. Jim
Moore, can you say a bit more to that point? In this wonderful room
we're in now, there are fossils on the round table behind you, of
course, there are books, there are photographs, as I mentioned, there's
an extremely attractively cluttered desk. Was there something more
than just a place to work that he needed?

JIM MOORE: You could almost say that Darwin came here incog-
nito. This house was a parsonage. The incumbent of the parish

lived in this house and Darwin purchased it from him. It helped seal his identity, at least for himself, with that of a country parson and after all he'd intended to become a country parson when he was at Cambridge. But he wasn't a country parson. In some ways he was quite the opposite, because he knew that this terrible burden he carried, of the belief in evolution, including humans in society in that evolutionary process, would open him to persecution if he let people know that he was working on that project.

So he looked like a parson, he wanted to be seen as a parson, he wasn't really a parson. But he could control access to himself here, that's the most important point. He is far enough away from railway stations and scientific societies. Actually, outside this window behind you he had a mirror installed so that he could see people coming up the drive. That's not paranoia, that's prudence in a man who was carrying the kind of burden that Darwin had – evolution.

MELVYN BRAGG: Although we talk about this as a sanctuary, he didn't exclude himself from local life, Steve Jones, he didn't live in total isolation, he was a magistrate, he acted as treasurer for Down Friendly Society and Down School. Was this tokenism or was this because he was properly interested in a country vicar way of getting involved in local society?

STEVE JONES: I think in some ways he was the ultimate Victorian. He knew that that was his duty as a gent, and as a gent he did his duty and he did it remarkably well. If you look, for example, at his role as a magistrate he was not a hanger and flogger, far from it, he was rather liberal. The Down Friendly Society, which was a sort of a local national health service, I suppose, and unemployment benefit service, he ran and ran very carefully and when it ran out of money he actually helped it along. So it's odd that a man of such gentleness and liberality, it's odd how quickly his theories were taken up as a sort of alibi by people with exactly the opposite view. Which really tells us, when you're talking about science, the person who does it is actually rather irrelevant to the discoveries that are made.

MELVYN BRAGG: We have various objects in this room, Steve, was this the centre of the laboratory – are these for ornament or was he using them?

STEVE JONES: Oh no, he was an experimental scientist, that's what people often forget. I mean *The Origin of Species*, which is a wonderful work, is really a work of reportage, it really brings together an awful lot of the information that he'd gathered using the Victorian internet known as the postal service, this huge number of letters he received. But at the same time, or a little later, he began to work and get his fingernails dirty, which is what scientists ought to do. If you're going to be a scientist you ought to be out there doing the job. And he most emphatically did. All these bottles and that microscope – the very primitive microscope you see over there – allowed him to make observations, do experiments and develop theories which have an astonishingly modern air.

JIM MOORE: It's interesting you should mention the microscope. Just here on the window seat behind you, where he had that mirror installed, just on this window seat is where he did his dissections. And he set his microscope up here because this is a north-east exposure on the house – the light is perfect. He had a specially designed chair, it's around here somewhere, on castors – there it is. And he could push himself from his desk over to these other tables and get every-thing done. He set up his dissecting blocks and he had his tweezers and that's what he devoted his life to.

MELVYN BRAGG: I mentioned the routine in his life, at his desk at eight o'clock in the morning and so on. Can you give us more of an idea of his routine and the rigidity of it?

JIM MOORE: This study was a you-shaped place for Darwin, it was for him, and his wife ensured that. He could come here and work and after doing the letters he would go out to the corner of his property, walk for a mile or so, and then he would come back and he would do another bout of work and then he would break for lunch and then he would have a siesta, smoke a cigarette in later years, and perhaps he would then go out and have another constitutional. He never really stopped working, even when he was out walking around he was noticing things, making notes on things – he was absolutely obsessive in all of that, it was part of Darwin's brilliance. And then in the evenings he would retire to the sitting room, next door, and he would play backgammon with his wife, listen to the piano – that's when he tried to relax. But even then in the middle of the night he would think of something that he had said or done during the day, an experiment that hadn't gone right, and he would either get up and do something about it or lose a night's sleep. He never let it alone. The important thing about Down House and about this space in Down House is that he was liberated to do science the way he wanted to do it – sequestered from intrusions.

MELVYN BRAGG: If Darwin were to carry out investigations on the scale and depth we've described it would help to have a laboratory close to home, and this is the space that solved Darwin's problem. We've moved out of the house now, into the garden. This is where he conducted his botanical experiments on orchids, primroses and cowslips, it's also where he studied bees, pigeons and worms – it must have been the most charming laboratory in the world. And down a gravel path is the kitchen garden and greenhouses which are really the HQ of Darwin's botanical investigations. To take us there is Nick Biddle, who oversaw the project that restored these gardens.

When you were given the job to bring these gardens back to what they were, what were you specifically asked to do?

NICK BIDDLE: The aim was to restore the gardens and grounds of Down House to the atmosphere and appearance during the last few years of Darwin's life here in order to illustrate and interpret his life and work to the visiting public.

MELVYN BRAGG: It was also a family garden. I've described it as a laboratory and it's a word we like to use about the garden because it gives it an extra stratum of significance but it's a garden where his family played, enjoyed themselves, and it looks very much like the garden of a small country house and not at all, frankly, like a laboratory.

NICK BIDDLE: I'm delighted to hear you say that because so many historic houses that you visit are about the political power, the wealth, they illustrate the idea that the occupant had about themselves. And it's quite appropriate that Charles Darwin's garden has that atmosphere of a family garden, because really before he was a scientist he was a father and a husband.

MELVYN BRAGG: So we have tennis here, we have croquet here, we have a swing in the yew tree, we had a sandpit.

NICK BIDDLE: Yes. His life and his work were just totally enmeshed, you can't really understand one without the other, and his family worked with him on all of his projects in the garden, especially on his study of insectivorous plants.

MELVYN BRAGG: This bit we're passing here, would he have done experiments there on our right?

NICK BIDDLE: Yes. He refers for example to the lobelia fulgens in these flowerbeds at the back of the veranda. And the point he makes about those is that they have a device to ensure that none of the pollen from any specific flower will go on the stigma of that specific flower. And this is really the key because the role of insects in pollinating plants in order to ensure cross-fertilisation is fundamental because that ensures the variability, which is part of the building blocks of natural selection, is there. He was aware that constantly self-fertilising plants just wouldn't produce the variability which is the raw material of evolution through natural selection. And just outside the veranda are six flowerbeds which were always planted out by Emma because really it was Emma who looked after the garden and Darwin would potter about, mooning about the garden, as one of his gardeners described it. 'I see him mooning about the garden and I just think it would be better if he had something to do,' he said.

MELVYN BRAGG: Darwin's garden was both a place for the children to play and the research centre for his work, a place to study, measure and experiment with the natural world, especially here in the kitchen garden. This is where Darwin did the majority of his plant experimentation. He called it his experimental bed and it's just in front of us.

NICK BIDDLE: Yes. The kitchen garden. When we started the restoration project here, the whole area was laid to grass but there's a fantastic record of what he did here. We were lucky enough to have a look at his gardener's catalogues with his annotations, and there's his copy of Loudon's *Encyclopaedia of Gardening*, because as well as looking at variation in the natural world he was also interested in variation under domestication, how variation occurs within cultivated forms, partly though the intervention of people breeding specifically for characteristics but also how those characteristics can become lost again through variation.

MELVYN BRAGG: He was running his domestic life along with the scientific life. This was a vegetable garden, vegetables for the family as well, I understand?

NICK BIDDLE: And for cut flowers. There's also a bed of roses which are referred to in the correspondence. I mean, as he did with everything really, he integrated the whole life and work together. He makes a reference, for example, to a very late frost in May and the effect that it had on a row of beans and how most of them were completely wiped out but there was just a very small number that were able to tolerate that degree of frost, and he really got quite excited about how just a small degree of variation could be really critical in the survival of those particular individuals which would then enable them to pass on that successful characteristic.

MELVYN BRAGG: Steve Jones, this looks like a vegetable garden, it doesn't look like the laboratory that we were referring to. He managed to do remarkable things here, can you give us a flavour of some of the experiments he carried out from this experiment bed in front of us – this vegetable garden?

STEVE JONES: This isn't just a vegetable garden, this is Bromley's Galapagos. There's an astonishing variety of brilliant things that he did here. In fact he was getting very close to something which he no doubt thought about but wouldn't mention to his wife which was the origin of sex, which remains one of the central issues of biology. The central question about sex is – why bother? I mean it's so expensive. And he actually found that there was a second series of sexes. If you were a primrose, not only did you have to be a male and mate with a female, you also had to pass the test, a second sexual test, of being a long style finding a short style. And what he found was that short could only make the long and the long the short. We now know that's universal. In humans too we have many, many sexual tests we have to pass before we're accepted by another mate.

So once again what seemed like trivial experiments, perhaps with the benefit of hindsight, but I think he had some foresight too, actually approach some of the most fundamental questions in biology. Another piece of work he did here, which in hindsight again is absolutely astounding, is to discover the first of all hormones. Who knows that Darwin discovered hormones? He only just realised it but he was interested in why do plants, when they're growing or shoot, why do they move towards the light? He did a simple but brilliant experiment, which was to shine a light on the tip and further down from the tip. Only the tip gave a response but the growth was further down. And so he suggested that some kind of molecular influence was passed from the tip further down the plant. That was a hormone. The actual very first animal hormone wasn't found until 1903, which is many decades later. So on that ground alone Darwin deserves to be famous and of course there's all the rest.

MELVYN BRAGG: We're also next to a greenhouse, which is next to the experimental bed. Given what we see of state-of-the-art laboratories and the effort that goes into them and the science created in them, this would seem extraordinarily primitive and yet he arrived at conclusions which have held to this day.

STEVE JONES: Yes. We're looking at his greenhouse now. Actually it was a state-of-the-art greenhouse in its day and was expensive – hot water and that kind of stuff. I think it proves that ideas are more important than equipment. Darwin was an anatomist both of plants and animals. Molecular biology is anatomy plus an enormous research grant – there's no difference, it's just cuttings things, not into nerves and muscles, but into the individual letters of the DNA. So I think it's the ideas that matter rather than the technology, and Darwin had the ideas.

MELVYN BRAGG: OK, let's go into this state-of-the-art greenhouse, as then was.

Can we start with you, Nick – did you have to put this together and restore this greenhouse as well as the garden?

NICK BIDDLE: The greenhouse was restored by English Heritage. When I joined the project it was almost there, we did a little bit more work just putting it together. But essentially it's three sections. Darwin had five sections, but there are three sections remaining and that's what's been restored.

MELVYN BRAGG: So what most leaps out at you here, Steve?

STEVE JONES: Well, this is a carnivorous plants section, and Darwin was slightly shocked to find that a plant ate an animal. Ruskin wrote eloquently that this had ruined the study of botany for him and it's disgusting, we shouldn't do that kind of thing. But Darwin was very curious about it, and he did a lot of clever experiments on sundews and Venus flytraps and the like. He got material from all over the world, much of which he grew in here. And he was astounded and he said to some extent terrified and frightened by the similarity between the behaviour of these plants as they ate insects and the behaviour of animals.

He found, for example, that the digestive enzyme of the sundew, as it breaks down the insect, needs to be in an acid environment, just like the human stomach. And he says again and again 'this is almost like an animal'. And many historians of science have wondered about the parallel between his own stomach problems and his interest in the gastric pastimes of the botanical world. As a mere scientist I'm not qualified to comment on that.

JIM MOORE: About these carnivorous plants and Darwin being carnivorous. Plants were little animals to him. If all the plants and animals that ever existed were suddenly to reappear – this is a very important point for Darwin – there would be complete continuity. From the first sensations all the way up to the development of mind. He learnt this early on when there was a great deal of question about whether marine invertebrates were plants or animals. And his very first professor, Dr Robert Grant at Edinburgh University, exposed him to this problem. The important point here is continuity and gradualism. Darwin's entire world was built very slowly without any gaps or any leaps or any jumps.

STEVE JONES: Yes, that's been much discussed recently, there's much argument between what's known as evolution by jerks and evolution by creeps. I think in the end the creeps have won, you know, and I think standing around in this greenhouse we've proved that to be true.

JIM MOORE: But Darwin's creeping was infinitesimal creeping and no one believes that the variations on which natural selection depend today were that small and this is where Thomas Huxley was closer to the modern view, that there were an intermediate level of variations which actually were the raw material of natural selection.

MELVYN BRAGG: I just get the impression while listening to you talk that this man was on constant alert for observation. How would you describe it, he never let up, whatever was going or growing he was learning something from it, or interfering with it in order to learn more?

STEVE JONES: I think in the end what you're saying is he was a scientist and a good scientist. He could never rest, he was an obsessive.

MELVYN BRAGG: You said he was trying to get at the origins of sex, I think that was the phrase you used earlier. There's a book that he published called *The Descent of Man and Selection in Relation to Sex*, can you talk about that?

STEVE JONES: It's a very important book, 1871, and in some ways it's perhaps his second most important book. It's an oddly disjointed book, it needed a good editor. The daring section is the descent of man, and in *The Origin of Species* he dared only say 'light will be cast upon man and his origins'. That caused enough of an uproar. But twelve years later he wrote this book about human evolution.

JIM MOORE: The story goes that Darwin discovered the theory of natural selection and something called sexual selection much later. And then he published his theory of natural selection in *The Origin of Species* in 1859 and when he saw that he was going to survive it he decided to go public with *The Descent of Man* twelve years later. That story has to be reconsidered at a deep level.

Darwin's theories were always about human beings and society. From the time he set eyes on Fuegans in South America he asked where had these people come from, can they possibly be related to me, are the races one or are they separately created species? Darwin didn't believe that the human races were separate species at all, he believed passionately in the equality of the races as human beings and he was deeply opposed to slavery. So Darwin works out his theory of sexual selection in the 1850s to establish the mechanism by which the races diverge from a single stock. And we know from his research project and his other letters that he was working up all of the evidence for sexual selection as the cause of racial divergence, and suddenly he dropped it when he wrote *The Origin of Species*.

So *The Origin* comes out shorn of human beings, which was a safe thing to do, wasn't it? And he plans to add a chapter to his enormous book called *Variation of Animals and Plants Under Domestication* and gradually the chapter he intends to add on human racial divergence gets bigger – typical Darwin – bigger and bigger and by 1867 or 1868 he said, 'it's going to be an essay, it'll be a small book' and it ends up being two volumes called *The Descent of Man and Selection in Relation to Sex*, two-thirds of which is his prize answer to the big problem of nineteenth-century anthropology – whence the races have come. Sexual selection.

STEVE JONES: The sad thing about the book is actually he didn't know anything about human evolution at all. There was one human fossil of what we now know to be a Neanderthal that had been found, and he didn't quite know what it was. He knew nothing about the enormous amount we now know about the age of human beings, the action of natural selection. And Darwin in the second part of the book explored much more deeply this question, the famous question of the peacock's tail – what use is a peacock's tail to a male peacock? None whatsoever. It's a pain in the backside in more than one sense. But for some reason the females find it attractive so the tail gets bigger and bigger over generations.

He had an odd feeling that actually attraction was important in humans, that maybe that was the reason why we got black people in Africa and white people in Europe, that it had to do with sexual preference. The interesting observation now is that isn't really true, biologists now can see in humans, as Darwin had seen in plants and animals, what I think of as the healing power of lust, which is that humans will mate in almost any combination, irrespective of race. And it's level of education that determines who we mate with more than skin colour. So I think when it comes to selection in relation to sex in humans he didn't get it right, but he had some very good ideas.

MELVYN BRAGG: When you think about the experiments Darwin did here at Down House and when you also bear in mind that for much of the time he was in poor health it's a remarkable body of scientific work. As we've said, Down House was a retreat for Darwin but it was also open to the world. If you wanted to speak with Charles Darwin you simply wrote a letter, part of the vast Darwin-shaped correspondence through which the man in Down House talked back to the world.

Alison Pearn is Assistant Director of the Darwin Correspondence Project. Alison, we're in Darwin's study again, and here he wrote about how many letters?

ALISON PEARN: Well, we know of around 7,000 that he wrote that still survive, but he spoke at one time about writing eight to ten letters a day. So there may be more out there.

MELVYN BRAGG: How important was correspondence to Darwin's science?

ALISON PEARN: It was enormously important. He coordinated almost a research group around the world from this study. It was of particular importance once *Domestication Under Variation* had been published and he was working on what became *Descent of Man* and *Expression of Emotions*. Once he was really working in earnest on human origins he needed that information from all over the world. And he used his existing friends, in particular Joseph Hooker at Kew, to tap into their networks of people around the world, particularly diplomats and missionaries. Darwin knew that he was using correspondence to get information out of people. He wrote to a naturalist, John Jenner Weir, in 1868, and at the end of a letter where he'd asked Jenner Weir for a lot of different information, a whole list of different questions, right at the bottom he writes: 'if any man wants to gain a good opinion of his fellow men he ought to do what I am doing – pester them with letters.'

MELVYN BRAGG: You've used the phrase 'all over the world', Alison, can you give us some idea of the geographical extent of his correspondence?

ALISON PEARN: Even a single letter may contain information on all sorts of different subjects. Darwin was always able to turn a source of information to account, so although he had talked with Fritz Muller, in particular, about botany, and that was Muller's primary interest, once Darwin was working on human origins he wrote letters to Muller saying 'and while you're about it, I'm sure it wouldn't cause you too much trouble if you would just observe the expressions in the native population, give me information about the people that you see and not just the plants'.

MELVYN BRAGG: This idea of relating everything or bringing everything back to people becomes a great theme, doesn't it? He corresponded with Sir James Crichton-Browne, I understand, a Scottish psychiatrist, a pioneer in mental health. Darwin was interested in child development and he'd write to members of his own family who had children, talking about the way that children developed. Can you give us some idea of that?

ALISON PEARN: Yes, once again very serendipitous in his sources of information. So when anybody wrote, usually wrote to Emma to say that a baby had been born, Darwin in writing back with congratulations passes on a questionnaire that he had designed, asking people for information about human expressions of emotion. And this is a letter that Darwin wrote to Thomas Henry Huxley, best known as 'Darwin's Bulldog', the man who argued so passionately for *Origin of Species*. Mrs Huxley had just recently had a baby, and Darwin writes: 'give Mrs Huxley the enclosed' – probably the questionnaire about the expression of the emotions – 'and ask her to look out for hints when one of her children is struggling and just going to burst out crying.' Then he carries on: 'a dear young lady near here plagued a very young child for my sake till it cried and saw the eyebrows for a second or two beautifully oblique, just before the torrent of tears began.' The relationship of expressions of sorrow and fear in young humans was something that Darwin was trying to relate to expressions of sorrow and fear in animals.

MELVYN BRAGG: In the early years, where he wasn't publishing or publishing very little, he was collecting specimens as well. He'd failed to bring a complete set back from his world tour, and he wrote to other people who'd been on board saying have you any finches? And I missed that out and can you send me what you've got?

ALISON PEARN: Yes, he did, and there are still in the archive in Cambridge University Library – there are still bits and pieces of plants in amongst the letters. There's one rather lovely letter from a correspondent in New Zealand which still has stuck on it some squashed bees, because Darwin was very interested in bees as pollinators and interested in competition among different species around the world and the driving out of native populations and the effects which came from trying to transplant, for instance, a native British plant to somewhere like New Zealand. If you didn't have the right pollinators then what were the effects of that? So he was sent squashed bees.

MELVYN BRAGG: What sort of information did he provide in return – it was an information barter, wasn't it?

ALISON PEARN: It was up to a point. The information flowed very much to Darwin, and increasingly. After *Origin* was published he was such a well-known man that people were very willing to help him. And they also knew about his precarious health, so they tended not to want to bother him for anything in return. What he did provide to the people who gave him information was a kind of patronage. He was very significant in promoting their careers in other ways. He would encourage people to publish on their own account. He would suggest lines of enquiry, suggest experiments. He would suggest observations they might make that were undoubtedly going to be of use to him and his agenda but at the same time he was very skilful at getting people to do what he wanted by recognising that he had to be really appreciative of the help they gave him.

MELVYN BRAGG: In that sense he was quite a clever politician?

ALISON PEARN: He was. To say that he was a manipulator, I think, would give the wrong idea, but he had to some extent an instinct for saying to people the things that would encourage them to help him and not discourage them.

MELVYN BRAGG: So apart from doing his own work out in the garden and writing here where we are in his study, his correspondence must have taken him an awful lot of time because these are often not short letters, they're detailed, so it's almost a third occupation, isn't it?

ALISON PEARN: Yes, very much so. But of course, being a Victorian gentleman, he had a wife and daughters who could help him to write the letters, so some of the letters that we know are in Emma Darwin's hand or Henrietta Darwin's hand. Henrietta actually became a support for Darwin's work in many ways. She became one of the people, one of the few people, to whom he gave the draft manuscript of *Descent of Man* for comment, not just to act as a secretary but actually to be a sounding board. She was away from home at the time when Darwin was writing *Descent of Man*, one of the books that he knew was going to be the most controversial. But there are letters. Darwin sent to Henrietta the proofs of the book, and asked her to comment on it, and she was clearly doing that, not just from a stylistic point of view, she was no mere copy-editor, she was commenting on the meat of the argument. And there are some hints that she did this for some of Darwin's friends and colleagues too. Even Hooker, who was no sufferer of fools and not terribly fond of women sometimes, relied on Henrietta as a sounding board for his writing.

MELVYN BRAGG: Did he get involved with people writing to him saying you must be wrong, your explanation is mistaken and evil and unacceptable. Did he respond to letters like that?

ALISON PEARN: He didn't respond very often. He was a man who avoided open controversy wherever he could. There are some letters that are not so much angry or critical as sorrowful, so there were some of his correspondents who were worried about him and about the health of his eternal soul.

MELVYN BRAGG: In October 1881, Darwin published his final book, *The Formation of Vegetable Mould Through the Action of Worms*, the result of forty years' work. The book sold well. Even at this late stage of life Darwin never lost his delight in the natural world but the fits and seizures were getting worse.

JIM MOORE: And worse and worse and then finally he stayed up late one night talking with his daughter, blew his nose loudly and then with a slow tired step he mounted these stairs in pain. And at the top of the stairs is the master bedroom. It was a cold spring night – 18 April 1882. There must have been a fire going here in this wonderful marble fireplace and no doubt right next to the fireplace is where the bed was up against this wall. And just before midnight there was a terrible attack and he was convulsed with nausea. Charles rang for Emma. She came running, the servants came running and it went on and on. He said, 'I wish I could die, if only I could die.'

And then he remembered to say, when his daughter arrived with her brother Francis, he remembered to say, 'I am not the least afraid to die.' Henrietta was writing all of this down because she wanted an eyewitness account that her father did not repent of his views on his deathbed. Somehow he made it through the night. The children sat on the bed with him and rubbed his chest lightly and he called them 'you dears'. And he referred to Emma as 'it's almost worthwhile to be sick to be nursed by you'. And then after breakfast he threw up again. The doctor was called. Emma tried to sleep and they called her again because the crisis had come by the middle of the afternoon. And this time he couldn't relieve the pain by lying back in bed or sitting up. And finally at the end of the culmination of all his heart attacks there was a great one from which he never recovered and he lapsed into a coma. Emma sat next to him and held his head on her chest and rocked slowly as he passed away.

MELVYN BRAGG: Even here in the bedroom where he died, as I understand it, Jim, different factions want to claim him and his legacy. From that moment.

JIM MOORE: Darwin wanted to buried amongst his friends and neighbours. He'd lived at Down for forty years, the family assumed that he would be buried in the parish churchyard. And a coffin was made and was brought here to the house, a plain oak coffin, his body was laid out in it and it stayed here in the house, probably in this room. But in London political forces were at work in the scientific establishment who wanted this body taken into the public domain where it could be seen to have the power that it had through Darwin's writings during his life.

And to make a long story short, the corpse was snatched and it was taken to Westminster Abbey and it was buried, according to the press, by the will of the intelligence of the nation. It was the new professional middle-class scientists, people like Huxley and Hooker, his best friends and defenders, who paraded this body through the nave of Westminster Abbey and laid it near the monument to Sir Isaac Newton at the north end of the choir screen. And around the graveside were the leaders of the government, the Liberal Party, and the Opposition, and there was a huge gathering of foreign dignitaries and there was not a dissenting voice. It was very, very important to Darwin's contemporaries that he should be honoured in this way because he had never been given a knighthood.

MELVYN BRAGG: What do you make of this snatching of the corpse, Steve Jones?

STEVE JONES: Well, the corpse had been snatched many times back and forth since then, the body snatchers are still out there on both left and right, on the atheistical side and the religious side, they're clawing at poor Darwin's remains. And I think we tend to forget, to be frank, that what's important isn't Darwin, it's Darwinism, and that's the thing which is alive. Darwin mouldered away long ago. I think Darwin himself actually would have been shocked at what happened to his corpse. He'd probably be even more shocked at what happened to his reputation. But he'd be very, very happy as to what happened to his science.

MELVYN BRAGG: What impact do you think Darwin had on the history of thought? First Steve Jones.

STEVE JONES: I think on the history of biology he had an absolutely stupendous impact, he almost invented the science. He was the Newton of biology and that's still true. Constantly his name comes up in conversations as shorthand for a whole constellation of different facts, which when we say 'Darwinism' we know what we mean. The history of science is slightly odder. He's turned out to be a sort of universal alibi for almost anything you think. Karl Marx was a keen Darwinist, he said that Darwin saw the workings of bourgeois society among animals and plants. Hitler was a keen Darwinist too. So was Mrs Thatcher. But what's quite remarkable is how what basically is only a science has become part of social, political, religious and artistic narrative. I have to say, as a mere scientist, I find that fairly baffling.

JIM MOORE: Darwin is hailed as a revolutionary, he was even hailed as a revolutionary in his own time, but the English do not bury revolutionaries in Westminster Abbey. Darwin's burial in Westminster Abbey was proof of his acceptability to the English establishment in his own lifetime, something he had never dreamt of when he was writing in his private notebooks. The fabric falls. The whole fabric of people's traditional creationist belief about the origin of life and God and man Darwin believed would have to be transformed. But he was never an atheist. He was not the revolutionary he was proclaimed to be. Darwin precipitated and symbolised a palace coup in Great Britain in the nineteenth century but it was not a revolution from below but the replacement of one set of largely clerical university-based religious experts on man and God and nature with another set who are themselves professional scientists who hailed Darwin and brought him to Westminster Abbey to be buried.

MELVYN BRAGG: Would you agree with that, Steve?

STEVE JONES: I'm only a scientist, so I think that's probably true. I mean science in those days was an aristocratic pastime – to be a scientist you needed to be rich and you only have to look at Down House to realise Darwin was rich. I think there's been a great proletarianisation of science since then, scientists became first middle-class and we're rapidly slipping down towards the lower class. But in the end what matters isn't who does the science, what class they belong to, who pays for the science, it's what the science is. And I think really the hagiography of Darwin is the hagiography of a man. What we really need is some understanding of the importance of his science.

MELVYN BRAGG: Do you think there's one aspect above all of Darwin's work that was the key to his success in formulating and publishing these theories?

STEVE JONES: I think the central thing which he stuck to from his youth was the enormous power of small means. Science does concern itself with trifles, science is trifles, but when you put the trifles together, perhaps rather unlike the law, you get something really big, and I think he was the first person to prove that.

JIM MOORE: Darwin's vision of nature was completely original, some say it could only have been articulated in Britain in the nineteenth century, not in France, not in Germany, not in Britain in any other time. His vision of a struggling progressive cosmos in which all life is related by common descent – we're all members of one family, we are all brothers and sisters – this was Darwin's vision and uniquely so in the 1830s, and it's become ours. I think if we had Darwin's humanity that accompanied that vision, his love of life and his hatred of cruelty, it would be the completion of his work.

MELVYN BRAGG: In making these programmes about Darwin, we've encountered exotic locations, radical thought, exceptional industry, experiments out there in the garden through the window beside me, but one of the things that strikes me most about Darwin is that the last book he published wasn't some grandiose world view, wasn't some old testament from the top of an intellectual mountain, it was a book about earthworms and here's part of the conclusion:

It is a marvellous reflection that the whole of the superficial mould over any such expanse has passed, and will again pass, every few years though the bodies of worms. The plough is one of the most ancient and most valuable of man's inventions; but long before he existed the land was in fact regularly ploughed, and still continues to be thus ploughed by earthworms. It may be doubted whether there are many other animals which have played so important a part in the history of the world, as have these lowly organised creatures.

And it's Darwin's observation, his humility, his work out there in the garden and his realisation of the connectedness of things which I think is one mark of his greatness.

TRANSMITTED: 8.1.2009

1

Agincourt

Owre kynge went forth to Normandy,
With grace and myyt of chivalry;
The God for him wrouyt marvellously,
Wherefore Englonde may calle, and cry
Deo gratias:
Deo gratias redde pro victoria.

It's not Shakespeare, though he was soon to go into the breach. The great victory was Agincourt, as described there in the Agincourt Carol, when the 'happy few' of Henry V's English army vanquished the numerically superior French forces on St Crispin's Day in 1415.

It is a battle that has resounded through the centuries, and has been used by so many to mean so much, not least what it is to be English. But how important was the battle in the strategic struggles of the time? What were the pressures at home that drove Henry's march through France? And what is the legacy of Agincourt?

With me to discuss the Battle of Agincourt is Anne Curry, Professor of Medieval History at Southampton University; John Watts, Fellow and Tutor in Modern History at Corpus Christi College, Oxford; and the medieval historian and writer, Michael Jones.

Anne Curry, can we look at the deep background first. We're talking about 1415, we're talking about a battle in France, but it does go back to 1066 when William of Normandy came over and from then on many great aristocratic families had holdings in England and France together, including the king himself. So there were pretexts from then on for going backwards and forwards.

ANNE CURRY: I think that's a very important point to bear in mind. William was Duke of Normandy, so when he became king of England he united the duchy of Normandy and the kingdom of England. From that point onwards English kings continued to hold lands in France and they actually got more because when Henry II became king of England in 1154 he was also Count of Anjou and Maine and through his wife, Eleanor of Aquitaine, controlled Aquitaine and Poitou. So in the late twelfth century the English kings held more land in France than the French kings, who were very much holed up around Paris and the Île de France.

MELVYN BRAGG: And there's a sense in which – although we're brushstroking decades and there's a frown, quite rightly – the two places were held together by a common ruler that worked. It was after 1204 when England, as we might call it, and France, as we might call it, which weren't that at the time, began to split that the trouble set in.

ANNE CURRY: I think you've got to mind my previous point. The French kings, as they became more powerful, didn't like this English king holding lands, even though they probably didn't see him as an English king, very much as a sort of French prince. But when John lost Normandy in 1204, that was very much because the French exploited feudal custom to deprive the Duke of Normandy, the Duke of Aquitaine, of his lands. After that point the English tried to get Normandy back and also other parts of their provinces.

They were unable to do so. They were left only with a part of Aquitaine that we normally call Gascony, the bit around Bordeaux and beyond, now Biarritz. And that was important for us because of the wine trade but it was nothing like that great Angevin Empire. Most importantly, we'd lost Normandy, the part that had been held for the longest.

MELVYN BRAGG: But there were still parts there that English aristocrats personally can claim and the kings can claim being heir to, most notably Edward III, who proposed himself as a king of France when the French had trouble finding a king. He had a fairly decent claim.

ANNE CURRY: There had been wars on and off after 1204, even though a treaty had been come to in 1259 by which the English had said, we give up our northern lands so long as we can keep Aquitaine and we'll pay homage to the French king for Aquitaine. There was a war under Edward I, a war under Edward II and a kind of cold war situation existed between the two kings.

But the claim to the throne is a new element and that's what really makes the fourteenth and fifteenth centuries so interesting. You're right. Edward III claimed the throne because he was the nephew of the last king of France, the last of the legitimate male line. But the French preferred a cousin of the last king because then the inheritance was entirely through the male line. Edward's claim was through his mother and that was a weakness for him.

MELVYN BRAGG: Michael Jones, what were the circumstances which led Henry to revive Edward III's claim to France?

MICHAEL JONES: We need to remember that Henry's father, Henry IV, had usurped the throne in 1399. He had taken the throne by force and he'd deposed the anointed king – Richard II. And Richard II was subsequently murdered on Henry's orders. This was not an auspicious start for a new dynasty and it led to bitter civil war and also a very dangerous revolt in Wales under Owain Glyndŵr. Young Prince Henry's upbringing was a civil war upbringing and his first battle – the battle of Shrewsbury – where he fought as a sixteen-year-old with considerable courage, was a battle where contemporaries were shocked by the devastating casualties inflicted by an English army against another English army. His upbringing and his political experience is the devastation of civil war and he's looking to move out of that and unite the nation with a very different vision.

MELVYN BRAGG: Can we go back to usurping the throne for a moment, Michael? You're not legitimate, you're not the appointed by God and in the natural succession. This is a serious matter, isn't it?

MICHAEL JONES: It is a serious matter and when Henry IV falls ill in 1406 – and we think he probably suffered from leprosy – many contemporaries were saying, 'Ah ha! That's divine judgement for the way you took the throne. You took the throne by force and God's judging you for that. That's the consequence of your action.' And it's very interesting that when Henry V takes the throne one of his first actions is a very important reburial of the deposed king, Richard II, in Westminster Abbey. In other words, Henry is recognising the seriousness of that and saying let's move on.

MELVYN BRAGG: You mentioned there the boldness of him as a fighter at the age of sixteen. The idea that we've got from Shakespeare, of his being a wild, untamed, roistering youth is largely borne out from what we know, is it?

MICHAEL JONES: Yes. I'm rather delighted by the fact that Prince Henry could combine both being a vigorous brave soldier and administrator and had a bit of time for roistering as well. Though when he took the throne he very definitely put that behind him. But I think one of the qualities of Henry as king is that, while bringing his sense of vision and purpose, he knows what it's like to talk to the ordinary man. He can understand the ordinary man in the street and he has a brilliant way of addressing ordinary people that makes them feel included not condescended to.

MELVYN BRAGG: It was also a time when Englishness was reappearing quite forcefully. The Normans, by breaking away from France had broken their powerbase. Norman French was being taken over by the newly re-emerged English language with Chaucer there and in parliament – they were very proud of parliament. Did Henry sense that and take advantage of it?

MICHAEL JONES: I think the answer is a bit of both. One of the things that makes Henry stand out is his skill in putting his case forward and using the English language to do so. And he does it in a way that's astute but is also not affected – it comes across as very genuine. He uses the English language when he's addressing the community of the realm, towns, his noblemen. He also has a way of using English very directly when he's talking to ordinary people as well. He certainly takes this up.

MELVYN BRAGG: And that feeling of Englishness and being English was built around the language in which, as you say, he was very astute.

MICHAEL JONES: Yes, I think he does sense the mood of the time but I also think he brings something to it. One of his instinctive skills as a politician is that he is a nation builder. He picks up on these things that are around. He not only brings them forward but fashions them into something and that's one of his superb intuitive skills.

MELVYN BRAGG: When he got his army together, was he exploiting the national mood in the way he brought that army together, because it was a rather unusual way to bring an army together for that time, wasn't it?

JOHN WATTS: I'm not sure it was particularly unusual. England has a national army which is funded through taxation. It's raised through the personal connections often of the nobility and the royal household, so it's a mixture of personal contacts and public funding. And Henry needs to make a case to parliament for his war, in order to justify the taxation which will pay for the army. But I think Michael's very much put his finger on something by saying that Henry has built an atmosphere of national unity and national energy in the early part of his reign and that energy has clearly carried forward on to the battlefields of France.

MELVYN BRAGG: What are the headlines of the case he makes to parliament for this war?

JOHN WATTS: The case he makes is that his just rights as king have been withheld from him in France. That's the textbook just law: just war case. He has to establish in terms of international law that his war is a just one and the just war has to be announced by a just authority. It has to be fought for a just cause and in defence of a just cause. And these things are all important because if you don't fight a just war your troops are vulnerable, they're dishonoured by the fact they're participating in a war that can't be justified.

MELVYN BRAGG: And it's also one Christian nation against another. This is the Christian idea from Augustine and Aquinas – if they're going to attack each other they must attack each other for reasons which make it a just war. It's as important in the thinking of the time as a king being a usurper, therefore not wholly legitimate, and Henry struggles in so many ways to be legitimate.

JOHN WATTS: Yes, it's a Christian principle and it's also a legal principle because war is the ultimate vindication of justice. Today we see justice as a domestic matter and war as an external matter. For the people of this time justice runs through into war. And a king who won't vindicate his proper rights on the battlefield can't be relied upon to uphold the rights of his subjects at home either.

MELVYN BRAGG: But who judges whether it's a just war? Does he say these are my proofs and parliament says aye and that's it? Or does he refer it to higher authorities in the Church?

JOHN WATTS: He's making a case he can rely on later. Though Henry does in fact send a copy of the Treaty of Bourges off to the Council of Constance, the international Church council which is meeting. That treaty had the signatures of French noblemen agreeing that the king had rights to lands in France. He was able to show international clerical opinion that he had been directly let down by the French.

MELVYN BRAGG: So when they meet at Southampton they're about to go off on a just war. They have the taxation to raise the army. How big was the army? Figures are going to play quite a big part in this discussion later, but that army then, Anne, what is it estimated to be?

ANNE CURRY: I've been able to do a lot of research in the Public Record Office, largely in financial records, and I think about 12,000 men.

MELVYN BRAGG: Would that be considered a big army for the time?

ANNE CURRY: Yes, it is a big army, in fact it's bigger than any army of the fourteenth century. I think it's probably bigger than the one at the siege of Calais in 1347. It's not matched again until two years later when Henry raises another 12,000 in 1417, otherwise it's not matched until much later in the fifteenth, early sixteenth centuries.

MELVYN BRAGG: And can you tell us how it breaks down?

ANNE CURRY: About 25 per cent of it are men at arms. The earls
and the dukes did fight as men at arms, so did the king himself. Men
at arms are anybody really who has the gear. You need a full set of
armour, you need a horse – not just to fight on but to get there – and
you're paid a shilling a day if you're a standard man at arms, perhaps
an esquire or a knight would be paid two shillings, the dukes get
paid thirteen and fourpence a day, so the pay is based not so much
on the way you fight but on your social status. The remaining 75 per
cent are archers. And that's actually rather clever. Henry's able to get
a big army together by increasing the proportion of archers in his
army. Michael mentioned 1406 earlier. I've been able to show that
it's at that point onwards in the Welsh wars that this idea of having
one man at arms to three archers becomes common practice and it
remains common practice all the way through to 1450.

MELVYN BRAGG: 'Archers' is a French word, isn't it, and so might
they have used the word 'bowmen'?

ANNE CURRY: Actually they called them 'valete' or 'valet', yeomen
in Latin. In fact, sometimes the Master of Rolls would indicate
esquires or gentlemen for the men at arms as a collective group and
valete, valet, yeomen for the archers.

MICHAEL JONES: This is a very, very important expedition, it's
a high status campaign, and although we're seeing this change in
military practice where more archers are coming in, there's a big
risk in such a high-profile expedition having such a high proportion
of archers. But at the same time there are good military reasons for
it, and if Henry combines this army together it will be a formidable
force. But he needs to make it work as a unit.

ANNE CURRY: But it's also a lot cheaper, because archers are only
sixpence a day. A man at arms is twice as costly. So you can have
more archers for the same amount of money.

MELVYN BRAGG: There was a plot – supposedly a plot – at
Southampton before they set off. There are some forced confessions,
as we think. Need that delay us or is it of any great significance?
John Watts.

JOHN WATTS: Hard to say really. These people are very unrepresentative in a sense and the person who's the chief intended beneficiary of the plot – the Earl of March – is the person who reveals it to the king. One of the things that's interesting about the Southampton Plot, as about the so-called Oldcastle Revolt earlier in the reign, the rising of a group of supposed heretics against the king, is the way in which these things are dramatised in Lancastrian propaganda to make it look as if the king is having to struggle against all these difficulties. I think we're going to be talking quite a lot about the way in which the war is publicised.

MELVYN BRAGG: And Shakespeare.

JOHN WATTS: Yes, indeed.

MELVYN BRAGG: Anyway, there they are, off they set and they go for Harfleur. What are they getting by going there, John Watts?

JOHN WATTS: Possibly two things. One is that the English had conventionally sought landing places on the northern French coast anyway, this has been quite a traditional posture of English armies in the fourteenth century. They controlled Cherbourg, for example, and Brest for a period of time, as well as Calais that had been triumphantly won by Edward III. So I think there's a desire to secure a bridgehead. Harfleur is also a base for Norman piracy against English shipping, so there's a certain amount of kudos to be won by putting a stop to that.

Perhaps more excitingly than both of these reasons is that it's Henry staking a clear claim to be Duke of Normandy, which is something he's been posturing towards in 1413 and 1414. If he lands at Calais and sets off down towards Normandy all he's going to do is intimidate his not altogether reliable ally, the Duke of Burgundy. But if he lands at Harfleur and conquers it he begins a conquest of Normandy, which makes him much more of a player in French politics.

MELVYN BRAGG: What made Harfleur hard to lay siege to? It was not an easy place to attack, was it, Michael Jones?

MICHAEL JONES: It was very strong, it was very well fortified, and it also has this system of water defences. It's on a small river, the

Lézarde, that runs into the tidal estuary of the Seine. So the defenders can use water defences. They very astutely flood the valley around the town and this creates a lot of difficulties for the English. It's got very strong fortifications. It must have looked quite a stunning sight for the ordinary English soldier when they turned up and saw it.

MELVYN BRAGG: We have to try to define in this programme how good Henry was as a leader and a military man, because that's part of the reality, certainly part of the myth. Was his use of cannon particularly cleverly done?

MICHAEL JONES: I think it was. And a lot of people say of this siege, 'well, it drags on rather a long time', as if Henry lost direction of the military operation. I see this as an exceptionally well-conducted siege. One of the reasons that he was choosing a tough target was he wanted to try out his artillery, he was very interested in artillery. And he does a number of things.

He sites it very well, he's got a clear idea of where he wants to effect that famous breach in the wall. It's going to be on the west side and that's where he concentrates his guns. But he doesn't just concentrate them, he takes a lot of care in defending them, getting them close in the trenches, in defences that will mean the French will find it very difficult to attack those gun emplacements. And we're told that he takes care of all this personally, he's there day and night sharing in the dangers, making sure that the guns are in the right places. So when they finally start to fire they deliver a very effective series of blows against the walls.

MELVYN BRAGG: It's six weeks, the siege, isn't it? And then they go in. What do they find, Anne Curry?

ANNE CURRY: Well, they go in really because the French don't send a relieving army. It's a negotiated settlement. It's not taken by assault. They go in to discover a rather depressed population because the king hasn't come to rescue them. And also when Michael said about the use of the guns, we mustn't forget that inside the town they'd actually tried measures against the guns. They'd filled the streets with sand, they'd mounted their own gun attacks, that kind of thing. They were probably running short of food to a certain degree, so I think they're feeling pretty depressed. Also there's evidence that Henry expels some of the population because he was going to turn it into a war base, rather like Calais, so he drives out the women and the elderly and the defenders of the city are allowed out as well.

MELVYN BRAGG: We've got to move on to Agincourt, but just one more – one massive thing that happened there, John Watts. We're told there's a huge outbreak of dysentery and considerable numbers were laid low by that.

JOHN WATTS: Yes, and the group that Henry takes off towards Agincourt, that probably amounts to, I think, 5,000 archers and 900 men at arms. Have I got that right?

ANNE CURRY: I think more than that. I think about 7,500–8,000 men.

JOHN WATTS: So it's played down in some of the Chronicles, then?

ANNE CURRY: He put 1,200 into garrison at Harfleur and possibly another 2,000 went home or died.

MELVYN BRAGG: Well, if he put 1,200 in a garrison, that takes it down to 10,800, and then he put 2,000 – went home or – that's about 8,000.

ANNE CURRY: So about 8,000.

MELVYN BRAGG: Then he decides to strike across country – now what's all that about?

JOHN WATTS: We have to accept that we don't really know why Henry does this. It may be that he can't get back from Harfleur. We don't know if the ships are still there to take him home. My view, I think, would be that he's actually looking for a battle and that he's wanting to repeat the great march that's carried out by Edward III, a blessed memory as it were, which of course culminated in a battle at Crécy, which is not all that far from Agincourt where Henry fights. So I think there's a degree of historical reconstruction here, though Henry's also signalling to the Normans that he's here, the Duke of Normandy has returned. And if you're going to attract the French to battle you have to make yourself vulnerable, you have to put yourself out there, they're not going to come and attack you in Harfleur where you're nice and safe. And it's in Henry's interest to return to England ideally with a battle won, rather than just one town conquered.

MELVYN BRAGG: What evidence do you have that he was out looking for a battle?

JOHN WATTS: I have no evidence except that this resembles the practice of previous military leaders and that one understands a certain amount about battle psychology, which is all about flirting, in a sense, with the enemy and making yourself look attackable.

ANNE CURRY: He had issued a summons at Harfleur to the Dauphin to meet him in single combat, so I think that that probably was a summons to battle generally.

MELVYN BRAGG: Michael Jones, the French then get out from Saint Denis one of their great sacred relics, the Oriflamme. Can you tell us what the significance of that was and what the consequence of that was in France at the time?

MICHAEL JONES: This was one of the magnificent trophies. It was an incredible red banner, a banner of war, and it was kept in great reverence in the Abbey of Saint Denis and it was believed that this was not only a token of good fortune but also it's a sign of determination, and in chivalric, the law of arms, it's a sign of no quarter given or taken. I don't think we should take that absolutely literally but it certainly is a gesture of defiance, determination and resolution. And I think that's needed because we've got a distinct leadership problem on the French side. We've talked about Henry V, we haven't really mentioned what's happening on the French side.

This is very relevant because the king of France, Charles VI, had suffered a mental collapse in 1392 and since then he suffered periodic bouts of insanity where he underwent the delusion that he was made of glass and needed to be bound in with wooden hoops. Not good qualities for leading a fighting campaign against the English. And there's a worrying resonance here for us because when he was suffering from insanity he refused to be called Charles but said his name was George instead. So that leaves us with the Dauphin, whom Anne has mentioned. The summons to the Dauphin is definitely a statement of aggressive intent.

But he's also injecting a bit of humour here and this is an example of Henry's common touch. The Dauphin was an eighteen-year-old corpulent youth whose daily regime consisted of getting up about four in the afternoon and banqueting and feasting, and he was so unfit that on a trip within Paris he actually collapsed of exhaustion. Henry is reminding people that there's a lack of leadership. So the Oriflamme is really an appeal to the broader French community.

MELVYN BRAGG: Well, it certainly brings a great number of Frenchmen from many parts of France together to fight this battle. And then we had the curious, for me very curious circumstance, where the French get ahead of the English and so the English are actually following a gathering French army across country and the French are trying to delay them all the way and the English are finding it difficult to get across rivers and that sort of thing.

It is very odd that the English are following them. And the French, presumably, are looking for a place to settle and to choose the ground, which is, as I understand it from what you've written and others have written, one of the great things in medieval battles – you get to choose the ground. And they did. Now can we talk about the ground they chose? Would you like to talk about it, John, and why they thought it was good for them?

JOHN WATTS: Actually I'll hand over to Michael or Anne who really know more about this.

MELVYN BRAGG: Anne.

ANNE CURRY: I think it's important it's near Calais. I think what the French were after was cutting them off near Calais and then going on to take Calais later on, and that's why they hang on for as long as possible. Agincourt isn't all that far, it's about an hour's drive nowadays, so that was why they waited until then. Also, Henry's getting weaker and weaker, shorter of food, and presumably his army was pretty depressed on 24 October, the night before, when they saw how many French were there.

MELVYN BRAGG: Right, but why do the French choose this particular ground, because a lot of mileage has come out of the fact that the
ground was not very good for them, and proved to be really terribly
very bad for them. Yet they chose it. What, when they chose it, did
they think its qualities were, Michael?

MICHAEL JONES: One of the problems in our accounts of Agincourt
is we end up with this caricature that either the French are incredibly over-confident or incredibly stupid or both and the plucky
English are fighting on this extraordinarily advantageous site. Now
once Henry is able to cross this great river barrier of the Somme –
and we must remember that the French had forced him further and
further inland by holding the bridging point, so as Anne has said
the army has got more and more tired and demoralised – they then
have the option of blocking his army on the Calais road, on his route
back, at a place of their choosing, and we know they had an initial
battle plan . . .

MELVYN BRAGG: The English were holding Calais at the time – it
was a fortified place of refuge, yes?

MICHAEL JONES: That's right, that was where Henry was aiming
for, that was where he was trying to get back to. So the French
needed to block him on that route. And the choice is really whether
they go for an all out aggressive strategy. And that was their Plan
A, they had an original battle plan drawn up by some very good
commanders, including the Marshal Boucicaut who was very highly
rated, he had international renown in terms of his military skill. Plan
A, an aggressive plan, was to tackle the archers head on by using
cavalry on the wings and to weaken the main body of English men
at arms with a missile attack, that's from crossbow men and some
bowmen, and then to use the full force of the main army on foot to
smash through the English line.

Now Plan A really needed open countryside and of course the final
battlefield wasn't open. But I think the reason for that is there's been
a change of plan within the French army. They've moved from the

aggressive Plan A to an equally astute Plan B, which is to block the route with these woods on either side – on either side of the road – and wait for the English to attack them.

ANNE CURRY: Of course one of the reasons may be that the English capture the battle Plan A. That's what the stakes are all about. If the archers put stakes in front of them the French wouldn't have been able to carry out Plan A. The defence of the archers must be related to the anticipation that the French would try to launch a special attack against them.

MELVYN BRAGG: That was a success of intelligence then?

ANNE CURRY: I think there's a lot of intelligence in evidence. They want to cross where Edward III had crossed the Somme at Blanchetaque, but they knew the French were there already so they moved further along the Somme. There's quite a lot of evidence of them sending out scouts, viewing the French army from the heights above – things of this sort. I think we miss out quite a lot of this military intelligence sometimes.

MELVYN BRAGG: What's your view of the way that the English set up their battle formation, John? The stakes that Anne's talked about. Henry instructed the bowmen, the archers, to use stakes sharpened at both ends, six-foot long, planted into the ground to surround them with a sort of blockade, didn't he?

JOHN WATTS: Absolutely, yes. And obviously they would break any incoming cavalry charge. And the archers are sensibly positioned in a sort of U-shape, so that as the French come forward they can be hit straight on and also from the sides. And of course the tragedy of the battle, for the French, is that as their massive army moved forward so it becomes narrowed and narrowed and narrowed in the gap.

ANNE CURRY: Of course the trees don't help the French at the end of the day because some archers are probably hidden by the trees. The French don't realise how many they are against them.

MELVYN BRAGG: The English are also helped at that time by the fact that it was very wet ground, but we just missed one little step.

The way you were saying it, and Michael was saying it, the first advantage of medieval war is to choose the ground, which they did. Then the plan got changed. The second is to be attacked because defence is preferable. But somehow or other the English provoked the French to attack, or the French became impatient, or they were over-confident. Why do you think the French attacked?

JOHN WATTS: Oh gosh, partly a matter of honour. One thing that's very striking from the fourteenth-century phase of the Hundred Years War is that it eventually becomes impossible to avoid attacking the English because their presence is such an insult, and we know that Henry has a great big gold crown that he's wearing on this battle-field, goading the French to attack.

ANNE CURRY: With *fleur de lis* on it.

JOHN WATTS: Right. And Henry's army advances at a certain point to get quite close to within our own crossbow range of the French army, to tempt them forward. And also the French are in the middle of a civil war, but part of being in a civil war is proving that you are the best defenders of France, so they're struggling with each other to put up the most honourable and chivalrous performance.

ANNE CURRY: One of the texts tells us they're actually fighting amongst each other for who should be in the front row to smash and particularly to capture Henry. That's what they were after.

MICHAEL JONES: I think the crucial thing here is that the French have not got an integrated system of command. And that one of the drawbacks in getting all these extra people ready to fight is that they're all coming in at the last moment and the command system breaks down. You've got a lot of aristocrats with royal blood now turning up. It's very difficult to decide on a clear command structure. And the great ace for the English army is that they've got a strong leader – Henry V – and clear decisive arrangements for conveying his orders. And Henry knows that if he can provoke the situation that moves from the initial disposition of the French army they will rapidly lose shape or cohesion once something starts to go wrong. So this is what he's aiming for, he's aiming to provoke the French.

MELVYN BRAGG: Let's get back to numbers. There's been an awful lot of talk about the English being massively outnumbered. We think there are about 8,000 English soldiers there of one sort or another. How many French do you think there were, Anne?

ANNE CURRY: Well, French historians are increasingly thinking there weren't many more, and in fact possibly fewer, but that's quite interesting. Obviously English texts of the fifteenth century come out with ridiculous numbers – 60,000, 100,000, whatever. I think it's hard to believe there were many more than about 15,000 there, but it's still two to one. I think Michael's got a very valid point – they're thrown together at the last minute and whilst it's great that they've got people from the Auvergne there, how well integrated were they with the force as a whole?

MELVYN BRAGG: Can I come back to your figures – how are these figures arrived at and do they surprise other people? Because I've heard figures ranging from 15,000 to 60,000, but the one that was settled on before you came up with 15,000 was about 25,000.

ANNE CURRY: The problem is we don't know, we just don't have the same kind of sources. That in itself is indicative of the state the French were in, both before and after the battle, I think. We just don't have the administrative records. So we rely on chronicle accounts, but those really are very unreliable indeed.

MELVYN BRAGG: Can we talk about the longbow for a second? Why was it so effective and why did it play such a big part?

MICHAEL JONES: Well, this is the high-quality weapon that the English are putting into the frame and it's internationally recognised at this stage. We even have the Knights of the Teutonic Order – and that's the highest kind of chivalric group you can get – looking out for English bowmen because they recognise their strength. The bow has range, it has speed.

MELVYN BRAGG: It's up to seven feet long, the bow itself.

MICHAEL JONES: Well, I'd put it around six feet, yes. Its firing range is much greater than the crossbow and by using special kinds of arrows and arrowheads some penetration of armour can be achieved, particularly in what we call the killing range, the last thirty to forty yards. But even before that range is reached, the arrow storm can inflict body wounds and it can bring down horses – very important.

ANNE CURRY: The thing is it can be reloaded very quickly and I think that's the key to it. You can fire off a very large number within a minute, whereas a crossbow takes ages to reload. So these archers could fire off a hailstorm of arrows, as one of the chronicles tells us.

MELVYN BRAGG: Let's talk about the legacy. The battle is very decisively won in quite a short time. The battle lasted for a number of hours . . . ?

ANNE CURRY: Three hours, perhaps even less than that.

MELVYN BRAGG: And one of the things about it was it was decisively won and Henry came back to a great welcome. John, how did he capitalise? We know he wrote his letters home in English and he asked them to be read out in the shires by the magistrates, to keep the people informed and to bring them round to him. When he came back, with his crown still on from the battlefield, was it recognised by him and by others that this had been a famous victory?

JOHN WATTS: Oh absolutely, and no opportunity is missed to spin the victory as well, great as it clearly is in itself. The king heads a slow procession through Kent to rest at his royal manor of Eltham, while the Londoners hastily prepare a suitable pageant to mark his arrival.

MELVYN BRAGG: The Agincourt Carol.

ANNE CURRY: And try to find forty virgins to sing it.

JOHN WATTS: Indeed. Everything we know about these London pageants suggests that there's a dialogue going on between the government and the Londoners about what would be a suitable way of welcoming the king. He comes into London and is greeted by a couple of giants, which immediately present him as David struggling against Goliath, and really that's just the beginning. As he moves into the city the sense is of Henry as Christ entering Jerusalem, he's clad in a simple purple robe, twelve angels sing to welcome him, twelve English kings welcome him home in triumph.

ANNE CURRY: It's God's victory as well, and that's the point he's trying to make.

MELVYN BRAGG: I was interested in what you said about the David and Goliath. At that time, whatever later research, there was a strong feeling that they had been very heavily outnumbered?

ANNE CURRY: Yes, because the point is that they bring home loads of French prisoners and so it'll be pretty obvious to people just how important the battle was. But it's an interesting point to know whether those who fought would have been able to tell how many were there. I don't think we're very good at guessing how many are in crowds. So I think they were bound to say that the odds against them were great.

MICHAEL JONES: I think a key point here is the way the victory is won. The English have a very small number of casualties – perhaps 100, 200 at most – and the French slain were between 5–10,000 and then there were all these impressive prisoners being paraded back. And this extraordinary disparity between English losses and French losses brings something miraculous into the equation and of course Henry can very effectively exploit this.

ANNE CURRY: He even sends lists of important French dead and prisoners around the shires. It's very significant propaganda. Parliament meets just before he comes back and votes another tax immediately, so this is really good stuff. It means he can go to war against the French in the future.

MELVYN BRAGG: He died a few years later, of dysentery, but by the time he died he'd gone back to France, he'd put himself in the position of being the heir to the French throne. Had he lived, there's alternative history – had he lived he could have been king of France and England – would that have been a real possibility?

JOHN WATTS: I think there were real problems with the idea of trying to be king of two countries and particularly with the terms on which Henry comes to an agreement with the French, namely that he will preserve the crown of France intact. On the other hand, I think had Henry been able to wriggle out of that with the English, maintaining a significant foothold in France, perhaps in Normandy and Gascony, and with a mixture of military activity and diplomacy, being able to hang on to those crowns seems to me to be quite plausible. I think there could have been a very different map of France emerging from the fifteenth century than the one that we're used to.

ANNE CURRY: I agree. I mean had he lived that would have been fine, but he was succeeded by a nine-month-old baby, and that baby wasn't going to be able to lead an army for really quite a long time to come.

MELVYN BRAGG: Did Agincourt begin to push itself towards that central point in English mythical history as well as military history from the very beginning?

JOHN WATTS: Oh yes.

MELVYN BRAGG: From the time it was fought?

JOHN WATTS: Just picking up on some of the comments that Anne made earlier about the unreliability of the chronicle sources – these are already dramatising Agincourt as a struggle of the few just against the many unjust, something that, as we've seen, has got Christian connotations. It's also got connotations of justice. It's interesting that the numbers in the English army are played down, the portrait of this army, hungry, tired and exhausted, with its inspiring leader who dashes hither and thither building up morale, is straight out of the pages of Agesius. This is absolutely textbook military leadership.

ANNE CURRY: It's interesting that the chronicler of St Albans, Thomas Walsingham, when he writes his account of the battle, inserts lots of quotes from classical texts. So there's already the linking of Henry to the past. Judas Maccabeus is linked to him in other texts, and Alexander. So this linking of Henry to the greats of the past, I think, is a very important way in which the victory is celebrated.

MELVYN BRAGG: There's a poem written in his praise which is presented to him, as Aristotle presented that poem to Alexander the Great, isn't there?

ANNE CURRY: Yes.

MICHAEL JONES: That's the 'Regiment of Princes'.

ANNE CURRY: Yes, absolutely. It enhances his reputation – back to what Michael said near the beginning – and it really makes him secure on the throne, so secure that he is able to raise another large army, that he's able to have the Emperor across the next year and make him a Knight of the Garter and when the Emperor goes home his entourage allegedly drop little bits of paper from their sleeves saying how wonderful it was to have been in England. It really puts Henry and England on the international map for the first time.

MELVYN BRAGG: And it stays very strongly in the literature, doesn't it? Shakespeare's coming along almost 200 years later and he's going straight for Henry V. The expectation from the directness of that approach is that the audience is going to be with him all the way, not only with the drama but with the history, because his story is their story.

MICHAEL JONES: The story is their story, and let's remember that this was seen as a triumph of the ordinary Englishmen. There were so many of the ordinary archers there and they did it over all these high-falutin French chivalry and this plays well to a popular gallery. And when Shakespeare brings his *Henry V* out of course there's another invasion of France going on. The Earl of Essex is taking an army into France, into Normandy, in 1592. And that's nicely echoed in the encouragement from Churchill to Olivier to do the film version when he has D-Day very much in mind. And again it's invoking this wartime spirit and this is the timeless echo.

ANNE CURRY: Interestingly they missed the Southampton plot out of the Olivier film because they didn't want it to look as though there was anybody who'd opposed the war. And I think the film was released in 1945, made in '44, made in Ireland.

JOHN WATTS: Whereas Shakespeare himself, I think, does pick up something of the concern with PR that we've been referring to at many points. Shakespeare's Henry is quite Machiavellian, as is very clear if you see the *Henry IV* plays before *Henry V*.

TRANSMITTED: 16.09.2004

Plate Tectonics

A merica is getting further away from Europe. This is not a political statement but a geological fact. Just as the Pacific is getting smaller, the Red Sea bigger, the Himalayas are still going up and one day the Horn of Africa will be a large island. These are findings from the theory of plate tectonics, a revolutionary idea in twentieth-century geology that saw the continents of the earth to be dancing to the music of deep time. A dance of incredible slowness, yet powerful enough to throw up the mountains and pour away the oceans and dictate the character of the planet.

Plate tectonics was a genuine scientific revolution. It made geologists and many more besides profoundly rethink what the earth was, how it worked, and how it related to all the things in it.

With me to discuss plate tectonics are Joe Cann, Senior Fellow in the School of Earth and Environment at the University of Leeds; Lynne Frostick, Director of the Hull Environment Research Institute; and Richard Corfield, Visiting Senior Lecturer in Earth Sciences at the Open University.

Richard Corfield, plate tectonics is the mechanism by which the continents move around the surface of the earth. It was developed in the 1960s. But let's go back, what sort of idea did people have previously of the movement of the earth, if any?

RICHARD CORFIELD: The sense that the continents may have fitted together goes back to the sixteenth century when Abraham Ortelius, a Dutch mapmaker, realised that the bulge of West Africa looks as though it could have fitted into South America. And this was taken up and thought about over the years – Francis Bacon, for example, was interested in the theory; Benjamin Franklin was also interested in it – this similarity in the way the continents looked, whether or not they might have once fitted together. But it wasn't until the early twentieth century that a German called Alfred Wegener actually proposed a mechanism by which the continents might have once moved around and at one point been part of the same single super-continent.

In fact, there are three components of the theory of plate tectonics, which is, as you say, a 1960s theory. You start with the idea of continental drift, which stems from this idea that the continents may once have fitted together. The second component is something which was discovered in the early years of the twentieth century, which is the idea of seafloor spreading. And then this was all synthesised in the 1950s and 1960s into the theory of plate tectonics. It's impossible to underestimate the importance of the theory of plate tectonics to the science of geology, it's really the royal oak of geology, it's the tree that dominates the forest and without which none of the science really makes sense.

MELVYN BRAGG: Can you tell us a bit more, though, before we come to the actual theory itself, about what people were saying about fossil distribution around the world and how puzzling that was with continents being so widely separated by ocean?

RICHARD CORFIELD: Well, on top of this idea that the continents look superficially as though they have shapes which would enable them to fit together like the pieces of a jigsaw you also have the distribution of rock types and similarities, for example, in the nature of glacial sediments of the Permian carboniferous age, about 300 million years old, broadly, which are found in South America and in Africa and in India. And the question then is how come you get sediments of the same age found so widely separated?

MELVYN BRAGG: What explanations did people come up with and when and who?

RICHARD CORFIELD: As well as the similarity of rock types, there's this distribution of fossils, which are Permian fossils, tetrapod fossils, very similar on a number of different continents. There's the so-called Glossopteris flora, very similar across four continents. So how could they possibly be so similar on four separate continents?

Well, the idea was that there may have been land bridges, which went up and down like a series of random elevators. Over the years they came up, and then they disappeared as completely as the lost continent of Atlantis.

MELVYN BRAGG: How long did the land bridges idea last and when did it come in?

RICHARD CORFIELD: I can remember as an undergraduate people still trying to defend the idea of land bridges. They were an older generation of geologists, it has to be said. But basically land bridges seems to have been around, the idea of those kind of things seems to have been around before, during and after the Second World War.

MELVYN BRAGG: Joe Cann, Richard's mentioned the seafloor spreading, can you explain how that idea developed through and after the Second World War?

JOE CANN: It started with Arthur Holmes, who was professor of geology in Durham and then in Edinburgh, who had the idea that the oceans were splitting apart in the middle and that the oceans were being carried on the back of giant deep earth currents, to one side and the other. And that was taken up after the war by Harry Hess, an American professor at Princeton, who was also a sea captain. All through the Second World War he'd sailed his ships to and fro across the Pacific and he had lots of time to make measurements and also lots of time for thinking. And he refined this idea. He was also the most amazingly persuasive speaker. He would stand there, put his elbow on the rostrum, chain smoking and talking away in a quiet voice but totally convincingly. And that was one of the great roots from which plate tectonics sprang. The other was the Second World War itself.

During the Second World War all sorts of marvellous marine tools were developed – magnetometers for searching for submarines, sonar buoys for listening to submarines, explosives for destroying submarines and all of these were surplus to requirements at the end of the Second World War, along with a lot of ship time, and as well as that there were scientists who'd been to sea during the Second

World War. So they set about exploring the oceans which had only been done in a most superficial way before the Second World War.

MELVYN BRAGG: And what primarily did they find that set them on the path towards the theory of plate tectonics?

JOE CANN: They first of all found the mid-ocean ridges. Along the middle of the Atlantic Ocean and going all the way round the world, was a range of mountains with a rift valley in the middle of the mountains that might indicate things were pulling apart. It coincided with a chain of earthquakes. And then when you took ships across these mountain ranges and towed a magnetometer across, you found these extraordinary big magnetic signals. Now I remember when I was a student looking at these records and thinking this is so weird because it wasn't so much that the lumps and bumps were there, it was the size of them, it indicated there were huge magnetic contrasts down on the bottom of the oceans and that was very strange.

MELVYN BRAGG: So just after the Second World War people were thinking that the old theories, whatever they were, which Richard began to outline, didn't obtain – were they moving towards any new theory of what this told them about the planet as a whole?

JOE CANN: This was where Harry Hess was so influential, because he really inspired all of us to start thinking about seafloor spreading and talking about seafloor spreading instead of it being a forbidden subject, as it had been certainly in America since 1928. In 1928 the Americans had a meeting where they declared continental drift as impossible, and so you couldn't teach continental drift in the American universities at all after that. But in Europe and in the southern hemisphere particularly there's a lot more sympathy to the ideas of continental drift and the ideas of seafloor spreading. So the ideas were there but it took these magnetic anomalies that people found to really bring them from being a happy idea, which is how it was when I was a student, through to being quantifiable fact where we could actually demonstrate what was truly happening.

MELVYN BRAGG: So, Lynne Frostick, can we go on from there then. Let's say we've come to the end of the Second World War, numerous observations have been made, as Joe pointed out, scientists had been at sea, there was a lot of shipping around, a lot of time on peoples' hands, and they went on doing experiments. Where were you in geology in terms of arriving at a theory?

LYNNE FROSTICK: When I was an undergraduate, which I started in 1967, plate tectonic theory wasn't there. We did learn about seafloor spreading. But the problem with seafloor spreading is if you're spreading the sea, making the sea bigger, you've actually got to destroy something somewhere else, if the whole earth is expanding. And people knew that there was no evidence that there was an expanding earth. So what you've got to do is find out where the ocean floor's going, because we've not got an ever-expanding ocean floor, so we must be destroying something elsewhere.

MELVYN BRAGG: So what was the theory before plate tectonics? What were you being taught?

LYNNE FROSTICK: I was being taught about things called eugeosynclines and miogeosynclines, which sort of dropped down and came back up again, for no explained reason. It was very much a jigsaw which didn't fit together, which had no underlying principles. And it was very confusing, actually, because that's what I was taught to start with and when the theory of plate tectonics was published, which was during my time as an undergraduate, suddenly the pieces fell into place, it was like a jigsaw coming together.

MELVYN BRAGG: Let's stay with the seafloor for a moment or two before we come to this eureka moment, plate tectonics, the extraordinary discovery which was quite recent. A lot of us were alive and ageing in the sixties. What were they saying about it – can you just say in more detail what they were saying about seafloor spreading? It's a very nice phrase, but you imagine two hands together, like that, the bottom of the sea, and they spread out from one another – was that what they were saying?

LYNNE FROSTICK: More or less that, that there was tension at the mid-ocean ridge which was opening up effectively large cracks and magma was coming up in the middle and then more tension and magma came up in the middle and solidified. And it was that solidification . . .

MELVYN BRAGG: Magma under the crust of the earth?

LYNNE FROSTICK: Yes, volcanic material, volcanoes effectively.

MELVYN BRAGG: Which comes up and then hardens?

LYNNE FROSTICK: And as it hardens, so little bits of iron, which there are in this very heavy very dense rock, orient themselves in the direction of the polarity of the earth, where the North Pole is and where the South Pole is. And of course there have been lots of magnetic reversals in the past and what . . .

MELVYN BRAGG: You're going to have to say what you mean by that.

LYNNE FROSTICK: Well, where the North Pole shifts to the South Pole and the South Pole shifts to the North Pole, so the whole thing turns round, and the earth does this repeatedly over time, again and again and again, and we know that and we know that it happens at relatively frequent intervals.

MELVYN BRAGG: And can you work out when it happens?

LYNNE FROSTICK: You can work out when it happens, yes. We've got evidence of when it happens, the age of these reversals. But you look at the seafloor and what you can see is stripes of rock magnetised with the North Pole where it is now, actually at the mid-ocean ridge. Then as you go out from it – reversal – you get the South Pole at the North, the North Pole at the South, and then another stripe with the North Pole at the North and the South Pole at the South. And these are repeated either side.

MELVYN BRAGG: This mid-ocean ridge you're talking about is down the middle of the Atlantic?

LYNNE FROSTICK: Yes, down the Atlantic, there's one. And in the Pacific, not complete. There's a whole string of them around the earth, and I think the description of it as a sort of tennis ball with these seams going all around the earth and joined up is a very good way of thinking of it.

MELVYN BRAGG: So what we're saying is it was the exploration of the oceans, more or less unknown until the Second World War and afterwards, which led to the revolution on this. To the theory of plate tectonics. Can you refine that now, Richard Corfield, how that came about – in Cambridge, these two people?

RICHARD CORFIELD: OK. Actually I wanted just to backtrack a little bit and say something that we'd missed, which is that the mid-ocean ridges, which is where new material is formed, comes out of the work of two American scientists called Bruce Heezen and Marie Tharp, and they were using another new technology – sonar – to produce remarkably detailed maps. So it was known in the 1950s that new materials were coming out at the mid-ocean ridges and it soon became clear that there were earthquakes located there as well, so it's obviously seismically active. Then, as Joe says, the other half of this equation is the work of Hess who, based on gravitational work, showed in the 1950s and early 1960s that the other half of the plate tectonics equation was where this material which is produced must go, which is at the edges of the oceans, that's by subduction. And a consequence of that is that the oceans are very young, the oldest ocean crust is only 180 million years old.

MELVYN BRAGG: And subduction is when one plate hits another and the plate goes under – one plate goes under and so it returns to just under the crust and it returns to the magma . . .

RICHARD CORFIELD: It's recycled.

MELVYN BRAGG: So it isn't lost, it neither expands nor shrinks. Can you just pinpoint for us now, though, Joe Cann, what these people did in Cambridge. They came up with the theory of plate tectonics. Can you say precisely what that theory is?

JOE CANN: It was a very exciting time. I was there as a research student and watched it all happen. The people who drove it forward were a young student called Fred Vine and his supervisor Drummond Matthews. And what Vine and Matthews did was to say let's suppose, let's just suppose, that the seafloor is being created by seafloor spreading. Let's suppose – and this was not established at the time – there are regular reversals of the earth's magnetic field. This should produce a regular stripy pattern as the seafloor spreads and that should be symmetrical about the mid-ocean ridge and we should be able to measure the rate at which the ocean is spreading apart. And that's what they found, that's what they demonstrated, and so we moved from a happy idea to a really quantitative foundation of seafloor spreading.

MELVYN BRAGG: And that theory, which you've called the eureka moment, I'm repeating myself but it's worth repeating, is something that was resisted in America and particularly in Russia. Lynne Frostick, can you tell us why initially it was so heavily resisted?

LYNNE FROSTICK: I think because there was an enormous amount invested in the previous ideas of what was going on. There'd been a lot of observations, a lot of ideas about how things worked and I don't think anyone was ready to give up those ideas. It was only people who really thought beyond the accepted idea that would take this theory on. But it was accepted relatively quickly. If you compare it with the ideas of Copernicus and how long they took to permeate through astronomy, seafloor spreading, plate tectonics, really did speak to a lot of people because it explained so much.

MELVYN BRAGG: How big an idea was it? I've used the word 'revolutionary' – can you tell us how big an idea it is in geology?

LYNNE FROSTICK: It's a huge idea, because it joins everything up. Before that point we didn't have anything joined up. It makes people look at things holistically, it makes you look at the oceans and the continents together, it makes you look at the sea and the atmosphere together, it makes you look at everything as one. In fact, it's the prelude to what are the ideas at the moment of earth system science – where the earth is one big system and it works together and the driving force of this is plate tectonics.

MELVYN BRAGG: Richard Corfield, before we move on, can you tell us how it works? We've used the word 'plate', we've used the word 'tectonics'. There are seven or nine large plates and innumerable smaller plates. What goes on specifically?

RICHARD CORFIELD: What's happening is that the continents which are granite are carried around on the oceanic crust, which is basalt, and the crust is continually moving. Imagine a conveyor belt in Sainsbury's – moving, moving, moving. Imagine two conveyor belts in Sainsbury's converging on each other. And that is the situation that you have with plate tectonics. Because the plates are continually moving towards each other and being subconducted underneath each other, the continents are moving closer and closer together. For example, even as we speak Africa is closing in on southern Europe.

The Mediterranean that we know and love for our family holidays is in fact the remnant of a world-girdling super-ocean which went right around the world, around the equator, called Tethis. So the Mediterranean is in fact a sad remnant of a once great ocean. And in 150 million years it won't be there, there'll be a range of mountains which will already be called the Mediterranean mountains. And in 250 million years the Mediterranean mountains will be even higher; the Atlantic will be only a sad little pond locked up a new super-continent called Ultima Pangaea. So this is what's happening. The continents are always moving and – as a function of plate tectonics – crashing into each other, continuously reshaping the surface of the earth.

MELVYN BRAGG: Joe Cann, what's going on underneath the plates – they're not only crashing into each other, they're pulling away from each other, they're converging and diverging? What's the deeper structure of the planet?

JOE CANN: The fascinating thing is that the sliding of the plates as they move along is almost silent. They are definitely moving, absolutely, but as they move you see earthquakes at the edges of the plates but you don't see a sheet of earthquakes underneath the plates. So the earthquakes are sliding on a soft sole about a hundred kilometres down and that soft sole is the earth's mantle with tiny little bits of melt in it. It's lubricated by these little bits of melt, drops of melt in a mantle at that depth, deeper down it becomes solid, above that it's solid but there's just a narrow zone where it's soft and it's the existence of that soft zone that allows the plates to slide so comfortably over the surface of the earth. And of course as they slide oceanic floor goes. There's about three square kilometres of new seafloor created every year and three square kilometres are destroyed. The plates move about as fast as your fingernails grow, about as fast as your hair grows.

But when the continents arrive, the continents are great thick objects, they don't sink, they can't be recycled, they smash into each other, they collide, they're complicated because continents have got all sorts of ancient fissures – they've got wrinkles and creases in them, just as we somewhat senior citizens have wrinkles and creases. And this means that when they're squashed, instead of behaving simply, as the ocean floor does, they break along old fracture lines, they're more complicated. So the Himalayas, the mountains where two continents are colliding, get quite complicated.

MELVYN BRAGG: Lynne Frostick, what happens when a plate is driven back into the earth? I just want us to be under no doubt as to what is actually going on. Things are moving, Joe's told us how they can move so, as it were, apparently easily, but they do collide and these collisions do result in the Himalayas and great ridges across the Atlantic. They do diverge and the result is the Atlantic is getting wider, just as the Pacific is getting smaller and so on. But when it's driven back into the earth, can you tell us what happens?

LYNNE FROSTICK: Yes. What happens is that the lighter plate, which is normally the one with the continent on it, because that's much lighter material than the ocean floor, when it meets the ocean floor plate – and it depends what's on the plates as to what happens – the ocean floor, because it's denser, heavier, it actually dips down beneath the continental part of the plate. And as it dips down so there's friction, so there's heat and so there's melting and this creates volcanic activity and creates mountain ranges. But this dipping down is a very strong feature and it occurs all round the edges, for example, of the Pacific, around the Rim of Fire there are what are called ocean trenches, they're the deepest places in the oceans.

MELVYN BRAGG: And also the Rim of Fire – that's where the earthquakes and volcanoes . . .

LYNNE FROSTICK: And that's where the earthquakes and the volcanoes are.

MELVYN BRAGG: Because of the plate boundary activity?

LYNNE FROSTICK: Because of the plate boundary and huge amounts of activity. You think about how much energy is expended by pushing or pulling the slab of oceanic crust beneath a plate. It's an enormous amount and that is realised as earthquakes and it also in the end causes the melting which forms the volcanoes. These huge volcanoes, such as those in the Andes and along the west coast of America, are all part of this whole melting system. And interestingly we only found this because of the atomic tests during the fifties where there were masses of seismometers set up around the globe to detect these bits of seismic activity. And as a result of that they detected seismic activity around these edges of the plates and particularly along a line which declines towards the continent at an angle of about 40–60 degrees, and that's called a benioff zone, that's the subduction zone, that's where the plate goes.

MELVYN BRAGG: Does this enable you more accurately to predict when earthquakes will arise and volcanoes will explode?

LYNNE FROSTICK: We can say where they're going to be and we can say that there might be earthquakes due because stress is building up, but predicting precisely when they occur is a very imprecise science. It's actually quite difficult.

JOE CANN: It's intriguing because before plate tectonics it was always possible to say that this earthquake was a one-off thing, and wasn't going to happen again, this volcano was a one-off thing. With plate tectonics we know how fast things are going, how fast they're slipping, we know they're doing it inexorably. So it's not possible to say there won't be another big earthquake on the San Andreas Fault because it's just stopped. It hasn't stopped, it can't stop, it's part of the whole plate tectonic system. The San Andreas Fault is constantly moving, building up strain, and of course eventually it'll snap.

RICHARD CORFIELD: And Los Angeles will disappear into the Pacific.

LYNNE FROSTICK: Could I make a point there, because there's an interesting fact about the South Island, New Zealand, which is along a plate boundary. There's a very large fault there which is overdue to move. We know that because there are stresses building up between the plates there. And that makes the probability of it moving most likely today and less likely to go off into the future. It's most likely to go today because it's so overdue. So we can make those probabilistic predictions. What we can't do is say it's going to happen tomorrow so therefore everybody move out.

RICHARD CORFIELD: The Boxing Day tsunami of 2004 is a good example of this. That strain had been building for a long time but, as we've discussed on this programme many times before, a long time to a geologist is not the same thing as a long time to everybody else.

MELVYN BRAGG: Richard Corfield, while I'm with you, what's this movement, where does the energy come from? I mean these massive continents moving all the time, the ocean floor moving, what is driving it?

RICHARD CORFIELD: Well, the energy ultimately comes from the radioactive activity in the centre of the earth, which causes . . .

MELVYN BRAGG: At the core, what's called the core . . . ?

RICHARD CORFIELD: Yes. Which causes the material above it in the mantle to flow like toffee. If you imagine a big cauldron of molten toffee above the heat on your stove, the convection currents in it are coming up towards the top. When they reach the top they move aside. There are variations on this whole great plate tectonic scheme. One of the most interesting is the islands of Hawaii. If you look at them they stretch north-west across the Pacific in a little chain and that is because underneath that sector of the Pacific is what's called a mantle plume and the plate, as it's moving across, is like holding a candle underneath a wax plate, the wax is bubbling, forming these volcanic islands which are the Hawaiian islands.

So plate tectonics, which is ultimately a function of this interior heat, is not only just about mid-ocean ridges and subduction zones, it's also about phenomena which happen in the centre of the oceans and on the continents as well. And the biggest volcanic or super-plume province in the world is the Ontong Java Plateau in the western equatorial Pacific when material bubbled up from the centre of the earth in a catastrophic outpouring about 150 million years ago.

MELVYN BRAGG: Lynne, Richard gave us a view of what might happen 100 million or 250 million years ahead where the Mediterranean becomes a puddle and the Atlantic Ocean becomes the size of the Mediterranean – what else do you think will happen if we wind the clock on forward in 100 million years?

LYNNE FROSTICK: I think those are the things which tectonically will happen. But if you think about it, the rearrangement of the plates on the surface of the earth actually affects our ocean currents and our ocean currents affect our atmospheric circulation patterns. So as the distribution of land and sea and the distribution of the oceans change, what happens as a consequence of that is that the ocean current changes and the atmosphere changes, which changes what lives or what can live on the surface of the earth. So the plate tectonic movements and the changes of oceans are very important.

One example of this I can give you from the past is that in the South Atlantic, as the Atlantic opened there came a point when the Benguela current, which is a really cold current coming up from the Antarctic, (it comes up the west coast of Africa), when that's switched on that actually caused a movement of cold sea to the north and it caused a complete change in the climate of Africa and a change in the climate across that whole area. So there are huge consequences for these changes. It's not just that land and sea changes but everything else changes in concert with the changes in the distribution of land and sea.

MELVYN BRAGG: Do you want to come in on this, Joe?

JOE CANN: Yes. The fact that we have an ice cap on Antarctica and that we have the weather patterns we see in the Southern Ocean is almost certainly related to the fact that about 30 million years ago

Australia split from Antarctica, South America split from Antarctica, opening up a circumglobal, circumantarctic current system, allowing the winds to blow, the currents to flow and that totally changed the weather pattern in the southern hemisphere.

MELVYN BRAGG: Why would you say that the ocean floor has been so special in the development of this? We've referred to it several times, but why so special, why was it that which caused things to move forward so dramatically and effectively?

JOE CANN: One of the great pioneers in this whole business – J. Tuzo Wilson – said if you want to know whether a ship is moving you don't look at the deck, you have to look over the side. And he argued that for hundreds of years geologists had been only looking at the decks of their ships and not looking at the water flowing by. And so they were able to disprove ocean floor spreading, plate tectonics, by a whole series of arguments based on what they saw on the deck of the ship. And fundamentally they were wrong. This was a very interesting example of the fact that they produced what they considered to be scientific disproofs of a theory when in fact these disproofs have been falsified. A philosophical point but a very intriguing one. We always talk about how science has these theories and they can be disproved but the disproofs themselves can be disproved. So science is a much more fluid thing than just saying I've managed to show you're wrong.

MELVYN BRAGG: I'd just like a footnote. I know that compared with Copernicus the theory of plate tectonics was accepted quite rapidly, but nevertheless it took a while in America and Russia for this to be accepted. When you went to talk about this in America you were hauled up next day by the head of the department who told you up with this he would not put.

JOE CANN: Yes. This was 1965, when in the UK there was no doubt about the plates moving – well, not in the University of Bristol, perhaps, but certainly there was in most other parts of the UK – there was no doubt that the ocean floor was spreading, plates were moving. I went for a job interview in Columbia University and it might not have been helped by the fact that at the time I had a

Beatle haircut and was wearing 1960s British clothes which didn't look too good over there in the States. But I gave a talk in which I said, 'I'm going to start by assuming that it is demonstrated that the seafloor is spreading and that mid-ocean ridges are where they're splitting apart.' And I was told, 'right, thank you.' I blew it right there. The next day the head of the institution called me and said, 'Cann, very interesting, very interesting, but I can show you you're wrong.' And he unreeled a great chart that his ships had made by dropping explosive charges over the side of the ship every minute for day after day showing the sediments in the South Atlantic. He said, 'if those continents were moving these sediments would all be deformed, absolutely all be deformed, they're not deformed at all, they're totally undeformed, so the continents cannot be moving.'

MELVYN BRAGG: Let's talk about how this discovery, this idea, fed into the notion of what the earth is in more detail. Can I start with you, Lynne? It's often referred to as a paradigm shift in scientific understanding. How has it changed the way that we think about the planet?

LYNNE FROSTICK: It's changed the way we think because now we can fit everything together and, I think I mentioned this before, we have this idea of a system science. It was a eureka moment because before that we had lots of people going around making huge detailed measurements of everything and having their own ideas about why this particular observation was made – why these rocks are there, why they're the age they are, why they look like they do – but nothing joined it together. So what it did was it made people start thinking laterally, to start thinking about both the underlying rocks – the volcanic, the sediments, the age. You couldn't get away from geophysics because you had to understand what the geophysical basis was, you had to understand seismic, you had to understand a whole load of things.

It stopped people being in their compartments. Before that I think geology was in compartments: you did petrology, you did fossils, you did sediments and you learnt it in compartments. What this did was it put the whole thing together and it put it together with the atmospheric sciences and the oceanic sciences and to me that's the most exciting thing.

RICHARD CORFIELD: The essence of plate tectonics is that it demonstrates the interconnectivity between things like the rock cycle and the climate cycle and ultimately the cycle of life, which somehow seems to be bound up with plate tectonics in a fundamental way.

MELVYN BRAGG: In what way?

RICHARD CORFIELD: Well, for example, the most obvious example is in the mid-1970s, when people started visiting the mid-ocean ridges for the first time in deep-sea submersibles. They found that the mid-ocean ridges teemed with life. Not life which is ultimately based on the character of energy by photosynthesis, which is what we have on the surface of the earth, but the capture of energy by chemosynthesis because there's no light down there. And so you have a very, very unusual community of organisms down on the mid-ocean ridges, the so-called black smoker communities, because the material which is pouring out from the centre of the earth is smoking blackly in the water. This has opened up a new discipline and there are those who say in fact that life may have originated at the mid-ocean ridges.

But a less obvious example of the way that plate tectonics would influence life on earth is the fact, as we discussed at the beginning of the programme, that the continents have moved. A very good example is the isolation of Australia, which is largely populated by an unusual type of mammal, the marsupials. When Australia separated from South America and the circumantarctic current formed and Australia was drifting away from Antarctica and South America, they became geographically isolated. This allowed the marsupial mammals to evolve in isolation into a whole series of parallel niches in the same way that their placental mammal cousins in the northern hemisphere were doing. That's an indirect example of the way that plate tectonics has influenced life on earth by isolating populations and powering evolution.

MELVYN BRAGG: Joe Cann, can you tell us how the movement of plates influences the oceans?

JOE CANN: It influences the oceans in a number of ways and I suppose the most striking way is that it makes it easier for organisms to grow shells. And it does this because over a few million years every drop of ocean water circulates through the ocean floor and as it does so all the magnesium in the ocean waters is stripped out and deposited as minerals inside the ocean floor and the fluid that comes out, this black smoker fluid that Richard was just talking about, has basically no magnesium in it. So having all of this plate tectonic activity going on and the oceans going through it means that the ratio of calcium to magnesium in the oceans is much higher than it would be in the absence of plate tectonics and because it's nice and high it makes it easy for molluscs and creatures to grow their shells with calcium carbonate. That's slightly indirect but it works.

MELVYN BRAGG: By indirections ... Can you tell us, Lynne, how this might tie in with what I'm sure people are thinking about, James Lovelock and the Gaia Theory, which came out in '69 around about the same time or near enough. Can you tell us how and if Gaia Theory ties in with the theory of plate tectonics?

LYNNE FROSTICK: I think it does to an extent, although I'm not a great fan of the Gaia Theory. I see plate tectonics being the heart and lungs, if you have a Gaia Theory, the heart and lungs of the planet. It's the thing which drives everything else. In a way you could say plate tectonics is the foundation of it because it fits every-thing together, because it creates effectively the opportunities for evolution, it creates the distribution of land and sea, it does all of that and therefore it is, if you like, the driving mechanism for the Gaia Theory, and it fits everything together. But I'd rather have earth system science. It is a systematic scientific basis of the earth and it physically, chemically, all fits together and I don't need any other theory than that.

JOE CANN: I disagree with you.

LYNNE FROSTICK: I know you do.

JOE CANN: I have to say I disagree with you. I'm a great fan of Gaia because Gaia is basically saying that it's the microbial communities on earth that control the environment, that arrange things to suit themselves. After all, we are just microbial colonised things, we are made up of a whole body of microbes that choose to live together to make our bodies.

LYNNE FROSTICK: But the distribution of the microbes relies effectively on the distribution of minerals, the distribution of water, the distribution of everything else. So the basis of it is plate tectonics and I'm happy with that.

JOE CANN: Microbes are extraordinarily flexible creatures . . .

LYNNE FROSTICK: Oh they are, yes.

JOE CANN: . . . they can adapt to almost any environment much better than we can.

MELVYN BRAGG: So it seems that they're slightly in opposition – the Gaia Theory and the theory coming out of plate tectonics – would you say, Richard Corfield?

RICHARD CORFIELD: The idea that the earth is a living organism, which is one aspect of extreme Gaianism, if I can put it that way, is patently absurd. The earth is not living, it has no other characteristics of life. The idea that human beings, for example, or animals or plants are colonisations of microbes is also, in my view, absurd. The idea that we are composed of microbes which billions of years ago fused and evolved together to form something new, for example, chloroplasts and mitochondria, is a function of evolution and so of course at that point you're no longer a microbe, in fact you're part of an organ system, which is like the earth but on a smaller scale. So I have to say I have no use, under any circumstances, in any way, for any aspect of the Gaia hypothesis.

JOE CANN: You two – Lynne and Richard – you're being so wimpish, I can't believe – I can't believe what I'm hearing.

RICHARD CORFIELD: Well, we're also being quite accurate.

JOE CANN: No, you're not, you're being – you're like the people before plate tectonics came in, you're like these people who stood up and said, as somebody said in 1928, if continental drift is happening, then everything that has been done for the last seventy years is wrong. That's what you're saying, that's exactly what you're saying.

RICHARD CORFIELD: Well, it's not what I'm saying, actually, Joe.

MELVYN BRAGG: I don't think it is what he's saying, Joe, to be honest. I think he got carried away – with the greatest respect – I don't think that's what he's saying. Do you want to say what you were saying, or do you want Lynne to come in?

RICHARD CORFIELD: Well, I will just reiterate the point that to call animals collections of microbes is patently absurd, we are constructed out of cells which may have evolved out of organisms billions of years ago, they are not microbes. Lynne?

LYNNE FROSTICK: I would agree with that. Microbial symbiosis started the whole thing off and we became multicellular organisms, but I would maintain that the distribution of those micro-organisms and their capacity to live originally came from plate tectonics. So whatever you say, plate tectonics is at the base of this.

JOE CANN: Well, I would agree with that, as it happens. I mean the way that you've just phrased it, Lynne, is acceptable.

LYNNE FROSTICK: Thank you.

JOE CANN: I mean, fundamentally life wouldn't exist without plate tectonics. Plate tectonics is there because the earth is wet, the plates are only moving across the surface of the earth because there's water that seeps down into the mantle and softens the mantle and lets the plates slide. And life originated in the oceans from the chemical energy that comes out of the source in plate tectonics.

LYNNE FROSTICK: This has implications for other planets and the potential for life on other planets and I think it's quite important to understand that the earth is relatively unique. There is evidence of some tectonics on other parts, in other parts of the solar system, but not much and I think that's actually very important for life and potential for life.

RICHARD CORFIELD: One of the interesting things about Mars is that it has this peculiar topographical distribution with this cratered high terrain in the southern hemisphere and uncratered low terrain in the northern hemisphere. That suggest that there may have been plate tectonics on Mars billions of years ago. It stopped, so we're quite lucky still to have ours. On the other hand, on Venus there is no plate tectonics, there is only volcanism, so we are quite lucky to have plate tectonics fuelling our planet.

MELVYN BRAGG: And so you can summarise by saying it is a revolutionary idea that has revolutionised the way we look at the planet?

JOE CANN: Yes.

LYNNE FROSTICK: Absolutely.

TRANSMITTED: 24.01.2008

Kierkegaard

In 1840, a young Danish girl called Regine Olsen got engaged to her sweetheart – a difficult and brilliant young man called Søren Kierkegaard. The two were much in love but soon Kierkegaard began to have doubts. He worried that he couldn't love Regine and stay true to himself and his philosophy. It was a dilemma, and Kierkegaard broke off the engagement – a decision from which neither he nor his fiancée fully recovered.

This unhappy episode has become emblematic of the life and thought of Søren Kierkegaard – a philosopher who confronted the painful choices in life in the light of his philosophy, and who endured dark times perhaps as a consequence. Yet Kierkegaard is much more than the gloomy Lutheran Dane of reputation. A thinker of wit and elegance, his ability to live with paradox, his admiration for both Socrates and Christ, his hatred of Hegel and his desire to think about individuals as free have given him great purchase in the modern world and he is known as the father of existentialism.

With me to discuss Søren Kierkegaard are John Lippitt, Professor of Ethics and Philosophy of Religion at the University of Hertfordshire; Clare Carlisle, Lecturer in Philosophy at the University of Liverpool; and Jonathan Ree, Visiting Professor at Roehampton University and at the Royal College of Art.

Jonathan Ree, as a young man at the University of Copenhagen, Kierkegaard was a devotee of Socrates. What did he admire about Socrates?

JONATHAN REE: He was a student, I think, for about ten years in the 1830s in Copenhagen University, a student of philosophy, and he would have been taught about the history of philosophy as a huge narrative that begins with Socrates. Socrates as the father of philosophy. Socrates is the first person who tried to use logical argument as a route to truth. And then the idea was that once that had been started in fifth-century BC Athens, it was carried forward by Plato and Aristotle and it grew into a great massive oak tree of metaphysics that flourished, perhaps over-flourished, in the Middle Ages and then was pruned by Descartes, the father of modern philosophy, and then it gradually developed again and it blossomed in the work of Hegel. Hegel provided out of the clues that had existed and been scattered around the previous history of philosophy a complete system, a theory of everything.

Hegel died in 1831, the very year that Kierkegaard began his studies at Copenhagen University, and Kierkegaard slowly began to become convinced that this whole story was a mistake and the idea that Hegel was the truest disciple of the Socratic tradition was a lie. In truth Hegel's ambition to create a whole system of philosophy was something that Socrates would have laughed at because Socrates' secret, according to Kierkegaard, was that Socrates reckoned everyone was a fool and he was the biggest fool of all – the difference was that he knew it. And he thought that the task of philosophy was not to build up a system of knowledge but to take down our pretensions to know more than we really do.

MELVYN BRAGG: Would it be correct, Jonathan, to say that one of the attractions that Socrates had for Kierkegaard was that, according to Kierkegaard, Socrates did not propose one correct point of view of the world?

JONATHAN REE: Exactly. The byword for Socrates is irony, Socrates was the paradigm of an ironist. That means not just that he's a joker, it does mean that, but it also means that he's someone who engages in conversation not in order to express the truths which he takes himself to be in possession of but to go with the ebb and flow. He thinks that truth happens in the ebb and flow of conversation, of engagements with other people. And the idea was that you could never tell from what Socrates said what Socrates really thought because all he was interested in doing was teasing out the inconsistencies in what his interlocutors were saying. That's what's meant by saying he's an ironist and that's exactly what Kierkegaard took from him because Kierkegaard then developed a theory – the theory of indirect communication – which said that with regard to the truths that are most important to us, they're not the kinds of things that can be transferred from one mind to another.

You may be able to provoke someone into discovering those truths – in fact Kierkegaard said you may be able to seduce someone or deceive someone into the truth. I suppose you could say he wanted to be the Socrates for the nineteenth century. Socrates famously never wrote anything down. There are all these stories of what he said. Kierkegaard wrote enormously but he wrote under many different pseudonyms, he wrote in different styles, he wrote in different genres. One of the great things about Kierkegaard is that you can never be quite sure whether what you read in his books is what Kierkegaard meant or whether it's some kind of stunt he's performing in order to try and kind of rearrange the furniture inside his readers' heads.

MELVYN BRAGG: Clare Carlisle, can we turn to Hegel? If Socrates was Kierkegaard's hero, this is a bit of a simplification, but not too much perhaps, Hegel was his villain. Now Jonathan has said something about that already, can we develop it? What had Hegel done to earn Kierkegaard's ire?

CLARE CARLISLE: As Jonathan says, Hegel is the epitome of a systematic philosopher. That's to say he wants to construct a self-grounding and all-encompassing totality of thought that incorporates nature, history, religion, art and of course the human being within that totality. Kierkegaard did accept that man is a part of nature, a part of history, a part of society to some extent, but he also thought that the human being has an inner life, inwardness as he calls it, that is separate from this outside world and that can't be assimilated into a system, that can't be rationalised, that can't even perhaps be articulated. And it's that inward sphere that Kierkegaard thinks Hegel's philosophy doesn't do justice to.

MELVYN BRAGG: Kierkegaard had been brought up by a Lutheran father, he was a Christian but he was very strongly against the Christian state Church, particularly the Danish Christian state Church. He thought that it was soporific and it missed the point, it was nothing to do with being a real Christian.

CLARE CARLISLE: Kierkegaard made a distinction between Christianity and Christendom. Christendom is the sort of social institutionalised religious state, whereas Christianity is to do with the inner life of the individual and that individual's relationship to God. And Kierkegaard said that basically to be a Christian is to have faith, i.e., to live one's life with a certain relationship to God. He identified a complacency in Denmark, precisely because Christianity had become so institutionalised.

Kierkegaard thought that everybody assumed that they were automatically Christians just because they'd been born into this Christian country, because they'd been baptised, because they went to church every Sunday and that that's what it meant to be a Christian. And it's that complacency that Kierkegaard wants to unsettle and to say that having faith is something that lies beyond the sphere of reason, it's not something that can just cleverly be grasped and then one has it. It's much more of an existential task.

MELVYN BRAGG: John Lippitt, because of his stance on faith – let's call it a stance although it's slightly wrong, given that he did do the philosopher in different voices – Kierkegaard has been accused of irrationalism, of going against reason as a basis of judgement. Would you like to explore this? Do you think it's true?

JOHN LIPPITT: The charge that's sometimes made is that he thinks reason is completely redundant and that really isn't his position. What he's rejecting though, I think, is not reason per se but reason conceived of – rather in the way that Clare was saying in describing Hegel – as some kind of timeless, Godlike faculty, Reason with a capital R, if you like. And instead what he's emphasising is the actual reasoning possibilities of creatures like us, historically and temporarily situated, finite, flesh and blood human beings who can't occupy anything other than a limited finite perspective.

So it isn't that he thinks reason is redundant, rather he's part of a long philosophical tradition that's trying to understand what the limits of human reason are. There's a religious dimension to this explicitly in the sense that Kierkegaard's view of human reason is connected with his view of our creatureliness. So our beliefs are always partial, provisional, divisible, we always see through a glass darkly, as it were.

CLARE CARLISLE: To try to construct a philosophical system is to take up an objective standpoint, almost a God's-eye perspective on the whole. Kierkegaard thought that's not a perspective that we as human beings are entitled to. In a sense it's a sinful self-assertion to try to occupy that Godlike position. So on the one hand there's a religious motivation for that critique but there's also a philosophical motivation for it too, namely that Kierkegaard thinks that we each of us are alive, we're living in the world, we're temporal beings, we're always in the process of becoming and if we do philosophy then we do so from a subjective perspective, from the perspective of what he calls the existing individual.

And from this perspective of the existing individual there are elements to our existence, elements to our life, that are unknown, that can't be rationalised. So, for example, we live our lives forwards, but as Kierkegaard famously said we can only understand them backwards, so we live our lives forwards towards the future and that future is something that's unknown. He thought we live our lives in relationship to God, God is something that's unknown. So for Kierkegaard there's an unknown, unknowable, unrationalisable dimension to human existence that can't be reduced to some kind of systematic explanation.

MELVYN BRAGG: John Lippitt, can I ask you something before we move into a more general discussion? When he was twenty-two he wrote: 'what I really need to be clear about is what I'm to do, not what I must know.' Can you fit that in?

JOHN LIPPITT: I think to understand that journal entry – Kierkegaard was famously a keeper of voluminous journals – we need to understand one or two of the other ideas that are in there. He talks about the need to find a truth 'which is true for me, the idea for which I am willing to live and die'. The contrast there between action and knowledge is in one sense slightly misleading. He does recognise in that very same journal entry an imperative of knowledge, so it isn't that knowledge doesn't matter. But he says 'it must be taken up alive in me'. So introduced very early on is this important idea of truth as subjectivity, which is again a slightly misleading phrase. It isn't the rejection of the objective truth, it's not relativism, it's not subjectivism, rather it's an insistence on placing this concrete finite human subject at the centre of enquiry.

MELVYN BRAGG: Can I go to Jonathan Ree here. There are no universal answers, as you said in your opening remarks, no final goal, but if truth is an objective where does Kierkegaard think truth is to be found?

JONATHAN REE: In a way he thinks it's going to be found in Jesus Christ, that's the short answer. But not in the way that most Christians think that. He was very preoccupied by a problem that was buried in 2,000 years of Christianity, about the relationship between classical pagan philosophy – Socrates, Plato and Aristotle – and the true, as he saw it, the Christian tradition that was written in Aramaic and Hebrew. It's true that both Socrates and Jesus were heroes to him, but he thought they pulled in different directions. Socrates thought there was such a thing as truth and that it's just that we can't get hold of it. And that truth existed eternally and pre-existed us, that's to say he thought that the task of learning was actually a matter of recollecting, that the really important truths are things that we knew in a former life, that we originally knew or that nature would teach us.

Kierkegaard says you can't be a Christian and buy any of that because if you're a Christian you think that at a particular date a new truth came into history, that Christianity is historical in a way that pagan philosophy is not, that a truth became possible that had never existed before. And that's why it's a rather confusing set of discussions that Kierkegaard has about the idea of repetition, about truth as something that is to be repeated.

I think the key to that is he's saying it's the opposite of recollection, truth is something that goes towards the future, it goes towards something that's open. And there are truths that exist, thanks to Jesus Christ, which didn't exist in the world before him and that was a thought that pagan philosophy couldn't have. It's not a denial of truth but it's an idea that truth is historical rather than eternal.

MELVYN BRAGG: How does this play to the idea of subjectivity, though, Jonathan?

JONATHAN REE: There is the slogan of Kierkegaard's which says that something like truth is inwardness, truth is subjectivity, in some of the books from the middle 1840s. But as I understand it, maybe I'm rather at the literary end of the interpretations of Kierkegaard, he's saying if there was a truth that could be directly communicated then it would be that the truth, at least truth in regard to the really important matters, is subjective and inward. But of course that can't be communicated and that's why we have to use all these roundabout storytelling, lyrical, dialectical methods rather than simply saying. The phrase truth is subjective – it expresses a truth that can't be expressed. In other words, by putting it like that you're deforming it.

CLARE CARLISLE: Just to add to that, Kierkegaard somewhere says that the distinction between objective truth and subjective truth can be understood as a distinction between what and how. So objective truth is a matter of what is known or what is believed. Subjective truth is a matter of how one appropriates that truth or, in other words, how one lives. So Kierkegaard thinks that we can live truthfully or we can live untruthfully and to live untruthfully involves self-deception. Hence the Socratic methods to try to illuminate that self-deception. Or we can live truthfully and that's, I think, what he means by saying that subjectivity is truth.

MELVYN BRAGG: Can I turn to you, John Lippitt? Kierkegaard had an idea of three stages in life – the aesthetic, the ethical and the religious. Let's start with the aesthetic. What is it to live an aesthetic life?

JOHN LIPPITT: The aesthetic emerges first and perhaps most clearly in a book called *Either/Or*, which is a particularly good example of the many voices that Jonathan was alluding to earlier. The book is divided basically into two parts: there's this story about the sets of papers having been found in a secret drawer of a desk – things are always being found in unusual places in Kierkegaard, in one case a locked box at the bottom of a lake. These seem to be papers which represent two different life views: the aesthetic and the ethical. And in the first the aesthetic papers seem to be the papers of an unnamed young man who is only known as A, who represents a state of extreme ennui and boredom with life.

MELVYN BRAGG: What did he mean by aesthetic? It might be useful to go into the word aesthetic because he didn't mean what it's now become. We're talking about a different interpretation of the word, aren't we?

JOHN LIPPITT: To understand that we need to understand a little bit about the tradition of German aesthetics – Kant and so on – which talks about the aesthetic attitude as being one of essential disinterest. So what the aesthete is trying to do is to bring this disinterested, disengaged, contemplative kind of attitude to life as a whole. And the result is that people become like pieces to be moved around on his chess board, manipulated. He's not prepared to engage with anything, he's not prepared to throw himself into existence.

CLARE CARLISLE: The aesthetic person is really one who organ- ises his life around the principle of pleasure. He's a hedonist in a sense. The irony of the aesthetic way of life is that actually it's self- defeating. It leads to despair, not just a kind of melancholy but more profoundly. What Kierkegaard means by despair is the loss of oneself or the failure to become oneself.

JOHN LIPPITT: So the young man sets himself the idea that the most important thing is to avoid boredom. And in order to do this he says one needs to avoid the things that might inspire boredom, such as commitments, so he advises to avoid marriage, avoid friend- ship, avoid a useful career. The ethical character – Judge William – will try to persuade him that this is precisely what is of value in life.

MELVYN BRAGG: Would you like to add to that, Clare?

CLARE CARLISLE: Kierkegaard thinks that the aesthetic sphere is what you end up with if you try to live in accordance with Hegelian principles. So in a sense part of his critique of Hegel is to say that doing philosophy, thinking abstractedly, trying to take up an objec- tive standpoint is, from an existential point of view, just to be confined to this aesthetic sphere, which Kierkegaard thinks is the lowest of the different kinds of existence that he outlines.

MELVYN BRAGG: Why does he think it's the lowest?

JONATHAN REE: Well, I'm not sure that he does exactly think it's the lowest. That's to say I'm not sure he's got such a clear sense of there being three different places, the aesthetic, ethical and religious.

MELVYN BRAGG: Mucks up my question! Yet he did claim the three stages.

JONATHAN REE: To think of it like that is to put it in an objectivising way already. And one of the great things about *Either/Or* is that it looks as though it's two sets of papers. Then actually the papers contain transcripts of some of the stuff by other people and then the editor says, actually I don't think they're by two people at all, I think they're all by the same person. And so you end up thinking it's not as though there's a choice between different ways of going about things.

The only bit that's actually called 'either/or' in the book called *Either/Or* is a little discussion, where the guy says: 'either/or – marry you'll regret it, don't marry you'll regret it; laugh with the follies of the world or weep over them, you'll regret it either way; hang yourself or don't hang yourself, you'll regret it either way.' In fact it's not as though he's saying you have to make the right choice, you have to be aware there are choices to be made. The most important thing is that you have to realise that your interests are vitally at stake in what you think and the important thing is not so much what opinions you have but how you live those opinions.

MELVYN BRAGG: Right. I got the impression, and if I'm completely wrong, I'm wrong, that there was a hierarchy. It was a three-tier view that the aesthetic was youthful and in the end inadequate and you moved to the ethical and you moved up or you improved or matured and on to the religious. Is that completely wrong, John Lippitt, and, if not, can you talk about the ethical?

JOHN LIPPITT: OK. I think this is where the many voices becomes important. In someone like the pseudonym Johannes Climacus, for example, I think it is quite clear that there is a hierarchy of stages and he uses this imagery of height all the time – ascending at various stages. But I think what I agree with about what Jonathan was suggesting is that it isn't like when you move on to the ethical stage you leave behind the aesthetic stage altogether.

MELVYN BRAGG: Sorry to interrupt and obviously I'm a total amateur here, but still. Judge William, who's also in this discussion with A, he's the older person. He says what you're doing will not be a satisfying life, he says marriage might require a sacrifice but if you stay with the sacrifice it will be well worth it and so on. So there is a distinction, there is a different attitude to life. And that is one of the things that fascinates people. I think Kierkegaard was the philosopher of choice for people who didn't read philosophy. He talked so much about these things that interest you at a certain stage in your life. But there is a difference there, isn't there?

JOHN LIPPITT: That's right, but in the case of Judge William, one of his two long letters to A is called 'The Aesthetic Validity of Marriage'. And part of the technique there is not to say, 'oi, young man, you've got this completely wrong.' In general the tactic – the communication tactic – seems to be to try to persuade A, the young man, the aesthetic, that what he truly values he will get in transfigured form if he moves on to the ethical. So for example A, he thinks, is besotted by the idea of first love, butterflies in the stomach and all that. What the Judge tries to do . . .

MELVYN BRAGG: Perpetually recurring first love?

JOHN LIPPITT: Precisely. What the Judge tries to do is to say the kind of beauty that you claim to see in first love – marital love gives you this squared. So it's an attempt to try to persuade A that what you're really valuing you can get by this kind of move, rather than just preaching at him directly.

MELVYN BRAGG: Can you enter into this, Clare. From your view of it, is there a sense of movement from the aesthetic? Jonathan has quite correctly fudged it and confused it and that's Kierkegaard, that's fine, but I would like to see if we can also make clear distinctions and I think a distinction has begun to emerge. Will you develop what John Lippitt has just said?

CLARE CARLISLE: Yes. I think one way of looking at this theory of the spheres or stages is precisely as an aid to self-reflection. Kierkegaard thinks people deceive themselves. They don't really know where they stand, they just assume that they're Christians. What Kierkegaard does in his texts is present characters who are living different kinds of life and invite the reader to identify him or herself with one of these characters. So, for example, what Kierkegaard's saying is that you can live what from the outside seems to be a Christian life but actually you're living in a purely aesthetic way. And then the ethical sphere has a different organising principle and that is the principle of living a moral life and having duties and responsibilities. And Kierkegaard says that ultimately that is self-defeating too, that's also going to lead to despair because the human condition is such that the ideal moral life is not attainable, because we're finite creatures, because we're not perfect or, as Kierkegaard would say, because we're all sinners.

And so the ethical ends in despair too because we're not able to live up to the moral standards that are required and that's where the move to the religious sphere comes. So the distinction between the ethical sphere and the religious sphere is the individual's realisation that he's not sufficient to attain the ideal by himself and that he needs to turn to God, he needs to open himself up to divine grace – he needs some kind of help and that's where the transition from the ethical sphere to the religious sphere takes place.

MELVYN BRAGG: Jonathan Ree, in his book *Fear and Trembling* he uses the story of Abraham's decision to obey the injunction to sacrifice his son Isaac to move from the aesthetic to the ethical, and he'll move into the religious sphere. Can you tell us what he meant by that and why that was an extremely pertinent story to tell?

JONATHAN REE: I think the first thing to say about the story of Abraham's willingness to sacrifice his only son, Isaac, is that by any ordinary moral or indeed aesthetic standards it's a completely outrageous thing to do. The Father of the Faiths turns out to be a child murderer, or willing to be a child murderer, and he did it just because God told him to. In a generation before Kierkegaard, Kant had said this was absolutely immoral. If Abraham seriously intended to carry out God's injunction then that was immoral of him, he should have told God, 'what you're demanding is impossible.' Kierkegaard is saying, actually there's something much more interesting here. And I love the way he begins this book, *Fear and Trembling*, subtitled *A Dialectical Lyric*, which is to say a kind of logical poem, a contradiction in terms, it's a generic nothing, this book. It has this wonderful little section called 'Atonement', where it says once upon a time there was a man and as a child he'd read the wonderful story about Abraham and Isaac and as he grew older he kept going back to it and the more he thought about it the more he loved this story and the more he was fascinated by it and the less he could understand it. And the idea is that the old man who recognised that there was something about Abraham's faith he couldn't understand was wiser than the philosopher Kant who said Abraham's faith was immoral. Because it was an acknowledgement that there is something about leading a good life that we're never going to be able to pin down and reason about. And that's what is involved in faith.

MELVYN BRAGG: But yet, as I understand it, Kierkegaard didn't necessarily think it was leading a good life. He said if a man in a church, in a Danish church, at the time, had stood up and said, 'I will now go and kill my son for God', the congregation would have lynched him or at least prevented him.

JONATHAN REE: Absolutely. There's a very useful phrase that Kierkegaard uses which is 'becoming a Christian', and you might think at first sight the idea of becoming a Christian, you might think, well, it means you grow out of being an aesthete, you grow out of being an ethicist and you become a person of faith. That's not really what Kierkegaard means by becoming a Christian. His idea is that the very idea of being a Christian is contradictory because to be a Christian would be to think of Christianity as a doctrine that you could relax into, like a comfortable armchair. But the whole point about being a Christian is that you always have to be on your guard against relapsing into taking things for granted.

MELVYN BRAGG: Clare Carlisle, how do you interpret this? Jonathan's given us a good outline of the Abraham and Isaac story.

One of the many things Kierkegaard does is to seek out what it is to be a real Christian, just like he seeks out or leads a truthful life. He doesn't seem to find or want to find any certainty, does he?

CLARE CARLISLE: I think there's a question that's raised in *Fear and Trembling*. In *Fear and Trembling* Abraham is represented as the Father of Faith and Kierkegaard says that normally Christians are very complacent about this. We admire Abraham because he's someone who has faith but in fact when we reflect on the story of Abraham we can't understand it. Can we really imagine ourselves doing what Abraham did? And so the question is raised here – is it really possible to have faith? Just as Socrates wanted to disrupt people's assumptions that they already possessed knowledge by saying actually I don't know anything, do you really know something? So Kierkegaard wanted to unsettle people's assumptions that they were already Christians by using his pseudonyms to say actually I'm not a Christian, I don't know if I do have faith, I don't know if I can have faith. Is it even possible to have faith because in the case of Abraham having faith involves believing something that's completely paradoxical and contradictory.

Abraham has faith because he is willing to hold that contradiction and to live his life and to live his relationship to God not just in spite of this contradiction but in full light of this contradiction. What Abraham achieves in the end is to receive Isaac back. He's prepared to give up, he goes through this movement of resignation, as Kierkegaard describes it, and then God changes his mind, Abraham receives Isaac back and so in a sense one always has to give up oneself or give up what is most precious to one in order to be able to receive it back as a gift from God. And it's that receptivity that is the essence of faith. It's not something that we do, it's something that we receive.

JOHN LIPPITT: Yes. There's this theme that comes up in Kierkegaard in a number of different ways and in a number of different voices, of giving something back and giving something up and getting it back in some kind of heightened or transfigured form.

MELVYN BRAGG: Let's move on, because he wrote about so many

different subjects. Let's take his ideas on love. John Lippitt, can you give us an introduction to this?

JOHN LIPPITT: There's a lovely line in the *Journals* where he says fear and trembling is not the prime mover of the Christian life, for this is love. Love is a theme that runs throughout the so-called aesthetic writings, like *Either/Or*, seduction versus married love, the aesthetic versus the ethical. But I think Kierkegaard's mature ethical and religious thought on love is found in an 1847 book called *Works of Love* where he's writing under his own name, so this is not pseudonymous. He unpacks some of the key New Testament passages on love. So, for example, you shall love your neighbour, which he divides up into three different parts – you shall love the neighbour, you *shall* love the neighbour – it's commanded, it's a duty – and you shall love *the* neighbour. So exactly who is the neighbour, as opposed to someone that you're inclined towards or have some kind of friendship with or whatever? And there are several themes that emerge from this. One is the sheer demandingness of Christian love. He has this notion of love as being a duty and he emphasises the Christian injunction that your neighbour includes your enemy and just the sheer difficulty of this. Yet it's commanded. Another is a worry about preferential love. He's forever contrasting Christian love, *agape*, with erotic love and friendship. The main point that he seems to be making there is that preference or inclination can't be the basis of responsibility for the other person.

MELVYN BRAGG: Can I just bring Jonathan in here on this? Be sure to love your neighbour as yourself – I mean a lot of people don't particularly love themselves, so if they give themselves a hard time they might want to give their neighbours a hard time. It sounds horribly flippant but it gets us to the next stage.

JONATHAN REE: But I think it's a really important point. As a kind of morose twenty-first-century secularist I find myself surprised sometimes at finding no one more interesting about these kinds of issues than the great Christian Kierkegaard. There's this old Christian thing about how the Devil has the best tunes, certainly as regards love. *Works of Love* is a very complex book but the main thing

I take from it is the idea that when you say you should love others as you love yourself, the usual way to hear that is to say – exactly as you were suggesting – that there's no problem, we have no problem loving ourselves. Then the question is how do we lend a bit of our self-love to other people, include them in our kind of favouritism towards ourselves? And Kierkegaard's point is that it's not like that at all and that the Christian teaching about loving others as yourself is also a teaching about loving yourself as another. It's a question about what your duty is to yourself as well as what your duty is to others.

JOHN LIPPITT: He makes a distinction, which I think is important in connection with what Jonathan's just been saying, between proper self-love and selfish self-love. So the real challenge is: what is it to love oneself properly as opposed to selfishly?

MELVYN BRAGG: What distinction does he make?

JOHN LIPPITT: Well, this is actually quite hard to pin down – exactly what proper self-love is concerned with. One thing that I would say is that in connection also with what he says about erotic love and friendship, he says the friend, the spouse, is first and foremost the neighbour. You have this important notion that God is the middle term. So both the friend, the spouse and the self need to be loved through God. God is the invisible third in these various kinds of love relationships. So proper self-love would need to incorporate that.

MELVYN BRAGG: Jonathan Ree, given Kierkegaard's religion and what he was trying to do, it's rather surprising that he is known as the father of existentialism. It's a philosophy that presumes the absence of God and the phrase wasn't around in his day. The German philosopher Jaspers coined it in about 1920. How did Jaspers carry Kierkegaard into existentialism?

JONATHAN REE: Well, I'm not sure you're right in the presumption that existentialism and Christianity are incompatible. I think a lot of the twentieth-century existentialists were Christians as well. So existentialism is a house with many rooms. I'm not sure on Jaspers, it's rather difficult to make out where he stood about religion. But what's definitely true is that you can't really object to Kierkegaard being classified as an existentialist, although it's true that the term wasn't invented till 1919–20. It didn't get into the English language until the 1940s, I think.

But Kierkegaard did talk about existences as being the particular quality of the being of the individual subject, as opposed to the being of other things. And Jaspers' is called existence philosophy after Kierkegaard. In a way existence philosophy is his name for Kierkegaard – Kierkegaardism. I think you're probably thinking of Sartre as the paradigmatic existentialist. He was an atheist but he paid enormous tribute to Kierkegaard. You know, there's this phrase of Kierkegaard's about how the problem for the Christian is becoming a Christian, it's something you can never settle into. For the centenary of Kierkegaard's death in 1955, Sartre gave a lecture saying 'for us atheists the problem is becoming an atheist', that it's as difficult for atheists to be atheists as Kierkegaard recognised it was difficult for Christians to be Christians.

MELVYN BRAGG: Clare Carlisle, would you like to develop this idea of becoming, which seems to pertain to what Kierkegaard says about being a Christian and about existentialism too?

CLARE CARLISLE: Yes, that's right. Kierkegaard in fact says that not only is Christianity a matter of becoming a Christian but he also says that to exist is to be continually in a process of becoming. So in a sense what it is to be human is to be a thoroughly temporal finite creature who lives towards the future. And to make that claim involves a critique of systematic philosophy and we can see both Kierkegaard and Nietzsche as two nineteenth-century thinkers who criticise idealism, criticise systematic philosophy in the name of becoming, in the name of life as it's lived from the perspective of the existing individual.

Kierkegaard and Nietzsche's philosophies are in many ways very different, but these two critiques, both very polemical, are then taken up in the twentieth century by philosophers like Martin Heidegger and Sartre and given more flesh. With both Heidegger's book *Being in Time* and Sartre's book *Being in Nothingness* there's almost an attempt to systematise this idea of becoming, to try to articulate an account of what it is to be an existing individual. Whereas we just get flashes of this in Kierkegaard and Nietzsche's writings. But these ideas are taken up and developed and worked out much more coherently in the twentieth-century existentialists.

JONATHAN REE: The other great twentieth-century existentialist who learned from Kierkegaard is W.H. Auden, who did regard himself as something of an existentialist. When Kierkegaard started being translated into English in the late 1930s, Auden absorbed it and he said 'it knocked me completely sideways'. And he became a Kierkegaard lover. There were things about Auden's Christianity that owed a great deal to Kierkegaard and also Auden's sense of the sadness of people who are excessively logical was something that he took from Kierkegaard.

MELVYN BRAGG: How significant do you think his work is now in philosophy and in the general run? Jonathan's indicated that through Auden and through a great number of others he influenced many creative writers and other artists. Where is he placed now, what's the view of him? Can we start with you, John?

JOHN LIPPITT: Clare's already connected Kierkegaard with Nietzsche and I think one thing that they have in common is the sheer range of different philosophical positions that have tried to claim both Nietzsche and Kierkegaard for their own. I think he straddles the often-made analytical continental kind of distinction. We've been talking mostly about existentialism, but one way in which a more traditional kind of Anglo-American philosopher might locate him is in terms of his contribution to the virtues. There's been a lot of work recently on virtue ethics and the significance of the virtues. And I think Kierkegaard is one source that we could draw on for an understanding of specifically theological virtues like faith, hope and love.

CLARE CARLISLE: Kierkegaard's a bottomless pit, really. His philosophy is so rich and so complex that there is a wealth of resources there in various different philosophical traditions that we find ourselves with. Because Kierkegaard has these theological categories that he operates with, people often would be reluctant to see the connection between him and more secular philosophers. For example, the French philosopher Jacques Derrida, I think, is very much indebted to Kierkegaard in a way that's perhaps not recognised. With someone like Derrida who's emphasising the fact that ideals are not necessarily possible or there's an aspect of language that always undermines itself, that there's never any sort of closure on concepts, on theses and so on, that kind of very modern idea is one that we can trace back to Kierkegaard and to Kierkegaard's imaginative reinterpretation of Socrates.

JONATHAN REE: I guess philosophy in our time is a heavily professionalised industry in a way that Kierkegaard would have loathed. He hated professors. He said, 'What's the difference between a thinker and a professor – take away the paradox and you have a professor' – it's a term he used. And it seems to me that he would think that contemporary philosophy is dominated by the professors. I think that contemporary philosophy would be in a much better condition if it would allow itself to learn more from Kierkegaard. There's a wonderful phrase he had in his notebooks: 'And even if you offered me a place in the great edifice of the system, I would rather be the kind of thinker who just sits on a branch.'

TRANSMITTED: 20.03.08

o

Tea

A fter air and water, tea is the most widely consumed substance on the planet. In this country it helped define class and gender, it funded wars and propped up the economy of the empire. The trade started in the 1660s with an official import of just two ounces. By 1801 24 million pounds' worth of the stuff was coming in every year and people of all classes were drinking an average two cups a day. It was the first mass commodity, and the merchant philanthropist Jonas Hanway decried its hold on the nation. 'Your servants' servants, down to the very beggars, will not be satisfied unless they consume the produce of the remote country of China' – in which it had been drunk and cultivated for thousands of years.

What drove the extraordinary take-up of tea in this country? What role did it play in the global economy of the empire and at what point did it stop becoming an exotic foreign luxury and start to define the essence of Englishness?

With me to discuss the history of tea are Huw Bowen, Senior Lecturer in Economic and Social History at the University of Leicester; James Walvin, Professor of History at the University of York; and Amanda Vickery, Reader in History at Royal Holloway College, University of London.

Huw Bowen, long before the British acquired the taste for tea, its consumption was widespread in China. Can you tell us when it's supposed to have taken hold there and how it was drunk and what significance it had?

HUW BOWEN: Tea had been drunk in China for thousands of years. Its significance was, in the first instance, medicinal and it gathered a reputation as an energising beverage. It's contact with that form of the commodity that first alerts the British, and indeed Europeans, to

321

its qualities. We find that by the early part of the sixteenth century, as European contacts are being made with the Far East and with China, that interest is being expressed in acquiring tea so that it can be brought to the benefit of the people in Europe.

MELVYN BRAGG: Let's stay in China. It was found on the borders of Burma, India and China and it was cultivated in many ways. There was green tea and black tea. Can you just develop the Chinese context.

HUW BOWEN: We're talking about two provinces in south-eastern China, Fukien and Wei Province. The tea plants, or trees more properly, were grown on mountains. They were harvested and then they had to undergo a process of either fermentation or roasting and firing to produce the quite distinctive forms of green and black tea that become so well known to Europeans in the eighteenth century.

MELVYN BRAGG: How widespread was it in China? You've said medicinal use – did it also have ceremonial uses, which it came to have in Japan by the eighth century AD. Did it have ceremonial uses in China as well?

HUW BOWEN: It certainly has social, formal uses, as it were, but not to the same degree that you're thinking of in Japanese tea ceremonies.

MELVYN BRAGG: Was it drunk by many Chinese, or was it drunk just by the rich Chinese?

HUW BOWEN: It's not an area that I know a great deal about, but my understanding is that its use and consumption is fairly widespread.

MELVYN BRAGG: And how did it trickle out to Japan, because as far as I can understand, the Chinese were very concerned to keep it a secret and a monopoly?

HUW BOWEN: It's very difficult to keep commodities secret and as China begins to expand its overseas trade and its overseas contacts during the fifteenth and sixteenth centuries, we find Chinese commodities of various types being traded throughout South-East Asia. It's really informally, I suppose, through links with Japanese merchants, that we find the commodity trickling in to other parts of the region.

MELVYN BRAGG: So when in 1660 Sam Pepys recorded having had tea – 'a China drink of which I have never drunk before' – he probably got a little taste from somebody who had smuggled it in?

HUW BOWEN: Yes. It is probable that the early tea that came into Britain came either via Amsterdam, where the Dutch would have imported it, or had been brought surreptitiously into Britain by a sailor on board an East Indiaman. At that stage, in 1660, the East India Company, which possesses the monopoly of trade with Asia and the Far East, was not importing tea at all.

MELVYN BRAGG: It's interesting to know that as late as 1660 nobody had the slightest idea of the power, the popularity, the influence this plant would have in the West.

HUW BOWEN: Not at all. And the most fascinating aspect of this is the speed with which the commodity begins to take hold in the years that follow.

MELVYN BRAGG: And changes so much. James Walvin, how did Britain enter the tea trade directly, and what was the environment that it discovered in China and how did it deal with it?

JAMES WALVIN: It's really the story of this extraordinary expansion of British influence and trade in the Atlantic and then in Asia and the establishment of the East India Company and the kind of pattern that was true to all the major European maritime nations. It's the sudden realisation from the 1690s onwards that here was something people rather liked but they didn't like it on its own. It wasn't just tea – and this was the key to it – they wanted it with something else.

MELVYN BRAGG: I want to come to that later. I just want to establish the trade. We're in 1660, King Charles II has been brought the magnificent gift of two ounces of tea, his wife comes from a place which knows a little bit more about tea, but tea is still nowhere, and the East India Company goes to Canton, the only port it's allowed to trade out of because China keeps the rest of the ports closed, and does the trade there. Can you tell us how it broke into the trade and who it had to deal with?

JAMES WALVIN: The East India merchants had to deal with local merchants that had a monopoly on the export of tea. The interesting thing is that they don't get any kind of access to the interior of China, they can only do it under very strict regulations and at first I think they do it through the good offices of local Jesuit priests.

MELVYN BRAGG: French Jesuit priests?

JAMES WALVIN: French Jesuit priests, but they don't really trade into China, it's just a toehold in Canton. They're very much at the mercy of the local Chinese traders.

MELVYN BRAGG: But these Chinese traders, as I understand it, the people who run it in Canton are called the Hongs – they sound like a terrific gang, don't they, they probably were! Anyway, ten or twelve of the Hongs have a monopoly deal with the East India Company, which also has a monopoly, so it's eastern and western monopolies, head to head.

JAMES WALVIN: It is. Well, that's the way trade evolves in the early years of European expansion into Asia and to the Americas. It's a monopoly system which breaks down because the people realise very quickly there's more money to be made on a freer trade system.

MELVYN BRAGG: The Hongs are very demanding of the East Indian men, aren't they? They want their guns, they want their powder and they want their sails, and they have to hand these over before they're allowed to do any trade at all. Where are the Hongs getting the tea from, James?

JAMES WALVIN: They deal with a group of merchants known as the Tea Men, who organise a very elaborate supply chain into the mountains and the provinces where the tea is grown. And we find them sending orders for particular types of tea up into the mountains and then the tea is literally carried to Canton by bearers and by boat in canisters and tubs. The important thing to stress is we're talking about a great variety of teas here. We've talked about green and black, but within that broad division, there are an infinite variety of different types of tea, and therefore the orders that are sent up are very specific in the type of tea that the Hong want and need to sell to the British.

MELVYN BRAGG: Can you tell us, Amanda, about the East India Company? Once they discovered there was a taste for tea in the late seventeenth century did they try to stimulate it, did they try to advertise it? There were coffee houses, there were chocolate houses, and this is rather a latecomer. They would have to 'market' it, we would say nowadays, wouldn't we?

AMANDA VICKERY: There definitely were attempts to market tea. But I think the first thing we've got to realise is that it's in the nature of this kind of mercantile exercise that people are going out, they're looking for exotic luxuries, they're bringing loads of different things back in the hope that something's going to fly.

MELVYN BRAGG: Such as?

AMANDA VICKERY: Well, for instance, a monkey or, later, pine-apples, or coffee and all sorts of spices. There's a bringing of these exotic luxuries back, they're rarities, and then they're hoping that one of these is going to take off. If you look in the letters of the East India Company in the British Library you can see that they're aware of what the Dutch East Indian Company is about. So they say things like, 'they've found this fantastic silk, the Dutch in Amsterdam, so why haven't we got it?'

They send out letters to their men on the ground – go and find this new thing. There's a complete flood of different sorts of commodities coming back and they don't know, it isn't written in tablets of stone, that tea is going to take off, and in any case coffee has the early lead, but gradually tea begins to build up a head of steam.

MELVYN BRAGG: I'll just go to James and then come back to you. James, you wanted to say?

JAMES WALVIN: I think one other element here is that, as in China, tea is promoted as a medicinal product in the first place. Tea, coffee, sugar, tobacco, are all on the shelves of the apothecaries. In fact, Pepys himself talks about taking it for medicinal reasons, so like the Chinese for hundreds of years previously, the British pick this up as part of the pharmacology of the early modern world. It's in the list of the pharmacologies that are recommended for various ailments. It's odd to think of it now, but tea, along with other exotic commodities, was promoted initially as a kind of health product.

AMANDA VICKERY: That's absolutely right.

MELVYN BRAGG: Was it a bit different then, the tea they drank? Was it more herbal, more healthy?

AMANDA VICKERY: Tea is certainly drunk, green tea is certainly drunk in a weaker brew than we would drink it today, when it first comes. But James is absolutely right, it's marketed as a tonic, it's a benign but refreshing pick-me-up, it is mildly narcotic, it has attractive intrinsic qualities, and quite quickly people realise they've got a bit of a heady buzz from it. There is a lot of health writing about it which may be *parti pris* – you made that point about marketing.

It does seem as if some of the people who were writing this medical literature may have been in the pay of the East India Company or the Dutch East India Company. There's one that I came across, Cornelius Bontekoe, who in 1685 writes a treatise on tea and says you should have between fifty and two hundred and fifty cups of tea a day. He was rumoured to be in the pay of the Dutch East India Company!

MELVYN BRAGG: Fifty entire cups?

AMANDA VICKERY: Yes. Medical and colonial interests are blended, but it is a tonic, as Jim was saying. It is at first seen as something that's incredibly healthy, and also people very quickly realised that it helps keep you awake, along with coffee. They say, well, it throws off lassitude, it slakes hunger as well as thirst, it keeps you up at night. I don't think it's an accident that the first coffee house is opened in Oxford, because scholars very quickly realised you can write much later at night if you've had a hot drink.

MELVYN BRAGG: But that is coffee, we're on tea.

AMANDA VICKERY: Tea is also full of caffeine.

MELVYN BRAGG: Twinings opened a coffee house and a tea house next to each other, didn't they, in the late seventeenth century?

AMANDA VICKERY: Yes. Twinings first opened their tea as a side-line for coffee and they think it's going to be coffee that's the winner, coffee comes sooner, but very quickly tea picks up the trade.

MELVYN BRAGG: So, tea's here, it starts with two ounces at the court of Charles II. That's where you try out new goods if you're lucky. You get to the court because lots of young, fashionable people consort there with very little to do except be young, fashionable people and then spread the news around town. Who's drinking tea in this country? Where is it? Can we go round the table, at the end of the seventeenth century, then get on to the bigger effects that it had? Who's taking it up, say, forty years on from Charles II?

HUW BOWEN: Take up is remarkably slow. The East India Company doesn't at first, as Amanda implied, realise that it's on to a winner, and if you look at the profile of its commodities that have been brought back to Britain in the late seventeenth century, tea is by no means up there as a leading commodity. We're talking about silks, lacquer ware, bamboo, rattan, that sort of thing, and therefore by the end of the seventeenth century tea, really, is only being consumed, I think, within a very narrow tight social circle. Those in the know, if you like. As you say, it starts in the court.

MELVYN BRAGG: It's an aristocratic elite genesis?

HUW BOWEN: Very much so.

AMANDA VICKERY: I would think that leading merchants and their families would also be drinking tea, because often taste is led not only by those at the very top but by those with access to the trade. A taste for novelty, a real pleasure in novelty.

JAMES WALVIN: No one could have predicted, let's say in 1690, that in fifty years' time, tea would be the national drink.

AMANDA VICKERY: No.

JAMES WALVIN: No one could have ever imagined that and yet that's what happens. It is transformed from being a kind of exotic luxury into the kind of commonplace necessity of every single person in the country, more or less.

HUW BOWEN: If you were to reduce it to numbers: at the beginning of the eighteenth century the East India Company is importing probably about 100,000 pounds of tea. By 1750 it's importing 5,000,000 tons of tea. That gives you an idea of the scale of the increase after the beginning of the eighteenth century.

AMANDA VICKERY: But it is seen as an exotic ritual and I think that's one of the things that's very hard for us to get back to now. When you sling your teabag in the mug, you switch on your kettle – that doesn't convey to us the glamour and the thrill of having it out of Chinese porcelain. The tea cups would have been bowls, as you would get now in a Chinese restaurant.

MELVYN BRAGG: The ballast from China, in the boats – the tea was very light – the ballast was Chinese porcelain. They were exporting a lot of porcelain.

HUW BOWEN: Yes, because it's one of the few commodities that wouldn't corrupt the tea. Porcelain will not corrupt it by introducing any smells, or it won't dampen it in any way, but Amanda again is, I think, quite right, it's all about the package around it, around the commodity. We're talking about china cups, saucers, teapots, lacquered tables and so on, and the ritual therefore that develops around that becomes hugely important in the identity of particular social groups.

MELVYN BRAGG: So we're not only getting tea from China, we're getting thousands, tens of thousands of pieces of porcelain, which we collectively call 'china'?

HUW BOWEN: Yes.

MELVYN BRAGG: Just as tea was called 'char', another Chinese word. Before we move on: we're drinking scarcely any in 1660, quite a bit more by 1700, by 1750 it's taken off, whoosh, and it's beginning to characterise the English. It's wonderful, isn't it, I mean, what characterises the English? An ancient Chinese custom which has been there for 2000 years. So why, briefly – no, take as long as you want – why did it take such a grip so quickly, why did it beat, as it were, in a very simple way, coffee and chocolate which would seem to be more exotic?

HUW BOWEN: There are two ends, aren't there? There's demand, which we've been looking at, but also supply.

MELVYN BRAGG: But why was there a big demand? Was it cheaper?

HUW BOWEN: It is seen as a commodity. The price does drop over time, but also there is this exotic quality that we've been talking about. I think the East India Company's very good at manipulating the commodity by producing different varieties of it. We're not talking about a standard type of tea here. We're talking about types that range from coarse black tea through to very fine green tea, and the Company manipulates the market accordingly.

JAMES WALVIN: Again, I think that if you consider tea simply on its own growing, then you're missing the point. What's happening is that the graph of tea consumption and tea sales almost parallels perfectly the importation and consumption of sugar.

AMANDA VICKERY: Quite.

JAMES WALVIN: And it's not that the British are just drinking tea, but they're drinking sweet tea and that's what really becomes this peculiar British thing. The Chinese didn't drink their tea mixed with sugar, cane sugar, they drank it on its own. But the British mix.

AMANDA VICKERY: It's this fusion, isn't it?

JAMES WALVIN: It is.

AMANDA VICKERY: In 1720 black tea overtakes green tea in popularity and the British do this great thing of adding sugar and milk. Amazing domestication of a product, and it's a hot sweet drink and I think it fills a place. There is a hole there before. It's a non-alcoholic hot drink that you can have at home.

JAMES WALVIN: I think there's something else. It does get cheaper, the unit cost gets cheaper, but it's also simple to prepare. It's not like chocolate. Chocolate, drinking chocolate, is very complicated to prepare in the period we're talking about. It's not like today. Even coffee's slightly more complicated to prepare, but tea is simple, you just put hot water on it.

MELVYN BRAGG: Right. Now this brings us to its financial and even cultural significance. There are two global triangles shaping up now, and Britain is at the centre of both of them. One goes from Britain to India to China and back to Britain. One goes from Britain to Africa to the West Indies and back to Britain, and for the purposes of this discussion, one brings back tea and one brings back sugar.

Can we talk about those triangles and how they worked and why they were significant? Start with you, Huw, let's talk about the eastern triangle. What were we taking to India? How were we getting the money from India to go to China, and using that money, because the method of payment involved is quite complicated?

HUW BOWEN: Yes. It's all very well having a rising demand for a commodity, but you need to be able to pay for it and the great problem that the British have in the eighteenth century is actually paying for this commodity. The Chinese want and require very little from Britain.

MELVYN BRAGG: In terms of goods? Not our wool, for example?

HUW BOWEN: They're not receptive to woollens, or to other sorts of things. There's an interest in mechanical gadgets and the like, but that is not sufficient to pay for the tea, and therefore this very unbalanced trade was always paid for by the export of bullion, silver. This caused a severe problem for the East India Company because it became the focus of criticism for those who condemned this trade as being a losing trade. It was all very well importing exotic products, but they can be seen to be of little use to society. Yet that society is exporting that which is hugely valuable to it, silver. Therefore while we find one level of criticism against tea, that it is a product that is undermining traditional British or English virtues and commodities, it's also damaging the national wealth because it's encouraging the East India Company to export increasing levels of bullion.

MELVYN BRAGG: So, how did we correct that problem?

JAMES WALVIN: You've got to look at the kind of trading systems in a much broader setting, because the trading systems of the East are actually plugged in to the trading systems of the Atlantic and the West and the generation of trade and wealth is interrelated. People don't use the word 'globalisation' but you're looking at a genuinely global economy by, let's say, 1750. Commodities from the Far East are being traded in London and then being added to by a product that's produced by labour from Africa and the commodities that you use for buying from the Africans are produced in London, and sometimes in Asia itself. For instance, you barter trades on the coast, barter for slaves on the coast of Africa with Indian textiles.

MELVYN BRAGG: African slave traders?

JAMES WALVIN: Yes, and if you think of it, it's a slightly bizarre-looking bird, in that you have Africans imported in their millions by the British, the British carry more than ever, to produce sugar, which you mix with Chinese tea to slake the natural thirst of even the lowest income people in this country. Quite rightly, critics in the eighteenth century said what is all this about? This is an extraordinary drain on the economy of this country when you're producing goods – it's Huw's point – producing goods that are simply unnecessary. You don't really need sweet tea. People have got by without it since time had a mind.

MELVYN BRAGG: On the other hand, the fact is this began to stimulate and even lubricate the economy. Would you like to take that up, Amanda?

AMANDA VICKERY: I think what this massive reorientation of the trade does is to change British geography. In the sixteenth and the seventeenth century, the key ports are on the eastern seaboard. If you go to King's Lynn today, it's this perfectly preserved port. By the mid-eighteenth century, you've had this massive reorientation, the continuing growth of London as the European port, but also the growth of the great ports on the western seaboard. You've got Glasgow with tobacco, Liverpool, Bristol, sugar and slaves, and the balance of the population starts to shift to the north and west.

MELVYN BRAGG: I still want to get back to this tea. Huw, how did it come to be paid for? As I understand it, it was the Mogul Empire who gave the collecting of taxes over to the East India Company and that's how they got their money in India.

HUW BOWEN: Yes.

MELVYN BRAGG: And that was the way they got round the problem of silver?

HUW BOWEN: I think that is a key development. Obviously, this growing demand is very important, but I think by 1750 the East India Company has reached a point where it can't really take the trade much further because it doesn't have the means to pay for it. The crucial development, therefore, is the British acquiring control of territory and revenue in Bengal in the 1760s. This gives them a huge surplus of funds which they can then use to invest in Indian textiles, raw cotton and the like, which can then be exported to Canton and the proceeds from the sales there can be invested in tea. So what we find happening between 1750 and 1780 is this connection of trade and empire which acts as a further stimulant to the growth of the tea trade.

MELVYN BRAGG: Before we move on, let me just ask you one last thing about this globalisation. You keep talking about it in terms of luxury and it does have a sort of sledgehammer cracking a nut quality, ships roving all over the world, slaves, Hongs in Canton, taking over the Mogul Empire, all for a cup of tea with sugar in it somewhere in the north of England, as it were. But it was a very big stimulus for the British Empire, it was in a sense one of the big financial lubricants, wasn't it, this trade?

JAMES WALVIN: Yes, absolutely.

MELVYN BRAGG: This tea and sugar trade.

JAMES WALVIN: It becomes the lubricant of the global financial system that makes Britain the great power in the world. By 1750, the British Empire is challenging the French, but by the end of the eighteenth century they've pushed aside the French and they've pushed aside the French in those areas – in India, in North America, in the Caribbean – where this whole economic system is being played out. It is a fight not merely for territorial possession, it's a fight for the material benefits of Empire. No one in the late eighteenth century would argue that this was an empire that actually didn't bring money into this country.

AMANDA VICKERY: No.

HUW BOWEN: No, and therefore the tea trade crucially becomes a means of transferring resources, imperial resources, from Asia to Britain. It's not any more trade for trade's sake, it has become a transfer mechanism and I think that's very important.

AMANDA VICKERY: And the British do think of themselves, emphatically, as a polite and commercial people, and I think the tea table seems to epitomise that. Because you've got your foreign commodities on your tea tray, you might have your Chinese porcelain, or by then you might have some British-made silver teapots. You've got milk, sugar, you've got all these exotic commodities all brought together. You might have a beautiful British-made mahogany tea table, you all sit around it and the woman predominates at the tea table and shows off her best manners, so she's polite, but she's also got the fruits of empire on her table before her.

MELVYN BRAGG: So, we've got it stimulating the empire in terms of money and trade, the key to this are these two global triangles with other geometric figures springing off from them. But back in this country, Amanda, it is actually penetrating society quite strongly, particularly through women's control of the teapot.

AMANDA VICKERY: I think women are, have always been, targeted by the tea trade. It's been a tonic that was aimed at women particularly. I think women do take a particular pleasure in tea and if you look at women's letters early on, if they're aristocratic enough or rich enough to have husbands travelling to Amsterdam at the end of the seventeenth century, they're saying and while you're at it, will you get me a bit of green tea? So we see that in their letters they start talking about it, or they comment on other ladies' tea sets.

As early as 1710, the tea table can become a shorthand for either a domestic grouping or a group of women. There are many poems and satires which tease women about how much they love tea and about how any gathering of women over the teapot is likely to produce scandal. But the other way you can map the incredible take-off of tea in the early eighteenth century is that if you look at inventories which record the property that people have at death. In the 1670s there are only one or two people who've got the equipment for hot drinks. By the 1730s it's almost universal amongst merchants, even urban craftsmen. It's something associated with towns. Everybody wants to have a teapot, and by the 1780s I've come across references to them giving tea in the workhouse when people are a bit sick. They think they deserve a little bit of tea.

MELVYN BRAGG: And its popularity was such that the British government not only was doing global trade but making an absolute fortune out of it for this country. The tax on tea, as I understand it, was 119 per cent. And we're bringing in millions and millions of pounds of tea – from the 5 million you said in 1750, it soon went up to 20 million pounds.

HUW BOWEN: Yes, tea contributes to about 10 per cent of government revenue by the end of the eighteenth century.

JAMES WALVIN: The problem was that the kind of tax on tea was such that it also spawned this other eighteenth-century industry, smuggling. Much of the trade in tea is actually in smuggled tea, isn't it? There's a substantial part of the market being satisfied by smugglers coming in via Europe, via the Channel Islands, via the Isle of Man.

AMANDA VICKERY: People estimate that as much as two-thirds of the tea drunk is either smuggled or adulterated.

JAMES WALVIN: Because it's not merely that it's made its way into fashionable homes but it's also – I was going to say percolated out, but that's the wrong word, it's spread down in life as well. It's not just fashionable society with its porcelain teapots and sugar bowls, but even the poorest of the poor, by the mid-eighteenth century, think that tea is absolutely basic to the way they live. If they can't afford tea they will pour hot water over burnt bread.

AMANDA VICKERY: Or they'll steal it as well. I've looked in women's diaries and they're always complaining that their servants have been pilfering the tea. They're saying the servants are at the tea again and they're breaking white sugar to have with it. What's to become of poor housekeepers? Canny servants then start demanding that they have an allowance for tea written into their contract.

MELVYN BRAGG: It's still rather bewildering, isn't it, that it takes off so spectacularly here? It doesn't take off to this extent in Europe. Although the Dutch were ahead of us in importing it, they stick far more with coffee and chocolate, but it really takes off here. Is it just the sugar that we're talking about, James or Huw? What is there, is there another element? I can't think it's any ingrained national characteristics that we like tea more than other Europeans. The Chinese have liked tea long before us. Perhaps we're like the Chinese. What's going on?

HUW BOWEN: I think we're finding the consequences of this demand spreading amongst the social classes but also the regularity and the strength of the supply is important here. The pushing of this commodity is hugely important to the government, to the East India Company, and they both have a vested interest in making sure that this commodity is consumed in large quantities. I think the effect of that is seen very much in a kind of attitudinal shift towards tea that occurs between 1750 and 1780.

JAMES WALVIN: I think the other thing that is also at work is the commercial pressure of the West India lobby. They're working hand in glove. The East India Company and the West India lobby both realise that the more tea or the more sugar you sell, the more you sell the other. The West Indian planters are also promoting the consumption of tea because they know full well that the more tea is bought and consumed, the more sugar will be consumed, and it's a double commercial pressure from two extraordinarily powerful groups. Both of these groups have extraordinary influence in London in politics, in economics, in banking and in the way distribution systems work, and they are both very actively promoting the produce of the other side.

HUW BOWEN: I think there is another dimension to that. We see the reduction in the opposition to tea drinking occurring. In the mid-eighteenth century tea drinking was often condemned as being of no benefit to the labouring poor. By the 1780s . . .

MELVYN BRAGG: There's a wonderful remark from Dr Johnson – I've got it written down here. He said: 'tea's proper use is to amuse the idle and dilute the meals of those who cannot use exercise and will not use abstinence.'

AMANDA VICKERY: Johnson describes himself as a shameless tea drinker and apparently he said that his kettle was always hot and he referred to it as 'that fragrant leaf, that special leaf'. He absolutely loved tea, but I've come across continuing criticism of tea for the labouring poor because a lot of the writers think, well, it's all very well for us in our drawing room, but if it means people rushing off, buying a little bit of tea, and a little bit of sugar it's changing the British diet. Before tea, the British breakfast was beer and porridge. Now that might not sound very healthy to us, but it was seen as such, and then tea, a hot drink with a little bit of bread, becomes the British breakfast.

MELVYN BRAGG: Burnt bread.

AMANDA VICKERY: Burnt bread. If you look at foreign commentators, they almost all comment on the British breakfast that is tea, newspapers, no conversation. Then they always comment on the bread. They say, 'they put the bread into the fire, they burn it on both sides, they add butter to it and this is called "toast".' Europeans are absolutely amazed by that. But I think you make a good point, though. It's still mysterious to me, really, why we don't go for coffee over tea when all our continental neighbours do, and of everything I've ever read, the only satisfying explanation isn't very satisfying, which is that the tax regime favours tea over coffee.

MELVYN BRAGG: And there's the landmark Boston Tea Party. The tea then goes across the Atlantic, having come across other oceans. It was chucked into the harbour at Boston. That is partly because of not wanting to pay tax. But there's also a cult rural statement there as well, isn't there?

HUW BOWEN: Very much so. It's important to recognise that an awful lot of the tea that came into Britain was re-exported, and huge quantities were exported to North America in the early eighteenth century. The elite in colonial America defined themselves by their consumption of tea. I think, therefore, when they get into political conflict with the British government in the 1760s, in particular they greatly resent the imposition of taxes. The throwing of the tea into Boston Harbour signifies opposition to a specific tax, but also rejection of particular types of British behaviour.

JAMES WALVIN: They become coffee drinkers. Americans self-consciously set out to drink coffee in the early years of the Republic, to be un-British.

AMANDA VICKERY: Before they really get established on coffee, I've come across many women writing piously about how they're having raspberry-leaf tea and they're all wearing homespun American goods. They're trying to – James is right – they're trying to assert their new status. I'm sure that coffee ever after holds the lead, but they're trying to say raspberry-leaf is just as nice as that terrible stuff the British are importing from China.

MELVYN BRAGG: We've just touched on America, but then back to China. The Opium Wars again, and this comes about through the tea trade.

HUW BOWEN: Yes, we're back to the problem of how do the British pay for it. And what begins to happen is that more and more commodities are exported by the East India Company or, crucially, by private traders, from India to Canton and the receipts from the sales of those commodities are paid to the Company's treasury in Canton so that they can purchase tea. What happens is that opium is recognised in the 1770s, 1780s as being a commodity that, although prohibited in imperial China, is greatly in demand. What the East India Company does is proclaim loud and long that it won't engage in a trade in an illicit commodity such as opium. Nevertheless, it turns a blind eye to those private British traders who are prepared to export it into China. Therefore we find during the late eighteenth century the growth of this illicit trade in opium, really to pay for tea.

JAMES WALVIN: The other story that lurks behind all this is that what makes tea accessible to everybody in this country is the emergence of the English shop. We've talked about tea being on people's tables, on their shelves. What makes that possible is this extraordinary proliferation of small shops throughout the length and breadth of not just of England, but Britain. This is actually on the back of these very commodities we're talking about.

People are able to buy tea and sugar and tobacco because people open up a corner shop. It becomes a very British institution, the corner shop. It emerges in these years and it emerges to cater for the very taste that we're talking about. Amanda's point about inventories of people's personal possessions – we know about shopkeepers' possessions – a substantial proportion of their wares are taken up by tea, sugar and tobacco.

MELVYN BRAGG: Amanda, you're bursting to speak.

AMANDA VICKERY: I think James is absolutely right. You get the rise of the small shop, first in the south, in the early eighteenth century, in the north in the later eighteenth century. I think he's absolutely right, it's about getting small amounts, these groceries, to the addictive consumer. You want to have a little bit of tea and sugar because once you get on to the hot drinks, you could be addicted to them. People don't want to let go the habit, and by the 1750s there were as many shops per head of the population as there were in 1870. It was Napoleon who said the British were a nation of shopkeepers, not Hitler.

JAMES WALVIN: Adam Smith said the same thing.

MELVYN BRAGG: The fact that the English, the East India Company, had trouble, always had trouble, getting tea out of China, although they shifted millions and millions of tons, made them want to grow it elsewhere, in India. They made several attempts to grow it there and failed. Finally they cracked it in India and the Indian tea trade grew and therefore you could more or less bypass China, as happened. Can you tell us more about that?

HUW BOWEN: The East India Company itself didn't grow tea in India, but it had long believed that it would be possible to grow tea elsewhere and therefore engaged in trials. In the 1780s Joseph Banks, for example, is promoting attempts to grow tea in Calcutta. The East India Company itself remains half-hearted about this and for a very good reason. In 1813 it loses its monopoly of trade in India and I think, therefore, it was quite reluctant to promote the growth of tea in India because it felt it would then be circumvented or undercut by private tea growers.

MELVYN BRAGG: But it keeps its monopoly in China?

HUW BOWEN: It keeps its monopoly in China until 1833 and therefore it's not until that monopoly is broken that we see the shackles come off everywhere. It's no coincidence that at that moment they seriously begin to develop, to grow tea elsewhere, notably of course in Assam in the 1830s.

AMANDA VICKERY: I don't think we should be surprised by this, though. It's a key colonial strategy, to try and control the trade of an exotic product and, if possible, control its production, and if not, its distribution. The same would be true of coffee. Coffee is originally found in the Yemen. Let's get the coffee out to the West Indies. The Dutch are trying, they're also experimenting on Java, trying to get the tea to take. But the knowledge of tea remains very confused. They think there's lots of different kinds of tea bushes. They don't realise that green tea and black tea come from the same bush. I don't know whether the Chinese absolutely block knowledge of tea or whether they confuse people. But I suppose when you can't even land in Canton, you can't get inland to where the tea is grown.

HUW BOWEN: Before the eighteenth century, before even the nine-teenth century, very few Britons had actually seen the tea process first-hand, and therefore a lot of half-truths are peddled about how tea is produced.

JAMES WALVIN: What you're looking at, through the history of tea and the efforts that flourish after the 1840s to grow tea some-where else, is part of this extraordinary colonial-imperial project of finding the ideal setting for all kinds of tropical and semi-tropical produce. I mean, sugar cane didn't grow naturally in the Caribbean, it was taken there from New Guinea through the Mediterranean.

The explorations of the eighteenth century are all largely to do with not merely mapping the world but finding areas where you can move one commodity and grow it somewhere else. Coffee and chocolate are the two examples that we've had, and they tried to grow tea elsewhere. They tried to grow cotton, and Kew Gardens is produced with this in mind. This is the whole purpose you have experimental stations, and ideally with an empire you have the world as an experimental station, so you can put the whole world to the task of producing things for your social and economic benefit.

MELVYN BRAGG: One of the romantic and beguiling things about the history of tea, though, is its move from the exotic to the common-place, isn't it? The move from being something which distinguishes Chinese people to something which is later supposed to distinguish British people.

JAMES WALVIN: Amanda touched on it earlier, and that is that here's a commodity that does become a commonplace drink. Even contemporaries couldn't understand how that had happened. If you look at any number of commentators talking about the poor, mid, late eighteenth century, even Frederick Eden writing in the terrible years of the 1790s, '95, '97, even he scratches his head. Why is it that this commodity brought tens of thousands of miles is still within the reach of very poor people? It is a social economic conundrum that they didn't fully understand and nor do we.

AMANDA VICKERY: But it does become a national symbol, does it not? If you see any Second World War war film, if there's ever a tragedy out comes the teapot, let's have a nice cup of tea. In fact, people joked at the time that if Hitler could only cut off tea supplies, it would bring the nation to its knees. When the war started the government went to great lengths to move the tea out of the warehouses along the Thames and to get it hidden, so much is it a part of the fabric of the nation by 1940.

MELVYN BRAGG: Where did they put it?

JAMES WALVIN: Like the pictures at the National Gallery, they hid them from the bombs.

AMANDA VICKERY: The tea and the pictures went together.

MELVYN BRAGG: I think that's a good place to stop, don't you? Thank you very much indeed. I enjoyed that.

TRANSMITTED: 29.04.2004

p

The Peasants' Revolt

'When Adam delved and Eve span, who was then the Gentleman?' These are the opening words of a sermon, said to be by John Ball, which fired a broadside at the hierarchical nature of fourteenth-century England. Ball, along with Wat Tyler, was one of the principal leaders of the Peasants' Revolt. His sermon ends: 'I exhort you to consider that now the time is come, appointed to us by God, in which ye may (if ye will) cast off the yoke of bondage, and recover liberty.' The subsequent events of June 1381 represent a pivotal and thrilling moment of England's history, characterised by murder and mayhem, beheadings and betrayal, a boy-king and his absent uncle, and a general riot of destruction and death. By some interpretations, the course of this sensational event threatened to undermine the fabric of government as an awareness of deep injustice was awakened in the general populace.

But who were the rebels and how close did they really come to upending the status quo? And just how true are the claims that the Peasants' Revolt laid the foundations of the long-standing English tradition of radical egalitarianism?

Joining me to discuss what has been termed as the greatest mass rebellion in English history are Caroline Barron, Professorial Research Fellow at Royal Holloway College, University of London; Alastair Dunn, teacher of history at Oakham School; and Miri Rubin, Professor of Early Modern History at Queen Mary College, University of London.

Miri Rubin, there was a range of economic and social difficulties towards the end of the fourteenth century – can you block that in for us?

MIRI RUBIN: To understand 1381 we must go back about a generation and this is the world in England and in Europe after the Black Death.

345

The Black Death, 1348–49, which recurred in the sixties and seventies. This is such a dramatic restructuring of relations between man, land, authority. People became scarce, in some places up to half the population perished, and as people became scarce labour became dear. Land was there in plenty because so many people working on the land had simply died. The immediate aftermath of the Black Death, we are talking the late forties, early fifties, meant confusion and disruption.

Prices of food were very dear. People were moving about and it was not clear how the economy would restructure itself and society and authority too, but the patterns soon emerged. The patterns were that with all the empty land and with fewer people around some sort of new order would have to emerge. What was clear was that those who owned the land, those who owned the vast agrarian estates with hundreds of thousands of serfs upon them, had to find a new order. What is absolutely clear is that those who are in a position to offer labour are now in a stronger position. Those on the land, though, are tied to the land, they are serfs.

They can't move freely, they can't marry freely and they can't charge for their labour according to its market value. Added to that, parliament legislates and tries to enforce a system that keeps people in place, in fixed terms of employment and at regulated levels of wages. All this creates extraordinary discontent but the interesting thing is that those in the best position to act politically and economically are not actually the serfs, the lowest of the low, the poorest population, but rather those who are active in their communities, church wardens, substantial tenants.

MELVYN BRAGG: And as I understand it the government passed a Statute of Labour in 1351 saying that despite the fact that there are far fewer of you and you have to work harder and there are more opportunities, we are going to cap your wages.

MIRI RUBIN: Yes.

MELVYN BRAGG: Running alongside the Black Death through these years, the second half of the fourteenth century and a few years before, were very expensive, over-expensive wars between England and France which caused the government of the day to need more money, therefore to go for more taxes.

MIRI RUBIN: Yes, to go for more taxes and they were experimenting with forms of taxation. It is an extremely creative period in that sense administratively. How do you extract wealth and taxation out of the wealth of England? Edward III, who is the king during the Black Death and during most of this phase of the war, invents new ways of taxation. Richard II, when he comes to the throne, is not at all keen to pursue the war in France, but again there are these expenses on fortification, particularly in the late seventies and early eighties, so what to do? New forms of taxation are introduced.

MELVYN BRAGG: Can you just give us an idea that this unrest wasn't confined to this country? There were the textile workers in Florence, as I understand it. Something similar was happening in parts of France and in parts of Germany. Let's call it Europe for the sake of ease – we have a western European movement going on here.

MIRI RUBIN: That's true and again it is so interesting to see how in each country or each region the discontent expresses itself in the appropriate local way. So, for example, in Italian cities it takes usually the form of activities in cities by workers who are paid by the day, who want to get organised and want the privileges of memberships and guilds. In France where, remember, parts of France are conquered, this is a land of conquests and war in the course of the Hundred Years War, there is terrible discontent in the population that feels absolutely let down and abandoned by its leadership.

MELVYN BRAGG: Caroline Barron, can we look at the poll tax? There were three poll taxes in about four years towards the end of the 1370s. Can you take us through that and the effect they had?

CAROLINE BARRON: The first poll tax was in 1377, the next one in 1379 and the third on, the one that sparked off the revolt, was 1380. And the point about the poll taxes was that they were a different way of taxing people, a per capita tax. The first one was to be paid by everybody over the age of fourteen. They were to pay four pence. The second one they tried to make a kind of graduated tax to make it fairer but it produced much less income, and so the third poll tax was back to the old system and that was to be three groats

— that is one shilling, twelve pence per head and that was everybody over the age of sixteen.

MELVYN BRAGG: Was this men and women?

CAROLINE BARRON: Yes. The poor were exempted and there was a general injunction that the rich should help the poor, which to us sounds a bit corny, but in fact that was something that medieval society accepted, that rich people should help poor people to carry their tax burden.

MELVYN BRAGG: What happened as a consequence of that third tax, which had trebled in three years, and how could that be said to be a match igniting the bonfire?

CAROLINE BARRON: It is worth making the point that, although there were three poll taxes in those years, there were also two grants of other taxation as well, so it was a period of very heavy taxation. There was, for the third poll tax, a great deal of evasion and so the money was not coming in as it was supposed to. They sent commissions of enquiry in the spring of 1381 to particular areas where they felt evasion was prevalent and it was those commissions of enquiry that seemed to have provoked the revolt, particularly in Essex.

MELVYN BRAGG: Was that because people resented paying tax or because of the way the commissions of enquiry behaved themselves?

CAROLINE BARRON: Probably both, but the stories about the way the commissions of enquiry behaved were developed and evolved later. You know — that the tax enquirers looked inquisitively at young women to see whether they were of an age to pay the tax and that kind of thing. Whether that really happened we don't know, but it is obviously something that was in the air.

MELVYN BRAGG: So you are fairly convinced that the revolt gathered round this and then other grievances came in?

CAROLINE BARRON: Well, I am convinced that it was the trigger, but I think it has to be remembered that in the statements and the demands they made to the king at Mile End and then at Smithfield the poll tax is not mentioned.

MELVYN BRAGG: Can we talk about the term 'The Peasants' Revolt'. Is it misleading? And if so why?

CAROLINE BARRON: If you are going to have a mass revolt in medieval England it is going to contain peasants, rural workers, because they are 90 per cent of the population. It really was a rural people. I think that the chroniclers called them '*rustici*' – people from the countryside. That was meant to be a pejorative term. But it was not only *rustici*, workers on the land, peasants, it included artisans when it got to London, it included Londoners, it included men from the lower ranks of clergy, it included some gentlemen. Whether they were coerced or whether they joined willingly we don't really know. It included a broad spectrum of people in late medieval England but not, obviously, the governing classes.

MELVYN BRAGG: So there was a touch of Middle England on the move after the poll tax . . .

CAROLINE BARRON: Absolutely, like the poll tax later.

MELVYN BRAGG: Alastair Dunn, why were the rebels, let's call them rebels rather than peasants at the moment, unable to exercise their demands in any other way?

ALASTAIR DUNN: The reason for this is that parliament is essentially representing those with property, those who own land, those who have property in towns. Thos people represented in parliament are going to want a system of taxation that hits them the least hard. Those poorer people who are now paying this twelve pence a head tax in 1380 don't really have any direct representation at all and there is no proper legal way for them to express their discontent and anger.

MELVYN BRAGG: Other grievances came into play. Can you give us some idea of what they were?

ALASTAIR DUNN: For a start, England is not a particularly well-governed country between 1377 and 1381. There has been a skip in the generation of kings. An elderly king has died, his adult son has died and the monarchy has passed to a teenage boy who is very reliant on the quality of advice from his government ministers. Not only are they making mistakes, like bringing in this third poll tax, they are also managing a war with France particularly badly as well. So there is a real sense that England is a poorly governed country in those years running up to the poll tax.

MELVYN BRAGG: What grievances did they bring to bear in terms of improving their lot? The idea is of the Peasants' Revolt trying to throw off serfdom and in the introduction I talked about releasing themselves from bondage. Can we bring that to bear?

ALASTAIR DUNN: Yes, many of those whose wages have been artificially depressed, who are wanting to make the best out of their lives, are effectively being prevented from doing so by the government. The government is being very aggressive, preventing people from actually trying to improve the quality of their lives.

MELVYN BRAGG: Is there any sense, inside the – let's keep calling it the Peasants' Revolt, because that is how it is in the history books – that they are attempting to throw off hierarchical systems, to go for liberties way in advance of liberties claimed in later revolutions further down the centuries?

ALASTAIR DUNN: Certainly. The two manifestos that the rebels delivered to the king during 14 and 15 June contained demands for the abolition of serfdom and the reform of the landholding system. So there is a sense that there is a real demand for radical change.

MELVYN BRAGG: Can we talk about the two most prominent persons in the rebellion? First of all John Ball. Most of the rebels that we are talking about came from the broad south-east, and on their way towards London they released John Ball from prison. He was a radical – you wouldn't use that word then – he was a radical priest who had been in prison for his views. Can you give us some notion of John Ball?

ALASTAIR DUNN: John Ball is a man with criminal form. He has been prevented many times from making radical sermons in the south of England. He has spent time in prison and his sermons have this unusual millenarian quality of predicting radical change, of social egalitarianism, and this is a very dangerous cocktail, especially if you are preaching them directly to ordinary people. This is very much not the kind of preaching that the Church is happy with and they have made strenuous efforts to shut him down and prevent him from preaching.

MELVYN BRAGG: And Caroline, what about Wat Tyler?

CAROLINE BARRON: Tyler is an interesting man because, unlike Ball, he doesn't have a past history, we don't know anything really about Tyler. He is like a meteor, he comes into view at the end of May and he dies on 15 June and the whole of his life that we know about is in that short period. We presume he was a tiler, a craftsman, one of the people that Miri was describing who were wanting to have higher wages and to be able to move around in search of work.

He seems to have come from Essex. He crossed the Medway and came into Kent and seems to have joined the Kentish rebels and maybe qualities of his own personality and character led him to the leadership. He seems to have been a disciplinarian, he seems to have imposed a kind of restraint upon the rebels, no mass plunder, no mass killings, but some sort of constraint and so he had qualities of leadership.

MELVYN BRAGG: Miri, can I come to the orchestration of this. There are a lot of people moving mostly on foot in the England of that time towards this powerful city with its impregnable Tower and its court. Can you give us any idea how it was orchestrated?

MIRI RUBIN: It is really important to remember here that the south-east is a very mobile place. It is served by wonderful rivers, people normally travel a lot in East Anglia. It is also the most commercialised part of England, people constantly come to London from Norfolk and Suffolk to sell to the market, provide their work and go for periods of domestic work. You can get letters literally within a day between the furthest outposts of East Anglia and the action in Kent.

People think of people in the Middle Ages not moving. This is a very mobile, very sophisticated group. Another important point is that the sort of men we are talking about in the leadership were involved in what we might call a vernacular, an English-language political culture. These are not neophytes, these are men who turn up in manorial rolls, who help collect taxes, these are not innocents taken from behind the plough, although, as Caroline said, surely ploughmen also joined in. So we have a very sophisticated, savvy lower and local government type of expertise to communicate, to send letters, to inform, to send emissaries and to say, 'London is where we go.' They have all the capabilities of organising.

MELVYN BRAGG: We really have good records for that period, do we?

MIRI RUBIN: Not an enormous amount, not as much as we would want to have, but we do have letters that circulated between them. We do know that letters went to Kent to activate people, and to Suffolk. For example, the group of men that ultimately created mayhem at Bury St Edmunds, which is a great privileged monastery in Suffolk, was activated by an order from the men of Kent. So there clearly is communication and remember: rivers connect people, they don't separate people.

MELVYN BRAGG: Alastair Dunn, the revolt took place during the first two weeks of June 1381. Two rebel groups arrived in London on the 12th and 13th. Why was that a propitious time for it to happen?

ALASTAIR DUNN: They come to the London rally at that time because they have already started their demonstrations out in the countryside, but they really want to get into the city to access those government ministers whom they are blaming for their difficulties and they think that it is really the time now to try and get hold of them.

MELVYN BRAGG: Have you any idea of the numbers we are talking about?

ALASTAIR DUNN: This is one of the thorniest questions. The chroniclers tend to go for very big numbers. They say that maybe 60,000 people came to London. We have to rather hedge our bets in the answer we give to that, but there certainly would have been thousands of people involved and many Londoners as well who actually join in with the rebels.

MELVYN BRAGG: Caroline?

CAROLINE BARRON: I think it is worth remembering that the population of London at this time was probably about 40,000, so the chances are that it wasn't 60,000 that came but, as Alastair says, a few thousand. It is perhaps worth pointing out that the day that they arrive in London is Thursday 13 June, which was the feast of Corpus Christi and the feast of Corpus Christi is a day on which there were processions, there was a lot of public activity in parishes. So I think on the network that Miri mentions of people in the south-east, the word went round that Corpus Christi is the day we make for London. I think that would have been the rallying cry and that is why it is not chance that they come to London on the 13th.

MIRI RUBIN: What is really exciting about Corpus Christi is that it is the great late medieval summer feast celebrating the Eucharist, celebrating the Mass, celebrating Christ's offering his body for the salvation of humanity, and this is the day in which you remember it with thanks. It is about sharing, it is about community, and this is exactly the sort of English vernacular rhetoric that anyone would understand.

MELVYN BRAGG: Given that they were organised so quickly and they came together from all over the place and you have London, then a great fortress city, why couldn't they be contained better, Alastair? Why, how did they get in? Were they allowed in?

ALASTAIR DUNN: They turned up at Blackheath on the south side of London and it seems that they effectively managed to negotiate their entry into the city. There seems to be some attempt by the aldermen and the corporation to try and deter them from coming in. However their numbers are fairly strong and they access the city from the south.

CAROLINE BARRON: And if I could just say, I think there is a problem for the city. It is worth remembering that since 1376, just a few years before, the city has got a new form of government. The mayor had always been elected annually, but from 1376 the aldermen are elected, new aldermen are elected every year, which means that the government of the city in 1381 is particularly vulnerable. They aren't a group of experienced men who have been doing this for a long time.

MELVYN BRAGG: And also, what you were saying earlier about Corpus Christi being a great feast and great festival, there could have been a feeling for a moment that these people are coming to join in the great feast and the great festival day.

CAROLINE BARRON: Perhaps, but they don't normally come in those numbers!

MELVYN BRAGG: Or bearing arms?

CAROLINE BARRON: I think also.

MELVYN BRAGG: I suppose many people did bear arms in those days though.

CAROLINE BARRON: But they come to London Bridge – that is the main point of entry from the south. I think they were let in under a kind of panic. If you were trying to keep the bridge, which only had a drawbridge, and these masses of people were swarming across, you didn't want the bridge destroyed. Remember, the bridge is absolutely crucial to the economy of London, so you didn't want them setting fire to it or damaging it, so in some ways it was easier to let them in than to try and keep them out. But I don't think it was the result of collusion, I think it was panic.

MELVYN BRAGG: Well, let's bring the second big player into this now. Not a person but the court, the king, the authority. We have a fourteen-year-old king and he had three encounters with the rebels, let's call them. One at Blackheath, they assembled at Blackheath, but the two more important ones were at Mile End, so let's talk about Mile End first of all, and then the Smithfield encounter.

ALASTAIR DUNN: Well, by 14 June the king has taken to the Tower of London. He has already spoken to the rebels briefly at Blackheath from his barge on the Thames but doesn't actually meet them face to face until on 14 June he takes the decision that he is going to meet them and hear their demands.

MELVYN BRAGG: Do we know that he himself took the decision or is he counselled to take the decision?

ALASTAIR DUNN: I think that Richard took the decision himself, and it is interesting that one of the consequences of the decision to meet the rebels is that he distances himself physically from his most unpopular ministers whom the rebels had already said they want to deal with. So it might be a strategy of making himself a little bit safer and leaving these unpopular ministers behind in the Tower.

MELVYN BRAGG: And at the same time as he is going to meet them at Mile End, what are the rebels doing to London?

CAROLINE BARRON: Well, they have been loose in London and I think one of the things to remember is that they are not just marauding, pillaging and sacking everything. They are very selective in their targets. There are two notable acts, or three perhaps. They sack the Savoy Palace, the great palace of John of Gaunt, who was the hated uncle of Richard II and held responsible for the various disasters that people were upset about. Luckily for him, he is away in Scotland at the time, otherwise I am sure he would have suffered. So they sack his palace, but they don't loot it, they burn it.

There is a restraint – we are not thieves – and it is a very different spirit. They also attack Lambeth Palace, the home of the Archbishop of Canterbury, Simon Sudbury, the Chancellor. But there again in the palace they burn the records, all the documents that are associated with serfdom, with taxation, with the things they are distressed about, but they don't burn the palace or the Archbishop's library, so they are not destructive of everything. And then they also attack the Hospital of St John at Clerkenwell, which was the seat where the Treasurer of England, Robert Hales, was prior.

MELVYN BRAGG: Hadn't they got into the Tower? Who is going to tell us how they got in the Tower – Alastair?

ALASTAIR DUNN: It is intriguing how they got in the Tower because the king would have had some form of bodyguard with him.

It seems that either they bluffed their way in or threatened their way in or there may have been some disloyalty on the part of the king's attendants. But while Richard is off at Mile End on 14 June, the rebels do gain access to the Tower and get the men that they wanted to get hold of. So the unpopular Sudbury and the Treasurer of England, Robert Hales, whose properties, as Caroline was just telling us, have been attacked by the rebels, are subject to very swift justice by the rebels.

MELVYN BRAGG: Their heads are chopped off.

ALASTAIR DUNN: Their heads are chopped off.

CAROLINE BARRON: Getting into the Tower was actually one of their greatest coups. But they had also already got into Rochester Castle, they had got into the prison at Maidstone, they had got into the Marshalsea Prison at Southwark, they had got into Newgate Prison, so in fact their ability to get into what appear to be strongholds of royal authority is quite striking.

MELVYN BRAGG: So the young King Richard goes to Mile End and promises them all sorts of things but not enough, it seems, or we may assume, for Wat Tyler, because he wants another meeting the next day at Smithfield.

CAROLINE BARRON: Well, remember at Mile End there was one group of rebels, perhaps not all the rebels, just some of them, and it is interesting that Richard promised them freedom from serfdom. We know that that night, the Friday night, a number of royal clerks actually wrote out Charters of Manumission, of freedom, and some of these have survived although they were all revoked later. But some of them have survived, so the king's party put into practice this idea of buying them off with a Charter of Freedom, and then the rebels would go away and some of them did go away, but not all of them.

MELVYN BRAGG: It is interesting that there doesn't seem to be any thought of regicide around. They didn't want to kill the king.

MIRI RUBIN: That's very, very important, isn't it? Again, to use modern terminology, it's almost reformist rather than revolutionary.

Who do we have but the king? As we have heard, they don't have representatives in parliament. Who do they go to over and above the heads of the landlords that are the problem? It is again deeply engrained in this type of vernacular preaching that this is sacred kingship, this is God-ordained, but he will be our help. We are his commoners and he is our king. And at some point one of the chroniclers says everybody is now a community, everybody now is a common, and everybody wants representation and the help of the king, the source of justice.

ALASTAIR DUNN: They seem to have this bond with the king, with the person right at the very top. They see the king as a protector and there is no sense that they want to get rid of the king. In fact, the password that they exchange among each other is 'Who do you hold with?' And the answer to that is 'With King Richard and the true Commons'. They really identified with their boy-king. I wonder if it was something to do with his youth.

MELVYN BRAGG: Let's talk about this encounter at Smithfield.

CAROLINE BARRON: Well, the king's party realised on Saturday 15th that the tactic had not worked in that only some of the rebels had dispersed from Mile End. The king, Richard, was obviously quite a brave chap. Maybe that was because he didn't quite understand the danger he was in, but in fact he is very brave, I think. Before going to Smithfield he goes to Westminster and consults with the anchorite priest, a special praying priest in the monastery there before he rides out to Smithfield. Then he rides out to Smithfield.

He meets Tyler at Smithfield, probably mid-afternoon, and he has this discussion. Tyler is summoned to speak to him and Tyler apparently, according to the chroniclers – but remember a lot of the chronicles are written by people who are not there, who only heard it from somebody who heard it from somebody – Tyler makes demands which are more radical than the demands they made at Mile End, much more, asking for disestablishment, as we would say, or disendowment of the Church. There was to be only one priest, one bishop. Everybody was to be free, there was to be no more serfdom. So it is a very milleniarist kind of view of society. And the king says, yes, you can have what you want, providing it is just or saving my regality or some kind of equivocal phrase.

MELVYN BRAGG: Can we just really go into more detail here, because it is so interesting? Tyler would have a lot of his men there with him, we presume, not everybody had gone away thinking we have got what we want. What forces did the young Richard have, because he didn't have a standing army, he would have had a household guard and then the mayor would have brought together the thieves and vagabonds, is that true?

MIRI RUBIN: He wouldn't have a standing army, you are absolutely right. So far we have concentrated on the constitution of kingship, but this is a city that is being invaded, this is a city that is feeling the effects, feeling the danger to the economy, to the fabric. So clearly a mayor does not sit idle, later to be blamed, accused of complacency, and he is organising.

It is interesting, people think of the Middle Ages as violent. Yet it's actually quite difficult to get together an army of willing people, to organise, arm, to coordinate them within forty-eight to seventy-two hours max. By the time of the last appearance of the king there is behind him, known or unknown to him, a phalanx of bodyguards, of bovver boys, whatever you might call them, of armed men who will act at the command of the Mayor of London.

MELVYN BRAGG: Can we look at this climactic moment, and I think it can be called that. They are facing each other across a piece of land in Smithfield and Tyler rides over on a small horse, summoned I presume by the king, and as Caroline said, demands more than he has ever demanded before. Just what happened in the next few minutes, Alastair?

ALASTAIR DUNN: A scuffle breaks out. It seems that words are exchanged between Tyler and the king's attendants, but it seems that somehow Tyler has been riled by some of the words of one of the king's squires, or maybe Willy Walworth, the mayor, who is there at the time, and this results in a scuffle, knives are drawn, and Tyler is struck by at least one knife, maybe more, and this is when there is the potential for there to be a real disaster at Smithfield because the king is out there, exposed in the middle of Smithfield, there are these armed rebels on the other side. It has the potential to go very badly wrong.

CAROLINE BARRON: And Tyler actually, as he falls from his horse wounded, apparently more or less instructs his army to shoot, because they have bows, and at that moment Richard rides forward and says, 'follow me, I am your leader, I will be your king' – giving them a kind of leadership. They have lost Tyler but instead they have young Richard, and he leads them out to Clerkenwell Fields. And it is a remarkable act of instinctive leadership.

MIRI RUBIN: Charisma.

CAROLINE BARRON: And in a sense that has interesting consequences because later, I think, Richard has a sense that he is a charismatic person, he is perhaps inviolable, he is untouchable, he is protected by God. I think that this has consequences for his kingship later, but at the moment it is exactly the right thing to do. It defuses the situation and the rebels follow him.

MELVYN BRAGG: That is surprising in itself, isn't it, just to go into it further. Tyler has been a charismatic figure, he has come out from nowhere, as far as you historians are concerned, but he has led this army, they have made a tremendous assault on London and they have attacked secure key places, they have scared the living daylights out of the authorities. They have done all that and yet he is struck down and left for dead and they turn away and leave him. Is it just the charisma of Richard, which of course I will accept, but do they think they have got enough now or what is going on?

MIRI RUBIN: I would have thought that actually the day before was the climax. They should have stopped there. That was the climax and I think that a lot of people felt quite satisfied.

MELVYN BRAGG: Yes, and also I would have thought it was quite scary, that scene of the scuffle, and people understood that this could become appalling and also here was the London force – I mean, do we know the size of it? A few hundreds?

CAROLINE BARRON: That the mayor was able to summon? One of the difficulties for the mayor was that it is one thing summoning a force, but if the streets are full of rebels it is not very easy to get your other aldermen around London to come together. But he does do that as soon as Richard leads the rebels away to Clerkenwell Fields. Then the mayor goes back to the city and rounds up the force to go and deal with the rebels.

MELVYN BRAGG: And now, not to put too fine a point on it, Alastair, revenge sets in, because Richard revokes all, he breaks all the promises he has made, pursues the rebels and revokes the pardons, no more freedoms.

ALASTAIR DUNN: Yes, the pardons are revoked and then a very aggressive clearing-up operation is set in place, not only in London but also out in the counties, especially in East Anglia, where the rising is almost running along its own timetable, and in the counties around London. There have been sympathetic revolts and groups of knights and men at arms with the judges are sent out in almost military-style tribunals to put on trial and effectively execute those rebels that they catch, and there is some resistance. There are a few small size battles that are fought by the rebels who want to hold on.

MIRI RUBIN: Yes, exactly. While some of the rebels were in London others were doing the job in a way parallel, in a way mirroring what is happening in the capital, making those demands on the ground, so they seek out the justices who deal with the Labour Statute and enforce it, and they seek them out for their summary justice. They go and they burn archives and libraries.

For example, the University of Cambridge has no sources from before 1381, everything was burnt because the Vice-Chancellor's court in Cambridge was seen to be a privileged one. Bury St Edmunds, St Albans – in all these places where great institutions, great land-owners, were seen to be holding people back, this was unfolding. East Anglia was a really scary place in 1382 and 1383. We still throughout the eighties get accounts of cases being brought against people who were suspected of acting in 1381. Government became very suspicious, so any people coming together were suspected of treason and are very quickly dealt with and we have inventories of confiscated properties.

MELVYN BRAGG: But are we talking about hundreds of people being hanged?

CAROLINE BARRON: I think, in fact, most of the chroniclers make a point that there were fewer people actually executed than you might have expected. I think we are talking about hundreds, certainly not thousands, and I think one of the things that the government came quickly to realise is that if you ask local juries to accuse their neighbours you get a great number of local grievances and grudges. Not everybody who is accused in the indictments probably took part but it is a way of settling old scores, and I think they began to realise they couldn't disentangle who had really taken part in the revolt and who was merely a victim of neighbourly grievance.

MELVYN BRAGG: Is there any sense in which you can summarise what was gained and what was not gained by this revolt? They came, they stormed the city, intimidated the king into giving them everything they wanted and more than most of them set out to want, and then they were turned and pursued. What was left?

MIRI RUBIN: Well, it is one of these cases where looking backwards we can be extremely wise. Perhaps they couldn't see what was happening right in front of them because the institution of serfdom was in serious decline already. The landlords simply could not hold on to that set of ancient controls of people's lives in an economy so volatile and they themselves needed labourers, they themselves needed people to be mobile.

For example, when the king has building done at Windsor he breaches the Statutes of Labour all over the place. You need workers, you need people, so the institution of serfdom was declining and a lot of the empty lands were then rented out, leased out, on contract without all the trappings of serfdom. That is what happened to a lot of the land of England. But it wasn't obvious and it wasn't palpable and the issue of representation will take us into the nineteenth century. These people do not gain representation.

MELVYN BRAGG: Sorry to be simplistic about this, Caroline, but on a simple level did they achieve anything that they set out to achieve or were they knocked back?

CAROLINE BARRON: Well, if we knew more clearly what they set out to achieve we could answer that question more easily, but we as historians looking back can see some things very clearly that they achieved. For example, there were no more poll taxes. Also I think they did deliver a wake-up call to the governing classes of England that there is a community out there, there's a group of people who may not be represented in parliament directly but whose interests have to be taken into account.

You cannot simply impose on the mass of the British or English population without thinking about the consequences. And I have to say that I think the fear that there might be another Peasants' Revolt, a mass rising, was a very important corrective in the evolution of policy, whether royal or parliamentary.

ALASTAIR DUNN: Richard himself responds to this by trying to avoid fighting a war with France. Ironically he gets into trouble for this with his nobility and it was one of the reasons he was overthrown. They want a war with France and he, in a sense, has learnt the lessons of fighting expensive wars that need taxation.

MELVYN BRAGG: So it does feed through. Do you think it feeds into what became a certain strain in English thought, that this is part of the beginning of a long route to radicalism in this country? The idea of liberty? Or is that too romantic a notion?

CAROLINE BARRON: I think the French would argue that they have a long tradition of liberty and egalité as well. One thing I think that is interesting is that it made the people who govern England aware that there was a class of people, a group of people, a large group of people who actually were much more able, were more literate, had more skills than they had any realisation of, and this is what really frightened the chroniclers and government.

These people are able to organise something on this scale and that was really frightening. If I could just draw a quick parallel, I think the attack on the Twin Towers in New York, which made people realise, my goodness, these people can actually organise something as sophisticated and as devastating as this has made the whole attitude to Islam, to radicalism in Islam, very different. I think it was the same in 1381.

MIRI RUBIN: And because there are these English-language preachers around the place, people who aren't licensed, they becomes a focus of attention of the government. From the 1380s and nineties on, England is extremely repressive on the expression of religious opinion. It is as if the fear that religion excites the lower classes meant that religion became the object of serious repression that continued well into the nineteenth century.

ALASTAIR DUNN: And in the longer term Tyler and Mayor Walworth in a sense become heroes to each side of the revolt. Tyler has a great posthumous history, appears in lots of different books, pamphlets and plays. Walworth is very celebrated by the Fishmongers' Company, who adopt him as their hero and even have him in their pageants. So everyone is able to take away something from the Peasants' Revolt and take it as their symbol.

TRANSMITTED: 28.12.2006

q

Black Holes

B lack holes are the dead collapsed ghosts of massive stars and they have an irresistible pull. Even light submits. Their dark swirling, ever-hungry mass has fascinated thinkers as diverse as Edgar Allan Poe, Stephen Hawking and countless science-fiction writers. When their ominous existence was first predicted by the Reverend John Mitchell in a paper to the Royal Society in 1783, nobody knew what to make of the idea – they couldn't be seen by any telescope. Although they were also suggested by the eighteenth-century Marquis de Laplace and their existence was proved on paper by the equation of Einstein's General Theory of Relativity, it was not until 1970 that Cygnus X 1, the first black hole, was put on the astral map.

What causes black holes? Do they play a role in the formation of galaxies? Will they eventually swallow everything up? And what have we learned of their nature since we have found out where they are?

With me on this voyage into the black hole is the Astronomer Royal, Sir Martin Rees, he's also the Professor of Physics and Astronomy at Cambridge University; Jocelyn Bell Burnell, Professor of Physics at the Open University; and Professor Martin Ward, Director of the X-Ray Astronomy Group at the University of Leicester and a consultant at the European Space Agency.

Martin Rees, you described them to us as collapsed stars, these black holes, can you give us a description of how a star collapses and how it becomes a black hole?

SIR MARTIN REES: The star is held together by gravity and the smaller a star gets, or the heavier the star is, the stronger gravity is. We know that in the case of the earth, gravity is what holds us down. That's why Gagarin had to have a fast rocket to escape from earth's gravity. To escape from the surface of a normal star you would have to fire a rocket at about 1,000 kilometres per second.

But if you imagine something which is much smaller than the star, or much heavier than the star, the speed you'd need to escape from it becomes much larger and eventually it may become so large that not even light can escape. A black hole is an object where gravity has overwhelmed all other forces and it has contracted so much that not even light can escape from it. So, a black hole is an object in space that exerts a gravitational imprint on its surroundings but which puts out no light, everything has collapsed, light can fall in, objects can fall in, but nothing can get out because space is so warped, as it were, that not even light can escape.

MELVYN BRAGG: What causes the collapse of the star in the first place? Can you tell us about what you call 'escape philosophy'? About getting out, like Gagarin got out, we fired a rocket: it's quite easy to get out of the earth, it's harder to get out of the sun, it's impossible to get out of a black hole. Now can you just go into that a little more?

SIR MARTIN REES: If the sun was smaller it would be harder to escape, and we do have objects which are not quite black holes, but where gravity is very strong. In fact, these are objects called neutron stars, which Jocelyn Bell Burnell here was co-discover of. A neutron star is an object which is as heavy as the sun, in other words, a million times as heavy as the earth, but is no bigger than the size of London. And on an object like that, gravity is clearly immensely strong, so strong that you'd have to fire your rocket at half the speed of light to escape.

If you were on a neutron star and you dropped your pen on the floor, it would not just make a noise, it would produce as much energy as a kiloton of high explosives, so that is a measure of how strong gravity is when you have a very large mass in a small space. Now, if you take a neutron star and imagine compressing it by a factor of three smaller still, down to a size of say three miles across rather than ten, not even light could get out and then it would be a completely dark object seen from outside.

It would have become a black hole, where something happens

inside it which we can never understand, but to the outside world is just something which exerts a gravitational pull and nothing else.

MELVYN BRAGG: I know these are enormous questions, but what is the main cause of a star collapsing?

SIR MARTIN REES: Well, a star is held up by a very hot interior, gravity pulls it in but it's very hot inside, and a star is kept hot in its interior by nuclear fuel. The same kind of fusion process that happens in an H-Bomb happens in a controlled way inside stars. When a star runs out of fuel it will face a crisis, and for heavy stars this crisis is solved by an implosion, which may lead to a neutron star, and may lead to a black hole.

So gravity always wins if fuel sources run out, and in a large star when gravity wins it pulls all of the material that was in the star together and much of it ends up in a black hole. Gravity always wins, if there's no pressure or heat to oppose it.

MELVYN BRAGG: Right. Jocelyn Bell Burnell, when the Reverend John Mitchell announced in 1783 a definition of the black hole, it was a brilliant three-line definition and it reads very clearly now. What interests me, because he was so ahead of his time, is how he got there without Einstein, without telescopes, without technology? Can you tell me how he arrived at that conclusion which has only over the last thirty or forty years been explored with any sort of certainty by people like yourselves?

JOCELYN BELL BURNELL: He was working with a picture of light that was invented by Sir Isaac Newton. It's called the Corpuscular Theory of Light, which is still a picture which we use in many, many ways in contemporary science. What Newton envisaged was that light was a stream of little bullet-like things, little particles, and each of these corpuscles actually had weight, and gravity would pull on that weight just like if you tried to lift a bottle of water. Light would have a weight like the bottle of water and gravity would be pulling it back, and what Mitchell was doing was saying how much gravity does there have to be to pull the light back and stop it escaping? And that at heart was what he was doing and Laplace, I think, a few years later, was doing the same thing.

MELVYN BRAGG: So it was a thought experiment?

JOCELYN BELL BURNELL: Yes.

MELVYN BRAGG: Working from Newton he got, as it were, beyond Einstein?

JOCELYN BELL BURNELL: It's an alternative way of looking at things. You quite often find in science there are parallel ways of looking at things, parallel pictures, parallel movies is perhaps the best way to describe them. As scientists we often use a lot of different pictures to help us understand. All the time you've got to remember it is a picture. It may not be the actual thing, and there are times when these pictures or analogies will let you down. So he was using a picture that one could still use today, though we don't happen to use it very often.

MELVYN BRAGG: Was that ever taken up? Do we know of the existence of his theory now because of what we know now, rather than people taking it up at the time and saying, ah, Mitchell said that in 1783 – I can build on that and develop on that?

JOCELYN BELL BURNELL: My guess is that we know of it because of hindsight. I think at the time it probably didn't make a great impact. People would have said, oh, that's an interesting calculation, pity it ain't relevant to the real world, and passed on. And it was only much, much later that the topic was revisited and I guess that Mitchell's quote and Laplace's quote were subsequently dug out again and people said, oh look, they thought of it this way back in 1784.

MELVYN BRAGG: Martin Ward, is it unusual in science that something discovered theoretically first is then found again much later, as it seems to be the case with the black holes?

MARTIN WARD: Not particularly. There are examples in particle physics where one has a certain model, and based on that model particles that have not yet been observed are predicted and then the particle . . .

MELVYN BRAGG: Can you give an example?

MARTIN WARD: Well, I am not a particle physicist but there are many examples of this. Many particle physicists build huge accelerators to test these particular models. So there are many examples, and of course a good theory will make predictions that one has to go and test. A theory that makes no predictions is not a very good theory.

MELVYN BRAGG: And so when did the practicalities catch up with the theory in the study of black holes?

MARTIN WARD: How do we actually observe black holes? I am an observational astronomer, Martin is a theoretical astronomer, so he interprets our observations, and of course observations are what we have to have to move forward. It turns out that black holes can be detected, observed, inferred, by various types of observations. I can't give you a complete list because it is very long. But the interesting thing is what happens to matter.

What do I mean by matter? I generally mean gas that comes from somewhere else outside of the black hole and is pulled in by gravity, as Martin explained, towards the black hole, just in the same way that the planets are orbiting around the sun. This gas is orbiting around the black hole and gradually it is pulled in, it spirals in, and one of the ways we can actually observe them, we can infer them, is because this gas gets extremely hot, it becomes very dense because it's compressed, and it emits X-rays.

My particular discipline of X-ray astronomy is important in the detection of black holes because that's what we use to see them. The hotter things get the higher energies they emit. It's the analogy of the furnace: if you have an ordinary furnace it glows red, if you wind up the temperature it gets to be yellow, and then blue, and then goes into the ultraviolet. The stuff that falls into black holes gets even hotter than millions of degrees and then we see it in X-rays – that has to be done from above the earth's atmosphere.

MELVYN BRAGG: So it took a development in technology to get that, because Martin Rees earlier referred to the gravitational imprint. If we're going to be strict about the word 'black', we cannot see them so we are inferring them from . . .

MARTIN WARD: ... processes that occur near to the so-called 'event horizon'. There are other ways to infer their existence, and that is by their effect on other bodies, not by making them very hot but just by disturbing the motions of stars, for example, near to a black hole such as we may have in the centre of our own galaxy. By looking at these stars as test particles, if you like, moving around the black hole, that can be another way to infer their existence.

MELVYN BRAGG: Martin Rees, what does a black hole do to space-time, in Einstein's General Theory of Relativity?

SIR MARTIN REES: The reason black holes are fascinating is that they exemplify the way in which Einstein's theory leads to surprising and counterintuitive conclusions in extreme situations. In our local context, on the earth, in the solar system, gravity is fairly weak, and Newton's theory is in effect good enough. But when gravity is very strong or when motions are very fast and things are moving at about the speed of light then we are not surprised that we have to go beyond Newton's theory. This is why we can understand black holes better now than Mitchell was able to 200 years ago.

We have a theory that can cope consistently in these extreme situations and according to Einstein's theory a black hole is an object where there's a definite sort of surface which is the place from within which no light can get out. And outside this surface we can calculate how gas or stars could move and that, as Martin Ward explained, is how we can infer the presence of black holes. But what fascinates scientists and physicists in particular about black holes is that deep inside them, in the region that we can't directly observe, there lurks a very basic mystery indeed.

MELVYN BRAGG: The singularity?

SIR MARTIN REES: Singularities, so called. The idea here is that deep inside the black hole gravity becomes stronger and stronger and stronger and eventually, according to the theory, it becomes infinite. And what this in fact means is that the theory which Einstein gave us breaks down and we have to find some new theory. Deep inside black holes there is a place we know for sure but we don't know enough physics to understand it. We need the kind of physics which unifies gravity, the force governing large-scale objects, with quantum theory which governs small-scale objects. We need the same sort of breakthrough in physics which we would need also to understand the Big Bang and the beginning of the universe. So, black holes point towards places we can actually observe in our universe, where physics transcends what we now understand.

MELVYN BRAGG: And also black holes bring in this remarkable business of light bending. Eddington in 1919 proved this empirically with the eclipse of the sun to justify, to validate, Einstein's theory. Can you talk about light bending, Jocelyn Bell Burnell? And in terms of the event horizon around the black hole – I'm using a term that I've got from you three, that is 'event horizon'. Sometimes if light goes towards a black hole it disappears into a black hole. I mean we're talking fantasy as far as I'm concerned, but here we go!

JOCELYN BELL BURNELL: It's good fun . . .

MELVYN BRAGG: Other times it bends around it. Now can you tell us why sometimes light just disappears into this hole and cannot get out? I think we must keep emphasising this because once you're in this black hole . . .

JOCELYN BELL BURNELL: You've had it.

MELVYN BRAGG: Not even light can get out, and light travels faster than anything we know and that can't get out, so nothing can get out. So light disappears into this singularity, which Martin says is beyond physics at the moment. But some light, seeing the black hole through the event on the horizon, as it were, bends?

JOCELYN BELL BURNELL: Yep.

MELVYN BRAGG: Now it's over to you.

JOCELYN BELL BURNELL: I have a picture of a table top and not a very smooth table top. It's a billiard table but it's got dents in it, and as you shoot a ball across this table it gets deflected by the dents. A black hole is not just a dent, it's like a plughole in your billiard table. It goes right through to the darkness underneath. Instead of a billiard ball we now have a ray of light, but it behaves in the same way. And where the space is flat it trundles straight, but where there's a dimple in space it curves, just like your billiard ball curves. And where there's a black hole and it heads straight for it, it goes 'whoops!' and down the hole.

Now, if you keep a bit away from the plughole, where space is still a bit curved but before it's got a bit plug-ish, hole-ish, then you can also get the light bent, but not falling in. If you aim light straight at a black hole it's going to go down, down the tube, but if you aim light a bit past the black hole it will just get bent. And what Eddington was doing in that eclipse expedition just after the First World War was checking out a prediction of Einstein's that mass and gravity would bend light. He wasn't using a black hole, he was actually using the sun, he was using the sun at the time of an eclipse so that the sunlight was blocked out and you could actually see what was happening to the rays of light from beyond the sun as they came past the sun. What Eddington was checking out was how much bend is there in a light ray as it goes round the edge of one of these dimples in the billiard table.

MELVYN BRAGG: And just before we leave the anatomy of the black hole, Martin Ward, could you tell us about the event horizon, can you describe what that is and why it's so important?

MARTIN WARD: Essentially it's an interface between what goes on inside the black hole and what goes on in the rest of the universe. The only way we can make progress in science is to make observations, experiments, and so on. And the importance of the event horizon is that after something goes through it, whatever that is, light or gas or anything, after that its properties become very simple. It adds to the mass of the black hole, and therefore the event horizon gets a little bit bigger, but then it can't communicate, by any means. Radio waves, any sort of communication is impossible after the event horizon. So we have to rely on theory to know what happens to matter after it's gone through. There's no more communication with the outside universe.

MELVYN BRAGG: As I understand it, your team at Leicester was the first in the world to discover physical evidence of medium-sized black holes. Is it possible for you to sum up the significance of that?

MARTIN WARD: Yes. This was a big collaboration involving many astronomers throughout the world, in the United States and Japan, because all these big instruments require huge investment of money. We were part of this collaboration. We'll probably go on to discuss massive black holes and not so massive black holes. The most interesting thing about science is that if you make an observational discovery there's always several interpretations. So this is currently one of the interpretations.

We looked at a nearby galaxy. Everything's relative terms, isn't it? It's about 9 million light years away, this isn't our backyard by our standards. And we looked at it with an X-ray telescope, and I won't go into technical details but it has tremendously fine resolution, acuity of vision, which we didn't have before for X-ray telescopes. The universe emits radiation across the electromagnetic spectrum, X-rays are one part. Previously we had a blurred view and now we have a clear view. We looked at this particular galaxy and we saw a bright X-ray source, which was so bright that if we used the standard argument that astronomers use to infer the mass of a black hole, one of them, then we believe it has about 500 times the mass of the sun. So this is in between . . .

MELVYN BRAGG: Not the size, but the mass of the sun . . . ?

MARTIN WARD: The mass of the sun, yes. This was in between the small ones, diddly ones, of a few times the mass of the sun, and the huge ones in the centre of quasars, which are perhaps a billion times the mass of the sun. Now, the significance is that this particular source was not in the centre of the galaxy. We would normally think that these massive black holes, because of gravity, as Martin explained at the beginning, would form at the very centre, because that's where the mass is.

But this is many hundreds of light years away from the centre, so the question is, first of all, is it an intermediate mass black hole? Another interpretation is possible: if it is, how do you form these things, not in the centre of the galaxy? It could be cannibalism, actually, it could have been a passing galaxy which had a black hole in its centre, which had an accident and crashed into the other galaxy. We are just as a snapshot seeing this little black hole, by chance, away from the nucleus.

MELVYN BRAGG: Or you're just making it up!

MARTIN WARD: It's one theory – but what's the significance? If it is an intermediate black hole, then how do you form these things? If we could understand that, and it's a nearby example and we studied in detail, maybe we'd get clues to how to form the really massive ones.

MELVYN BRAGG: Martin Rees, did you want to come in on this?

SIR MARTIN REES: Well, I think what Martin Ward has just said emphasises that black holes are now one of the zoo of objects which astronomers study. They study stars of all kinds, galaxies, exploding stars, and they find evidence for different classes of black holes. We try and put these together into some grand evolutionary scenario as to how the universe has evolved and formed these objects. But one thing which we should be clear about is perhaps the sizes of these black holes, the different masses.

The black holes that were first discovered and which are thought to be what happens in a star when it runs out of fuel and it collapses, would be a few miles across, whereas there could be black holes – indeed, we think there are black holes – in the centre of galaxies which weigh as much as millions or even billions of stars and they are proportionately bigger. The size of a black hole scales directly with its mass, so a black hole weighing a few million times as much as the sun would be a few million times larger and, indeed, would have quite a large volume inside it. So if you fell inside you would have quite a long time for leisured observation before you got to this other singularity . . .

MELVYN BRAGG: Let's be completely clear about this. This difference in size, mass. If the sun were to turn into a black hole, what would be the diameter of the black hole?

SIR MARTIN REES: The black hole from the sun would be about two or three miles across. A few times smaller than the neutron stars which Jocelyn Bell Burnell discovered. But a black hole of a kind which might exist in the centre of our galaxy would weigh as much as about three million suns, and that would be about ten million miles across, because the size goes with the mass. So there are these much bigger black holes and there may be even the medium-sized ones which Martin Ward was talking about.

But the theory of gravity doesn't have any sort of preferred size built into it, so in principle, according to Einstein's theory, there could be black holes of any size. And perhaps to pre-empt what we might come to later, there could also even, theoretically, be little tiny black holes, the size of an atom, which would weigh as much as an asteroid or a mountain. There are loads of theoretical constructs that probably don't exist, but according to the theory there could be black holes of any size and any mass, and it's up to the astronomers to discover which of these actually exist in our universe and which are formed by different groups.

MELVYN BRAGG: And what that might be for and what that might do. But just to keep mapping this out, Jocelyn, Martin Rees said you'd found these small black holes – what is the difference, are there any distinctions between the small black holes and those of intermediate size and super massive size?

JOCELYN BELL BURNELL: Could we just clear up what we mean by size. We've talked both about the mass of black holes and their physical size. The physical size of a black hole is perhaps more confusing because one moment we're saying it collapses right down to this singularity, to point size. When we as professional astronomers talk about the size of the black hole what we're usually talking about is the size of the event horizon, that mythical surface round the black hole, which is its Rubicon, and if you cross that event horizon you are going down the black hole come hell or high water. If you can keep outside the event horizon you may escape. And for the sun that's about three miles across, and for the bigger things it's much, much bigger.

The physics of the star size, the intermediate mass, the super mass of black holes are all very similar. They are large, large gravitational masses with this so-called singularity at the centre and round them this event horizon. But, interestingly, the effects that you would feel as you fell into these different kinds of black holes are different. The star-size black hole, as you cross the horizon you would feel the effects, not just of gravity but of the gradient of gravity tearing your body apart. Whereas if you were going into a super massive black hole at the centre of a galaxy you actually don't feel that effect until much, much later, which in that case is too late. But the basic physics is very similar, yes.

MELVYN BRAGG: Can I come back to you for a moment, Martin Rees, and then go from there? Is there a super massive black hole in our own galaxy? And what role do you see it having? Are there words – I'm stumbling around for words – are there words like role and function? Are they relevant at all in this? Does it have a role? Does it have a function? Does it have a place you can see which is interdependent on others, is helped by others, the way we like things to fit in, in engineering and, if we're lucky, in the rest of life?

SIR MARTIN REES: It is certainly part of the picture. If you wish to understand galaxies and stars, the picture we have is that the universe started off as an expanding amorphous fireball after the Big Bang and at some stage galaxies and stars condensed out, and they eventually evolved, and around some of those stars we had planets, etc., etc. So we picture cosmic evolution spread out over a bit more than 10 thousand billion years, and at some stage black holes have become part of this scenario, and they do indeed play two important roles.

One is that they are the end point of stars. If we came back and looked at the universe in the far future a lot more of the stuff would have ended up in black holes, in this dead remnant, because gravity will have eventually won, and swallowed up the vast material. So there's a general trend towards more and more of the material ending up in black holes. But they're also important to astronomers in trying to understand the universe because they are able to manifest their presence in a very conspicuous way. Although a black hole doesn't put out any energy, something falling into a black hole releases a tremendous amount of energy. I mentioned that if something falls on to a neutron star it releases a lot of energy and an explosion, but if something falls into a black hole it releases far more energy, per kilogram, than you can get in any kind of explosion, even a nuclear explosion.

What this means is that black holes, when they are not in empty space but are surrounded by stars and gas, shine very brightly, and indeed some of the most spectacular optics in the universe that we observe, things called quasars, objects sending out jets, and indeed exploding stars of various kinds, are energised black holes which are interacting with stuff close to them. So they are very important to us as astronomers because they are conspicuous objects to study and therefore allow us to probe distant parts of the universe because they're the brightest things that we can see out there.

MELVYN BRAGG: Martin Rees referred to the Big Bang 12 thousand million years ago or slightly more and it has been suggested by Hawking that maybe black holes were there at the start of that. They could be something to do with creating and 'seeding' the galaxies. Can you just discuss that possibility?

MARTIN WARD: I think it's a chicken and egg sort of argument. The fundamental question is – what's the dominant energy output process of the universe? There are two contenders really. One is star formation in the same way that the Orion Nebula is an example of stars forming in our own galaxy. It's called a stellar nursery sometimes. And these processes are nuclear processes, as Martin Rees has said.

They're not terribly efficient, in fact, in converting matter into energy, by the e=mc². Black holes are more efficient, ten times or even more than ten times more efficient. We don't actually know, at the moment, in the early stages of the universe, what the dominant energy process was. Whether it was accretion, that's a technical word that means material falling on to the black hole, accreting through the event horizon, and that produces a lot of energy, or is it star formation? It's a big open question. The early generation of black holes, say the ones that were formed just a billion years after the Big Bang, these are hypothetical but they could have provided the seeds for galaxy formation. This is work that Martin Rees has done. And one of the efforts in observational astronomy, particularly X-ray astronomy these days, is to look for signatures of black hole activity in the early universe to try and quantify whether it was star-forming regions or whether it was accretion that was producing a lot of the energy in the early stages.

MELVYN BRAGG: Are black holes always on the retreat? Because if they're always on the retreat then the idea of them being a seeding wouldn't seem to me to make any sense. But what I've heard so far is that they get smaller and smaller and more and more mass, pull more and more in, eventually reach a singularity in which you've got infinite density and zero . . .

JOCELYN BELL BURNELL: . . . size . . .

MELVYN BRAGG: Size, yes, that's right, zero size. And so are all black holes destined to disappear in that way and, if so, how can they be part of an expanding universe?

MARTIN WARD: I think there's a misconception here. They don't disappear . . .

MELVYN BRAGG: . . . Ah well, if you could clear that up I would be very obliged.

MARTIN WARD: They can't get smaller. The event horizon can only be what it is now, or larger if it accretes more material. As it accretes more material the event horizon will scale up and become larger, as I think Martin referred to earlier. The sense of their disappearing – the misconception is to do with whether we see evidence for them. It's believed that these very energetic things called quasars that were formed in the early universe emit tremendous amounts of energy, as much energy as the entire star output of energy from our galaxy, in a region the size of the solar system.

But that only works if they're feeding, another rather colloquial term, if material is falling into them. If that dries up, if they stop feeding, then the black hole becomes really black, because it is only the effects of the matter falling through the event horizon which produces the energy. So it may be that there are black holes sitting there which are not feeding, which we can't observe. The era of black holes producing huge amounts of energy may be over but they're still there. They haven't disappeared.

MELVYN BRAGG: Jocelyn Bell Burnell.

JOCELYN BELL BURNELL: An analogy due to a colleague of mine at the Open University: you see a child, a small child, with chocolate all over its face. You rightly infer that the child has been eating chocolate; you don't have direct evidence that the child has eaten the chocolate but you do see the side effects. It's a bit like that with material going into a black hole. You don't see the material that has gone in, but you see the effects that happen as the stuff goes in, the plastering around the mouth.

MELVYN BRAGG: Martin Rees, this would lead me on to the conclusion that if black holes are sucking everything in that comes anywhere near them then eventually everything will be sucked in to one black hole or another. We're all destined, the future of the universe is that we all end up in a black hole.

SIR MARTIN REES: Things aren't quite as apocalyptic as that. Black holes are indeed growing but we are, for instance, at an extremely safe distance from the one in the centre of our galaxy. There's no danger of that swallowing us up, so indeed although they are growing it would take a very long time before they swallowed up more than a tiny fragment of the galaxy.

MELVYN BRAGG: But also, not to be apocalyptic but to look far forward – you people around this table speak very easily of 12 billion years ago and that sort of thing – let's just take the odd billion or so years ahead. Are black holes not going to go away, or are they going to go away, or are they going to grow? What's going to happen there?

SIR MARTIN REES: They're going to grow, but there is a very interesting effect which will happen in the very, very far future, which does perhaps mean that they will not actually exist for ever. This is that there are tiny effects which are beyond what Einstein predicted in his theory which allow for the micro-structure of space, and the effects of quantum theory. These will gradually erode away black holes. This is an effect which wasn't in Einstein's theory but has been included later, and this will cause a so-called erosional evaporation of black holes. But the time we're talking about, at which this operates, is far, far longer than the age of our present universe.

And this I think indicates two things about the importance of black holes. One is that although we understand black holes well enough to interpret some of the astronomical observations, there are still mysteries about the details. And also they do point towards new physics, new physics that may manifest itself deep inside black holes, and will manifest itself in present-day black holes in the far future. So they are important because they are made, as it were, from the fabric of space and time. And if you want to understand space and time, not only on the large scale of the universe but on the tiny microscopic scale of atoms, you are going to have to have some new ideas to make sense of this. And black holes are going to be the kind of places where we can perhaps test these theories.

MELVYN BRAGG: Jocelyn Bell Burnell, is it possible to tell us what the effect on space and time is of the black holes? I mean, if this studio went into a black hole, what would be the effect on our space and time?

JOCELYN BELL BURNELL: If this studio right now started falling into a star-sized black hole, a star mass black hole, as opposed to one of the bigger ones, the first thing that would happen is that we'd begin to feel our bodies being pulled apart, because not only was the gravity strong but there was a very strong gradient of gravity, which means the gravity on the lower part of your body is much bigger than the gravity on the upper part of your body and it would ultimately rip things apart in the most unpleasant manner.

MELVYN BRAGG: Spaghettification.

JOCELYN BELL BURNELL: Spaghettification, yes, you get long and thin, you go in sort of strands . . .

MELVYN BRAGG: A lot of people would pay for that!

JOCELYN BELL BURNELL: Yes, but it's not a pleasant experience. If there was somebody else on another planet able to observe us and the studio falling into the black hole, if they could see the studio clock, which I'm sure is very precise, the closer we got to the event horizon the slower the clock would go. We wouldn't actually notice that effect because our hearts and our whole metabolisms would be slowed in the same way. So actually what we'd just notice was the gravity. But the mass of a black hole or indeed of any massive object does alter clocks.

One of the things that people in my speciality have to be aware of, where you're dealing with pulsars which are very accurate clocks, we have to be aware that our watches, our clocks run at different rates between new moon and full moon. It's only about a millionth of a second difference, but it is there, and it's because at new moon, sun and moon are on one side of the earth, at full moon sun and moon are on opposite sides of the earth and so earth experiences slightly different gravity, and the two circumstances now clock slightly different rates. It's a much bigger effect near a black hole.

MELVYN BRAGG: Martin Ward, is there any purchase at the present time on the idea that something, this terrible greed that we have, that something could come out of a black hole which would be useful, which we could harness?

MARTIN WARD: Can we tax it? That sort of argument. I frankly think – no. I mean in principle and I emphasise – in theory, I should say – we could possibly extract energy from a black hole, because if you had two particles falling into a black hole it would be possible that one could fall into the black hole and the other one could be – they call it sling shot – shot out of the black hole with more energy. It could be extracting energy, if you like, from the black hole. In theory. But I think the practicalities of this would be so difficult, I'm interested to hear Martin's view that this would really not be the way to go. I think we'd be better off trying to solve how to do fusion effectively or something like that. The European Space Agency isn't necessarily interested in making money out of space missions and so on. What they are interested in is making new observations.

And in the future there's a very interesting new satellite. ESA, the European Space Agency, is like NASA, slightly less money than NASA has, but it does many things in space. And a European mission, which may be a joint one with NASA, is to look at the effect on the fabric of space of black holes as they merge together. We haven't talked about this, but we've talked about material, gas, falling on to a black hole. You can have a situation where two black holes are going around each other and they can spiral in and they can merge into one black hole. And it turns out from the Theory of General Relativity when this happens there is a pulse of gravity waves, so called, which propagate out, presumably at the speed of light, though that depends on whether they have any mass.

This can be detected. Jocelyn gave an analogy, a nice analogy, of the billiard table and the indentations which are caused by mass. So an experiment is to put a bit of graph paper, if you like, on the billiard table in space. Separate spacecrafts, separated by about 5 million kilometres, look for the wobbliness of the curvature of space as the gravity waves permeate through the universe towards us. And so we should be able to hear a chirp, there's an analogy with sound, it has a certain frequency, so you can imagine it almost like an orchestra, playing different notes, different chirps, as different massed black holes merge together. This isn't fantasy, this is actually scientific theory.

MELVYN BRAGG: Martin Rees, you've talked about two black holes joined together hurtling quietly through the universe – you didn't use quietly, I did, because it sounds ominous – can you discuss that in a second? But can you first go back to the previous point? Roger Penrose has talked of the 'hypothetical plan' for using the powers of a black hole – is there any potential in this at all?

SIR MARTIN REES: I think this is futuristic and almost science fiction, the idea of getting energy from them. The other thing that in principle happens near a black hole, if you go into the right orbits but stay just outside the black hole, is the converse of what Jocelyn Bell Burnell was saying about the clock. If you fall in, down there near the black hole, you see everything else in the external universe happening in a speeded-up way. So if you go to a place near a black hole you can in principle see the external universe speeded up and see its entire future – but that is science fiction.

Turning to the more direct motivations for doing this sort of work, I should mention that the corrections to Newton's theory due to Einstein are in fact significant enough to be used in the GPS satellites for getting out positions, that's one application. But the main reason why we study black holes is twofold. First they're clearly an important part of our cosmic habitat, which is really part of our environment. And secondly, gravity is a fundamental force of nature and there's a limit to what we can do experimentally on earth. The cosmos provides us with a way in which we can study the laws of nature and the forces of nature which are far more extreme positions than we could ever simulate on earth. And so as you understand forces such as electricity, nuclear forces and gravity, then we can learn a great deal from these observations. Black holes in particular are objects that extremely strongly manifest the effects of gravity, so that's the motivation, I would say.

MELVYN BRAGG: Jocelyn Bell Burnell, can I ask you one simple question – is there a possibility of white holes?

JOCELYN BELL BURNELL: Yes, the equations that predict black holes can be run in the opposite direction of time and in theory there could be white holes, places where material suddenly appears out of nowhere and spreads out into the universe. But we've not seen any yet.

TRANSMITTED: 21.02.2008

r

Avicenna

I n the city of Hamadan in Iran, right in the centre, there's a vast mausoleum dedicated to an Iranian national hero. Built in 1952, exactly 915 years
after his death, it's a high conical tower with twelve supporting columns. It's
dedicated not to a warrior or a king but to a philosopher and physician. His
name is Abu Ali al-Husain ibn Sina, but he's also known as Avicenna and is
arguably the most important philosopher in the history of Islam.

With me to discuss Avicenna, his world, his ideas and his influence on the
way that both Muslims and Christians think, an influence which continued
for centuries, are Peter Adamson, Reader in Philosophy at King's College,
London; Amira Bennison, Senior Lecturer in Middle Eastern and Islamic
Studies at the University of Cambridge; and Nader El-Bizri, Affiliated Lecturer
in the History and Philosophy of Science, also at the University of Cambridge.

Peter Adamson, we know a great deal about ibn Sina's life from his
autobiography. It was, it seems, finished by his pupil. He was born in
980 in Central Asia – and can you go on from there?

PETER ADAMSON: The biography – autobiography – is a very
useful text for Avicenna. Not only do we learn a lot about his life
from that but we learn a lot about what he was like as a person,
partially because we have his own words telling us what he was like.
There are two things that really come out of that autobiography. One
is that he was immensely pleased with himself. The other, which is
rather connected to this, is his kind of independence and originality
with respect to the tradition that came down to him.

First of all, why was he so pleased with himself? Well, he tells us
that he was a child prodigy and that by the age of ten, for example, he
had mastered the Koran. He went on to study arithmetic, medicine

389

and logic and in these disciplines he was so impressive that he was able to outstrip the ability of his master within a year. He also tells us that by the time he was eighteen he had already formulated most of his ideas and that the rest of his career was just spent spinning them out in ever more refined ways. He seems to have had a prodigious memory. We've already seen he memorised the Koran at a very early age. And, for example, because his life was spent often moving around through Central Asia and then into modern-day Iran, he often had to work using only his memory without any sources available to him, as it were, on his desk and yet he still manages to engage with a very wide range of Islamic ideas and also ideas from the Greek tradition.

MELVYN BRAGG: His father was a scholar, as I understand it, as was his brother. You say he was very pleased with himself, but from what you've said he had good reason to be, didn't he?

PETER ADAMSON: Absolutely. He's a genius, in fact, and he knew he was a genius and this really comes out in the autobiography. As I say, he's very emphatic that not only was he able to accomplish these prodigious feats of memory, he was able to write voluminously in a very short period of time in a way that really impressed other people. He was well acquainted with his own abilities.

MELVYN BRAGG: Do we know any more about his family than that his father and brothers were scholars? Is it an intellectual family – can you set it in context? We're talking about a thousand years ago, the tenth into the eleventh century?

PETER ADAMSON: I think that there are two things that are important to know about his father. One is that he was a governor under the Samanids who rule parts of Central Asia and what's called Transoxania and northern Iran. He was part of a politically well-favoured family, at least when Avicenna was young. The other thing to know about his father was that he had apparently some kind of Shiite leaning. It's not clear how far to take this but his father was apparently attracted by the ideas of a group of Shiite thinkers called the Ismailis, who were in turn very influenced by ideas from the Greek Platonic tradition.

But Avicenna, with his customary originality, rejected these ideas when he heard them being discussed in his father's house and struck out on his own. I think that's a sign from Avicenna's childhood of his independence of mind, which is not something that should be underestimated. If you think about medieval philosophers, he's probably the medieval philosopher who's most self-consciously original and a lot of the ideas that we'll talk about shortly are not ideas that he presents as interpretations of Aristotle or anyone else but, to the contrary, they're ideas that he presents as deliberate departures from the tradition that comes down to him.

MELVYN BRAGG: There's a tendency, a sometimes useful cliché, that philosophers are in ivory towers or minarets and are apart and dry and ascetic, but he seems to have been a worldly and provocative figure. Can you develop that a little?

PETER ADAMSON: Yes. Something that's important to remember about Avicenna is that for the people around him it was at least as important that he was a medical physician as that he was a philosopher. For example, again when he was a teenager, he gained access to the very impressive library of the Samanids.

MELVYN BRAGG: I want to come to that in a minute. I want to talk about his character first. We haven't quite got there. You've told us he was very pleased with himself, you told us he was a polymath, we know a little about his father, but – in the autobiography – he drank a lot – can you flesh it out a bit? Don't spend more than half a minute on it but just . . .

PETER ADAMSON: Maybe the most salacious detail from the biography . . .

MELVYN BRAGG: Not only salacious, I just want to round it up a bit because it's interesting.

PETER ADAMSON: I think it's right to say that he was someone who really enjoyed life and that these prodigious feats of memory and his willingness to depart from the tradition was of a piece with, for example, the fact that he did use wine to keep himself up at night. That's actually connected with the fact that he was able to write so much. Another example is that his student tells us – and this is not a criticism on the part of the student, this is sort of praise – that he had a very well-developed sexual capacity and that one of the reasons why he became ill and died at a relatively young age, in his mid-fifties, is that he didn't follow his own medical advice and continued to indulge in this wider range of things. On the other hand he wasn't a hedonist. But he was clearly more than anything else a serious scholar and thinker. He's not what you'd expect from a medieval philosopher.

MELVYN BRAGG: Your embellishment can cease, Peter! We can put the life aside and concentrate on the ideas from now on. But I do think it is part of the mix in this particular case and rather surprisingly, and it might, who knows, be significant.

Amira Bennison, can you give us a sense of the political situation in Avicenna's early life? The Islamic world was under the sway of the Abbasid caliphs, but wasn't that breaking up? They were in Baghdad, Avicenna was in Uzbekistan, part of the Persian Empire. Can you just tell us what the politics were?

AMIRA BENNISON: It's a very interesting period from a political perspective. Whilst you do still have the Abbasid caliphate situated in Baghdad, the caliphate had become much more of a symbolic religious institution and much less of an actual political institution. We've already heard of the Samanids who ruled in Transoxania in northern Iran; they were a dynasty of autonomous governors who recognised the Abbasids but acted in a completely independent way in terms of governing the regions of which they were in control. However, although Avicenna's father worked for the Samanids, during Avicenna's own lifetime the Saminids' state came to an end, it fragmented, and you have other political powers coming in.

At the centre, in Baghdad itself, the caliphs were really under the de facto control of a dynasty called the Buwayhids who were actually a confederation. There was a Buwayhid ruler based in Baghdad in Iraq, also one in Rai in northern Iran, situated near the site of modern Tehran, and also in Fars to the south. And in fact there was this multiplicity of smaller political units, there were numerous patrons. If you wanted to take up the previous role, which the caliphs had held in Baghdad, of stimulating and patronising knowledge, this made it such a fertile time in terms of philosophy and other ideas – Shiism, Sufism. It's a very important time politically. You have almost a contradiction. On the one hand you have political fragmentation occurring but at the same time that's actually stimulating cultural efflorescence in a number of different relatively minor centres, including cities where Avicenna spent a lot of his time, like Isfahan in southern Iran.

MELVYN BRAGG: Can we go back to his early days? When he was about seventeen or eighteen, as I understand it, Dr Avicenna healed a regional governor and he came to the attention of the local Samanid dynasty. He was invited to their court. What advantage would it give him, being part of the court?

AMIRA BENNISON: This era's one in which inter-personal relationships were of primary importance for advancement. So the mere fact that Avicenna came to the attention of the Saminids was very important in terms of him developing his thought and his career. It opened up career prospects to him. He would begin to meet with other individuals like himself who served the Saminids in some capacity, other scholars, people who served as ministers advising a ruler, other physicians. He became, if you like, part of a courtly elite made up of scholars and advisors.

MELVYN BRAGG: His primary discipline at that time was that of a physician, a man of medicine. Nader El-Bizri, at that time, the Saminids had, as I understand it, a vast library to which this young man, this teenager, was given access. What would be in the library?

NADER EL-BIZRI: That library would have been on a par with the libraries that we find in Baghdad or Basra or Isfahan or even in Cairo under the Fatimids. It would have had titles that related to many works that came down from the Greeks, some related also to ancient Indian traditions and to Babylonian. And also a variety of texts and studies that had been developed since the time of the translation and transmission movement which started towards the end of the eighth century. So he encountered no less than 200 years of commentaries and textual criticisms and expansions of whatever was encountered in terms of the translation and transmission movement within the Islamic civilisation.

It would have had titles that relate to all the branches of the exact sciences and mathematics and medicine, including works on geometry, on arithmetic, works related to the newly related discipline of algebra, works on astronomy, on mechanics, various treatises related to logic, metaphysics, studies in the realm of psychology, or what we might call treatises on the soul, the anima. And a variety of textual traditions associated with the development of the medical profession, including texts that were established by prominent physicians in the Islamic medieval civilisation. Titles like Euclid's *Elements* . . .

MELVYN BRAGG: All in Arabic – are these translated into Arabic?

NADER EL-BIZRI: All translated from Greek and Syriac into Arabic. The translation movement started around the end of the eighth century, intensified in the ninth century, further refinements and revisions of translations happened throughout the ninth and tenth centuries. For instance, the *Elements* of Euclid had three versions of translations in a span of not more than thirty years. And besides the texts that were transmitted from the Greek traditions there were processes of adaptive assimilation and expansion of the various branches of knowledge.

MELVYN BRAGG: So there was a golden cave there for him. He also drew on the Islamic and Persian ideas as found in *kalam*. Can you explain what that is?

NADER EL-BIZRI: It's a tradition that we might describe as a dialectical doctrinal theology. It developed in response to the initial assimilation of Greek ideas within the intellectual milieu, particularly in Iraq and Mesopotamia. It was a way of introducing methods of argumentation that are based on rational deliberation or reasoning in the pursuit of addressing fundamental questions pertaining to Islamic theology. One of the debates, the heated debates, was around divine essence and the divine attributes and how to account for them in a manner that does not compromise the centrality of the idea of divine transcendence or the centrality of the idea of divine unity.

MELVYN BRAGG: So an enormous amount was there for him to draw on, Peter Adamson. But, as you said, he took those ideas and self-consciously or not, made them original, made them his own. This originality we have to keep in mind and the massiveness of the man's achievement across the board. So let's look at one or two of his main philosophical ideas. He devised thought experiments and one was called the floating man or the flying man. Can you tell us about that and what he was driving at?

PETER ADAMSON: This is a famous thought experiment that he gives us in his works on the soul. He was again very pleased with himself for having thought of it, so he mentions it several times.

MELVYN BRAGG: I don't quite see why he shouldn't be pleased with himself. It's a great idea.

PETER ADAMSON: Absolutely. Actually it occurred to me, maybe I can slip in this one other . . .

MELVYN BRAGG: It doesn't accord with our stiff-upper-lip English modesty. Nevertheless . . .

PETER ADAMSON: No. In fact you might think it's not so much that he's pleased with himself as that he's just telling us the facts. I thought of another good anecdote which you might want to hear. He was once accused of not being very good in Arabic, so he went off and wrote an entire work collating various obscure references to the Arabic language and various aspects of it to show up the person who had made this accusation against him, so this was the kind of thing he was able to do.

MELVYN BRAGG: Back to the floating man.

PETER ADAMSON: The floating man argument is an example he gives in several contexts where he's talking about the relationship between the soul and the body. He says, well, imagine the following scenario. Suppose that God creates an adult human who is perfect in terms of all of his cognitive capacities but this person is created in mid-air, floating or falling. And he's blindfolded, he can't see anything, there's nothing to hear, there's no wind and his limbs are stretched out so that he's not touching his own body. Avicenna then makes the assertion that a person in this situation would still be aware of his own existence.

The reason this is remarkable is that he's aware of his existence even though he's never had any sense experiences at all, and more to the point he doesn't know that he has a body because he can't see his body, he can't touch his body – his limbs are stretched out, his fingers are even extended so they're not touching each other. Because of the centrality of the claim that the flying man or the floating man would know of his own existence this is sometimes compared to the famous argument of Descartes: I think therefore I am. Descartes says could I doubt everything? No, because there's one thing I can't doubt, I can't doubt my own existence.

Avicenna seems to be alluding to the same philosophical idea, the idea that we have this intimate awareness of our own existence. Yet I think that's not the point of the floating man argument. So what is the point? Well, as I said, it gets mentioned in contexts where he's talking about the relationship between the soul and the body. The point is not so much that there's one thing the floating man can't doubt, it's that he's aware of his existence even though he's not aware of the existence of his body. I think it would be fallacious to infer from that that the soul is not the body and is therefore immaterial. What Avicenna is trying to point out with the thought experiment is that it's conceptually possible that we are not identical with our body. Why? Well, because I can clearly conceive of myself and know that I exist without conceiving of my body or knowing that it exists. So if I can be aware of one thing without knowing another thing exists then, although that doesn't prove that the two things are distinct, it shows that it's conceptually possible that they're distinct.

MELVYN BRAGG: That was a great summary. Can you add to that, Nader El-Bizri? Do you see it as presaging 600 years later, Descartes' 'I think, therefore I am'?

NADER EL-BIZRI: It has some elements, yes. It is close to what we find in terms of Descartes' argument, but the purposes behind the thought experiment are different from what we find with Descartes. I would say the motivation is more in the sense of ontology rather than epistemology, in the sense that ultimately with the flying man argument there is a convergence between that affirmation of the existence of his own self and the affirmation of the fact that there is something rather than nothing.

It is an affirmation of being-ness, even though it is mediated with reference to his own self. It is actualised in the sense that the flying man is able to affirm that there is something rather than nothing. And ultimately this connects with what we find in terms of his reflections on necessity and contingency in terms of ontology or reflection on the question of being. This affirmation of existence is ultimately an affirmation of a connection with that which is necessary existent due to itself.

MELVYN BRAGG: We'll come back to that in a moment. Amira Bennison, at the time he was a court physician – that was the title he had – as well as philosophy he wrote a book *The Canon of Medicine*. Can you give us a sense of what Avicenna saw fit to put in this *Canon of Medicine*, which at the time was probably his most famous work and continued being used until the seventeenth century?

AMIRA BENNISON: As we've heard, Avicenna mastered medicine by the young age of eighteen, according to his own account, and he got his first official jobs, if you like, as a physician. He himself comments in his autobiography that medicine was by far the easiest of the sciences. Philosophy was the hard intellectual game but medicine was fairly straightforward and simple. So what he set out to do was write a compendium of all the known knowledge about medicine which is his medical canon. It was based to some extent on Galen and Hippocrates but also on Islamic medicine, as it had developed over time.

It's divided into five volumes looking at various aspects of medicine. One of the volumes looks at general issues of the human body, its health, therapeutics. Other volumes look at pharmacology, the use of herbs in medicine and various other remedies. There are also volumes on fevers, wounds, dealing with these kind of problems, pathologies, different kinds of disease and how one might address them. And in addition to the *Medical Canon* he also wrote numerous separate treatises on various aspects of medicine. Some of the most famous are things like the *Cardiac Remedies* and other books which he wrote on the use of different herbs and plants in the healing process.

MELVYN BRAGG: But he also spoke of diseases being infectious, perhaps being carried not only in the soil and water, which you describe, but also perhaps being carried in the air. He writes about diet, he writes about psychology, he writes about quarantine. You can see why it lasted for 700 years.

AMIRA BENNISON: Absolutely, yes. He's seen as being quite innovative, particularly in terms of his theories of experimentation and issues – you've mentioned quarantine and issues of contagion. I think it links up with the fact that he is in some ways a very practical thinker and he does try to apply the knowledge that he has. He was a practising physician, as well as writing on medicine. He's not an otherworldly character, he is embedded in daily life as well as being a philosopher, as well as being a physician, and he brings those things together in a remarkable and unique way. Hence his lasting fame in both the Islamic and then the Latin Christian worlds.

MELVYN BRAGG: To go back to philosophy now from medicine, although in his mind they would inform each other all the time, I presume? Nader El-Bizri, rather deceptively his major philosophical work was called *The Book of Healing*. It was also translated as *The Cure For Ignorance*. You began to touch on it in your last answer. He developed an argument for the existence of God which depended, as I understand it, on a distinction between essence and existence. Now is there any way you can tell us that – explain that to us – so that we understand it at this time in the morning?

NADER EL-BIZRI: Perhaps I will mediate the possible response to this question by accounting for what we might refer to as the modalities of necessity and contingency. He treats them in his logic but also he has applications of them in terms of his . . .

MELVYN BRAGG: What's he trying to prove, first of all, before you get going?

NADER EL-BIZRI: There is a conflict that he faced at the beginning when he started reading Aristotle in terms of how can we have a science, or a body of knowledge, that is universal, that accounts for the ultimate principles of reality. There was a conflict in his mind between on one side metaphysics or ontology, particularly the study of the question of being or existence, and on the other side theology. How ontology or a reflection on the question of being would lead us to a reflection on aspects that pertain to divinity, to the divine essence and attributes and to the notion of creation. It was al-Farabi's commentary on Aristotle that opened up the possibilities for him to reconcile ontology from one side with theology. But still that tension, at least in terms of the interpretation of his work, that tension I would think remained associated with his reflection on the question of being.

It is related in a way to what you could call an ontological argument, ultimately a form of proving the existence of God. There is a moment in it that could be taken as pure ontology, a pure reflection on the existence of being which ultimately, to be translated into a term that accords with the religious faith, requires the introduction of a theological notion. So he deploys in the ontological context, in the context of the metaphysics, the term 'the necessary existent because of itself' or 'the necessary existent due to itself'. And this could be translated in theological terms into a notion of the divine, into a conception of God. But this conception of God pertains to his own metaphysical endeavour. It was not accepted by theologians.

MELVYN BRAGG: Can you just take that on a bit, Peter Adamson, this idea of the necessary existent. Would it be too crude to boil it down to the first cause that all other examples of essence and existence are possible, or not possible, but there's infinite regression until you put a stop to it. And he says the whole universe exists, it must exist, because of some necessity, some necessary thing which is on its own, which is outside the essence and outside what Nader was talking about. This is an outside force and that can be called God.

PETER ADAMSON: Right. This I think is exactly why it's such an interesting proof of the existence of God, because if you think about why most people who believe in God believe in God there's a fundamental intuition. If you look around the studio or at home, if you're listening to this on the radio, think about the radio, the radio could not exist, there's no reason why it has to exist, look around at the whole of the world, the world doesn't have to exist. That's the intuition. There's no absurdity in supposing that it doesn't exist.

MELVYN BRAGG: If we didn't have a wireless . . .

PETER ADAMSON: Right. If you think about this in a slightly more technical way, what Avicenna would say is that there are two kinds of essences, or three kinds. The ones that are impossible – like round squares; the ones that are possible or contingent in themselves, and things like the radio, the radio doesn't need to exist. In fact Avicenna said something even more interesting about this, which is that if the radio doesn't exist there has to be a reason for that too. So the idea being that anything that's contingent or possible in itself, doesn't deserve to exist any more than it deserves not to exist.

So if it exists or doesn't exist there has to be an explanation for that. And the proof for the existence of God is really quite simple. He just says, well, suppose that everything were merely contingent, how would we explain that it exists? We can't, because in itself it's merely contingent, there's no reason why it has to exist. But if you hypothesise . . .

MELVYN BRAGG: Including us?

PETER ADAMSON: Including us. If you hypothesise a necessary existent, then what you're hypothesising is something that needs no cause in order to exist. In fact, what you said about it being the first cause is a good way of thinking about it. So really all that it means for something to be possible in itself or contingent is that there must be a cause to explain why it exists, if it exists. And then Avicenna says if you take all of the things that are contingent, all of them together as one set, that would be the world, the world is just one big contingent thing.

So you have to suppose that there's a cause for it and the cause would be God. The point you made about the infinite regress is just that. If I said that there was a cause for that cause I'll just keep having more and more contingent things. So in order to put a stop to this chain of causes I say there's a necessary existent and that's God.

MELVYN BRAGG: Can I bring in Amira now. Can you just tell us to whom these thoughts were addressed, the sort of intellectual network at the time. Was it in fact a network?

AMIRA BENNISON: There is definitely an intellectual network, partly through these numerous courts through which Avicenna moves, again . . .

MELVYN BRAGG: Yes, he goes from court to court as he gets chucked out of one after another . . .

AMIRA BENNISON: Yes, from the Samanids to the Buwayids, he serves a number of different masters. And all these different masters have entourages which include scholars around them. It's very much part of the intellectual life of any court in this period that there should be regular discussions, often presided over by the ruler himself, on various points of theology, philosophy or other items of interest. But in Avicenna's autobiography he mentions that he had gatherings of pupils in his own home every evening. He worked at court and he had a role there and he engaged at court with other thinkers but he also taught numerous pupils night after night in his own home. He also engaged in correspondence with various different intellectuals of his time, including the philosopher al-Buruni and other individuals, and correspondence with his own pupils. He is very much part of an intellectual circuit, there is an exchange of ideas going on. And then he subsequently does become part of the philosophical tradition within Islam.

MELVYN BRAGG: And also his critics – al-Ghazali was someone who criticised this idea, his proof for God, strongly.

AMIRA BENNISON: With al-Ghazali it's quite interesting, because early on in al-Ghazali's career he writes what is in effect a commentary on one of Avicenna's works. And he's very, very knowledgeable about philosophy, although he's not generally described as a philosopher because his major interests lay more in theology and jurisprudence and later Sufism. Al-Ghazali was deeply influenced by the philosophical tradition and he has sometimes been described, ironically, as one of Avicenna's most true disciples.

MELVYN BRAGG: But he objected to the main idea that Nader outlined to us?

AMIRA BENNISON: Yes. He does object to some of Avicenna's ideas and certainly later on in his life, when he writes *The Incoherence of the Philosophers*, one can see a sort of critique of philosophy in general emerging very strongly.

MELVYN BRAGG: Because philosophy was rather dangerous, wasn't it? It was thought to be dangerous to theology and Avicenna's idea wasn't, as it were, theological enough by any means for those who upheld theology as the central thinking place inside these Islamic courts?

AMIRA BENNISON: I think that's very true, but of course again it's somewhat ironic that in the process of debunking someone's ideas you have to become very familiar with their ideas. So what you actually see happening is pure philosophy increasingly being rejected by the theological establishment but at the same time that establishment being deeply imbued with its concepts, with its tools of dialect and disputation. It's an interesting relationship.

MELVYN BRAGG: Peter Adamson, can I come back to something you said near the beginning of the programme, about his originality? We know from what Nader said about that magnificent library that he was able to take – which he did – from Aristotle and so on and so forth. Can you give listeners some idea of this originality, because his ideas are very striking, he's called the most innovative logician since the second century BC. Can you give us a taste of that?

PETER ADAMSON: I think it goes on with what Amira was just saying. The history of Islamic philosophy I would say has two phases. This may be oversimplifying. You have the phase up till Avicenna and then you have the phase after Avicenna. And the reason for that is that after Avicenna everyone needs to respond to Avicenna, so they don't necessarily, except for Averroes, write commentaries so much on Aristotle any more as writing commentaries of Avicenna. And in fact what Averroes was doing in some ways was his own response to Avicenna, it was a response of conservatism, of trying to get back before these original ideas. But if you think about something like the idea of God as the necessary existent, that's a big challenge to Islam, a challenge that's not present in Aristotle's works.

Why is this? Why would someone like Ghazali find this to be a threatening idea? On the one hand Avicenna thought he could derive all of the divine attributes that Nader was mentioning from the idea of necessity. If you take, for example, the idea that God is omniscient, why is God omniscient? Well, because if He didn't know everything there would be some things He couldn't know and doesn't, so there'd be some possibilities that are unrealised for Him, so He wouldn't be necessary, He'd merely be possible. That sounds good, but then Ghazali responds to that by saying if everything about God is necessary, then it would be, for example, necessary that He creates us, it won't be a gratuitous act of generosity on His part, it would be something that He's forced to do by His own nature.

That move by Avicenna, of trying to think about God almost purely in terms of necessity and then derive all the other features of God out of necessity, is a very original move. It's not something that someone had done before. And I think it's a very intuitive move because it does capture the way that a lot of theists think about the world, calling out for an explanation which doesn't need its own explanation.

MELVYN BRAGG: Can I just come back to Nader? These ideas of Avicenna, are they still being disputed in Islamic philosophy today, as well as being recognised in the West? Is he still part of the picture?

NADER EL-BIZRI: I would say it is mediated by responses or the development of traditions that responded to Avicennism at large. If it's in contemporary times, it would be in the context of mainstream academia. It tends to be in most instances focused on establishing an accurate or relatively accurate documentation of his thought and the channels of its transmission or influence on a variety of traditions within Islam, within the history of ideas in Europe. But in terms of contemporary practices that take it as a living tradition it would be more associated with extensions of his thought or impressions that he had on later philosophers. One of them is Mulla Sadra, a seventeenth-century theologian.

MELVYN BRAGG: Can I come back to Amira here. He was clearly important in Islamic thought. Can you tell us how he became translated into the European mainstream in the eleventh to twelfth centuries and on from there?

AMIRA BENNISON: There were a couple of points in the Mediterranean basin where translation activity began to occur. Toledo, after its fall to the Castilian kings in 1085, became a site of a flourishing translation school and numerous scholars moved down to Toledo. One of the most famous is Michael Scott, who travelled to Toledo. Scott was born in 1175, to give you some idea of his time frame. He learned Arabic in Toledo and then subsequently went on to the court of Frederick II, where he translated a lot of material, including some of Avicenna's works. And they begin to appear in various places in Europe in the thirteenth century.

MELVYN BRAGG: Peter Adamson, I've read that he has influenced directly people like Duns Scotus, Roger Bacon and Aquinas, can you just ... I'm sorry, we're coming to the end of the programme here ... but ...

PETER ADAMSON: So just one example. Both Aquinas and Scotus take up this proof of God's existence. Scotus's proof of God's existence is a more complicated version of Avicenna's. And Aquinas, very early in his career, wrote a work called *Being In Essence*, which is essentially an exploration of this essence/existence contrast that Nader was talking about. I think this is one reason to say what you said at the beginning of the programme, which is that Avicenna is the most influential medieval philosopher. That's because he had a huge influence on the Islamic world, but also in Latin and also in Hebrew. The Jewish tradition in Maimonides, for example, the greatest Jewish medieval philosopher, is very deeply influenced by Avicenna. He's the only medieval philosopher to have an enormous impact on philosophy in all the faiths in the medieval world.

MELVYN BRAGG: Amira, you want to come in?

AMIRA BENNISON: I would just agree, he does have this incredible reach and it's not just the philosophy. It's also the medical tradition, which was translated into Latin and used extensively up until the seventeenth century.

MELVYN BRAGG: Nader?

NADER EL-BIZRI: Avicennism, in terms of ontology and meta-physics, could prove to be the foundation for the renewal of the philosophical impetus in Islamic thought.

MELVYN BRAGG: Would you agree with that, Peter?

PETER ADAMSON: Yes. What's really key – and we've talked about this – is the relationship between ontology and these logical ideas about modality, necessity and contingency and you can trace a line that goes from Avicenna through scholastic Latin philosophy and into someone like Leibnitz who is doing the same thing. He's got this project of thinking about metaphysics, possible worlds, this is all in some ways spinning out of intuitions about modality and how it relates to existence that we find in Avicenna.

TRANSMISSION: 8.11.2007

The Origins of Life

S cientists have named 1.5 million species of living organisms on the land, in the skies and in the oceans of planet earth, and a new one is classified every day. Estimates of how many species remain to be discovered vary wildly, but science accepts one categorical point – all living matter on our planet, from the nematode to the elephant, from the bacterium to the blue whale, is derived from a single common ancestor.

What was that ancestor? Did it really emerge from a 'primordial soup'? What is in the explanation of evolutionary science and what provided the catalyst to start turning the cycle of life?

With me to explore the scientific explanation for the origin of life is Richard Dawkins, the Charles Simonyi Professor of Public Understanding of Science at Oxford University and author of *The Ancestor's Tale: A Pilgrimage to the Dawn of Life*; Richard Corfield, Visiting Senior Lecturer at the Centre for Earth, Planetary, Space and Astronomical Research at the Open University and author of *The Silent Landscape*; and Linda Partridge, Biology and Bio-technology Research Council Professor at University College, London.

Richard Corfield, can we start with the time the earth was formed. What time scale was that and what were the conditions of earth then?

RICHARD CORFIELD: The earth was created out of the primordial solar system disc about 4.5 billion years ago. The convention in geology is that we call a billion ga, so you might hear me refer to it as ga from time to time. A more helpful analogy, though, when you think about the span of geological time is to consider one single day, twenty-four hours, and midnight is taken as 4.5 ga, 4.5 billion years – that is when the earth formed. From then on the first aeon of the history of the earth is called the Hadeon, so called because the earth and the other planets were forming at the same time. The solar system was created at the same time as the earth was being continuously pummelled by a rain of asteroids and meteorites. That is where the name Hadeon comes from. That is called the heavy bombardment period of earth history and that ended at 3.9 billion years before present, 3.9 ga, which is, if you're thinking about the twenty-four-hour clock, equates to twelve minutes past three in the morning.

MELVYN BRAGG: And then we move on to the time when life may have emerged. What were the conditions on the planet, this planet earth, then?

RICHARD CORFIELD: The first thing to say is that the early earth was quite, quite different to the world we know today. The green and blue planet which was famously shown from the Apollo 8 mission is the result of oxygen, photosynthesis and the greening of the world. There was no oxygen at the end of the Hadeon. Indeed oxygen at that time would be toxic to the organisms which were just beginning to evolve.

MELVYN BRAGG: But there was an atmosphere, wasn't there? There was a gravitational field which would hold an atmosphere. Can you tell us how important that was?

RICHARD CORFIELD: There was. The atmosphere was the so-called 'reducing atmosphere' to distinguish it from an oxidising atmosphere. It had carbon dioxide, methane, hydrogen, ammonia, nitrogen, carbon monoxide, and this broth of basic chemicals was continuously cooked by lightning discharges and the surface of the earth was pocked by continuous volcanism. It was a very unpleasant place indeed.

MELVYN BRAGG: So the three things there, if I can pick up the word 'reduce' and reduce it: there is an atmosphere around with the gravitational pull, there were volcanoes bringing stuff out, including water, carbon dioxide, methane and so on, and there were flashes of lightning coming in. This is what was there then.

RICHARD CORFIELD: That is the condition of the earth at 3.9 billion years before the present, when the late heavy bombardment period had just finished.

MELVYN BRAGG: Richard Dawkins, can you just take up the point made by Richard Corfield which will surprise a great number of listeners. It surprised me when I came across it. There was no oxygen then and oxygen was not necessary for this process, the origin of life, to begin. Can you develop that?

RICHARD DAWKINS: It is a surprising fact that the oxygen that we breathe and that we utterly depend upon is itself a biological product that comes from green plants and green bacteria. I think many people are surprised by that, as you say, because they feel there is something fresh and wonderful about the oxygen in our atmosphere and as Richard Corfield said, it was originally a pollutant, it was toxic, it was poisonous.

When green plants and green bacteria released it into the atmosphere it then became the condition that life had to adapt to. And we are the end product, we are the product of that. We are now the product of natural selection in an oxygen-rich atmosphere. Not only did we tolerate oxygen, we depend upon oxygen and we have taken biochemistry much further because of oxygen.

MELVYN BRAGG: But can I go back again, Richard, because it is a fascinating point. When there was no oxygen, when it was being drawn out by iron and so on, are the conditions for life being set up despite the absence of oxygen? Was the fact that there was no oxygen initially a help?

RICHARD DAWKINS: You are asking was it essential that there was no oxygen? Could you imagine life arising on a planet that was rich in oxygen?

MELVYN BRAGG: That is a better question than I asked, yes.

RICHARD DAWKINS: I don't know. I mean if you look at the kind of life we have it is now normally accepted that it needed to have a reducing atmosphere, but I could easily imagine somebody speculating on some alternative chemistry, some alternative biochemistry that would have evolved in an oxygen-rich atmosphere. I don't know what my colleagues think about that.

MELVYN BRAGG: Just a second. This oxygen – how did oxygen arrive here then if it was toxic – it would have been toxic to us?

RICHARD DAWKINS: It was here but it was compounded with other things. When we say there wasn't oxygen, what we mean is there was no free oxygen, there was no oxygen as an element. It was compounded in the form of carbon dioxide, water and so on.

MELVYN BRAGG: And it grew powerfully as a pollutant?

RICHARD DAWKINS: Yes. It was produced by photosynthesising green organisms, and yes, it would have been a pollutant.

MELVYN BRAGG: You have this mix there, then, and in the 1950s a man called Stanley Miller performed an extraordinary experiment. Can you tell us about that experiment and why I use the word 'extraordinary'?

RICHARD DAWKINS: He got together the ingredients that were thought to be present in the early earth atmosphere.

MELVYN BRAGG: Around the 3.9 billion mark?

RICHARD DAWKINS: Yes, and set up an apparatus in which he had a flask that represented the sea and a flask that represented the atmosphere above it and put into the atmosphere the ingredients, the non-oxygenated ingredients of the early earth. There was a circulation tube going up, tube going down, there was electric spark which was simulating lightning strikes and he just left it for a couple of weeks. At the end of this time there had accumulated in he sea, the lower of the two flasks, the one with water in, a thin brown liquid which when he analysed it turned out to be pretty much what G.B.S. Haldane had speculated as the hot brown soup. It contained numerous organic compounds, many of which were vital to the origin of life, amino acids of various kinds, including several amino acids from the twenty that life actually uses.

MELVYN BRAGG: But we are not talking yet about the origin of life. That in itself would not have led to the development of life?

RICHARD DAWKINS: No, there was nothing living there.

MELVYN BRAGG: So what did it prove?

RICHARD DAWKINS: It proved that the conditions of the early earth were right for the synthesis under the ordinary laws of chemistry of many of the basic building blocks of life. It was a pre-condition for life, it wasn't life itself.

MELVYN BRAGG: Linda Partridge, can you tell us the place that carbon played in all of this and why it is so fundamental?

LINDA PARTRIDGE: Carbon is an absolutely critical atom for this process to occur. The reason is its structure. Each element consists of a nucleus surrounded by electrons and the interesting thing about carbon is its electron space is only half filled so it is very eager to interact with other elements and make more complicated molecules. It can form bonds with oxygen, with nitrogen, with sulphur, all of the elements that make the ingredients of living organisms.

Its bond structure and the fact that it is so keen to interact with other molecules allows it to make large complex polymers, molecules with complicated shapes, that make it such a vital building block in living creatures. And almost certainly I think if life has evolved somewhere else in the universe it will be based on carbon for that reason. There is no other element that has this set of properties that make it such an ideal building block for living things.

MELVYN BRAGG: What part did that play in this experiment conducted by Stanley Miller?

LINDA PARTRIDGE: It was crucial that carbon was present in the various gases that were present that he passed the electrical discharges through. It was present as methane and carbon monoxide. Richard raised something very interesting earlier, which was this issue of . . .

MELVYN BRAGG: We are going to have to use surnames here. There are two Richards.

LINDA PARTRIDGE: I am sorry – Richard Dawkins raised an interesting point earlier about whether the presence of oxygen would have actually been a problem in the early atmosphere for the formation of these organic molecules. I think the evidence is that it would have been because a reducing atmosphere would have to be there and stable for this kind of organic synthesis to take place under the conditions that prevailed at that time.

MELVYN BRAGG: As a digression, but as we will be coming on to it, Darwin wrote a famous letter to Hooker in 1871 – can you tell us about that, Linda, and why you think it is significant?

LINDA PARTRIDGE: It was a quite extraordinarily prescient letter that Darwin wrote. He almost described the conditions that existed on the primitive earth and almost seemed to foresee the experiments that Miller did with the gases and the electric discharges and the organic synthesis. He described it in a rather cosy way compared with the picture that we have been given of what the conditions on the early earth were like. They were almost certainly extremely hostile. Darwin described a nice warm little pond and that is almost certainly not the circumstances under which life evolved. But he did foresee the importance of this mixture of organic compounds and the possibility that they would form larger and more complicated molecules and eventually give rise to life.

MELVYN BRAGG: Would you like to comment on that letter, Richard Dawkins?

RICHARD DAWKINS: I think it was typically prescient, as Linda says. Darwin got things right so many times. Actually, at the end of that little passage from the letter Darwin said that actually it was futile even to speculate about the origin of life. He was confining himself to talking about what happened after the origin of life and he was just allowing himself a little brief speculation. He did remark that if such a thing should ever happen again it would promptly be eaten so we would never know about it.

MELVYN BRAGG: Yes. Linda, you are waving your hand.

LINDA PARTRIDGE: One of the things that Darwin didn't foresee and that has been so exciting about all this was the possibility that people would be able to do experiments that would throw light on the sequence of events.

MELVYN BRAGG: I was going to ask what has changed since Darwin wrote that, as it were, prophetic thing in 1871, 130-odd years ago. Why can we talk about it, why can you three talk about it now in terms that were not available to him?

LINDA PARTRIDGE: I think partly because there is a lot more experimental evidence than there was. We know a lot more about the molecular basis of life, we can use molecules to trace back to what the primitive organisms would have looked like. By looking at what molecules control events now we can get an idea of forms of life that have disappeared completely and which therefore you couldn't get evidence on simply by doing the sort of things that Darwin was doing, just looking at organisms.

MELVYN BRAGG: Well, that is a platform, I hope. Now then, Richard Corfield, can you give us a working definition of life before we start talking about the origins. What would life be?

RICHARD CORFIELD: Thank you very much! Right, well that, of course, is a non-trivial question and I was rather hoping you would give it to Richard Dawkins! But to be blunt, a definition of life is something that we have to strap on immediately so we all know what we are talking about. I was looking at a paper recently and I saw that there are 102 criteria to define life but they can be boiled down into about four really, and the question is whether even those four are all mutually applicable.

Life replicates itself. It makes copies of itself but that doesn't make life unique. Crystals do the same thing. Life is about metabolism, it builds things up as opposed to letting things break down, and that leads me to my personal favourite definition of life, the single thing that I happen to think is most important, and I have done since I was a schoolboy, which goes back to Schrodinger's 1944 definition of life, is that life is reverse entropy. And that is based on Boltzmann's formulation of the second law of thermodynamics which, simply put, means that systems will tend to run down to the lowest energy level. I have a glass of water in front of me, eventually that will assume the same temperature as the rest of the room, that's entropy occurring.

Life does the opposite thing. It forms complexity, so it runs uphill against the entropy gradient. If I can give you an example, an analogy. I have the builders in at the moment. I watch them knock down my study. That is entropy. Now they are building it up again, I hope, and that is negative entropy, OK, and that is my personal favourite definition of life. A reversal of the entropy gradient.

MELVYN BRAGG: You said 102, and you have given us replication, metabolism and reverse entropy. Do you want to give us others?

RICHARD CORFIELD: Replication, reverse entropy, metabolism, which is kind of part of the reverse entropy thing. And the thing which perhaps Richard Dawkins should address which is susceptibility to Darwinian evolution. You know – visibility to natural selection.

MELVYN BRAGG: I think you three should just take this programme over! That is perfectly OK by me. Richard Dawkins, can you talk here especially with relevance to heredity, because that is a point you make very firmly in your book.

RICHARD DAWKINS: I think that when you ask what is life, one could treat that as 'what would life be wherever one found it anywhere in the universe?' Or it could be 'what do we happen to observe about life here?' And I suspect that the four which Richard Corfield has mentioned are universal. I don't think they are just particular to life on this planet and I think the really fundamental one is susceptibility to natural selection or a product of natural selection.

Life is what you get when the ordinary laws of physics and chemistry which pervade the entire universe find themselves filtered through this remarkable process of natural selection and natural selection will arise on any planet in the universe wherever you have true heredity, and true heredity means that you have entities which are self-replicating, with high accuracy but not perfect accuracy.

You get a population of such replicating entities which are not all identical, therefore some of them are better at replicating than others, some of them die away, others increase in the population of replicators and that is the starting point for natural selection, because once that starts then everything else follows which we call life.

MELVYN BRAGG: But the real question is how does it start? How does the first replicator replicate and how do we know that with any degree of accuracy?

RICHARD DAWKINS: That is exactly what we don't know and that is exactly what the whole field of origin of life research is about. It is how do you get from the ordinary laws of chemistry . . .

MELVYN BRAGG: To biology?

RICHARD DAWKINS: Well, to an entity which is self-replicating in this peculiar sense, and that must have happened. It did happen because we are here. If it happened anywhere else in the universe there will be another kind of life.

MELVYN BRAGG: Well, let's just stick to this planet. It is quite hard enough!

RICHARD DAWKINS: Right.

MELVYN BRAGG: At some stage, at one time or at several times, let's say at one time, there was a spontaneous generation of something that then became susceptible to natural selection which then became divergent as soon as it became susceptible to natural selection and then the whole game was afoot. But what is the scholarship now about that first spontaneous generation? We are thinking it was between 3.9 billion and 3.5 billion years ago? What happened?

RICHARD DAWKINS: Well, when you say spontaneous generation, spontaneous is right, but of course spontaneous things are happening all the time with the ordinary movement of atoms and molecules in chemistry. The particular spontaneous thing that had to happen is that a molecule arose which, whatever other properties it had, had also the property of making copies of itself. A chemist might call that auto-catalysis. A catalyst is a molecule or a chemical agent which facilitates a chemical reaction without participating or rather without being used up. An auto-catalyst is a catalyst which facilitates its own production.

MELVYN BRAGG: If I remember correctly, in your book you use the word 'luck' – it could have been luck that caused this. Some people

– creationists and Christians and other religious people listening to this – would say this would be the divine spark. One has to say that because it is what a lot of people believe did happen – you use the word 'luck'?

RICHARD DAWKINS: It simply means an improbable event. We know it is an improbable event because if it wasn't it would be all over – there would be life on Mars, Venus, Jupiter. It is certainly a very improbable event. We don't know quite how improbable. I have speculated it could be absolutely vanishingly improbable because we don't know there is life on more than one of the billions and billions and trillions of planets that exist, so it could have been very, very improbable indeed, in which case we are totally wasting our time trying to speculate about it.

MELVYN BRAGG: It is a wonderful waste of time though.

RICHARD DAWKINS: I don't actually believe that. I think it is sufficiently improbable to be present here and probably dotted around on isolated islands as well, but it was very improbable and that is another way of saying 'luck'.

LINDA PARTRIDGE: It may have been very improbable but it happened extraordinarily quickly in geological terms.

RICHARD DAWKINS: Good point.

LINDA PARTRIDGE: I mean 3.9 billion years ago we stopped being bombarded. And 3.6 billion years ago we have the first fossils, so life presumably evolved well before that.

RICHARD DAWKINS: Yes.

LINDA PARTRIDGE: So one could argue that if the conditions are propitious it is extremely likely to happen.

RICHARD CORFIELD: One of the interesting things is that the oldest sedimentary rocks we know on this planet are from the Isua complex in western Greenland and there is evidence to suggest that these rocks are 3.8 billion years old. That is a hundred million years younger than the 3.9 when you know the starting gate went up and life could have got going. That is only half an hour on our twenty-four-hour clock. Now if there is evidence for photosynthesis, as some suggest there is in the rocks of 3.8 billion years before the present, that means you got from no life to photosynthesis, i.e., quite complicated life, in a hundred million years, which is like Michael Schumacher going down a straight. It is not hanging around.

MELVYN BRAGG: Could you speculate on how this might have happened? What formations are inside, how the thing got going in the first place. Richard Dawkins, you have talked about it not being DNA but possibly RNA that could have been the cause of it. Can we bring that in?

RICHARD DAWKINS: Yes. DNA is what Graham Cairns-Smith has called a high-tech replicator. It needs a lot of machinery, rather like needing a Xerox machine to make a copy of a piece of paper, so it almost certainly wasn't DNA.

MELVYN BRAGG: And there is a Catch 22 in the DNA?

RICHARD DAWKINS: There is a Catch 22. DNA is needed to make protein and protein in the form of enzymes is needed to make DNA.

MELVYN BRAGG: So it is a closed system?

RICHARD DAWKINS: That is the Catch 22 of the origin of life and it is very difficult. We have these two fundamental properties of molecules that you need. Replication, which DNA is brilliant at, and catalysis, which proteins are brilliant at, and you seem to need both and it is not clear how you can get one without the other. RNA seems to have some of the properties of both. RNA is a good replicator though not as good as DNA. RNA can act as an enzyme, can act as a catalyst, so the hope of the RNA world theory is that RNA might have actually done both jobs and then later the job of replicating was, as it were, handed over to the really streamlined high-tech version DNA.

MELVYN BRAGG: Linda, can you spell out RNA?

LINDA PARTRIDGE: Ribonucleic Acid. It is one of the two main nucleic acid molecules that occur in modern organisms, As Richard says, it has this extraordinary property – it can act as a genetic template to direct its own replication but it can also behave like modern-day proteins do as a catalyst that makes chemical reactions far more likely to occur easily in cells. In fact, that is one of the areas where there has been a lot of experimental work on the origin of life because it is possible to evolve in the test tube RNA molecules that can do all kinds of chemical jobs that in cells now are done by proteins. So it is very plausible that this whole RNA world existed.

The other point is that again if you go back to the chemistry and the pre-biotic soup, if it was a soup, RNA forms far more easily under those circumstances than DNA would just chemically. But it may not have been the first genetic template. There may have been other worlds before it for which we have no evidence now.

MELVYN BRAGG: Richard Corfield, what could have come before RNA?

RICHARD CORFIELD: What I wanted to say before we actually get up as far as RNA is there may be one place where the conditions of the early earth still prevail. And we hope to be there at Christmas time. I am talking about Titan, the moon of Saturn. One of the main reasons for the Cassini Huygens mission to Titan is to drop the Huygens probe on to Titan, because the atmosphere is dense, has carbon dioxide in it, nitrogen, methane and ammonia. In other words, it appears to be an analogue for the way the earth was 3.9 billion years before the present.

So the ultimate holy grail of this kind of expedition would be to go there and get evidence that there are amino acids floating around in the atmosphere as there were, and I agree with Richard Dawkins that there were, in the early earth. And the other thing that you need is the basic building blocks, the nucleic acids floating free in some kind of broth, so you have your amino acids and you have your nucleic acids – you need both of these before you can start to build RNA and ultimately come to the DNA protein world. I am very excited about the possibilities of Titan as an analogue for the early earth.

MELVYN BRAGG: Richard Dawkins, can you tell us what might have happened before we move on to complexity? It is speculation but how, in your view, did the first forms come into being, those which allowed natural selection to begin? Because what you say is that once replication and heredity had taken a grip of any sort, then the game was afoot.

RICHARD DAWKINS: When I speculate about it I suppose what I imagine is that originally there were self-replicating molecules which made copies of themselves and which were subject to natural selection and some of them were better than others, so you have got in a population of self-replicating molecules increasing efficiency at self-replication. A major step in the subsequent evolution under natural selection which by now was properly going was the formation of something like the first cell, because when you had the first cell that meant that a membrane of some sort, a wall, separated units of self-replication and kept their chemical products together instead of having them streaming around free in the soup. And I think that enabled the possibility of building up complex collections of molecules which work together with each other which is what a cell is, as opposed just to having them streaming out into the sea. The first cell wall seems to me to be a very crucial step.

LINDA PARTRIDGE: One of the most important problems, I think, which Richard Dawkins is almost alluding to, is that the molecule somehow had to get concentrated, the different things that were going to form life had to somehow get together as well as be compartmentalised, and one of the most interesting suggestions that is around, I think, is that perhaps it wasn't a primitive soup. Perhaps it was a primitive pizza and the surface of some sort of mineral, perhaps clay, perhaps iron pyrites charge could have acted as a surface on which these molecules concentrated and came together and also acted as the primitive substrate for the formation of the cell membrane. Because these surfaces, it turns out, can concentrate the lipids that are so critical to make the membranes of living cells.

RICHARD CORFIELD: I am very excited by that. I think of that as the cat-litter world because the clay in question is montmorilonite, which is well known as the major ingredient of cat litter.

MELVYN BRAGG: Is that your contribution?

RICHARD CORFIELD: That is my contribution! No, what is interesting is if you think that early life could have formed on mineral surfaces like montmorilonite or iron pyrites these most basic organised mineral structures are actually giving rise to the most complicated structures that you can possibly imagine, which is life itself.

MELVYN BRAGG: There is one point in Richard Dawkins' book, I will come to Richard Dawkins in one moment, when people say life came from the sea and people say life came from the land but the suggestion is that life came most likely from on rocks. Does that fit in with what you are saying?

RICHARD CORFIELD: I think Graham Cairns-Smith had an interesting idea which goes back to the question of prebiosis, things which were before life. Cations could exactly arrange themselves on mineral surfaces and this would then provide a self-replicating template which is below the level of RNA, below the level of PRNA and TNA, and would be completely inorganic and eventually this built up, but nobody has actually thought of a way of testing this at the moment. So I think you have to go with the idea that there are amino acids and nucleic acids required to start biology. They have carbon in them but biology only gets going when these are formed into some kind of primitive RNA molecule.

MELVYN BRAGG: Richard Dawkins, you speak of the great historic rendezvous, which is the complex multicellular which is the eukaryotic cell. Now why is that such a big event?

RICHARD DAWKINS: Living cells are conventionally nowadays divided into two main types: eukaryotic and prokaryotic. Prokaryotic cells are bacteria of various kinds. Eukaryotic cells are those of the cells of all the rest of us. They are enormously larger than prokaryotic cells, they are much more complicated and they have a nucleus within the cell which contains the genetic material separated off from the rest of the cell. The rest of the cell is filled with complicated systems of membranes including mitochondria, which we now know are themselves originally derived from bacteria.

   The great historic rendezvous was a moment in history when

several different kinds of bacteria, it is now thought, came together to form a kind of social unit, a bigger cell, which was a combination of different kinds of bacterial. To this day mitochondria still reproduce themselves with their own DNA so there is a population of mitochondria inside every one of your cells which are reproducing themselves just like bacteria. When your big eukaryotic cells divide they each take with them their own set of mitochondria which then carry on dividing, so there is reproduction of mitochondria going on quite independently of our main reproduction.

The great historic rendezvous, as I say, was a moment – not a moment in history because it was spread out in several different episodes – when the eukaryotic cell was formed by the coming together of several different kinds of bacteria and they were so smoothly merged that it was only very recently that people even realised that they had come together. People didn't realise until recently that the eukaryotic cell is a fusion of prokaryotic cells.

MELVYN BRAGG: Once we have got that, are we on the road to natural selection?

RICHARD DAWKINS: We are on the road to natural selection long before that. It was a major milestone in the history of life on this planet. After the formation of the eukaryotic cell, a whole flowering of life took place, a fusion at a higher level, multicellular life, the forming of large creatures we could see with our naked eye came about after the formation of the eukaryotic cell, but natural selection was well under way for a long time before that.

RICHARD CORFIELD: Just to give you some perspective on the time. By the time the eukaryotes evolved you are effectively two billion years before the present, we are half of the way pretty much towards where we are now. So the evolution of the eukaryotic cell is actually quite a complicated long-term thing. In terms of natural selection it is a major platform from which life can then step up on the way to multicellularity. What Richard Dawkins has mentioned about this fusion actually adds a whole new level of complexity to what we know about evolution because at the very base of the tree of life, if indeed it is a tree, you have the two phenomena.

They are called horizontal gene transfer, where coexisting organisms, prokaryotes, without their nuclear material packaged within membranes with the cells, can actually exchange nuclear material directly with each other, which provides a lot more variation on which natural selection can work. Then you have a bigger version of this horizontal gene transfer which is called endosymbiosis, and the evolution photosynthesis is probably some form of endosymbiosis as well, when the chloroplast formed inside the eukaryotic cell by the arrival of another bacterium, similar to the way Richard Dawkins described the arrival of mitochondria in the eukaryotic cells.

MELVYN BRAGG: Linda, you wanted to come in – can you take this forward to the further developments from this eukaryotic cell? What happened after that?

LINDA PARTRIDGE: One of the things about it, just before moving on, is that this may have been one of the very improbable steps in the evolutionary tree because as well as this endosymbiosis it turns out that eukaryotes are almost certainly derived from a very basic fusion of two quite separate bacterial lineages, one of which brought in the information transferring processing machinery in the cell and the other of which brought in the metabolic bits, the things that actually do things within the cell. And they seem to have had quite separate evolutionary origins, which makes sense of why there have been such conflicting results of evolutionary biologists trying to ask the question where did the eukaryotes come from? What are they most closely related to? Well, the answer is they are closely related to several things, because essentially the eukaryotic cell is a committee of separate bacterial lineages.

The next big event was the evolution of multicellularity, cells coming together to form more complex organisms, and the evidence on that is that it has happened more than once, it has happened separately in the plant, animal and fungal lineages and also several lines gave rise to multicellular algae from single cell forms, so that seems to be quite a common easy step to take.

MELVYN BRAGG: So by going for the cells, as it were, we are finding commonalty right across the planet, whichever way you cut it?

RICHARD DAWKINS: Yes. The new findings Linda has just been talking about, of two separate genomes merging, is immensely exciting and that is quite a new thing which I am still trying to digest. But yes, after multicellularity then you have the evolution of life as we have known it for a long time and life as Darwin would have known it. Big life, life that you can see, creatures that swim and walk and fly and climb – all that seems to have come about through the modularity, the building up of lots and lots of cells. Each cell having fundamentally the same structure but modified for different particular purposes in a kind of society of cells.

MELVYN BRAGG: But enormous similarity in the cells themselves across the animal world, plant world, bacterial world?

RICHARD DAWKINS: There is. The eukaryotic cell has fundamentally the same properties wherever you look at it and it becomes modified into detailed differences between liver cells and muscle cells and woody cells and so on, but it is fundamentally the same kind of cell.

MELVYN BRAGG: A point that has been raised, and it was raised a long time ago by Fred Hoyle, was that life or the beginnings of life or the things that could make life begin came from asteroids, came from extraterrestrial sources. What is your view of that, Richard Corfield?

RICHARD CORFIELD: Well, carbonaceous chondrites, a particular type of meteorite, are so called because they have carbon compounds on them and in fact the basic building blocks of life, amino acids and probably nucleic acids that came before them, the things they are formed from are available in stardust in outer space. There is nothing particularly unique about the basic chemicals of life, it is just the way that they were put together on this planet. If you take that one step further and say was life seeded from outer space, the panspermia theory, well, it may have been, but that doesn't help you very much because it means you have to go somewhere else to figure out how it started in the first place.

RICHARD DAWKINS: I thoroughly agree with that. The thing that really irritated me, if I may put it that way, about Fred Hoyle is that before putting forward his interesting ideas about panspermia, he put it in the context of trying to pick holes in Darwinism, as though one could get away from Darwinism. You have got to have Darwinism somewhere, even if it is outer space. You have got to have Darwinism to produce the life that is then going to be transported by panspermia or you do it here. It seems more economical to do it here, but I have no objection to doing it elsewhere and bringing it here.

LINDA PARTRIDGE: I quite agree with all of that. And even if life did in fact evolve here and didn't come from outer space, some of the information that gave rise to it may have come from elsewhere and there is plenty of evidence that the early earth received a large amount of organic input from outside, from more widely in the solar system. Sometimes the sorts of molecules that come have a particular handiness to them which doesn't tend to happen when they are formed under the conditions that prevailed at the early earth. That handiness may have acted as a source of information for modern biological systems.

MELVYN BRAGG: Once it got going, Richard Dawkins, once natural selection got going, once there was the ability to enter into Darwinism as it were, was it inevitable, was there a sense of the inevitability of the massive multiplication of species?

RICHARD DAWKINS: That is very interesting. I think there may have been more than one very difficult step to get over. It has already been mentioned that the formation of the eukaryotic cell with all that followed from that could have been a very, very difficult step. It could be that there are all sorts of beginnings of life elsewhere, none of which reached that point. There could be other major steps. Multicellularity might have been a difficult step. I don't think in fact it was, because, as Linda said, it happened many times, so we know that multicellularity is not that difficult.

But maybe intelligent life, the sort of life that is capable of language, technology and of broadcasting itself by radio to other planets, maybe that is a very, very difficult step indeed, and that may be the answer to the riddle of, as Enrico Fermez said – where are they? Why haven't we received radio communications from outer space? It could be that there is plenty of life out there but only we have reached the technology threshold.

MELVYN BRAGG: Briefly, Richard Corfield.

RICHARD CORFIELD: I was just going to say that the interesting thing about the origin of life question is that you need three different sciences to get at it. Palaeontology can only get you to about 3.8, then you need biology and the structure of the cell, and then you are thrust back on theoretical chemistry.

TRANSMITTED: 23.09.2004

t

The Siege of Constantinople

When Sultan Mehmet II rode into the city of Constantinople on a white horse in 1453, it marked the end of a thousand years of the Byzantine Empire. After holding out for fifty-three days, the city had fallen. And as one contemporary witness described it: 'the blood flowed in the city like rainwater in the gutters after a sudden storm.' It seemed to mark the end of the classical world and the crowning of an Ottoman Empire that would last until 1922.

Constantinople was a city worth fighting for – its position as bridge between Europe and Asia and its triangular shape with a deepwater port made it ideal both for trade and defence. It was also rumoured to harbour great wealth. It was a place of fabled splendour. Whoever conquered it would reap rewards both material and political.

Earlier attempts to capture the city had largely failed. So why did the Ottomans succeed this time? What difference did the advances in weaponry such as cannons make in the outcome of the battle? And what effect did the fall of Constantinople have on the rest of the Christian world?

With me to discuss this are Roger Crowley, an author and historian; Judith Herrin, Professor of Late Antique and Byzantine Studies at King's College, London; and Colin Imber, formerly Reader in Turkish at Manchester University.

Roger Crowley, in the fifteenth century the Byzantine Empire was in decline, it had lost most of its territory. Why was that?

ROGER CROWLEY: It was the result of an extremely long process of external pressure and internal decline that goes back many centuries. At the end of the eleventh century the empire started to come under pressure externally from the East and the West. From the East this came in the form of Turkish tribal raiders who started to push into Anatolia, Asia Minor. At the same time it was coming under military and economic pressure from the West as a result of the crusades. The crusaders passed through Constantinople and eyed it covetously as a rather rich place and in the aftermath of that one of the signal disasters of Byzantine history was the Fourth Crusade of 1204, which the Venetians hijacked from going for Jerusalem and sacked Constantinople instead.

The upshot of this was catastrophic for the Byzantines. The emperors were in exile for sixty years, the Turks pushed on into Asia Minor and out of these warring bands one emerged under a tribal leader called Osman, whose people became known subsequently as the Ottomans. The fourteenth century in Europe was equally calamitous for the Byzantines – civil war, population decline, plague. Constantinople was the first city in Europe to be hit by plague rats coming on ships from the Black Sea. The Ottomans continued their advance and they crossed into Europe as guests of one of the warring factions in the civil war and by the end of the fourteenth century they had established themselves in Europe. They smashed the Serbs. They created a capital of Irdini 140 miles to the west of Constantinople and the emperors of the empire were reduced effectively to vassals of the Ottoman sultans. They were in a very weak position.

MELVYN BRAGG: That is a wonderful overview. Can I just pick out two points? So it had reduced from what to what? In about 1453, how big was it? What was it – it was a city and what else?

ROGER CROWLEY: It had a tiny footprint. It was a city with some small hinterland and effectively the Peloponnese in southern Greece and that was more or less it. There wasn't much more.

MELVYN BRAGG: And this amazing sacking of it by Christians, the attacking of a Christian city by Christians in 1204, that was extraordinarily debilitating. Can you elaborate on that a little? I mean, the glories that we see in Venice were looted from Constantinople, many of them, weren't they?

ROGER CROWLEY: That's right, and one of the real symbols of the decline of Constantinople was the four empty plinths in the Hippodrome which, of course, had housed the four horses which had been carried off to Venice. These were the ultimate symbol of the decline of a great empire and the events of 1204 left a legacy, a long legacy of bitterness between the Catholic and the Orthodox world.

MELVYN BRAGG: Judith Herrin, until 1453, apart from this unchristian incursion, there had been other attacks on the city and they had been beaten off. Can you give us some details about that?

JUDITH HERRIN: Many, many attacks, starting in the seventh century with the Avars and the Persians in conjunction in 626. This is a very important, a symbolic moment, because the Byzantine victory was attributed by the inhabitants of Constantinople to the Virgin Mother of God, and she became the defender of the city and gave it her very special protection. And the inhabitants believed firmly that she would come to their aid, as she did in all the subsequent sieges when she was frequently seen allegedly fighting on the walls beside the Byzantines.

So they had great faith in the divine protection that had been accorded to them and they managed to beat off the Bulgars in the early ninth century, attacks by the Russians in the tenth and numerous other sieges right through to the major siege of 1422, when the Sultan Murad II was absolutely confident of capturing Constantinople and even sent out instructions to his subjects to come and prepare to plunder the city because he knew and they knew that it was very rich. They were all lined up to come and enjoy the booty. That was not to be, but in 1453 that is what happened.

MELVYN BRAGG: What was the great strength of the city? Why could they not conquer it? They turned up again and again. We'll get to 1453 in a moment or two. What was the city's strength, apart from divine protection? Was it simply the depth of the fortification?

JUDITH HERRIN: The depth of the fortifications was very impressive. These early fifth-century walls were a major architectural achievement, a feature which is still very impressive today, even though they have been much destroyed and now patched up and restored. But there was a very simple triple system of a major inner wall with many towers, an outer wall and a huge moat, three barriers which every besieging force had to tackle one by one.

MELVYN BRAGG: Let's fit another piece into the jigsaw. There was
a growing isolation of Constantinople, not least following the schism
with Rome when they set off as equal cities and equal, let's call them
patriarchies. Then Rome began to demand supremacy and that the
Byzantines should kowtow to it.

JUDITH HERRIN: This too has a very long history and I think it is
quite clear that the notion of two major centres of Christianity – Latin
in old Rome and Greek in new Rome – had developed over many
centuries. Originally the five great patriarchies included Alexandria,
Antioch and Jerusalem and the five together were said to constitute
the pentarchy. This rule of five was the way in which the councils,
the universal councils of the Church, were organised right up to the
ninth century. That authority was vested in the five great sees representing Christendom. Of course, the three that were conquered by
the Muslims in the seventh century never regained the strength that
they had had before, or the wealth, although they had the authority
and the tradition and continued to govern the Christian populations
still living under their control as minority churches within the world
of Islam.

The real problem is that the notion of the primacy of the heirs of
St Peter, the founder of the Church of Rome, gave the Bishops of
Rome a greater authority, which they played on, and they called it
the primacy of the Bishop of Rome, which was superior in honour
to anything that the Bishop of Constantinople could provide.
Constantinople had been a very small church in the fourth century
AD and when Constantine made it his capital the bishop had to be
rapidly promoted to a patriarchal status. Nonetheless, there had been
good relations between the Christians and these were only vitiated
by the question of the primacy of St Peter and the wording of the
creed, which was of course an impossible theological conundrum
that was never entirely satisfactorily resolved.

MELVYN BRAGG: What this resulted in, as I understand it, is that
come critical times the Church of Rome for various reasons was not
very willing to send allies and help to what should have been an
equal Greek Christian Church in Constantinople.

JUDITH HERRIN: There were of course very successful crusades in the eleventh and twelfth centuries, but subsequent to the great sack of 1204, for which Pope John Paul II apologised on the two hundredth anniversary of the sack of 1204, these relations were deeply embittered, as Roger just said, and therefore the Byzantines were put in a very difficult situation. In order to gain military aid from the West to combat the Turks there were certain conditions that the Bishop of Rome imposed, and the first was the submission of the Church of Constantinople to the authority of St Peter.

MELVYN BRAGG: And they wouldn't do that. Colin Imber, if we turn to the Ottomans, they clearly are enjoying great success. Can you give us, can you tell us about their strengths in the mid-fifteenth century?

COLIN IMBER: The strengths of the Ottomans seem to have been the manpower they could muster from both the Asian provinces and the European provinces and also an extraordinary organisation in that nearly all of the troops at the siege of Constantinople in 1453 were there because they had to be there. Their names existed in registers and they received either fees from the sultan or they received a salary from the sultan. In return they had to perform military service and if they didn't – curtains – they would be sacked. So the sultans could muster troops very quickly.

What they had also shown themselves able to do was to master military techniques very quickly and I think the thing which concerns us particularly in 1453 is the use of cannon. Now cannon were used in 1422, a Greek source calls them '*bombardi*' – in fact using an Italian term, but saying they were ineffective. What had happened in between? I think the Ottomans faced a major crisis in 1443–44 when a crusade with the Hungarians attacking from the west, the Emirate of Karamar attacking from the east, with the Venetians, the Gandians and indeed the Byzantines blocking the straits, they could have failed. But they didn't.

What were the reasons for their success then? Partly an alliance with the Genoese, who ferried Murad II's troops across the Bosphorus for him. They also provided him with cannons. The reasons the Hungarians had been very successful in those wars was in fact their use of cannons. The Ottomans learnt this very, very quickly. They had used cannons before that, but now cannons became a major part of the Ottoman military machine and where did they get the expertise from? Home-grown expertise – they could already make them. But in 1444 the Genoese from Pera, the city opposite Constantinople, provided them with cannons in order to go and fight the Hungarians. Also they procured the famous cannon of 1453, which was produced by a Hungarian, Urban, and it is worth noting that he got a house in the newly conquered city afterwards as a reward for this.

MELVYN BRAGG: His famous cannon, as I understand it, had to be dragged across the route from Hungary by sixty oxen and 2,200 men on either side pulling it to its place for the siege.

COLIN IMBER: Yes. The number of men, let's say, varies according to your source.

MELVYN BRAGG: I am quoting from one of you three.

COLIN IMBER: It certainly was a very, very large number of men.

MELVYN BRAGG: Why did the Ottomans want Constantinople so much?

COLIN IMBER: Constantinople was, from an Ottoman point of view, an annoying city state in the middle of what you might call their empire. The Byzantines had of course no military or naval power to speak of, but they had a very good diplomatic service and they were able, as in 1443–44 to quote just one example, to stir up the foreign powers against the Ottomans. Secondly, they had another weapon in that members of the Ottoman dynasty who failed to make it to the sultanate tended to take refuge in Byzantium and if an emperor at any stage wanted to cause trouble he would release one of these Ottoman princes and start a civil war – so that was a reason. Also it was an enormous centre of stage, particularly coming from the Black Sea, coming from the Mediterranean. And it was wealthy and the sultan would rather have his hands on that wealth than leave it with the Byzantine emperor.

MELVYN BRAGG: To round off this part of the programme, Roger Crowley, there is also a lot of superstition in the city on both sides.

There was a rumour that Mohammed's standard bearer was killed at one of the early sieges in the seventh century and other myths surrounding the city and its capture. Can you take us through those?

ROGER CROWLEY: I would say that both sides were obsessed with prophecies. A lot of them had a very millennial nature, particularly for the Byzantines. Some of these go back to the Arab sieges which Judith mentioned in the seventh and eighth centuries when Islam failed to take the city. The death of Mohammed's standard bearer designated the city a holy place for Islam and it left behind a deep longing for Islam to take this city and a set of prophecies which were attributed to Mohammed, but which are probably apocryphal, foretold this cycle of defeat, death and final victory. They also had this image of the city as a red apple, this centre of wealth and power.

MELVYN BRAGG: Let's look at the two leaders. Constantine is the Byzantine emperor. Let's talk about him first.

ROGER CROWLEY: He was a member of the ruling house of Paeleologus who had been emperors of the city for 200 years. He became emperor at the age of forty-four. As a young man he witnessed the siege of 1422, which was quite a serious one, and he had spent twenty years of his life, more or less, in the Peloponnese trying to shore up the Byzantine influence and push back the Ottomans, with disastrous consequences. He was a practical man, a soldier not a theologian, very straightforward, unlike his brothers who were rather treacherous. He was deeply aware of his inheritance as emperor and he was prepared to fight to the end for this.

MELVYN BRAGG: What about Mehmet II, Colin Imber, the Ottoman leader who was twenty-one years old?

COLIN IMBER: Well, it's difficult to say anything about medieval characters but he is described by Doukas the Greek, who knew him, as being, in contrast to his father, insolent and violent. Indeed, I think the cliché 'ruthlessly ambitious' would sum him up. He was highly unpopular with his subjects because he drove them to exhaustion both from the military point of view and the taxation point of view. He never stopped until he died. His ambition was boundless.

MELVYN BRAGG: Judith Herrin, this was often seen in religious terms and we have heard about the Virgin Mary fighting on the walls of Constantinople and defending the city and we have heard about Mohammed's standard bearer falling in Constantinople. There was talk about the Turkish heathens and the infidels, Christianity versus Islam. Does that hold water?

JUDITH HERRIN: Yes. I think the Christians really felt this was the last Christian outpost in the Near East. It was a very ancient Christian city. It had been a centre of Christianity for centuries and the Muslims had conquered all the other major centres of ancient Christianity. They did feel that this was a very Christian city with an enormously long tradition and their pride and their ability, their willingness to defend it to the last man is clearly evident, and of course some western Christians came to their assistance. It is not to be thought that there weren't western Christians who arrived in the years 1452–53 to support the Christian defence, knowing that the city was completely surrounded. The defenders were totally outnumbered.

MELVYN BRAGG: Let's get some idea about the numbers now, Roger Crowley. How did they measure up on terms of fighting force and weapons as we close in on 1453?

ROGER CROWLEY: There is no contest on paper really. On the one hand you had the Ottoman army, described as being as numerous as the stars – very difficult, I think to estimate the quantity of men that they had. Possibly 60,000 fighting men, but a huge non-fighting force of ordinants, labourers, people who could dig trenches, carry out earthworks, drag cannons, incredibly powerful mining engines, that kind of thing. Mehmet had also built himself a fleet of an unknown number of ships, possibly about 140, a lot of which were quite small, and about fifteen to eighteen war galleys, because he realised you had to surround the city by sea as well. And Murat had not been able to do that.

Inside the walls it was depressingly easy to count the number of men. Constantine organised a muster and there were 4,773 Greeks and about 3,000 foreigners, some of whom were Venetians, Genoese,

Catalans, Cretans. There was one Brit there, a Scotsman called John Grant, who played a small but significant part. He was a siege mining engineer. It was an unequal struggle. They did have some ships as well, mainly Venetian and Genoese ships in the harbour – about thirty. But sieges tended to favour the defenders, or had favoured the defenders until 1453, so they were reasonably confident that they could hold out, that their walls were strong, until Mehmet came along with his cannons.

MELVYN BRAGG: The big cannon, Colin Imber. As I understand it, it was so big and difficult to load and difficult to cool it could only fire seven great cannon balls or rocks a day, but these really hammered the walls. Can you tell us about how the siege began and the effect of these cannon and the other cannon. But the big cannon is the one that seems to have done the damage.

COLIN IMBER: Yes, the big cannon was against the St Ramanos Gate, and that is in fact where the Turks finally entered. So I think you can say it is the big cannon that did the job, but there were a lot of other siege instruments involved, as Roger has mentioned. Mining, which in the end was unsuccessful. Incidentally, the miners were brought from the silver mines of Serbia and indeed there was also a large contingent of Serbian cavalry provided by George Brankovich, the despot of Serbia, who was a vassal, if I can use the term, of Mehmet.

They also used siege towers which some sources say were very useful in the final conquering of the city, but it seemed ultimately that it was the cannon that made the breach. And the ships were held out of the Golden Horn which provided a moat on one side of the city by a large boom, which was successful in keeping them out and that is what precipitated the famous incident when Mehmet ordered the ships to be brought overland from the Bosphorus into the Golden Horn. Incidentally, he was to do the same thing in the siege of Negroponte in 1470, so it was obviously a tactic he favoured.

MELVYN BRAGG: It is a chance for us to get into detail, which is great. Contemporary sources paint a vivid picture. We have got bows and arrows against this massive cannon, so it is a wonderful moment – I mean horrible to be killed, but still it is a wonderful moment. But we read as well about a terrific amount of noise. Can you just give some idea of how it started and then away it goes?

JUDITH HERRIN: Medieval warfare was always very noisy, I think. The Byzantines used to take an organ and a lot of percussion instruments out when they were fighting in the field and they used to have these huge organs, water-powered, hydraulic organs, sounds very blaring, horrid noises to frighten the enemy. By the fifteenth century there was a great deal more in the use of trumpets and drums, lots of drumming, lots of real racket, of noise on both sides. We hear from Greek sources that the bells would be run in the city to tell everybody that the attack was commencing, the day's attack was commencing, and that they should take up their positions.

Women and children then joined the lines of people lifting stones up to the walls to be thrown down at the attackers when they got too close. So everyone was involved, everyone inside the city was involved. The monks would go to pray in the churches, if they weren't actually involved in ferrying water and supplies to the defenders, but the noise must have been something tremendous, and of course that is where Mozart got his notion of Turkish military music which we find some hundreds of years later. It is an astonishing tribute to the fact that the Turks had developed this very noisy style of musical accompaniment to their warfare.

MELVYN BRAGG: And the great cannon thumping through the day.

JUDITH HERRIN: That must have been a terrifying sound for everybody concerned.

MELVYN BRAGG: So, Colin Imber, it goes on. The Ottomans have this incredible superiority everywhere you look – ships, men, cannon. Constantine is there with his 7,500 men, as Roger has told us. Judith earlier pointed out that some Christians did come to his aid. Can you tell us about the most significant ones who did?

COLIN IMBER: The most significant was the Genoese Giustiniani, who took up his position on the wall where the cannon was firing, so he put himself quite literally you can say in the firing line, and he seems to have been a highly effective leader.

MELVYN BRAGG: He brought 700 professional soldiers at his own expense.

COLIN IMBER: Yes he did. The final signal for the fall of the city seems to have been Giustiniani receiving a wound and going away to have the wound dressed. The Venetian sources, the Venetians hated the Genoese, say that Giustiniani ran away, which is probably not true, but it seems that his absence from the wall certainly encouraged the attackers and disheartened the besieged and that really was a key moment. Giustiniani does emerge, I think, as one of the heroes of the defence of the city and also the tragic figure in its fall.

MELVYN BRAGG: How close are they getting at this stage? We are not quite at the nub yet. Roger, you have talked about these three boundaries, the obstacles, before they got there – the outer wall and the rest. How near are they getting? It takes fifty-three days, so let's say we're on day forty-eight.

ROGER CROWLEY: They have blasted a lot of holes in the wall but the Byzantines have been quite successful in replacing them with a kind of earth barrier that was actually more effective than a stone wall because rather like throwing stones into mud it disperses the effect of them. It reached a point where both sides were pretty exhausted and Mehmet decided it was do or die. His troops were starting to get a bit edgy about the whole thing. The prophetic atmosphere was getting to everybody, the weather was very bad, which added a kind of 'this is the end of the world' moment, particularly for the Byzantines, so he just decide he was going to have to go for it.

There was no secret about an Ottoman attack. You could see it coming. They would have three days of fasting and ritual prayer, light huge bonfires at night. The Christian sympathisers in the Ottoman camp fired arrows over the walls telling them what was about to happen and at 1.30 in the morning on 29 May he decided to march. There was no cunning plan, three waves, he marched forward in waves. The most expendable Christian troops were first, working up to his most valuable troops at the end. Constantine decided he was going to do or die, so he marched all his men between the inner and the outer wall and locked the doors behind him.

So they were going to go for it basically, and they held out pretty well for about five hours until Giustiniani was wounded and his men asked for him to be taken back into the city and Constantine didn't want him to go but he said, no, I have got to go. The gates were opened, everybody panicked and tried to run for the gates and of course most of them were locked and they were surrounded and massacred. The actual moment of collapse, I think, happened very quickly and people were surprised how quickly it happened inside the city.

MELVYN BRAGG: Judith, can we just come on the side of Constantine in Constantinople. Roger has given us a graphic idea, there are waves and waves, there are upwards of 60,000 coming at the city. Have we any notion of what Constantine thought? He believed the Virgin would protect them as she had done for over a thousand years. Do we know what his position was in those last hours?

JUDITH HERRIN: He hoped for a miracle and he ordered all those who could pray to pray and the great church of St Sofia on 29 May 1453, when the city walls were breached, was full of those praying to the Virgin for intercession and divine support. The night before the major attack, as we know, he and his grand advisor Francis rode out together and Francis later gave a vey moving account of how they looked at the bonfires and saw the advancing troops and knew that the end was near. And Constantine looked at his city and told Francis that he was there to defend it and in fact, since his body was never found, it is quite clear that he preferred to die leading his troops against the Turks than to negotiate any sort of compromise and handover.

Francis himself was captured and imprisoned and later ransomed and in his old age he was able to write about this. It is a little sentimental but I am sure he reflects the truth when he reflects what Constantine perceived to be his role. He had a duty to defend the city and as the Christian emperor he would do that even if it cost him his life.

MELVYN BRAGG: Roger, can you say when was the moment when the city fell. Was it when Giustiniani had to be taken in through the gate and therefore the gate was open? Was that the moment when it was all over?

ROGER CROWLEY: More or less, yes. The Ottoman troops got up on to the walls, trapped the resistant soldiers, then opened the gates and their army flooded into the city and started to ransack it. There was a kind of ceremonial moment when Mehmet entered the city, one which is much reflected in nineteenth-century Turkish paintings of this moment. He takes on the epithet of the Conqueror, as it is called in Turkish, and this is the moment when it is considered to have fallen, but effectively it had fallen before he entered it.

MELVYN BRAGG: But before he got in there were three days, Colin Imber, and as I understand it those three days were allowed for the soldiers to loot, pillage and rape. There was some sort of almost official license given. What is all that about?

COLIN IMBER: Yes, there is an official license but I think the Ottoman sultans knew perfectly well the reason why troops, particularly volunteers, were there and the things that could keep all troops busy was the promise of plunder, and an immensely wealthy city did indeed promise plunder and some people did become very wealthy. I can in fact quote an early sixteenth-century Ottoman historian who said: 'it is a proverbial saying that if there is any person who seemed to have wealth far beyond his humble status in life he must have been at the siege of Constantinople.' And this was true in all Ottoman sieges.

ROGER CROWLEY: Just briefly on the motivation of the troops, we don't know a great deal about the motivation of the Ottoman troops, but there is a rather grumpy letter during the siege from Mehmet's spiritual advisor saying most of these men are not interested in dying for God at all, but they will run for death if there is booty involved. The idea of material reward was infinitely more attractive than the hereafter.

JUDITH HERRIN: I think they assumed the city was full of gold and silver and silks and wonderful things that they all wanted. This was possibly not as true as it had been in 1204, but nonetheless there were sources of gold and we know from one of the Byzantines who was later captured that he offered the sultan a great deal of gold for his safety and the safety and ransom of his family, and the sultan turned to him and said, 'why did you not offer this to your emperor before?' So that was Notoras who lost his head as a result.

MELVYN BRAGG: Can we just conclude this business of the three days of license which fascinates me. Was it some agreed deal, was it written down somewhere?

ROGER CROWLEY: I think it was written down in Islamic law, and Colin might be able to correct me on that one, but it was general. It didn't pertain just to Islam, it pertained to all siege warfare – that if you didn't surrender you could expect to be sacked, and three days was the allotted term for this, but actually within a day they had stripped out everything of value and Mehmet was keen to preserve the fabric of the society intact so he was very keen to put a stop to it.

MELVYN BRAGG: Is there any hard evidence that day two or three this looting and pillaging and raping stopped?

JUDITH HERRIN: In sieges prior to that, the siege of Jerusalem, for example, by the crusaders, was followed by days and days of looting and there wasn't nearly so much control. So to the extent that there was only a three-day period and that was the limitation, that was very much more civil than the unrestricted looting that had taken place in medieval warfare before.

ROGER CROWLEY: It wasn't a complete sack. The Christian churches did survive this process. The church of the Holy Apostles, I believe, survived and was put under guard by Mehmet. Some of the other Christian churches, in some of the villages within the walls, surrendered and took the keys of their little stockade to Mehmet and they survived the siege as well.

MELVYN BRAGG: And also a lot of the looting was of people. There was a big slave trade, so younger people and handsomer people, I presume, in terms of women, were kept and looted for this live trade. Colin . . . ?

COLIN IMBER: Not only everyday humble domestic slaves but also members of the imperial family. We find a Governor General of Rumelia, of the European Provinces of the empire, in 1470 trading under a Turkish name, Hass Murad Pasha, but he was a member of the Palaeologus family, and indeed Mesih Pasha, the Ottoman commander at the failed siege of Rhodes in 1480 and later Grand Vizier, was also a member of the Palaeologus family, and another Greek Vizier of the 1406s is known in Turkish as Rumi Mehmed Pasha, or Mehmed Pasha the Greek, so we know there were Greeks, the old aristocracy if I can call them that, continuing to trade but under different names.

MELVYN BRAGG: Can we just develop what Roger said, Judith, a little about the treatment of the Christian monuments in Constantinople?

JUDITH HERRIN: We know that St Sofia, the cathedral church, was rapidly converted into a mosque and remained a mosque, of course, until it was secularised under Ataturk and it is now a museum. Of the other churches we learn that some of them were converted to mosques, one was preserved for the Greek Patriarch Skolarios, who became leader of the Greek group, the Greek ethnic group, under the Ottomans. The church of the Holy Apostles where the Emperors of Byzantium had been buried was razed to the ground on Mehmet's orders in order for him to construct a very beautiful mosque called the Mosque of the Conqueror, which survives today, and is a very fine fifteenth-century mosque. But it was clearly a symbolic replacement of the imperial mausoleum, a magnificent church dedicated to the Holy Apostles, by the Mosque of the Conqueror on the same place. It shows how insistent Mehmet was that he should become the master of this city with all its traditions.

MELVYN BRAGG: And that leads me, Colin Imber, from what Judith has said to the business of its traditions. There was a policy, was there not, of keeping people in Constantinople from different traditions, from different faiths, from different ethnic groups?

COLIN IMBER: Yes there certainly was, and also in order to revive the city there was a policy of bringing people in from all over the empire. That was one of the reasons why Mehmet was so unpopular. He deracinated people and put them in the city. But there is another interesting incident from 1539 actually which tells us a bit about the survival of the Greek churches. There is an over-zealous Chief Mufti who wished to close them down on the grounds that the city hadn't surrendered. A rather more clever Chief Judge produced a 110-year-old man and a 130-year-old man who gave evidence – that is two witnesses as required in Islamic law – that the Christians and Jews of the city had made a secret agreement with Mehmet to surrender. Therefore the churches can stay.

MELVYN BRAGG: I would like to develop this. The Christians had their own quarter, they stayed, and the Jews stayed. They were penalised with taxes and some of them converted to evade the taxes and to get on better, but Mehmet is definitely attempting to establish this sort of cosmopolitan place, isn't he? Can somebody just give it a bit more colour?

JUDITH HERRIN: I think the whole tradition, the whole history of Constantinople had been one of a very cosmopolitan, polyglot, multicultural city which Mehmet knew about and wished to preserve and strengthen. Not only did he wish the craftsmen all to stay in Constantinople, so that they would continue to service the city but, as Colin said, he brought in a lot of craftsmen and inhabitants from other places and made them live in Constantinople so that it would flourish again, and indeed it did.

Under his rule Constantinople became again a very prosperous city and it was to become even more prosperous, of course, in the great Ottoman cultural renaissance of Suleiman the Magnificent in the sixteenth century. So we have a clear policy of reinforcing the multicultural traditions of the city, which required tolerance which demanded that those who didn't want to adopt Islam pay an extra tax and keep themselves and their religious celebrations at a low key, no ringing bells or riding horses. Nonetheless they could carry on and it is quite evident that there was a very determined policy to build up Constantinople to make it again a great city and a great capital.

MELVYN BRAGG: Roger Crowley, how did the other Christian countries in, let's call it Europe, react to the fall of Constantinople?

ROGER CROWLEY: They had as far as I can see a sort of 9/11 moment. When you read the accounts you feel that people could remember where they were at the moment that the city fell. We know that people wept in the streets of Rome about this and it recreated a kind of zeal for crusading. Pius II, the pope, shortly afterwards tried very hard to get crusading going as a project, not with a great deal of success. The news of this rippled across Europe incredibly quickly.

There were songs, there were poems, there were all kinds of diatribes written against the Turks. It was bad luck for the Turks, for the Ottoman reputation, that they arrived just as printing was being developed and what you see in the latter half of the fifteenth century is a huge amount of literature in Europe about the terrible Turk. You start to see this whole projection of the terrible Turk in European thought and literature. Yet it was obvious that the Turks were established in Europe and were going to be there for a long time.

MELVYN BRAGG: Colin, what about the reaction inside the Ottoman Empire to this?

COLIN IMBER: The immediate reaction, to judge from very exiguous sources, seems to be not very great. What is remarkable is that the Byzantine Emperor has no special titles, is not regarded as anything very special in contemporary sources, and accounts of the siege are actually very small. It is later, I think, that the siege starts to acquire a symbolic significance. For example, in part of the coronation ceremony as developed from 1595, the sultan took a trip up the Golden Horn to the shrine of Abu Ayyub, then he came round the outside city walls, entered the city through the Edirne Gate, visited the tombs of his ancestors and then entered the palace.

This was, I think, a symbolic re-enactment of the conquest of the city which somehow emphasised it was an Ottoman city. I think also by that time the Ottomans had begun to treat Istanbul, Constantinople, in the same way the Byzantines did. It was their city and the inhabitants were extremely snobbish and thought that anybody in the provinces wasn't worth anything. So in a sense the Byzantine culture was replicated in the Ottoman city. It seems to me it was a history written by the losers, there is very little contemporary Ottoman material that we can point to in any detail, and it seems to me that everything we know was written by people who lost it.

MELVYN BRAGG: Well, that is a very good ending!

TRANSMITTED: 28.12.2006

Alchemy

At the end of the sixteenth century the German alchemist Heinrich Khunrath wrote: 'Darkness will appear on the face of the Abyss; Night, Saturn and the Antimony of the Sages will appear; blackness, and the raven's head of the alchemists, and all the colours of the world, will appear at the hour of conjunction; the rainbow also, and the peacock's tail. Finally, after the matter has passed from ashen-coloured to white and yellow, you will see the Philosopher's Stone.'

This is the language of alchemy. It is cryptic, encoded, symbolic and secretive. Isaac Newton wrote more manuscripts on alchemy in like language than on anything else and Ernest Rutherford, the father of nuclear physics, described himself as an alchemist.

What was the essence of alchemy? What is its history and legacy? And how much more was it than a rapacious desire to turn base metals into gold?

With me to discuss alchemy is Lauren Kassell, Lecturer in the History and Philosophy of Science at the University of Cambridge; Stephen Pumfrey, Senior Lecturer in the History of Science at the University of Lancaster; and Peter Forshaw, Lecturer in Renaissance Philosophies at Birkbeck College, University of London.

Peter Forshaw, alchemists are keen to see the origins of their art in the Bible, but there was one key non-Biblical text that was very important. It was called the Emerald Tablet, supposedly written by Hermes Trismegistus in about 500 BC in Egypt. Can you describe why that was so significant?

PETER FORSHAW: One thing was that it was one of the first texts ever translated into Latin when alchemy hit Europe in the twelfth century. It appears in a text attributed to Aristotle called *The Secret of Secrets*, so it was guaranteed to whet people's interests. It is very important because it is a pithy text of about twelve or thirteen lines which has the phrase 'as above so below', which became really one of the major maxims of magical philosophy and alchemy.

MELVYN BRAGG: That phrase keeps recurring, so can you tell us what you think it means and why it was so resonant?

PETER FORSHAW: I can do better. I can tell you what some of the alchemists thought it meant. Thomas Aquinas's teacher Albert the Great, for example, suggested that reading the Emerald Tablet 'as above and so below' refers to the influence of the heavens. The seven planets of the Ptolemaic cosmos from the Moon up to Saturn influenced the growth of seven metals in the earth. So for example Saturn influenced the growth of lead, the Sun the growth of gold and so forth, and there was a correlation between the planets above and the metals below. Others say it is form in a neo-Platonic sense and matter below which are the two components of all substances.

MELVYN BRAGG: So it is the relationship between what is up there and what is down here. A material and a spiritual relationship, which is where the Bible comes in. There's a dynamic going on between the earth and let's call it the heavens.

PETER FORSHAW: Yes, and also what was very interesting was that in some ways it is a pre-Christian creation myth which is equated with the Book of Genesis. People when they read things like the Emerald Table said hey, this sounds almost like Genesis at times. It is foreshadowing Genesis maybe. In the Book of Genesis, you have light being created which correlates with 'as above' and then you have the formless and void earth and water below which ties in with the 'as above so below' of Hermes Trismegistus and the Emerald Tablet.

MELVYN BRAGG: You say this was translated in Latin. Did the idea of alchemy take form then? Or did it take form later in the seventh-, eighth- and ninth-century development of Islamic culture?

PETER FORSHAW: It is very influential in Alexandria even earlier, but certainly in the Arabic tradition you have got very famous names like Jabir Ibn Hayan, also famous for being a Sufi. His works were translated into Latin or at least ones attributed to him and the figure Geber in Latin tradition became extremely influential. Ideas of mathematics, quantification of substances were introduced which influenced people like Robert Buller later on.

MELVYN BRAGG: So is this wholly theoretical? Or at this time, pre Middle Ages, are they talking about turning base metals into gold and the elixir of life?

PETER FORSHAW: You are certainly getting that in the Arabic tradition. You are also getting discussions even then of the properties of things like alums and salts and how they can be used in medicine as well, but certainly there are discussions of the transmutation of one substance to another. Aristotle is talking about it, the Arabs pick it up and then people like Roger Bacon in England in the thirteenth century develop these ideas.

MELVYN BRAGG: Lauren Kassell, can I talk to you about the English monk and natural philosopher Roger Bacon and how he took up the practice of alchemy. What did the practice of alchemy mean for him in the thirteenth century? What had happened to it that it arrived at his door, as it were, and he embraced it so rigorously?

LAUREN KASSELL: I am not an expert on Roger Bacon. My sense however is that he picks up the notion of distillation and he is very much interested in coming up with a sense of pure substances which can be used for medical purposes. If you separate out the pure from the impure you can then enhance the powers of substances. This is what distillation does and then you come up with something that has not simply physical properties but spiritual.

MELVYN BRAGG: So we are talking about a third thing now. First of all we are talking about this almost philosophical idea, 'as above so below', a way of understanding the world, then we are talking about how you can turn base metals and now we are talking about its uses in medicine. Was the drive towards medicine part of the alchemy as Roger Bacon saw it?

LAUREN KASSELL: Absolutely, he along with a series of others. Texts attributed to many thirteenth- or fourteenth-century alchemists are talking primarily about distillation and they are interested in the elixir of life. They are interested in that which makes one healthier and enables one to live longer. This is a tradition that becomes one of the dominant traditions through the later period.

MELVYN BRAGG: So what is Bacon doing? Is he going into a laboratory? In the thirteenth century does he have a laboratory? Are there glass bottles? Can you tell us what he is doing for this distillation? Is it like an old-fashioned chemist's laboratory that I used to see at school?

LAUREN KASSELL: Yes, probably. We have a lot more textual evidence than we do actual physical evidence, but yes, he knew an awful lot about the way that many different physical properties worked. Roger Bacon is known not primarily as an alchemist. In the literature he is thought of as one of the first experimental philosophers. That is an anachronistic way to put it, that is more of a seventeenth-century definition, but what he is doing is observing things and questioning the standard approaches to how they were understood. So he does work with light, he does work with distillation, he explores all of these things hands on.

MELVYN BRAGG: But it seems to me that we are still talking in nice parallel lines. We started with the idea of 'as above and so below' and we had the idea of Genesis, God, all things were made by Him, so we have two ideas. Is Roger Bacon working on the idea, as I understand it, that there is a substrate, there is a basic substance which is the same in everything and if you can find the key to that then you can move it around?

LAUREN KASSELL: Quite possibly. Am I allowed to throw this open to the others? I thought when you asked Peter the question of what were the two books – you have the Bible, you have the texts by Hermes Trismegistus – I thought you were going to ask about the Book of Nature. What Bacon is doing is trying to understand what is going on in the physical world that he is observing. If you are looking for whether he is part of what is referred to as the corpuscularian tradition, whether he is picking up on this pseudo-Geber set of texts where all things are positive as coming from sulphur and mercury, then yes to some extent he is looking to isolate and then to manipulate physical properties.

MELVYN BRAGG: Stephen Pumfrey, can I turn to you? In the quotation at the start of the programme the Philosopher's Stone was referred to. How does that link in with what has been said so far?

STEPHEN PUMFREY: I think it links in quite nicely with this idea that alchemists and indeed many philosophers had that there was some prime matter, some kind of underlying substrate common to all things, and individual types of species of metals were differentiated by some kind of properties added to this prime matter. The Philosopher's Stone was the ultimate secret, I suppose, of the alchemists and I think it brings together a lot. The Philosopher's Stone was that kind of magical ingredient. I suppose one might think of it as a catalyst that would bring everything to perfection as different kinds of species of metal or whatever were growing or developing from some primitive base form such as a base metal of iron through to its perfection as a noble metal of gold.

The Philosopher's Stone was something that would work and bring about perfection at various levels. At the material level the example would classically be the transmutation of base metals into gold, but that was just one example. The Philosopher's Stone also had effects at the organic level, particularly on the human body. So the Philosopher's Stone, if one could somehow grind it up and make a medicine out of it, would bring the body to perfection, would cleanse it of impurities and bring it to the most perfect health that was available. Not eternal life but certainly the prolongation of life.

It also connects not just at the material and the organic but to the spiritual level in a theological sense as well because the alchemist's language is often loaded with religious language and allusions to theology. Some alchemists made connections between the Philosopher's Stone and Chrysus, the stone rejected by the builders, so the Philosopher's Stone could also be seen to refer to the perfecting work of Christ or the Holy Spirit bringing the soul from its state of original sin to perfection and union with God in eternal life. It works on all these three levels, that is why it is so central to alchemy.

MELVYN BRAGG: And is the turning of metals into gold to make them more perfect, is that in order to find the Philosopher's Stone? Is it something like a kidney stone which the body turns into stone which is one of the things that fascinated people at that time? Is it rather like that?

STEPHEN PUMFREY: No. The Philosopher's Stone as I understand it – and it is obviously quite difficult to understand it, they don't give us much help – but the Philosopher's Stone as I understand it is something that one adds to one's chemical operations or other kind of matter. So you might take a big lump of lead, add a small bit of this kind of secret ingredient that someone has given you, and if you are very lucky three hours later, wham, bam! the Philosopher's Stone has acted to allow nature to work faster than she normally does and effect this lead into gold. What exactly it is we are not clear about. An alchemist like Paracelsus said you make the Philosopher's Stone by taking the rose-tinted blood of the lion and mixing it with the gluten of the eagle, which doesn't get us very far . . .

MELVYN BRAGG: We have not had Paracelsus. Paracelsus comes just after twenty past nine. We are not at Paracelsus yet. Peter, why this obsession with metals?

PETER FORSHAW: Metals were seen as the most perfect manifestation of basic matter. Also metals I think are significant because a lot of natural philosophers who are interested in alchemy as well are reading Aristotle. Aristotle in his work *Meteorologia*, even though that sounds as though it is about the weather, in Book Three he calls it 'the formation of metals and minerals and rocks and so forth from two substances'. There is a watery vapour which later on is understood as being mercury by Geber and an earthy smoke which is understood as being sulphur.

Natural philosophers really take to this Aristotelian idea. It is developed by the Arabs and more firmly equated with sulphur and mercury and the idea is in Aristotelian theory that all things are growing to perfection. So all metals will eventually grow, mature or ripen into gold and, as Stephen mentioned, the alchemist is looking for something that will catalyse the process. You can take lead. The idea in Aristotelian theory is that lead and gold aren't a different matter, they are both basically primal matter which is matter without form and what you do is you strip away the form of lead, reduce it to primal matter and then encourage nature to put the form of gold.

MELVYN BRAGG: It seems to me that as the Middle Age goes into the cusp of the Renaissance, Aristotle is standing for a great number of things to do with the search for the divine. It is to do with the interaction between the heavens and the earth. It is to do with what you do with things themselves, and it is to do with the purification of yourself, and it is always going to be alchemy. At the same time because of this we are going to turn this into gold and make people, including ourselves, very rich. It netted an awful lot of fakes and charlatans who were called 'puffers' at the time. Can you give us an example of one or two of the puffers?

LAUREN KASSELL: There are many puffers, and one of the problems is that you have stories that are told, now referred to as transmutation stories, in which people say I am a real alchemist and this is my claim to legitimacy and I have got the text or the stone because I married the widow of the dead alchemist or I met this itinerant on the road. All of these stories posit a bad alchemist against a good alchemist, the good alchemist being the one who is being written about. Any number of practitioners would be referred to as puffers, these charlatans. Paracelsus – I know we are not quite twenty past! – Paracelsus was famously decried as a charlatan. Virtually everyone who practised had this label attached to them at some point or another.

There are people who, you can think of them as sort of market-stall alchemists, people who are swindlers of some sort or another. In order to understand alchemy you have to understand that it has always been suspect. It has always been thought to be fraudulent and there have always been frauds. So I don't know of particular ones from the early date. The evidence about these guys is hard to track down, largely because they don't write.

MELVYN BRAGG: But there were people, weren't there, like Nicolas Flamel and George Starkey – do you know about those people? Can you give us some idea of how they were getting away with it? Presumably nobody turned up saying, 'look, I have turned a base metal into gold', so in a sense how did they all get away with it?

ALL: But they did.

STEPHEN PUMFREY: Take Edward Kelly, John Dee's sidekick, as it were. John Dee is Queen Elizabeth's astrologer. They found, supposedly in the monastery of Glastonbury, a powder of the Philosopher's Stone and Edward Kelly allegedly did transmutations in front of the Emperor Rudolph in Prague and actually was knighted. He did really well from it, but he was always accused of being a charlatan and fraudulent.

MELVYN BRAGG: But do you believe that he – that Kelly did turn it into gold with the means then available? We can come to the present day as to how the idea is by no means foolish or nonsensical, the idea of changing things, but at that time with the means available, do you think that he did or that he was just a cleverer charlatan than the others? Maybe charlatan is the wrong idea because some of them really were searching for solutions that were important. But it was just at the age a few hundred years ago when they had not the means that people have now. To deride them is perhaps foolish because that was then, and what they had and with what they had, they went a very long way, as we can now see.

STEPHEN PUMFREY: I think historians of science and especially historians of alchemy don't like being forced to talk about what they think was really going on, but let me take a chance. The alchemists' understanding in our terms of what kinds of metals there were and purification was rather different. I think we can imagine that some of the operations did result in pure gold being smelted out when they didn't expect it to be there in the first place and there may have been a few kinds of tricks and indeed some minerals and amalgams can look a bit like gold. So I think what we can say is the results of these operations sufficiently often produce material that was sufficiently convincing to count as gold at that time to give the whole thing a serious credibility.

PETER FORSHAW: Yes, when you buy a gold watch, how do you know it is gold?

MELVYN BRAGG: I don't know anything about that sort of thing.

PETER FORSHAW: Precisely. It was the same then. It is a yellow colour, if it is heavy, if it is malleable, then it is sort of gold. You find for example in museums gold coins and medals which have been struck, some of them . . .

MELVYN BRAGG: From fools' gold?

PETER FORSHAW: Yes, and iron pyrites, yes. But you find some that are really closely approximating gold. They may be amalgams as Stephen implied, and that is one of the things the more sceptical alchemists, or the more realistic ones, say you have got to test.

MELVYN BRAGG: So even on this level, which is a greed level, enough of them were showing emperors and kings results sufficient to keep things ticking over. We will come back to the association with ideas of how the universe operated in a moment or two, but another public demonstration that they were alchemists was to do with the pursuit of the elixir of life. Can you talk about that, Lauren? What were they pursuing when they were looking for the elixir of life?

LAUREN KASSELL: Well, they are pursuing – this brings us partly back to Roger Bacon and the distillation – they are pursuing the quintessence, the fifth essence, that which was present at Creation . . .

MELVYN BRAGG: So they are referring back to the Bible?

LAUREN KASSELL: Oh yes, it always refers back to the Bible. What the alchemist does is what God does at Creation. The alchemists are pursuing a way, as has been talked about before, of replicating what happens in the bowels of the earth but at a greater speed. This is God's work. So they look for the processes that enable them to do this and one of the most important products as well as gold is this quintessence. If you imagine alcohol, it evaporates quickly, it is like air, it is a water that burns, it is a divine substance of some sort. So they are looking, through distillation, for some sort of quintessence which then has positive effects on the body and that is the elixir of life. It preserves health.

PETER FORSHAW: Quintessence is spirit and spirit at the time has so many different ramifications. You get it equated with the Holy Spirit, the spirit of the world, the spirit in your body and there is a continuum between them.

MELVYN BRAGG: When you say it all goes back to the Bible, we are talking about the Fall, aren't we? So where exactly in the Bible are they referring to when they are talking about the elixir of life?

PETER FORSHAW: The elixir of life? I can't answer that question.

MELVYN BRAGG: Can somebody answer that question?

LAUREN KASSELL: I can answer that question. The story is that Adam and Eve sin and we know it is Eve's fault. Adam and Eve sin, disease is the result, so before the Fall there are different stories about whether they were giants, whether they had genitals. It is very interesting, the debates about what the existence of Adam and Eve was like before the Fall. After the Fall they suffer disease and they will suffer death, the angels come along at the behest of God and they tell Adam what he needs to know in order to heal his disease. Now this is the story that Paracelsus likes to tell in various forms and after Adam comes the knowledge of medicine. Adam has the first true knowledge of medicine and men begin to live less long. What Paracelsus is saying is we have lost this knowledge, it is no longer present in books, we need to recover it from nature, from studying nature. His whole programme is to find this true Adamic knowledge, this angelic knowledge that Adam and Eve had just after the Fall, in order for us to be able to heal ourselves better. It is the only source of this practice. It cannot be found in the corrupt classical tradition.

MELVYN BRAGG: Paracelsus about five minutes late, but here he comes! Can you just give him a date and take on from what Lauren has said, just to place him. What is he bringing to the table?

STEPHEN PUMFREY: He is born of humble origins so we are not quite sure of the date, but he was born somewhere around 1493 or 1494, dies in 1541. The date I think is significant because he is developing his ideas in that very turbulent time of the Reformation.

And he himself is a firebrand radical character with strong ideas on religion and medicine, alchemy, everything. What I think he really brings to the table is first of all an evolution of our chemicals. We have talked about sulphur and mercury. Paracelsus adds a third principle, which he calls 'salt'. So he is refining our chemical theory.

But perhaps more importantly what I take him to do is to argue very forcefully that these three prime chemical principles are not just the basis of the transmutation of metals they are the basis of all matter. The entire creation. What Paracelsus successfully does, or certainly his philosophers do on his behalf, is to advocate an entire alchemical model of the whole universe, which he deliberately opposes to the corrupt bookish tradition of people like Aristotle and Galen and the four traditional elements. He and his followers are effectively setting up an alchemical or chemical philosophy as a rival way of understanding the whole of nature to attack the philosophy of the Schools and the traditional medicine of the Galenists of the time.

MELVYN BRAGG: Some people give him great regard for bringing all sorts of things to medicine. For instance, introducing the idea that illness comes from germs that are external and not internal. We haven't really got time to go into that now but to move to another big person in this story, Simon Forman, a follower of Paracelsus, Forman the English alchemist. Lauren, can you tell us what he did that was important to this story?

LAUREN KASSELL: Forman is not a great scientist, he is not a great figure in the history of science, but what he does is he writes constantly. He is born in 1552. I have spent the last ten years of my life working on him. He wrote. Fifteen thousand handwritten pages survive from a single decade. Most of what we have is the decade between 1590 and 1600. What he documents is the life of an alchemist, astrologer, magician in London in the 1590s. This is a period when the great commercial commonwealth enterprises are under way, great improvements in navigation are taking place, people are interested in making sure that navigators and merchants have practical knowledge and that they are taught this practical knowledge so there is a lot happening. There is a high literacy.

MELVYN BRAGG: He goes to see Shakespeare's plays.

LAUREN KASSELL: He goes to see Shakespeare plays. He is doing all of this stuff in London and what he documents is that there is a huge circulation of alchemical Paracelsian medicine in this period which is being passed in scruffy handwritten notes from person to person and being practised in conjunction with astrology and magic at the most dispersed level on the streets of London.

MELVYN BRAGG: This is alchemy in the thriving 1590s – Elizabeth I, John Dee, Shakespeare's writing, the East India Company about to be formed and so on, in comes alchemy to the highest courts. The Queen and the Privy Council back alchemy, literally put their money where their alchemy is. So it is roaring away. What, though, did Forman do that convinced the people around him that it was alchemy that was a key way into a real knowledge of the world?

LAUREN KASSELL: He practised astrology. That is a backwards answer. That was his service. You could come to him and, based on the moment of the question that was asked, he would tell you what was wrong with you and he would give you an answer that he could help your illness and either help it with straightforward remedies or not.

MELVYN BRAGG: We are back to the beginning of the programme, because astrology had a bearing on medicine, given that the heavens had a bearing on what was happening on earth. 'As above so below.' But he also used the elixir of life idea, didn't he, on himself when he got the plague?

LAUREN KASSELL: OK, now you want the story.

MELVYN BRAGG: No, I don't want the story, I want to get moving! In 1591, he is bringing into play the elixir of life as well as the astrological ideas behind alchemy, isn't he?

LAUREN KASSELL: Yes, he is probably giving everybody this stuff he has distilled. He says he can cure the plague with it. At the time there is a separation between medical practitioners who write the prescriptions and an apothecary fulfils those prescriptions. Forman

refuses to work within the established hierarchy. He is not a legitimate physician and he says, 'you get the full service from me. You
get these potions that I am making', which may or may not have
magical, alchemical, astrological properties. They may be straightforward herbal things. He enables people to be treated by him in
what is a comprehensive coherent framework.

MELVYN BRAGG: So in some sense you have the apotheosis of
alchemy but at the same time it isn't studied at any university. You
are going woof, woof, Peter.

PETER FORSHAW: I am going woof, woof. We are talking about
the 1590s and early 1600s. These are the heydays of Paracelsian
revival. He died in 1541 and then you find, in the 1580s particularly, his texts appearing. Paracelsus wrote in German most of the
time. People are translating them into Latin and you find that Simon
Forman is very Paracelsian. Hands on, getting dirty, making your
own medicines. And astrology is necessary – you know the 'as above
so below' – the as above, the stars. Paracelsus says there is a Heavenly
Arcana, and there is a star also inside you. The physician identifies
your ailment through astrology, the alchemist then makes the arcane
which is the secret remedy which is good for you.

MELVYN BRAGG: You didn't answer my question, though, which
is why isn't it studied at universities as astrology, as astronomy are?
There is so much knowledge here, it is taken up by very intelligent,
influential people in society – why isn't it a subject at university?

PETER FORSHAW: Because it is very hands on. For example, take
medicine, university medicine. Steve mentioned Galen. There was a
strict hierarchy. A doctor at university had the theory and then he
had some underling like a barber-surgeon do all the physical work.
Alchemy is hands on, you don't get a pharmacist to do it, you do it
yourself. This is not what university dons do.

MELVYN BRAGG: Is it the secretiveness as well? The language
that I read at the beginning of the programme, the language which
Newton writes, is it because of the secrecy? They want to keep it out
of any public domain for all sorts of reasons.

STEPHEN PUMFREY: Oh yes, they certainly write in this secretive cryptic way. We are dealing with codes and I suppose there are several reasons why that might be. Some of them frankly are writing in this way because they are trying to obscure the fact that they are pretending to more knowledge than they have. I am sure that is one reason.

Another reason is this – if it is true then alchemical transmutation is powerful knowledge which you don't want the vulgar to have. And in this case the vulgar means the unadept, the uninitiated, not just the common people. Even peers of the realm don't count as initiates. You are keeping it from the unitiated and the reason for that perhaps is that the true alchemical adept imagined himself to be particularly chosen by God as part of a succession of people who had been initiated into this kind of revealed knowledge which was the ultimate key to the understanding of nature.

MELVYN BRAGG: I am going to move radically now. Boyle – yes, I am sorry it is that far, never mind. Robert Boyle, 'the father of modern chemistry', wrote in 1661 and paid great tribute to alchemy. Can we talk about him as an alchemist as well as a chemist, because it would seem that we are dealing with chemistry, a most practical hard subject, and with it this ancient subject that comes trailing clouds of Genesis and Egyptian lore. Can we talk about Boyle?

PETER FORSHAW: Good. Boyle is interesting because of this sceptical chemist, everyone thinks oh, he is totally against alchemy. Certainly early on he does make remarks. For example, he loathes the obscurantism of alchemy, the way it is transmitted – green lions and dragons and so forth. He said, 'no, we have got to have a far more open language so that we can share knowledge.' In some ways it is the end of one style of alchemical transmission, but he is fascinated with alchemical processes.

You mentioned George Starkey, an American who has far more laboratory experience than Boyle. He introduces him to this work and they really do practise, they are theoreticians on the properties of matter. Boyle is fascinated by the property of mercury as some sort of universal solvent. He even gives a paper to the Royal Society in 1678 on the degradation of gold by an anti-elixir. He can't make the elixir that makes gold, that perfects it, but he has made one that at least dissolved gold, which is a start. He is critical of Paracelsus for his bombast, critical for the odd language he uses, but has a great deal of respect for adepts.

MELVYN BRAGG: Lauren, do you see the alchemy in Boyle's work?

LAUREN KASSELL: Absolutely, and I think it is very useful for Peter to have pointed out that Starkey taught Boyle. From around 1600 you have this coalescence of different schools of alchemy, and Boyle and Starkey, or Starkey teaching Boyle, are following a mercurial school of alchemy. They are less interested in the medical applications. They are much more interested in the matter principles, although there are still medicinal applications. There are these other schools as well, and Boyle is setting himself up as one sort of proponent against these other schools. He is looking for this red powder which has been circulating in Europe for about a hundred years. He is looking for missing texts which tell you about how to make this red powder. He is recovering very assiduously, as does Newton, the process and the history of alchemy both through the textual and the practical study.

STEPHEN PUMFREY: But I think . . .

MELVYN BRAGG: I want to go to Newton – sorry about that, Stephen. People will be surprised that he wrote more about alchemy than about mathematics and seems to have been just as devoted to alchemy as he was to his science. There is a body of thought that it was the ideas behind alchemy which may have influenced his own thinking on the laws of motion and gravity more than what he discovered in mathematics. Is there anything in that, Stephen?

STEPHEN PUMFREY: Yes, I think there is a lot of truth to that. I think what we have to start from here is that when Newton is beginning to think about this in the 1660s, the dominant way of thinking about nature is the mechanical philosophy that the world can be explained in terms of lifeless corpuscles. None of this spirit, none of this connection through intermediaries with God, although God is there, and Newton is deeply worried about that. He is deeply worried that developments in natural philosophy are squeezing out the divine and the spiritual.

I think it is clear that his calculations for the inverse square or of gravity don't come out of the maths alone. He starts thinking what is going on here and it is clear that both in the 1670s and indeed right to the end of his life he is deeply interested in alchemy because he thinks what have these alchemists been studying? They have been looking for that extra kind of spiritual, non-material, non-mechanical element which is the key to God's creation and upholding of the universe. So Newton is an alchemist in his way of thinking. He is a decoder, he is trying to decode the alchemical texts.

By the end of his life Newton thinks that he has managed to arrive at a kind of inverse square law, mathematical inverse square law of what the alchemists were talking about in terms of sulphur and mercury and he thinks he has arrived at an ethereal, attractive and repulsive model of the law of gravity which is derived from a modernised form of this alchemical tradition of thought which he thinks holds the key to nature. You have got to remember that Newton thought that Pythagoras and other ancients knew the law of gravity but expressed it in code.

PETER FORSHAW: Going back to Boyle, whose writings after Boyle's death Newton is desperately trying to get hold of. Just to change people's perspectives on Boyle. Yes, the father of chemistry, but don't be under any misapprehension that this is just physical chemistry. Boyle towards the end of his life wants to leave a 'hermetic legacy' as he calls it, and one of the most fascinating quotes is when he says: 'the Philosopher's Stone may be an inlet into another sort of knowledge which will allow us to actually have intercourse with good spirits.'

He and Elias Ashmole, who founded the Ashmolean Museum in Oxford, believed that the Philosopher's Stone has supernatural qualities which allows communication with angels. So it is interesting to equate — they are smiling at me! — the physical chemist who is the prototype of the father of modern chemistry with someone who has these very spiritual beliefs that Newton has too.

MELVYN BRAGG: But do you think that the repudiation of alchemy by people in the last hundred or more years is itself being again repudiated? The search for fundamental particles through nuclear physics, particles that seem to be able to transform themselves or to be transformed from one thing to another. Do you think that alchemy was a very good early push at it, with insufficient means to get there?

STEPHEN PUMFREY: Yes, I think there clearly is a legacy in terms of the attempts to try and transform one kind of substance and try to understand the relations. But that kind of model of physics, of the change from one thing to another, completely lacks this spiritual religious side. That universe has gone.

MELVYN BRAGG: Has it gone completely?

STEPHEN PUMFREY: Well, it certainly has gone out of modern particle physics. If we are looking for the survival of modern alchemy it is perhaps worth looking at modern alternative health practices where by a rigorous disciplining of the body, of eating the right foods, of purifying yourself you somehow become a better person. That I think, as it were, kind of maps on to the lingering psychological interest in alchemy.

PETER FORSHAW: Yes. Paracelsus is often touted as the founder of modern homeopathy for example. Homeopathic websites have him as one of their authorities.

MELVYN BRAGG: It seems a bit of a comedown after all you've said. To end up with keeping fit.

PETER FORSHAW: It is. But the elixir was for prolonging life and all of these things at the end of the day are aiming for perfection. Perfect body, perfect spirit, perfect soul, and alchemy is all about that. The three principles of mercury, sulphur and salt are spirit, soul and body.

STEPHEN PUMFREY: But if we go back to the very limited idea of transmutation of metals I think we can see there has always been a place for that. Aristotle has it, our mainstream alchemists have it and in the time when Newton was working there is a mechanical philosophy argument. After all, if you believe that the only difference between gold and iron are atoms arranged in different ways, if you can smash them with a hammer enough you can rearrange these particles physically and generate gold. So there has always been a tradition. You don't have to buy into the whole spiritual element to allow this belief that metals are related and we are understanding something of the fundamental nature of matter.

TRANSMITTED: 24.2.2005

Shakespeare's Language

William Shakespeare 'was not of an age, but for all time'. That was in the seventeenth century and it's a claim that has often been repeated since, but is it really true? Is what we see in the theatre and increasingly at the cinema the work of a playwright whose works live on, or are we merely watching historical reconstructions – and even museum pieces – with any contemporary meaning obscured by the reverence we pay to the author? And if Shakespeare is for all time, what is it about him that makes him so eternally special?

With me to discuss Shakespeare in our times is Professor Frank Kermode, recently described by John Sutherland as Britain's most distinguished living critic. He has just brought out a masterly book, *Shakespeare's Language*. Also with us in the theatre director Michael Bogdanov, who is to give a lecture called *Shakespeare is Dead!* at the Royal Festival Hall next week; and Germaine Greer, Professor of English and Comparative Studies at Warwick University.

Frank Kermode, one of the things you say in your book is that around 1600 Shakespeare as a poet, Shakespeare's language as a poet, changed because of the theatre. Could we start by your developing that?

FRANK KERMODE: I think the idea, not entirely new, is that in the earlier plays there is a kind of rhetorical quality which really belongs to the printed page rather than to the stage. And that as time went by, and particularly as he saw possibilities of showing people in the act of thought, painful, anxious thought, you got a new kind of language, far more resonate, far less explicit and sometimes very much more difficult. So that the audience itself had to be prepared for this development, this change in the quality of what people said. No longer were they just laying out an idea or a scheme and embellishing it, but they're actually like people who have got something terribly serious to think about and are thinking about it there and then on the stage.

MELVYN BRAGG: When you talk about the rhetorical nature of the early plays, you are also referring to rhetorical devices which you refer to when you discuss the early plays in your book. Could you give us some idea of some of these devices, the device of repetition for example, and others that he uses?

FRANK KERMODE: Yes. You get passages which are just as they would be if the work was a poem and not a play. That's to say if you have a man lamenting that he's lost a battle he will find four or five different ways of explaining that, and saying losing a battle like this is like being a lion who's killed by a hunter, is like this, is like that. All that disappears later, everything becomes more urgent, tighter packed, harder to unpack, so the strain on the listener gets greater and greater as time goes by.

MELVYN BRAGG: Before we move on to that, which I suspect will be the meat of the discussion, can we just talk a bit more about the early plays? You start off with *Titus Andronicus* – one of his very early plays. The man is speaking to Lavinia for three minutes whilst she's got no hands and her tongue's been cut out and she's been raped – describing what we see in front of us for three minutes – these repetitions are called 'anaphora' that you describe?

FRANK KERMODE: Well, there are all sorts of rhetorical tricks in the passage you've used where the girl's uncle comes upon here with her hands cut off and her tongue pulled out and has about forty-five lines comparing her to a lopped tree, a fountain, and all the rest of it. Clearly nobody thought perhaps he should go and try to help her, or do something for her, because everybody was perfectly happy with this sort of pretty set of verses saying 'but of course she can't speak' so she can't tell, obviously she can't tell me what's wrong with her, because she can't say anything. The sheer implausibility of it is not relevant in the context of drama at that time because it's much more like a poem than like a play.

472

MELVYN BRAGG: So actually by responding to the needs of drama at that time as he saw it is one of the things that made Shakespeare's poetry more dense?

FRANK KERMODE: That's right. So that the reason for picking 1600 as the turning point is not to say that the plays before 1600 are all inferior because that is not so, but because this new kind of intensity really came in with *Hamlet*. The soliloquy Shakespeare used is quite unlike any other soliloquy. He discovered that it was possible to represent somebody thinking, on the stage, as if he was in some dreadful moral situation and he had to persuade himself what to do in it. The speech of the king in *Hamlet*, for example, where he's contemplating his own guilt, wondering whether he can keep the rewards of his offence and yet be pardoned for his offence, and deciding of course that he can't, but deciding that question with a language of a new kind of intensity.

MELVYN BRAGG: We'll come back to that in a moment. Germaine Greer, do you find this intensity of language, this denseness, something you agree with? Because I have read that you have said that you think the language is simple, it's the meaning that's difficult.

GERMAINE GREER: Well, it depends. I mean when I was listening to Frank talking about what happens in *Hamlet* it seems to me there's something a bit more complicated going on. I would say the first time you get that contrast between highly figured language and the real heroic blank verse of Shakespeare is in *Romeo and Juliet*, and it's Juliet who does it. Everybody around her speaks in rhyming couplets, even in sonnets. Her mother speaks to her in a sonnet, a hideous sonnet, a sort of spoof sonnet in a way, an obscene sonnet as it happens, and that is also Shakespeare's most obscene play. So you've got all this highly figured language which is – 'the bawdy hand of the dial is now upon the prick of noon' – oh please! I just asked the time!

Then you've got Juliet, this fourteen-year-old, we get told a thousand times that she's fourteen years old. We all know what that means, to be fourteen, I think, and it wasn't that much different then. She was very young in everybody's estimation. And we have this language of strong passion and a disordered imagination, as the child goes straight down this sort of solipsistic path to nowhere with this dark Romeo who also speaks in figured language. And she has to shut up, otherwise he's gonna wreck the play, you know, 'swear not by the moon' etc. So I think that this opposition is something that Shakespeare was very well aware of. He, after all, made up the new language of the theatre, other people didn't speak it until he did.

And the other thing that's important to remember is that the people loved all that figured speech. It's like opera. You don't want them to suddenly start talking the language of real feeling in opera because you understand the game that's being played. I always wondered why directors didn't have someone bring on a blanket for Lavinia, in *Titus Andronicus*, but they never do and there's nothing in the play that says they couldn't or shouldn't because the uncle can emote as much as he likes and you could still have the servants making sure she was wrapped up, but they never do that. And so I think that Shakespeare's got to be given credit for this contrast.

The thing that I always say to my sixth-formers when I talk to them about Shakespeare, when they already think they're jaded and fed up with Shakespeare, is that they have to listen to the way they talk in real life. We don't speak prose in real life, we speak an intensively suggestive and extraordinarily mysterious language which has got to be interpreted with a great deal of other assistance.

And I usually give them the example of people passing each other in the street and saying 'Alright?' and the answer, what's the answer? 'Alright.' What on earth are they saying? They're saying, 'I'm all right, I'm in a hurry, don't talk to me now, I hope you're fine.' That's what is packed into that word, and when you speak normally your voice is governed, the way you speak if you're not, like me, talking like an academic to a microphone. But normally the way you speak is governed by the way you feel, by your heartbeat, by your breath length. You are actually speaking a rhythmic and figured language of intense suggestivity.

If you then look at Shakespeare's language, it's not a question of hard words, and it's not a question of purple effects – it is if you're Polonius of course, but that's the whole point about Polonius, he's incapable of talking directly to anyone. If you look at the language you'll see that you understand as much and as little of what

Shakespearean characters are trying to say as you do of what your mother said to you this morning, or what your mate said to you in the playground. That it's this openness, this strange partiality, that Shakespeare's language needs, 'men that can breathe and eyes that can see', it's only as alive as the registration mechanisms of human beings. And he didn't think he was for all time, I don't think. He knew that he was only for as long as men breathed and eyes saw and black ink shone on a page and so on. Much more modest than Ben Jonson in every way.

MELVYN BRAGG: Michael Bogdanov, you've directed Shakespeare in the theatre and you did a film. From what I've read from a lecture you gave, you're hammering away at the way Shakespeare is received, the way Shakespeare is regarded, the way Shakespeare is ignored by 90 per cent of the population. Do you think the language stands in the way?

MICHAEL BOGDANOV: Yes, I do. I think that the education system has been at fault, and still is at fault for surrounding the language and the plays and the stories in particular with an aura of mystery. The problem is that when you make Shakespeare compulsory and you teach him in certain ways to answer examination questions, it means that you start to negate the very fundamental thing that the man was about, which is a working playwright. I think that far from there being a change in 1600, I think it was a maturing of a playwright over a period of twenty-five years, who started off as a swashbuckler and used all kinds of dramatic devices in the raw, including language, which he kept repeating, and also ideas, just in case people didn't understand them, and gradually honed his craft and his way of telling his stories to a point when you reach *The Tempest*, right at the end, when it's like a mosaic and every word is very carefully placed and you take one word out and the thing falls apart.

The key to Shakespeare has always been, for me, live performance and not treating the audience as if they already know the story. Shakespeare when he put the plays on was putting them on with a bunch of actors who were also contributing, improvising and changing, and even after his death writing different bits to put in the Folio, perhaps from false memory or whatever. He was working with a live audience, live material, telling stories that a lot of them had never heard before. He had to put them across in a way that people could follow.

So while I accept the fact that the audience wouldn't have understood everything that was being said on stage, their points of reference and their cultural frame was much more equipped to deal with the plays than we are today. And as long as you treat Shakespeare as literature and something on the page rather than something on the stage I don't believe that the plays will last in any form. In fifty years, a hundred years' time, with the rate that words are dropping out of the English language and being struck out of the Oxford English Dictionary, the plays will be the province of academics. It's an elitist affair in that respect and that's why I welcome films like Baz Luhrmann's *Romeo and Juliet* because they awaken the consciousness of young kids who are brought up on Spielberg and arcades and Nintendo and need some other frame of reference in order to work with the stories.

MELVYN BRAGG: I thought that was a terrific film too, but one has to face up to the fact that he used 40 per cent of *Romeo and Juliet* and left the rest of the text out.

GERMAINE GREER: But what's more important, Melvyn, is that he didn't change what he used and that was amazing. It's very helpful for kids to realise that Shakespeare writes . . .

MELVYN BRAGG: I agree. I want to ask whether that's for you, Michael, a way forward, to say, look, we'll just take the highlights, the best bits, and that's the way to get it over?

MICHAEL BOGDANOV: Well, I'll return to you with a question, a similar question. How much do you think was cut from Olivier's *Hamlet*, for example?

MELVYN BRAGG: A massive amount.

MICHAEL BOGDANOV: Which became . . .

MELVYN BRAGG: It's the same question.

MICHAEL BOGDANOV: Which became, if you like, a benchmark of thinking about *Hamlet* for about thirty years. I mean it put thinking back on *Hamlet* basically because he managed to strip it of all the politics, and yet people look at that film and say 'that did Shakespeare a service'. Now I would say the same for Baz Luhrmann's *Romeo and Juliet*, and you don't do *Romeo and Juliet* on stage usually without cutting about 25 per cent. And he's also using the cinematic technique of visuals to say what Shakespeare sometimes used repetitive language to describe in images on the stage. Because you're using your imagination and you had to listen to words and conjure these pictures, *Romeo and Juliet* is full of the things Frank was talking about, repetition and back up, in other words you repeat things in order to make sure the audience are there with the story or you repeat and make sure they've got the idea and the image.

FRANK KERMODE: All right. Well, one of the most interesting lines of *Romeo and Juliet* is: 'well, Juliet, I will lie with thee tonight.' In other words, we've stopped all fancy talk and we're really down to a life situation: she's dead and he's going to join her.

MICHAEL BOGDANOV: But what about that thing that comes out of left field? Suddenly when he's with the apothecary and he says 'this is' – and he's got the poison – 'this is the real poison in the world, this gold that I give you, this is the thing doing the more mischief than these compounds thou may'st not sell.' Suddenly out of the blue comes this extraordinary, if you like, pre-Marxist statement about gold being the corrupting force and that actually that's the more evil in the world than anything else.

FRANK KERMODE: Fine. There are a lot of good things in his plays, we know that, but I think as an experienced director you must have had to recognise sometimes that there are parts of the later plays where the audience is catching the drift rather than actually understanding what is being said. And I believe that must have been true even in the 1600s or, say, the time of *Coriolanus*. There are passages in *Coriolanus* which nobody understands and nobody can have understood. They're not due to textual corruption, they are just due to this tremendous overuse of rhetorical force that comes out of Shakespeare.

MELVYN BRAGG: Can I turn back to the soliloquies for a moment, because you took me back, Michael, by talking about the Olivier *Hamlet*. One of the things that thrilled people like myself when they saw it was that he sat silently and the soliloquies were spoken, as it were, in his voice, out of his head. And you thought gosh, he is thinking, I'm listening to thinking. Do you think that Shakespeare developed that, he alone developed that? And can you give us just a little bit more about how important you think that is?

FRANK KERMODE: I think it's important. I think that the soliloquy was an easy dramatic device for telling the audience something that the author felt they ought to know, at a particular point. When it developed into something else, into the soliloquies of *Hamlet*, it became a very powerful new agent in drama. That period was the period of Shakespeare's writing after 1600. Nobody else did it, and after Shakespeare nobody did it again. It was, as far as I'm aware, the period where soliloquy was so important because it opens up the whole question of character, for one thing, during that period. And that period was a very short one and the experiment of it was Shakespeare.

MELVYN BRAGG: Is this as near as you can get to the way people think?

FRANK KERMODE: It's a representation . . .

MELVYN BRAGG: Of thinking?

FRANK KERMODE: Of agitated, sometimes, unusually agitated thought, yes.

MELVYN BRAGG: Would you agree with that, Germaine?

GERMAINE GREER: I would, but I think a lot more thinking was done aloud then than is done aloud now, because all reading was done aloud, for example.

MELVYN BRAGG: That's a good point.

GERMAINE GREER: And I think if you want to find someone thinking in a similar way, in a different context, you've got the sermons of Donne. Donne also shows processes of thinking in his elegies and in his sonnets where actually he's going from thought to thought, sometimes in a free associative way, which adds up to something marvellous and something very compact. It is still a rhetorical device. It is still the device of plain speech, the device of simplicity and it's all as thoroughly documented as any other device is. It's not accidental that Hamlet's interlocutor is called Horatio and is silent through the play and stands in the play as a representative of the audience. He is the auditor on stage who is left at the end to draw his breath in pain, to tell Hamlet's story, as only the audience can do, because they're the only people who've been privy to it, because they have been privy to this long and painful journey.

I would place it in another context too, which is the maturing of Protestantism and the notion of earnestness and sincerity in religious experience as opposed to ritual and lip service. There's this long struggle in *Hamlet* to escape from figured utterance and lying and courtly manipulation to a world where you can speak frankly one to another and the fact that he does that with the audience is the central core of that play. And it exists in the text. It doesn't always exist in the theatre because it gets messed about with, because you have him speaking to his armpit, or muttering, and not bringing the audience into his confidence, and because he's played as mad – which is outrageous – he's not in the least mad, although he's being subject to maddening circumstances.

The audience can't follow someone who's mad because mad people speak a private language. The whole point about Hamlet is he doesn't, and that's why he'll always be the greatest hero because he goes into the world that we actually live in, the world of frustrations and lying semblances, and he takes us with him, on his back as it were, and keeps talking to us all the way. We are involved.

MELVYN BRAGG: Frank, can you just bring us up to speed on one other thing in *Hamlet* – this business of 'doubling'.

FRANK KERMODE: Hendiadys.

MELVYN BRAGG: Hendiadys. Now what's going on there, because that seems to be almost a disease that goes through the play?

FRANK KERMODE: Yes, it's a very peculiar thing and it's escaped notice for a very long time, that habit of doubling adjectives. Now that you asked me, I can't think of an example!

MELVYN BRAGG: House and home.

FRANK KERMODE: House and home is a stark instance of hendiadys. In *Hamlet*, not only in the part of Polonius but in other parts, there's a habit of providing two adjectives for every noun and sometimes these blend with each other in a very strange way to make a new compound. This has been traced statistically, it happens far more in *Hamlet* than anywhere else. The next play is *Othello*, and then after that he just gives it up, he gives up the practice. And my idea was that there's something that this intense concentration on doubling everything that extends to the characters. Why do you have Cornelius and Voltimand? I mean, there's no need for two of them, but they're ambassadors to Norway. I don't think Voltimand actually says anything.

Rosencrantz and Guildenstern. You have a revenge plot and another revenge plot, Fortinbras' revenge plot, Laertes' revenge plot, the play within the play has a revenge. That doing everything over and over again is an absolute characteristic of *Hamlet* – you double: the play within the play doubles the main action of the play, and so on. This makes *Hamlet*, of course, a very long play and also in a play, very hard to take in. I agree with a lot of what Germaine said. I think for example that Donne was a poet who cultivated harshness, he says so – 'I am harsh.' There was a cult of harshness which at this point actually does begin to invade theatrical language too.

But there's more to it than that, I think. What you have to do when you think of these plays is – of course you don't *have* to do it, but this is what I try to do – is to look at this peculiar disease that *Hamlet* has and think then on to other plays where you have a different kind of semantic version of it. In *Macbeth*, for example, there is this intense concentration of a small group of words which are repeated again and again, and you find that in all the mature plays, an intense application to language which cannot necessarily be something that the audience is intended to pick up completely. That's why I think the intense reading of the plays should be complementary with the performance of the plays.

MELVYN BRAGG: Michael Bogdanov, when you come to direct soliloquies, do you think you're dealing with an antique form or do you think what Germaine has said is the central clue to the way you direct it?

MICHAEL BOGDANOV: I have to try and make that contact with the audience that the Elizabethans made with the audience. That doesn't mean to say you necessarily are appealing to them directly and asking them questions because I think those soliloquies were a two-way process. I think that it was a debate with the audience and it is inconceivable that when questions were asked in those soliloquies of the audience – 'he who knows better how to tame a shrew?' or 'who calls me villain?' – that it would not have opened up a debate.

Those kinds of moments are lost to us in the mist of theatrical history, but that kind of debate which was opened up originally I think has to continue in any modern form. We believe in a kind of naturalistic approach so therefore people go into themselves in soliloquies. The rhetorical approach to the audience that you often see in contemporary production strikes a false note a lot of the time because you have to go with the conventions of theatre that exist in the day and that's why I believe that the only way in making Shakespeare live is to be modern about him.

MELVYN BRAGG: What do you mean by 'being modern about him'?

MICHAEL BOGDANOV: To treat the material as organic, living material.

MELVYN BRAGG: You can chuck it away if you don't think it works?

MICHAEL BOGDANOV: Absolutely.

MELVYN BRAGG: And substitute if you don't think it works?

MICHAEL BOGDANOV: If there are key words to a passage that would be unlocked by the changing of one word, let's say ten lines can be unlocked with one key word, I see no reason why that can't be done. It's a process of developing theatre in a form that will make it live. Now you can put it in a box and you can do the plays uncut, you can do *Hamlet* at five and half hours without belting through it, as Peter Hall's productions do, just to prove you can do it uncut and give it the pace that it needs. But the audience won't sit through five and half hours, it's for academics and purists. So if you want to do a play that gets people home to the last bus, and they don't leave Swansea after a quarter past ten because they can't get home to the hinterlands, then you need to find a way of doing these plays that retains the integrity of the language, the story, the dynamic. I believe they're like arrows, straight to the heart with the stories, and you have to distil that story and anything that is a superfluous meandering you can take away, as long as you don't destroy that dynamic. You can do the plays in that form, that's what I call being modern.

FRANK KERMODE: I agree with that. I agree with that absolutely.

MELVYN BRAGG: Well, I don't.

FRANK KERMODE: If it doesn't live in the present, it doesn't live at all.

MELVYN BRAGG: Except that if we're talking about Shakespeare's plays, 'the life of the plays is in the language'. You're talking about cutting. It worked well with Olivier, it worked well with Baz Lurhmann, but if you're talking about changing the language, is this not really on the way to using Shakespeare as a peg to hang another play on?

MICHAEL BOGDANOV: But in Frank's book he points out that editors have already made choices about the words that you actually use to say those lines. In any one of the plays you could take maybe a couple of hundred words and you have a different choice with different editors, and so what am I going to do? Am I going to do the Folio version? Am I going to do the First Quarto, the Second Quarto, the Third Quarto?

MELVYN BRAGG: But that's one thing, but using a completely different word, saying, you know, 'eff off!', which is not Shakespearian at all, which is not in any of the Folios? Your documentary *Shakespeare in the Estate* was a terrific documentary – you took Shakespeare to an estate in Birmingham, people who had never heard of him did parts of Shakespeare and it had a real dynamism, it was a terrific piece of work all the way through. But words were flying around that were very late twentieth century. So what are we talking about? Are we talking about Shakespeare or again about using him as a peg?

MICHAEL BOGDANOV: I had to unlock the ideas and the stories for those people, who had no interest in Shakespeare whatsoever. Some couldn't read, had never heard of any of the plays, *Romeo and Juliet* maybe. The only way was to take the passages, explain what they meant, and get them to work them back dramatically in their own way and their own language. There was one boy who said he wanted to try the part of Romeo in the original, and he did, and he started as nothing and he made a fair fist of it by the end. Others wanted to rewrite it, to make it live for them in their context and in their way. A number of those kids have carried on, they stopped breaking shop windows and shooting and started taking a few things seriously in their lives. Theatre in that respect can be therapeutic. I'm not saying that Shakespeare's necessarily the vehicle for that, but that was the effect of that documentary.

MELVYN BRAGG: OK, Germaine Greer.

GERMAINE GREER: I listened to that with interest. *King Lear* is the worst case because it's actually two plays cobbled together and it probably makes more sense to do one or the other. But then you lose some of the best bits whichever way you decide and no one can bring themselves to do it, so in the end we do this huge, inclusive and rather disturbing play. But I think in the end I've no problem with people building on Shakespeare's text in order to understand it. But it's curious because I want to ask what is it that they're understanding? Because ultimately dramatic language is not expository language, it's not explanatory, it's not narrative, it doesn't get understood, you can't paraphrase it. In the end you come back to that precise emotional colouring that even the tortuousness of the language brings with it. 'Oh that this too, too sullied flesh should melt' – 'sullied', 'solid' – in the end it doesn't matter, because you know what he's saying. He wishes he could slip out of his genetic garment at that point, and so would I if I was heir to the throne of Denmark at that moment in time.

I think it's fine for the kids to build on the numerousness and suggestiveness of the language, but in the end they will come back to the charm as originally added by Shakespeare because everything they've got out of it is still in it. When you expand something, explain something, my students used to complain, 'oh, you're breaking it all up, you're destroying it', and I'd say, 'no, look, it's still there, in black ink, it is still shining bright, go back, use it, learn it.' It's like all incantations, in the end you have to learn them without knowing exactly what they mean.

There are sonnets of Shakespeare's that I learn something about every day and in fact there are bits of *King Lear* that I am only going to understand as I grow older and as I see my mother, for example, embarking on the same journey of personality disintegration. These are common experiences. What Shakespeare gives them is this grandeur, this mystery, and that's really where the sublime comes in. Something is only sublime if you don't quite understand it. If you've actually got it all tickety-boo, and you've got it all well compartmented, and it's all done and dusted, then it's not sublime any more, you have missed it. Shakespeare survives because of his ultimate ungraspability, and that's got something to do with his deep humility before the actor and the audience.

Now there's one place where you will get that impact, perfectly modernly with a perfectly modern audience, and that is the Globe, which we still don't know how to use. People are still playing in the Globe as if they're playing in a picture frame theatre, not under-standing that they can actually feel the breath of the audience. So that some small thing happens on the stage, the audience draws in its breath, you can feel the breeze in the Globe. You are, as it were, suspended in an egg of drama and you see the faces of other people reacting on the other side of that space. It is the most exciting dramatic situation to be in, and audiences behave – guess what – in an old-fashioned way. They actually do affect the action by the very atmosphere that they generate, when they laugh or when they cry, or even when they simply draw in their breath. It's the most exciting thing, and that's one of the things we have to do, get back to that very simple theatrical dynamic. The cinema's messed us up for Shakespeare to a large extent, I'm afraid.

MELVYN BRAGG: Frank Kermode, do you think there's something about the Shakespeare heritage industry, including the academic heritage industry of Shakespeare, which takes it away from the plays and which takes the plays therefore away from the largest possible audience?

FRANK KERMODE: Well, I hate the enemies of Shakespeare, people who refuse to treat him as a human author, who make him part of the heritage industry of Stratford. The great misfortune is that you have to go through Stratford in order to get to the theatre, but that aspect is deplorable. The other modern Shakespeare scholarship doesn't interest me very much because it's not interested in the language, with the ink on the paper that Germaine was talking about. What I think is, as I listen to this discussion, is what a huge responsibility the director has because it is he who is going to make the choice as to what is present, what is modern and what can be discarded. The most impressive production of a Shakespeare play I've seen in the last couple of years was the Moscow production of *A Winter's Tale*, at the Lyric Hammersmith, where of course the language was Russian and we could read Shakespeare's texts on the surtitles. I don't know whether you saw it, Michael, but the director took enormous liberties with the way that he presented the closing scene of the play where the statue of Hermione comes back to life as an awful and kind of tragic affair. And when they were all grouped together in attitudes of dismay, the little dead boy is led on to the stage to bow before his mother and father and then is removed. None of that has anything to do with what Shakespeare wrote but it seemed to be absolutely successful. This presentness has to be judged from one production to the next. I think you would accept that?

MICHAEL BOGDANOV: Absolutely. Other countries are much bolder with their treatment of Shakespeare and therefore much more radical and most of the time much more exciting because Shakespeare in translation isn't archaic. When the equivalents are found in translations it's normally in a modern sense. Nobody tries to translate Shakespeare in Spain into sixteenth-century Spanish and with the archaic words in place. So while the rhythms are often observed in, for example, Germany, with the twelve-syllable line, and the same in France, nevertheless the language is much more modern and therefore much more accessible and people are able to respond to the plays much more immediately than English audiences. The heritage industry is responsible for putting a gloss on Shakespeare, a conservative gloss, making him an icon that is actually unassailable.

MELVYN BRAGG: Would you favour an updating of the language for performance?

MICHAEL BOGDANOV: There is no reason why one shouldn't do that. Just as there's no reason why one shouldn't perform them for 10,000 people or for ten people, or in plush surroundings or in rough surroundings. It's just different. But if you want to find a way of opening up the plays, as Germaine was saying, for a young audience who basically are turned off at a very early age, even if they are taken to plays or even if they have to read the plays, the only way you will be able to do it is by finding some point of reference to their own lives and making them own the material. If they don't own the material from the beginning, then they are never, ever, really going to enjoy them as pieces of theatre instead of pieces of literature.

GERMAINE GREER: Yes, but I don't think you have to worry about the language, you know. I taught kids you would think had nothing in common with *King Lear*; and I talk to sixth formers all the time about *King Lear*. Now they may not know what a fitchew is until they've actually looked it up, it doesn't hurt them to know what a fitchew is. If it's rap talk, they learn rap and new words every day. Learning more words is actually enriching you, it's giving you a bigger store to lug around with you. I'd be very happy if the word 'fitchew' came back into circulation and meant a particular kind of trail bike or something, it would make me very happy. I think it really isn't a problem, because the language is only archaic as long as it's not spoken. The key to it all is familiarity, and it's easy to remember. I meant there's the inbuilt mnemonic in Shakespeare. Once you do your Shakespeare play in school you may find it dreadfully tedious but you can also relive it and it will keep on coming back to you and you'll begin to understand the iceberg that each word is. You'll begin to understand the submerged bit.

FRANK KERMODE: The trouble is . . .

GERMAINE GREER: I don't think you have to water it down . . .

FRANK KERMODE: . . . they always pick what are thought to be the easier plays, don't they?

GERMAINE GREER: Like *Julius Caesar*.

FRANK KERMODE: Which is a great mistake because it teaches people to despise Shakespeare. What I want to do is set the difficult plays like *Coriolanus* and *Timon of Athens*, so that they know they're up against something.

MELVYN BRAGG: Do you think that Shakespeare will continue in a popular form only through the cinema, Frank?

FRANK KERMODE: I feel ill-qualified here because I haven't seen the *Romeo and Juliet* film you keep talking about, but I did see the Olivier film and I think I regard these things as allusions to Shakespeare rather than the plays themselves. And, as such, I think the Olivier film was very fine, and I dare say that Lurhmann's film is too. I'll take your word for that.

GERMAINE GREER: Well, we learnt Olivier's Shakespeare off by heart when I was twelve, but that also meant that we did performances of the whole play, where we played them in Olivierish sort of ways and really the whole thing didn't make any sense at all, but the play survived. The whole point is that play will always survive even a very astigmatic director, even someone doing an ego-trip at Shakespeare's expense. The cloud-like wreck will fade and the text will still be there.

MELVYN BRAGG: But Michael Bogdanov has challenged that view, Germaine. You think that. I think that. I'd guess that Frank might think that. But you don't think that is necessarily true, that whatever happens Shakespeare will survive, do you?

MICHAEL BOGDANOV: Yes, he will survive but he will survive in a very rarefied form. I don't believe the plays will be accessible to a large audience. I don't believe they are now. I believe that he's not a popular writer as such. He's forced to be shown to a lot of people who are taken to the plays, in other words, young people, but there is very little Shakespeare production that you can see in this country at the professional level. Not compared with Germany or America for example. With regard to film, the problem is that a lot of the films that have come out recently have only reinforced a lot of people's prejudices. They've reached a wider audience but they're basically reworking old ideas, old conservative ideas, out on screen.

MELVYN BRAGG: Last word, Frank Kermode.

FRANK KERMODE: Well, I'm just wondering. When I was in America I taught a huge Shakespeare class in Columbia and when the Royal Shakespeare Company came to do *All's Well* on Broadway I asked would they like to go, and they said yes. Then I asked them how many of them had ever seen a Shakespeare play in the theatre and about 20 per cent of them had. These are people in New York, so I think the enthusiasm is not something we can count on.

TRANSMITTED: 11.5.2000

W
—

Angels

George Bernard Shaw made the observation that 'in heaven an angel is nobody in particular'. Perhaps he is referring to a hierarchy of angels drawn up in the fifth century, but there is nothing commonplace about this description of angels from the Book of Ezekiel:

> They had the likeness of a man.
> And every one had four faces and every one had four wings.
> And their feet were straight feet; and the sole of their feet was like the sole of a calf's foot; and they sparkled like the colour of burnished brass.
> As for the likeness of their faces, they four had the face of a man, and the face of a lion, on the right side; and they four had the face of an ox on the left side; they four also had the face of an eagle.

With angels like that, it is easy to see why they have caused so much controversy over the centuries.

What part have angels played in western religion and western thought? How did they get their halos and their wings? And how did the medieval philosophers use them to explain the world?

With me to discuss angels are Valery Rees, Renaissance Scholar from the School of Economic Science; Martin Palmer, theologian and Director of the International Consultancy on Religion, Education and Culture; and John Haldane, Professor of Philosophy at St Andrews University.

Martin Palmer, can we start with the etymology of the word and tell us where it came from?

MARTIN PALMER: It is the Greek word *angelos*, which means messenger, and it is a translation of the Hebrew term meaning precisely that – the messenger of God. In fact in the Torah, in the Hebrew Bible, what we call the Old Testament, the angels are described as the Angel of the Lord in the same way that you might say the Word of the Lord or the Message of the Lord. It is giving a sort of pedigree to what they are saying and saying listen to this, it is worthwhile, it is trustable.

MELVYN BRAGG: What is their role in the books of Ezekiel and Isaiah and in earlier books in the Bible?

MARTIN PALMER: It changes actually, it is quite interesting. The earliest account of angels, if you take them from Judges for instance, or some of the earliest . . .

MELVYN BRAGG: Can you give us a date?

MARTIN PALMER: Judges – we are looking round about 800, 900 or 1000 BC, but in the oral traditions that are collected together in the Book of Genesis which is probably edited round about the fourth or fifth century BC, the stories are much older. Angels are essentially simply instruments. They are rather like the postmen of God or the telegraph boys of God. They come down and deliver the message, they stop certain things happening. They warn people. They have a function but nobody's terribly concerned about what they look like or what their powers are, they are just simply part of this rather wonderful mystical, spiritual world in which, remember, at this time Israelites aren't entirely sure there is only one God, there is God among the Gods, so they are not too worried about having lots of different deities and beings. When you get to that extraordinary vision of Ezekiel you are moving into something quite different. Here Judaism or the Israelites . . .

MELVYN BRAGG: This is about . . . ?

MARTIN PALMER: We are talking round about 580 or 590 BC.

MELVYN BRAGG: Is this before Genesis is collected but after Judges?

MARTIN PALMER: That's right. And you have got the early experience of the exiles. Many of the Israelites are now captives in Babylon. They are being exposed to a tremendously more sophisticated powerful culture than they have been used to. Earlier in the text, for example, Ezekiel says that the glow around God is like the glow around amber and it is quite clear that they have never seen amber until that point. Amber was so rare, traded from the Baltic, that only the Babylonians could afford it.

So you have got this relatively unsophisticated tribal group that suddenly find themselves in this great empire and they are confronting the most extraordinary system of angels and deities and beings coming out of what we now call Zoroastrianism and these are not messengers, these are demi-gods to all intents and purposes. These are immensely powerful beings and Ezekiel is trying to make them servants of God but he ends up really creating almost a subset of divine beings and that is where part of the problem comes in.

MELVYN BRAGG: Valery Rees, can you take that idea on? Can you tell us more about the cultural influences at play – the Syrian influences, the Zoroastrianism Martin has led us to?

VALERY REES: As Martin has said, the figures that people saw during the Babylonian captivity must have made a huge impression on the imagination.

MELVYN BRAGG: When you say 'saw', saw in sculptures, you mean?

VALERY REES: Saw in sculptures, yes. You only have to go into the British Museum and see those fabulous winged creatures at the ends of the friezes to realise these are very powerful presences. Now the difference between the vision in Ezekiel and the earlier appearances of angels in the Bible is that Ezekiel's is a sort of dream vision whereas the earlier angels that people have been familiar with through the stories of their ancestors appear as human beings and they don't have wings. You only know they are an angel because they have brought a message that you realise was a divine message that you needed to hear.

After Ezekiel, in fact after Isaiah, there are winged beings but in Isaiah they are not angels, they are not messengers of God, they are the seraphim that Isaiah sees and there are also cherubim or keruvim, to use the Hebrew term, which is much closer to these winged protective beings. When the Ark of the Covenant was made for the tabernacle in the wanderings in the wilderness, the box that held the tablets on which the words of the Lord were written had two figures at the ends which do seem to be borrowed either from the Babylonian tradition through some kind of early contact, or more likely there is a possibility they are a reflection of ideas that were present in Egypt. In the Cairo Museum you can see wonderful gold-covered boxes with winged figures at the ends protecting very valuable contents.

MELVYN BRAGG: Can I just go back a little bit on what you have been saying, Valery, so we are absolutely clear? We are not talking about angels as being an invention of the Israelites, as being first discovered in the Torah, the Old Testament, we are talking about the idea of angels being very much around in civilisations running co-incidentally or even before that. What you said was very vivid but I am not quite clear what is happening to whom and when. So can you just give us some chronology and chart the influences.

VALERY REES: The chronology is very difficult. I would rather stay off that. But the winged figures that were known from Egypt and that were later encountered in another form of winged figures in Babylon . . .

MELVYN BRAGG: How long ago from Egypt? Can you give a date?

VALERY REES: Well, the Exodus may have been in the fifteen century before the Common Era – there are different views.

MELVYN BRAGG: And the Israelites encountered the winged figures in Egypt – is that what you're saying?

VALERY REES: Yes. There were winged figures in Egypt. Moses grew up in the palace. He would have been familiar with all these images, but the big difference is that in the Egyptian religious beliefs, and in the Babylonian too, these are divine figures with powers of their own. When they come into the Israelite tradition the angel is only a servant of God, they are not gods themselves. By the time angels get into the Bible, whether they are the messenger angels of the early books or whether they are the winged figures of the visions of Isaiah and Ezekiel, they are servants of God, they have no power except that of carrying out the divine will.

MELVYN BRAGG: Can you tell us something about the influence of the Book of Enoch, the apocryphal book, Enoch who walked with God and was never seen again?

VALERY REES: Yes. These writings were after the Babylonian exile and they were not included in the Bible. They were considered to be beyond the canon of what was totally acceptable. In these books great variety and profusion is introduced into the angels and levels are given and heavens. Enoch goes on incredible journeys and he meets all different kinds of angels and he goes through the different heavens meeting different types, so you have here a wealth of angel literature which begins to colour people's ideas, but they don't have quite the authority of the biblical angels.

MELVYN BRAGG: Can you take us on from that, John Haldane. Can you explain how apocalyptic Judaism started to emerge and what that does for the idea of avenging angels and why this prolif-eration? I am sorry to ask you three questions at once, but why are they drawing away from what they encountered in Babylon and in Egypt and perhaps even before?

JOHN HALDANE: So far what we have are two strands and we are going to add perhaps a third and a fourth. The first and second of them is the angels' role as intermediaries or messengers that we began with, and then we have got this picking up on an iconog-raphy of minor deities or powers unto themselves that Val has just been speaking about. And now we move to a further strand in which angels become aides or assistants divinely provided to the people of Israel and this is going to introduce the notion of avenging angels.

Now there is an ambiguity in the idea of an avenging angel, whether they are good or bad, and that introduces an even further dimension. But let me just pick up the first of those elements, the avenging angels. What happens with the Jews is to some extent there is a separation in the experience after the return of the exiles in their relations with the governing powers. They are pretty much left to themselves to get on and on they do. But then among Palestinian Jews, I mean Jewry in Palestine, there is the development of a force which sees itself as set against earthly powers. It is very important that it develops itself in the direction of Messianic Judaism.

So now we have got this chosen race of people set apart who are special in God's sight who the world might reject and rebuff and that is not surprising because the world doesn't recognise the true God. So they see themselves in an oppositional relationship with some of the governing powers and of course this produces a certain amount of trouble and a period of disturbance in which they themselves come to be abused by some of these governing powers or see themselves in these terms. This gives rise to the idea that this good God who has chosen them as a people set apart will provide for them, and one of the ways in which he is going to provide for them is by providing powers greater than those of their enemies.

So this sense of spiritual beings or angelic beings who now become avengers on behalf of God or God's people against their persecutors starts to develop and this is part of a Judaism which shapes the world into which Christ enters. But it is a Judaism which includes things like the eschatology, the final things, this account of what is going to happen in due course. And these people start to build up ideas of the resurrection of the dead, of the triumph of final times, of a Messiah who is going to come and be a great ruler, and the avenging angels enter into that world, I think.

MELVYN BRAGG: And then – I am rushing it a bit – but there begins a long period of using angels for thought as well as thinking about angels for religion. What is immaterialism and what is a Fall? There is a curious passage in Genesis, if I can read it to you, John:

> And it came to pass when men began to multiply on the face of the earth and daughters were born unto them,
> That the sons of God saw the daughters of men that they were fair; and they took them wives of all which they chose.

The sons of God – these are presumably angels – or are they? Over to you . . .

JOHN HALDANE: Well, sorry, not that simple, I'm afraid.

MELVYN BRAGG: You are rolling your eyes there!

JOHN HALDANE: I mean, look, we won't start to go too far into the roots of biblical scholarship. We don't really know quite what that means. But I think that some people see this as perhaps a source of the idea of fallen angels and in some of the translations it comes out as such, but even in early times this was disputed. And as soon as people reflect in a systematic way on scripture they are beginning to ask questions about what this kind of thing means.

One possibility here is that the sons of God are a strand within the lineage of Adam because what you get in the passages that precede the one you just quoted is one of those genealogies – so-and-so is the son of so-and-so and all the rest of it – and one possibility is that the sons of God are just some preferred strand within the lineage of Adam. It is really quite hard to know what to make of it except that what I think is significant is that some people see that passage as being connected with the idea of fallen angels, so the notion of fallenness is important.

MELVYN BRAGG: Fallen because if they desire the daughters of men and saw that they were fair they obviously had lusts and ... so here, Martin Palmer, it takes us to the point of how close to angels were gods, were they gods or were they not gods, and if they were gods how were they gods, how could he create gods himself, being God, how could immaterial create immaterial and so on ... Can you take that on?

MARTIN PALMER: Well, it is a huge problem for any faith that claims a monotheistic view of the world. Angels travel out of the Babylonian Middle Eastern world both in to Judaism and Christianity and Islam but they also go into Buddhism and Taoism. In Buddhism and Taoism there is no problem. You have a pantheon of deities, you have a vast celestial empire and they can fit in very easily, there is no theological problem for them, but introduce them into Judaism, which is trying to define itself as a strict teaching, exactly as John has captured, and you have got a real dilemma. What exactly are they? Are they to be worshipped, for example?

And you find quotes both within the Jewish sources and within the New Testament saying don't go worshipping angels, worship God only, so there is clearly a problem. Are they interceders? Can we go through them to God or does God only come through us? Are they divine? Are they material? Do they have lusts? Do they fall? Are they temptable? If they are temptable, are they really instruments to help us?

A huge raft of questions arises which essentially fractures the attempt to create a monolith of monotheism in which there is only one God, only one source of power. So you begin to get the idea that they are emanations, that they are instrumental, but then if they are instrumental how can you have one angel fall, because if the angel falls he must be capable of free will, so it raises a vast . . .

MELVYN BRAGG: We will come back to this when we come to Aquinas. But it seems to me that theologians are using this in order to explore the world with the knowledge they had.

MARTIN PALMER: I think you are also pushing how far you can actually be monotheistic.

MELVYN BRAGG: Let's just get there when we get there. There are a couple of steps to go first. Valery, Dionysius, a Syrian monk in the fifth century trying to make sense of all this, made a hierarchy. Can you tell us what that hierarchy was and why it was important?

VALERY REES: It was assumed that there were angels. We mustn't leave out of account that angels were accepted by everybody and their presence was welcomed and in particular in all the liturgies, both the Jewish liturgy and the Christian liturgy and the Eastern Orthodox liturgy. The angels are seen as joining in human prayer and there is an unbroken song of praise that goes from the angels to God with humans joining in to complete the circle. Now this is the picture that Dionysius is looking at when he studies the scriptures and pulls out nine levels, taking the Old Testament angels and also references in the New Testament, particularly in St Luke. And he comes up with three sets of three, which is very appealing numerically. The first group, who are closest to God, are the seraphim, the cherubim and the thrones, and what unites all those three levels is that they are in constant contemplation of the divine. They are close to God.

They are constantly turned towards the divine, absorbing the light in full measure and passing it on to the lower levels, and what distinguishes the three is that the seraphim are ablaze with love of God, the cherubim are characterised by knowledge and the thrones are to do with divine power. Then the second set of three is less clearly defined but has to do with universals and then the third and lower set of three of the hierarchy is the principalities, archangels and angels. So even archangels, who we think are very high, actually come quite low in this hierarchy and they are the ones who move down from the heavenly realm and move among mankind bringing messages we have been speaking about.

MELVYN BRAGG: So, John Haldane, we see a very clear exposition there, we see that angels have moved in, not only into thought. There are hierarchies, scholars know about them in detail. They move into medieval thought and this is held to be true.

JOHN HALDANE: Yes. Just one thing that might be useful to understand is that the author that has just been referred to, Dionysius or St Denis, is referred to in different languages. His works enjoyed enormous prestige in the Middle Ages and the reason for that goes back to scripture and St Paul, who himself talks about angels a fair bit. When St Paul went to Athens and took this religious message to the philosophical world his experience was not a terribly good one. He goes up on to the Areopagus Hill in Athens and is rebuffed there. But, he says, one good thing came out of this experience in Athens which is that he made a convert and he refers to this man Dionysius.

Then in the later world these texts show up in the fifth, sixth century and are commented upon later. The author claims to be that very person, Dionysius the Areopagite. So what you have are texts that are of the apostolic period and written by a philosopher. These are of enormous prestige. Because what they seem to represent is a turning of the philosophical world towards the new religion. The medieval authors themselves begin to suspect these are actually later works and by the thirteenth and fourteenth centuries that suspicion has developed, but in the early stages these are regarded as enormously important works, blending Judaism, Christian thought and Greek philosophy.

The medieval writers take Dionysius and all he says very seriously and the subject of angels certainly does begin to feature. It features in a number of ways but I will just take the greatest figure. People will know of Thomas Aquinas. Aquinas has quite a number of questions that he addresses in his great *Summa Theologica*: angelic knowledge, the question of whether or not angels move through space, how angels relate to God, how they relate to man and so on. It is there that some people seem to think that we get the famous question about angels on the point of a pin.

MELVYN BRAGG: Can we develop this? We'll keep the pin out of it because that is apocryphal. Can we develop this, Martin? Could you tell us what is happening to angels in the New Testament, just to distinguish it, and take us on to how Aquinas and the great thinkers, minds as great as any there have ever been, take this on and examine the world through it.

MARTIN PALMER: I think in the New Testament you have a very interesting shift again, rather like the one that Valery has discussed earlier. You have a continuation of the notion that they are the messengers. For example, when the Angel Gabriel comes to tell Mary that she will bear the Christ, that is very much in the tradition of the Old Testament messenger. Indeed, when the angels come to the Magi, to the Wise Men, on their way and warn them to go on, you have a traditional role.

   You also have hints of something that has developed very much from what John was discussing, from this sense of a personal relationship with angels, which is guardian angels. Christ refers to children having guardian angels and when St Peter is released from prison it is his angel that does this and there are all sort of accounts around that. You are also getting this very powerful tradition, particularly in Revelations, of avenging angels, that angels in a sense represent the power of God when all other powers have failed on earth. You are a persecuted minority, you are up against it, the Romans are out for your blood, everybody is out for your blood – who is going to stand with you?

   Well, you know God is going to stand with you, but then suddenly you know that you have angels with flaming swords, you have hordes of angels, you have multitudes of angels. Suddenly you are caught up – and I think this is terribly important – you are caught up into a much more glorified and, exactly what Valery is saying, a glorifying world, so you are not just part of what goes on down here.

And, as Valery said earlier, this gets reflected in the earliest Christian liturgies where not only do you join in worship with those who are present there and those who have died, the saints as they become, as we know them, but you also worship with the heavenly hosts. So you enter into the Christian faith, you enter into the New Testament, into a world where you are given access to greater levels of existence than if you were just a simple ordinary human being.

MELVYN BRAGG: Brilliant. Now can I go to Aquinas who tried to bring Aristotle to bear on theology. How is he putting the angels into that, what was he using them for and how was he squaring it with Aristotle?

VALERY REES: I think one of the main things he is trying to do is to discover where the angels fit in philosophically and to address this question of whether they have bodies and, if so, what are their bodies made of, which is something that had exercised people from early on and it is a real theological issue. When were they created? And what from? And what for?

MELVYN BRAGG: It is like particle physics in that sense.

VALERY REES: It is in a way. There was an old tradition that they were half fire and half ice, but whatever it was, by the time of Aquinas, I think, there was a general agreement that their bodies were subtle not material and that they didn't have desires which sort of negates the whole concept of fallen angels. Because they don't have free will and they don't have desires and they do have this access to the heavens and they become a model for humans and you get a discussion going on, for example, among the Franciscans, who thought St Francis had become an angel after he died. They thought he had gone into one of these vacancies caused by a fallen angel and, as I understand it – and correct me if I'm wrong, John, you know far more about this than I do – Aquinas's view was more along the lines that there was no possibility of angels becoming involved in this sort of way and they represented something much more ethereal that spanned the realms between heaven and earth.

JOHN HALDANE: There are many things going on here. Melvyn mentioned the relation between Aquinas and Aristotle. In Aristotle, for example, there is a philosophical puzzle which is how a movement is transmitted through the cosmos. And he introduces a series of intermediary movers, one transmits its motion to the next thing and so on. Motion in this context means activity and so he thinks that there are intermediary moves between the material objects that we encounter and whatever is the ultimate cause of those, which becomes God in Christian understanding.

Now Aquinas to some extent is caught up in that metaphysics of activity and the angels certainly have a function in that, but he is much more interested in the theological philosophical structure than in the mechanics of the universe. He, in his understanding of the angels, sometimes uses the notion of angels as subsequent philosophers do, even philosophers we wouldn't associate in this. People like Locke and Descartes and later on Spinoza will mention angels from time to time, in part to explore certain ideas.

So, for example, could there be non-experiential knowledge, knowledge not rooted in sight or hearing and so on but in some sense intuitive or direct and when they think about that they say, well, imagine angels for a moment. They don't have eyes or ears, so how do they know? So it is a way of exploring that. But one thing I might just add here is that the Church gets involved in this in terms of dogma and you get Councils of the Church, these great convened meetings of the Church, when they are setting out questions about what one ought and ought not to believe and this becomes important again after the Reformation. We will say what is and what is not permissible with regard to the questions of angels. So for instance in 1215 they insist that angels were created, they may be eternal, they are immaterial beings but they are not co-existent with God in any sense as minor deities.

MARTIN PALMER: It is interesting because the same debate is going on at the same time in Judaism and Islam. In Judaism you have the whole debate about when the angels were created and it is decided that this is on the second or third day, so they are not pre-existent before the Creation. In Islam this debate about what they were and what their powers actually were rips apart early Islam. Because early Islam does develop the story that first appears in the Book of Enoch that Satan is a fallen angel who refused to obey God, this being called Iblis who refuses to worship man when man is created.

All the angels are called in, according to the Koran, and told to worship man because man is now the most important being and Satan says – quite legitimately, one feels – 'you have made a pretty good universe, why on earth are you handing over power to this bunch?' and refuses to worship man and is thrown out. But the question then arises incredibly sharply for Islam which will not even permit the Trinity and the notion of God's son – what exactly is this force that we have allowed? You begin to get in the medieval writers particularly in Spain the notion that angels are in a sense the distillation of the thought of God and that sometimes that thought was so dark you are left with the conundrum but you are left with the sense that you are entering into the ambiguities of divinity as much as you are into the certainties.

MELVYN BRAGG: Valery, how does Neo-Platonism come into this?

VALERY REES: It picks up this idea that Martin has just mentioned of the angels being a distillation of the thought of God because there is a great mystery as to how you get from one primal divine force to all this incredible variety we see before us in the physical world and there has to be a philosophical way of explaining that. How the one becomes multiple and doesn't just make multiple things that it plays with but enters into his creation fully. So the angels really are seen as part of that series of manifestations, or emanations as they are called, where the light and fire of the one gradually goes out and becomes absorbed in different degrees by the different levels of creation and the angels are the nearest to God.

From God the next level of emanation is angel or the divine mind. So you have got this very clear sense of the thoughts of God and then the next level is soul, which means the human soul, the rational soul, and after that the soul takes on qualities and eventually takes on bodies. That is the Neo-Platonic picture as it becomes elaborated in the Renaissance.

JOHN HALDANE: I just want to say there is a connection here. We spoke about Dionysius earlier on and the hierarchy of heaven. You see Dionysius is a Neo-Platonist, so this story of emanation is there within that, but one thing that is interesting to think about is the parallelism between this kind of story, so-called emanationist metaphysics, in which the world comes out as concentric developing circles out of this inner core of being, and modern cosmology. If you think of the idea of the expanding universe originating at some point of energy and we now have the physics that tells us of how energy is transformed into matter and so we can think of a sort of process of transformation whereby some originating point of intense energy about which we can say nothing except there was an originating point of intense energy is transformed into this enormous variety. So in a way, in contemporary physics, we still have to think about something that is not so very different to what these people had to think about when they thought about Creation.

MELVYN BRAGG: It is very striking, isn't it?

JOHN HALDANE: It is a very striking parallel, yes.

MELVYN BRAGG: Now then, Martin. Luther nails his pamphlet on the church door and Protestantism comes on board. How does the Reformation affect the position of angels in western thought?

MARTIN PALMER: I think we fell the angels rather than have fallen angels in the sense that Protestantism chucks it out, not quite with the baptismal water because we do retain that as one of the sacraments. But Protestantism does a very thorough expunging of a great deal of the tremendous system that Catholicism has implemented.

MELVYN BRAGG: What is driving Protestantism to do that?

MARTIN PALMER: I think in a sense it is – I mean, John's image is a wonderful one, the parallel with modern cosmology – what Protestantism does is demolish the medieval world view of concentric rings by saying let's go back to that original one point, that one principle, and in a sense see angels simply as a reflection of political hierarchies. To a great extent the angel orders and the divine orders and the order of saints and so forth do reflect society. It would have

to do because of the imperial courts and the kingly courts of medieval Europe. Protestants want to get rid of all that, they want to
have a personal relationship with God, no interceders, and not even
priests really have the role that they used to have.

So Protestantism throws out the angels and yet it doesn't. We have
this dilemma. I am an Anglican, I go to moderately rational services
as we like to see them in the Church of England and our churches are
stuffed full of angels, our hymns are absolutely heaving with angels.
We pray exactly as Valery said, we join with the angels in giving
praise, we even use the section from the Old Testament of what the
angels say when they sit before the throne of God and say 'Holy,
Holy, Holy'. And yet we don't discuss them, we are acutely embar-
rassed by them. It is as though in order to get back to a personal
relationship with God we have shed everything, with the one exception of guardian angels, because the guardian angel appeals to the
Protestant notion of the individual soul finding its way back to God.

MELVYN BRAGG: Can you take us further, Valery? Martin has
been graphic about the Reformation of the sixteenth century. Take
us to the next century, the dying off of interest in angels as the
Enlightenment grows. Is it as simple as that? It can't be as simple
as that.

VALERY REES: Well, I am sure it is not simple at all and interest
in angels did continue and certainly there was a resurgence of it in
Victorian times. You only have to look at the art and the art I think
should be our key much of the way through this. For instance, when
angels stopped being strong stocky men and start being rather ethereal feminine figures in the appearance.

MELVYN BRAGG: When is that precisely? Is there a century for that?

VALERY REES: Yes, around by the thirteenth century the change
has happened.

MELVYN BRAGG: Why is that, do you think?

VALERY REES: Well, in a way it could be to do with sending angels
back to heaven rather than having them around us here on earth. I
think that the early very masculine figures . . .

MELVYN BRAGG: Nothing to do with the liberation of painting itself? They couldn't paint women and this was one way to do it and get away with it, as it were.

VALERY REES: That would surprise me, because you have figures of the Madonna much earlier.

MELVYN BRAGG: That's true.

VALERY REES: No, I think it's to do with wanting to push the demons back into hell. We haven't spoken about demons, but they're . . .

MELVYN BRAGG: There isn't time, Valery!

VALERY REES: I know, and anyway we should keep them out of this. But there, in the philosophical side to this discussion, there is this whole idea of demons, the good ones which were identified with angels and then the dark ones who caused lots of mischief in the world and should be pushed firmly back into hell, and the concomitant of that is that the angels go right up into heaven and interestingly therefore out of reach. So the angels are no longer all around us and I think that is reflected in the art and I think that is also what carried on into the seventeenth century when the interest is much more in science and you have got a lovely period in the sixteenth century where science and angels are rubbing shoulders all the time, and you have people like John Dee trying to talk to angels to gain knowledge about the physical world.

MELVYN BRAGG: Mathematician, magus and advisor to Elizabeth I.

VALERY REES: Elizabeth's scientist.

MARTIN PALMER: You have the Jewish tradition, this magical incantation tradition, in the Kabbalah which goes through also into the Jewish experience of the Renaissance, which is that you could access these greater powers in order to understand better the world in which you lived, in order to control it better, to make it better. You have a fascinating tension between 'they exist but now they are our servants almost, aren't they?'

VALERY REES: There is a blend of a mystical approach and repairing the world.

MELVYN BRAGG: Can I use what you just said, Valery, and go over to John? This question of art, this taking up the idea of the prolif-eration of angels in art, how far was that reinforcing, how far did it develop the idea? At the beginning – I don't know if it was the beginning – anyway, six wings and so on, and now we have got two-winged angels and we have got very feminine angels and we have little cherubs, we have halos, and it begins to set in its ways, doesn't it? And in every church around the place.

JOHN HALDANE: I think the depiction of angels in art is very interesting as a way of keeping track of what is happening theologi-cally and philosophically, if you like. I would say this happened in relatively recent times and this is in part to do with the Protestant tradition of failing to think theologically about angels. Their depictions of angels is fairly well disciplined. For example, angels up until the time of Constantine in the fourth century of the Christian era, where angels are depicted, and that is very rare, they are not equipped with halos or with wings, they just appear. I think there are two or three depictions in probably the third century where they appear as young men. The Annunciation scene, a young man stands before Mary and is announcing that she is to conceive Christ is later, after Constantine.

Then angels start to acquire the accoutrements of these strange beings and then they leave earth and they start to hover in the sky and they are flying around and so on. Now I think one thing that is happening is that up until the period of Constantine when Christianity was a minority, and an oppressed minority, the last thing they wanted to do was to give their opponents material to accuse them of being believers in lots of deities, so they didn't want to get tangled up in this. Once they become more confident they can start to use angels pictorially, iconographically and so on. As it moves through, some of this rediscovered mythology of the ancient world starts to be used but it is used within a theological Church context that is very self-confident and so it doesn't worry too much about this, because it has got its dogmatic definitions.

Everybody knows what you can believe and what you can't believe. I think the really interesting period is the liberalisation of angels in art when they are unconstrained, particularly in the nineteenth century. The angelic depictions move precisely into the area which would have horrified early Christians. It moves into the area of superstition. The contemporary interest in angels would for most Christians seem utterly superstitious.

MELVYN BRAGG: Can you talk about the contemporary interest in angels, Martin, bring us right up to where we are?

MARTIN PALMER: One of the interesting things that emerges out of Protestantism is two of the most strongly angel-directed new versions of Christianity. First the Swedenborgians, who emerge in the mid-eighteenth century out of the teaching of Emanuel Swedenborg, who believed that he was in touch with angels and was receiving a true message about the real Church. Then of course the most famous angel in contemporary history is Moroni, the angel who appears to Joseph Smith in the 1820s and reveals to him the Book of Mormon and founds the Church of Jesus Christ of Latter Day Saints.

We tend to forget that angels come back when people need them, as did Mohammed, when he received the revelation from the angel Gabriel. Angels reappear when you want to say everybody else was wrong and I have now got the real truth. And that lays down the foundation of an idea that angels are going to bypass conventional religion, angels no longer are in hock to the church or to the synagogue, they are free and I think that is what John is talking about, the notion that angels have escaped out into popular belief. As Chesterton said: 'when you stop believing in God you don't believe in nothing, you believe in everything', and that I think lays the foundation for today's New Age angel massage, angel therapy, etcetera.

VALERY REES: Those angel therapies are also performing a very useful function of opening people's eyes to universal forces and really breaking free of the mould you spoke of earlier. There is me and there is God and the idea of bringing back the angels with all its strengths and weaknesses is about allowing people to become more aware of universal forces. The fact that you sitting opposite me could well be God's messenger and so I should listen, I should be aware of everything around me as being part of what I have to meet in the world.

MELVYN BRAGG: Could I just point out that you are addressing John Haldane!

VALERY REES: I happen to be looking at him.

MELVYN BRAGG: Good to clear that up. It was terrific and we could go on for a long time but we can't, so thank you all very much indeed.

TRANSMITTED: 24.3.2005

The Fibonacci Sequence

I , 1, 2, 3, 5, 8, 13, 21, 34 . . . I could go on ad infinitum. This is the beginning of the Fibonacci sequence, a string of numbers named after but probably not invented by the thirteenth-century Italian mathematician Fibonacci. It may seem like a piece of mathematical arcana but the Fibonacci sequence is found to appear, time and time again, among the structures of the natural world and even in the products of human culture. From the Parthenon to pine cones, from the petals on a sunflower to the paintings of Leonardo da Vinci, the Fibonacci sequence appears to be written into the world around us. But what does it signify?

With me to discuss the Fibonacci sequence are Jackie Stedall, Junior Research Fellow in History of Mathematics at Queen's College, Oxford; Ron Knott, Visiting Fellow in the Department of Mathematics at the University of Surrey; and Marcus du Sautoy, Professor of Mathematics at Wadham College, University of Oxford.

Marcus du Sautoy, the Fibonacci sequence is named after a thirteenth-century Italian mathematician. He was called Leonardo of Pisa at the time. Can you tell us about him?

MARCUS DU SAUTOY: Yes. He is an incredibly important person in the history of mathematics because Europe, before Fibonacci, was in the Dark Ages mathematically. They were still using Roman numerals, they hadn't got the developments that had been happening in the East. India had developed these wonderful new numerals 0, 1, 2, 3 up to 9 and it is Fibonacci who learnt about this and brought a lot of these ideas to Europe. He is a key lynch pin in the whole history of mathematics and he learnt it by travelling in northern Africa with his father who was collecting taxes and a merchant for the state of Pisa. So it was there that he became aware of exciting developments that had been happening in the East mathematically. You mentioned in your opening that maybe the numbers shouldn't be credited to Fibonacci and you can find in India the discovery of these numbers much earlier, say in the sixth century, related to rhythms. Mathematics and music were very connected in India.

And these numbers can be used to count how many rhythms there are, if you have got long and short beats. So, for example, in poetry, if you have got four beats in a bar, how many different rhythms can you fit in with long beats and short beats. Well, you can have two long beats, four short beats or long, short, short, short long short, short short long and that is five and that's a Fibonacci number. You find that actually these numbers were used and discovered in India to be able to count the number of rhythms, so maybe Fibonacci had also been aware of these numbers through his travelling in northern Africa. But he is really seen as the beginning of mathematics in Europe because he brought these ideas to Italy from northern Africa.

MELVYN BRAGG: You have talked about numbers developing in India and then going into the Arab world. What about the Fibonacci sequence itself, can you tell us a bit more about where that might have come from?

MARCUS DU SAUTOY: He describes it in a book to do with a problem about rabbits, which I am sure we will come on to, but the idea is that this is a natural sequence about growth and I think actually this idea of Indian rhythms is a nice place to look at it. For example, if I want to count how many rhythms there are with 5 beats in the bar that is built out of the ones with 4 beats and 3 beats, you add either a short beat on the end of that or a long beat, so the Fibonacci sequence is got by adding the two previous numbers together.

We haven't actually said what is really important. The Fibonacci sequence – how do you build it up? Well 1, 1, 2, 3, 5, 8, 13 you get the next number in the sequence by adding the two previous numbers together. So it is a sequence which is very much to do with growth, the information you have got beforehand, the two numbers before the number you are trying to work out are used to get the next number in the sequence. You add those two together to get the next number and that is why we see it in so many different problems because it is about growth, about learning from what you have done before to get the next piece of information.

MELVYN BRAGG: Jackie Stedall, he wrote this in a book called *La Libre Abaci*, a book of calculation. It was written in 1202. Can you give us some overview of what was in that book because the Fibonacci sequence is only part of it. Was he bringing vast tracts of new mathematics to Europe?

JACKIE STEDALL: Yes, he was. I don't quite agree with Marcus that Europe was in the Dark Ages before that. Islamic Spain had a very rich mathematical and scientific culture for two centuries before Fibonacci brought this work to Europe. But his book was important in spreading these ideas and in writing them as a textbook. It was the first European textbook in mathematics. It is an enormous work. The modern English translation has 600 pages, so imagine that written by hand in manuscript, it is a very large work. The beginning of it is introducing the Hindu Arabic numerals, the very first line of it introduces those numerals and explains to you how to write them and also how to calculate with them because you need to know that, not just how to write them.

MELVYN BRAGG: 1, 1, 2, 3, 5, 8, 13.

JACKIE STEDALL: Well he writes them backwards in the Arabic way. But he has to explain to you how you add, how you subtract, how you multiply, using place value which comes with the numerals.

MELVYN BRAGG: Can you explain place value?

JACKIE STEDALL: Yes if I write the numbers 666 the first 6 stands for hundreds, the next 6 stands for tens and the final one is units, so according to the place that the digit takes that tells you something about the size it is representing. It means you only have to learn nine digits plus zero and you can do all the arithmetic you want to do. It is a very powerful system.

MELVYN BRAGG: So he started with that. What else did he develop inside this book?

JACKIE STEDALL: Well after seven or eight chapters on teaching you how to use these numerals he then goes on to lots of practical calculations. There are lots of problems in commercial arithmetic. For instance if you buy so many yards of cloth as such a price how much will it cost you to buy so many other yards. That kind of problem. Also converting currencies, because at that time every town had its own currency more or less, so you needed to know how to convert currencies between different places. Lots of problems of that kind. There is a long chapter on recreational problems and that is where the rabbit problem comes. There is more, I mean there is a very short chapter on algebra and there is a very short chapter on geometry. So it is really a compendium of the known mathematics of the time that he had gathered from his travels in North Africa, the Middle East.

MELVYN BRAGG: You pointed out that some of this had been going on in Islamic Spain for a couple of hundred years but would it be true to say that Fibonacci brought it to Europe in a more general and a more influential manner?

JACKIE STEDALL: He brought it to Italy. Spain was enormously influential and lots of material that eventually found its way to northern Europe actually came through Spain not through Italy. Fibonacci's book had a relatively limited circulation but it was important because it spread the numerals through Italy and eventually into France and Germany.

MELVYN BRAGG: Ron Knott, in chapters 12 or 13, or so I have been told, Fibonacci sets out various problems which are in need of mathematical solutions. One problem he talks about is the Fibonacci sequence and he uses rabbits as an illustration. Can you bring the rabbit out of the hat? Sorry.

RON KNOTT: Yes it's about doing what rabbits do naturally and he has just introduced the idea of perfect numbers. Then there is this big chapter that Jackie mentioned. It's about a whole quarter of the book and it looks as if it might have been an arithmetic exercise because it is about rabbits. You put a pair of rabbits in the field and they can reproduce after one month, and each month they produce a pair. So he says, if I put a pair in an enclosed field how many will there be in twelve months? Well, each rabbit continues to the next month. We are assuming there are no foxes around or other diseases that we hear in the news these days and so he says that after one month you have still got your original pair, they produce another pair and then the next month the original pair have produced a new pair and the pair that were there from the month before have now become reproductive and so you get one pair and then the original pair plus the new pair too, then the original pair plus the new, new pair and the original one three and it goes on in that way and these are the numbers.

Each month is a sum of the two before. It is a sum of the two before because all the rabbits that were alive the month before are still there and then all those who were alive two months ago are the ones that are reproducing. So for each one of those you get a new pair so it is the sum of the last month and the new ones from the month before. So that is why it is the sum of the two before. You are starting with a pair when you start and a pair when they are a month old, you start from one and one and it builds up in that way. It is just a very small problem in this huge chapter and, as Jackie says, he sets all sorts of practical problems about ploughing fields and cloths and things.

MELVYN BRAGG: And you end up with 377 pairs?

RON KNOTT: That's right yes. 1, 1, 2, 3, 5, 8, 13, 34, 55, 89, 144 – 1 shall stop because I have forgotten ... It was only later on that a French mathematician Eduoard Lucas, writing in the 1800s, who wrote mostly about the sequence, gave it its name. It wasn't known as the Fibonacci sequence, it was one of many sequences like the perfect number in the chapter before, the sequence of perfect numbers. Lucas was the one that gave it its name, 'Leonardo of Pisa, he calls himself Fibonacci'. We are not sure whether that means the son of the Bonacci family or the son of good fortune but that is the name that has stuck from the 1800s.

MELVYN BRAGG: Why did it take so long to get out and get taken up?

RON KNOTT: It was known before. Lucas looked at the mathematics of it and other similar sequences starting with 1 and 1. If you start with 2 and 1 you get a different sequence called the Lucas numbers: 2 and 1 were the same principle, 2 and 1 make 3, 1 and 3 make 4, 3 and 4 make 7 and those two are very much tied up mathematically. But they were known beforehand. Kepler writes about them in the 1600s. He hints at the idea of patterns in the vegetable kingdom, as he calls it, and he writes about the golden section as well which is another number related to this series. They are all very much linked together, the Fibonacci numbers, the Lucas numbers and the golden section pair of numbers really.

MELVYN BRAGG: Well, let's look at the golden ratio. Marcus du Sautoy, this golden ratio, how do you get it out of the Fibonacci sequence and what does that signify?

MARCUS DU SAUTOY: You get it if you look at the ratios of one number to the previous number. So for example 8 over 5 and you keep on doing this, so let's take the next one 13 over 8, so these fractions as you go through the section converge more and more on a special number which we call the golden ratio and the golden ratio has been studied since the ancient Greeks. It expresses what we believe as the perfect proportions for a rectangle. A rectangle is in the golden ratio if the ratio of the long side to the short side is the same as the ratio of the sum of the two sides to the long side and it is a very aesthetically pleasing sort of ratio. One starts to find it everywhere. People find it in too many places, I think, but for example the Parthenon is believed to be constructed in this beautiful ratio and a lot of frames in the Louvre for example like this sort of shape, they don't like squares, they like this rectangle.

MELVYN BRAGG: And postcards.

MARCUS DU SAUTOY: And postcards. You find it in a lot of places and Ron is showing me his ticket from the train, apparently that is in the golden ratio as well, and your credit cards and things like that. There is this relationship then, this very special ratio and the Fibonacci numbers converge on this golden ratio. And it is a very important relationship between these numbers because what mathematicians want to do is to find efficient formulae for example for calculating the Fibonacci numbers. If I want to calculate the millionth Fibonacci number I don't want to have to count all the pairs all the way up to a million because that is terribly inefficient. We are very lazy at heart, mathematicians, so the golden ratio gives you a lovely formula. You take powers of the golden ratio essentially and you can use those to get the millionth Fibonacci number without having to do any work at all. So if you are calculating and want to know what Fibonacci numbers are, the golden ratio is extremely important in capturing them.

MELVYN BRAGG: Jackie Stedall, Marcus has mentioned the ancient Greeks knowing about the golden ratio. Would Euclid write about that?

JACKIE STEDALL: The construction that Marcus is talking about appears in Euclid, in Book Six of Euclid, where Euclid sets as a problem how do you divide a line into two segments so that the ratio of the whole line to the longer segment is the same as the ratio of the longer segment to the shorter segment. This is exactly what Marcus is describing and this is quite a difficult construction in Euclid but he tells you how to do it, he explains how to do it, and it became very well known. It was known as dividing a line in extreme and mean ratio. All later mathematicians knew this because they knew Euclid very well, so it is there. I am not sure that Euclid calls it the golden ratio, I don't know where the term golden ratio comes. Plato knew about it and talked about this particular ratio.

MELVYN BRAGG: What is your view of the notion that buildings like the Parthenon followed this ratio?

JACKIE STEDALL: I don't know. As Marcus said, I think people can see this ratio too often in too many things. It does give pleasing proportions, so maybe people just built in pleasing proportions and that happens to be close to the number we now know as the golden ratio. Whether they actually had that in mind as they built is doubtful I would say, but I don't know.

MELVYN BRAGG: Does it suggest that if they didn't have Euclid in mind the very fact that they did build something which does seem to follow those proportions means that it is instinct in human beings?

JACKIE STEDALL: Yes, it is certainly an instinctive . . .

MELVYN BRAGG: Where does it come from?

JACKIE STEDALL: I don't know. I am not a psychologist.

MARCUS DU SAUTOY: It's again about growth and building things up because you can build this perfect rectangle by using the Fibonacci sequence in a way. I mean you take a 1 by 1 box and then you add on the side of that another 1 by 1 box and then you have got a 1 by 2 building. Now what do we know, we have got a number 2, so let's add a 2 by 2 box on to that, so now I have got a 2 by 3 box. Well, I have got 3 now so let's add a 3 by 3 box, so I have now got a 3 by 5 box. You can build up what is actually a sort of spiral of boxes and that natural thing is growing into a rectangle which is getting closer and closer to this golden ratio, so I think it is naturally . . .

JACKIE STEDALL: But a building like the Parthenon wouldn't have been constructed on those principles . . .

MARCUS DU SAUTOY: Absolutely not. I think that is why we are naturally drawn to this shape because it has this growth in it and that is why you start to see it all over nature as well.

MELVYN BRAGG: Ron Knott, Euclid, I am told, seemed to relate the golden ratio to the five platonic solids. Can you take us into that?

RON KNOTT: These appear in the Euclid *Elements* as well and people think that one of the aims of Euclid's thirteen books was to describe the five shapes that Plato mentions to the most symmetrical 3D shapes. In other words, if you are trying to design a dice, you want the edges to be the same length, all the angles to be the same and the faces to be identical. And so the usual shape we use is six squares to make a cube but there are five shapes; the simplest one has four faces which are regular triangles, four faces, tetrahedron; the next one is two square-based pyramids glued together on their squares and that makes eight triangular faces, the octahedron; there is the hexahedron, the cube; and there are two other ones as well, with twenty faces triangular called the icosahedrons, and then another one with twelve pentagonal faces called the dodecahedron and these are the five most symmetrical ones. If you look at the mathematics of the icosahedron and the dodecahedron it is full of ratios to do with the golden section.

MELVYN BRAGG: So was Euclid thinking about that in much the same way or was the Fibonacci sequence a refinement?

MARCUS DU SAUTOY: It is interesting. I think the golden ratio was around before the Fibonacci sequence was ever around and I think it reflects that the ancient Greeks were more interested in geometry and ratios of lines. I think you can even find this ratio in a simple pentagon and the pentagon of course was a very spiritual figure amongst the Pythagoreans. So it is interesting that then you get the numbers, these Fibonacci numbers, starting to mix in much later, in medieval times and then this connection between geometry and numbers which is a very late idea. That is really what Descartes did, to fuse geometry and numbers. Before that they were not really seen as two things together. I think that is quite an exciting moment when you see the Fibonacci numbers actually giving rise to geometry.

JACKIE STEDALL: I agree this is the extraordinary thing about it that the golden ratio was known for a long time. The Fibonacci sequence is a quite separate development. It comes from separate roots, it comes from Arabic and Indian roots whereas the golden ratio comes out of Greek mathematics and tying these two things together is very interesting. I don't know when it was first discovered that these two went together. I might just say that the ratio that Marcus is talking about, if you calculate it, it is a number which begins 1.618, I think it goes on. It is an infinite decimal. There's an exact definition for that. It is 1 plus the square root of 5 divided by 2 which the Greeks would have known. They would have known it in that form, which is a very precise measurement.

MARCUS DU SAUTOY: Which also is interesting because it is an irrational number, so although the Fibonacci numbers are giving you fractions they are the fractions which approximate but never quite meet the golden ratio.

RON KNOTT: And in fact they gave the best approximations as well to the golden section. If, as Marcus said, you take the ratios of the numbers, the larger over the smaller, you will get very quickly to 1.618 and if you take the smaller to the larger you will get 0.618. The interesting thing is that it is exactly one larger and that is what defines these two numbers very precisely and makes them unique.

MELVYN BRAGG: We will stay with Euclid for a moment, Marcus du Sautoy. Mathematician Luca Pacioli published *On Divine Proportion* in 1509, illustrated we think by his friend Leonardo da Vinci, and we have the golden ratio in that. Can you tell us about how it went over into painting?

MARCUS DU SAUTOY: Well there are certainly sketches which Leonardo made, Leonardo da Vinci rather than Leonardo da Pisa, which seemed to indicate that he was setting up proportions, for example, in faces and this is another place you can find if you want to the golden ratio, in the proportions of the structure of the face. Leonardo da Vinci had a lot of mathematical background, he drew a lot of these platonic solids as an exercise in perspective. I think again what you find is a square. If you have a square your eye is naturally drawn to the centre of the square and that is uninteresting actually. But if you have a rectangle in this golden ratio there are other focal points, partly due to the Fibonacci spiral you get with these squares.

Build up this sort of shape and there are natural places in a picture that your eye is drawn to which aren't the most obvious places that you might think, and if you look at pictures done by someone like Leonardo da Vinci you will find these four focal points. Interesting things are happening there. Now again you might say is this someone who has intuitively drawn that or has he actually programmed this in and constructed a picture which has these focal points because he knows that the golden ratio naturally draws you to these four points so he puts something interesting in those places.

MELVYN BRAGG: Would it be fair to say, Jackie Stedall, that mathematics in this period was underpinning aesthetics?

JACKIE STEDALL: I think it is difficult to say. As Marcus says, you don't know how deliberate these things were, whether this is an instinctive thing to do because it is naturally pleasing or whether there is some deliberate construction going on.

MELVYN BRAGG: Well, if we look at *The Last Supper*. That has been said to be following the rules of the golden mean. Can you tell me if you think that it does or if it could have been arrived at naturally?

JACKIE STEDALL: I really can't say. I think you can't say unless you know what the painter had in mind at the time. It's impossible to know whether it . . .

MARCUS DU SAUTOY: I would suggest they were so aware of mathematics because of perspective and how that worked and that relied on a lot of mathematics, it was full of platonic solids in the paintings of the time and so they would have known about the relationships with platonic solids to the golden ratio, so I think . . . again it is speculation but I will come off the fence and say I think they probably did know what they were doing.

JACKIE STEDALL: OK. I won't come off the fence.

RON KNOTT: No, I think I am with Jackie. I think when you look at pictures there are so many lines you can draw and somewhere in there you will find one that is more or less around .618. Now whether that is deliberate or is a product of psychology, I will sit on the fence.

MARCUS DU SAUTOY: But it is only in more modern times you find a lot of artists and composers deliberately using all these things.

JACKIE STEDALL: Yes, definitely.

MARCUS DU SAUTOY: We can't say anything about that time but we know now that a lot of composers and architects and artists like Salvador Dalí, who was deliberately using the golden ratio in some of his work.

RON KNOTT: And Corbusier as well.

MELVYN BRAGG: Ron Knott, can you tell us about the maths we touched on in the aesthetic equation. What purchase did it have on other areas of mathematics?

RON KNOTT: The Fibonacci?

MELVYN BRAGG: Yes.

RON KNOTT: Well around the 1800s in Victorian times there was a lot of interest in unifying mathematics and finding theories for things and they had noticed that the Fibonacci was appearing in nature, in plants as opposed to animals. For instance if you cut a tomato across the middle you will find it is in 2 or 3 segments but if you look at the outside there is a little green bit which has got 5, 4 is missing. If you look at a cauliflower the florets are actually in little spirals, there are about 5 spirals in one direction and 8 in another. If you look at a pineapple there are 3 fairly obvious sets of spirals on the outside, one of them is 5 spirals going round fairly shallow, 8 are a little bit steeper and 13 steeper still. In these particular numbers 4 is missing, it is very often not there in the world of nature. So when you are looking at the food we eat every day, this is a series you are eating every day when you are getting your five a day. It was defined, the Fibonacci defined the five.

It seems to be that it is to do with the packing problem. If you are trying to arrange leaves around a stem you don't really want them to overlap and cut out the sunlight or not catch the rain. If you are arranging seeds on the seed head you really want efficient packing and it was only proved relatively recently in the 1990s that the best form of packing is to do with arranging seeds with a golden section; you put .618 seeds per turn, it is a little rotating stem. This is the original stem cell at the end of a stem where the plant grows and it is as if it goes .618 of a turn and produces a new stem cell which might become a new leaf or a branch or a petal and then it goes another .618. When you plot that out, quite magically, the human eye picks up spirals near the middle, spirals in two directions, 3s and 5s, 5s and 8s, 8s and 13s and then the mathematicians have proved that is the most efficient packing no matter how large you go. There are no seeds squashed in one direction and spaces in another, so mathematically it fits into nature and there was a lot of interest in that before it was proved around the 1990s.

MARCUS DU SAUTOY: I think again it relates to this way of building up this spiral of squares. I mean if you think a cell starts off with just one cell and then it has to add something, so it adds this other cell so you get the one. Then you add, it has grown, and it needs to enlarge and actually this is why you see the Fibonacci numbers coming up in the way that snails grow. The spiral of a snail actually has the Fibonacci numbers embedded in it as well and if you take these squares and you build them up and draw a spiral through it, you see a natural shell appearing. The other one we have to mention is petals on flowers and that again seems always to be Fibonacci numbers or a double of a Fibonacci number. It is very rare plants that don't have Fibonacci numbers and if you do go out to the garden and test it in the summer and it hasn't got a Fibonacci number, I bet you it's because a petal has fallen off the flower which is how mathematicians get round exceptions.

RON KNOTT: Yes, it certainly is prevalent there in nature but actually in the plants. Not so much in animals. With animals we have got this bilateral symmetry, the mirror symmetry which is very rare in flowers and that seems to be the distinguishing factor, we can't find the golden section very much in animals. Then again you look at a fuchsia which has got four petals and a daffodil which has got six and those aren't the Fibonacci numbers.

MARCUS DU SAUTOY: The explanation for that I have heard anyway is that it is a double flower basically, it is a three on a three and a two on a two. We can find any way to get round these things.

RON KNOTT: That can be if you are an ardent Fibonaccist.

MARCUS DU SAUTOY: Well somebody did send me a picture of a flower which had seven petals on and that I can't do, I give up with that one.

JACKIE STEDALL: When you say it is not in the animal kingdom, of course there is the very famous drawing by Leonardo of the man in the Pentagon.

RON KNOTT: And his picture of Vitruvius. This is the one you see on the front of pads of paper, the man on the square in the circle, but it is very much to do with fractions. He gives a little scale at the bottom to show it was done with fractions. The whole thing about the Fibonacci numbers and the golden section is that it is an irrational number, these fractions are the best way to get at it.

MELVYN BRAGG: You have described it very reasonably in terms of packing, Ron, these numbers pack well as it were. Are there any other reasons why that numbering sequence should be so widespread?

RON KNOTT: If you look at cactus and succulents you quite often find the arrangement of the spines are 4s and 7s, 7s and 11s and in fact that gives us another sequence starting with 1 and 3, 4, 7, the same principle, add the latest two together and the next 11 and that gives us these Lucas numbers. But the thing is, no matter what two numbers you start with, start with any pair of numbers and keep adding those to get the next; all of them get to the golden section and it seems to be that mystery that is the golden section is behind this. It manifests in the Fibonacci numbers but also in the Lucas numbers.

MARCUS DU SAUTOY: I think it is an important point because mathematically this is a very important idea. This is called a recursive sequence because you use the previous numbers to build the next one in the sequence. The Fibonacci is the most simple version of that. You use the two previous, add them together and get the next one. But in mathematics, certainly in the twentieth century, we have been looking to find more complicated versions of this in many sequences of numbers. In my own work I deal with trying to count numbers of symmetries but what I am trying to do is to show that there might be a similar process to build my sequence of numbers. They are very nice sequences because you get very explicated formulas for them and so Fibonacci just kicked off this sequence, just kicks off a whole way of looking at number sequences. We are trying to find Fibonacci in as many sequences as we can of that style, recursive functions, so it is a very important mathematical idea.

JACKIE STEDALL: There are many very beautiful properties within the sequence itself as well, apart from the relation to plants.

Just looking at the numbers themselves for instance. If you take the consecutive numbers 2, 3, 5 – if you square 3 you get 9, if you multiply 2 and 5 you get 10, which is one more. This happens all the way along the sequence. If you square any of the numbers it is one more or one less than the product of the numbers either side. And there are many, many, many such properties.

MARCUS DU SAUTOY: Yes, it is amazing.

JACKIE STEDALL: Absolutely fantastic.

MARCUS DU SAUTOY: Which is why there is a whole journal, a *Fibonacci Quarterly*, which is dedicated to discovering all these weird and wonderful things.

MELVYN BRAGG: Could we have some more examples, please?

JACKIE STEDALL: Ron is the expert.

RON KNOTT: The other one is if you start from 1 and 1 as your indexing sequence, the first Fibonacci is 1, the second is 1, the third is 2 and the fourth is 3 and so on. Using that number sequence since 3 divides into 6 as just numbers, then the third Fibonacci number 2 divides into the sixth which is 8 and this happens whenever you start with that number system. So in fact the Fibonacci numbers in the prime positions are the ones that become important and this relates to Marcus's work because each of these is distinguished by a unique prime which is itself the divisor of the Fibonacci number and it acts as a marker all the way through . . .

MARCUS DU SAUTOY: Yes but there is an open problem which is there are infinitely many Fibonacci numbers which are prime numbers, indivisible numbers we don't know. Thirteen, for example. It is a Fibonacci number and it is also an indivisible prime number but it is an open problem about Fibonacci numbers.

MELVYN BRAGG: What does that mean?

MARCUS DU SAUTOY: Are there infinitely many Fibonacci numbers?

MELVYN BRAGG: No, what does 'open problem' mean?

MARCUS DU SAUTOY: It means that we don't know.

MELVYN BRAGG: It's far more elegant! I am going to use that, it's an open problem … rather than I haven't a clue. Well, why don't you know if you can calculate your Fibonacci ad infinitum, why don't you know?

MARCUS DU SAUTOY: Very good. Because I am a finite being therefore … that is a very fair point. Mathematicians are finite beings at heart and to be able to analyse an infinite sequence like this we have to find clever ways to show why infinitely often a prime will pop up and this is a mystery. The other interesting place, I think, where Fibonacci numbers come up is in generating Pythagorean triples. Pythagoras's theorem is about right-angled triangles, so you can build a right-angled triangle which has a short side three, next side four, longest side five units. Three, four, five is called a Pythagorean triangle, but if you want other examples of right-angled triangles each of whose side is integer lengths, actually it turns out the Fibonacci numbers are a wonderful way of generating these triangles, so it shows that these Fibonacci numbers are just embedded everywhere. They are embedded in geometry, they are embedded in nature, and also aesthetic things like music, architecture.

MELVYN BRAGG: It comes back to . . . it probably isn't accurate, but a fairly accurate paraphrase, Galileo said: 'I discovered the book of the universe, it is written in the language of mathematics.' That is what you seem to be saying now.

MARCUS DU SAUTOY: Yes. I think that it is nature, it is built by very simple operations which can produce things with immense complexity and the Fibonacci sequence is a very simple way of generating growth and suddenly you have a very rich sequence.

MELVYN BRAGG: Ron, you mentioned earlier Le Corbusier. Can you tell us how Le Corbusier took it on and incorporated it and made it central to his work.

RON KNOTT: It was the early 1900s and he wanted to design buildings which had a human feel, of human proportions, and so he had this model of the human which is if you look at the position of your belly button, it is about this golden section; if you raise your hand, if you look at your arm, the length of your hand to the length of your elbow looks as if it is a golden ratio and the elbow to the arm, so he formalised that in a structure called the modular and he used that to tell his architects how to design buildings. On the other hand he did say, if it is not working, if it is not really fitting then abandon it, but certainly he was trying to use it as a guiding principle in designing buildings.

MELVYN BRAGG: And once the Fibonacci sequence came out, which was centuries after it had been in its original form, it was taken up or developed. There is a Scottish biologist called D.W. Thompson's *On Growth and Form* in 1917. How did he come in on this argument?

RON KNOTT: Yes, he wrote the book *On Growth and Form*. Again, looking at the 1900s when they were trying to find principles behind things, major principles, that led to a whole growth of mathematics in the 1900s. He was writing about patterns. Can you take the shape of a horse's head and lay it to a sheep's head, they are similar. He wasn't the first to write about this. It relates to a book by Church. He was the first person in about 1910 to formalise shapes of objects in nature and then there was a big chapter in there about the golden section and the Fibonacci numbers.

They didn't know quite why they appeared but they were noting they were there and also the properties. There was another interesting property we haven't mentioned about the golden section which I call Phidian, which is usually called Phidian after Phidias, the architect who designed the sculpture in the Parthenon. If you take the powers of Fibonacci you can add the two powers; the squared plus the cubed power adds to give you the fourth power; the third and the fourth power add to give you the fifth. Well, you would expect a multiplication but you can do it with an addition and again that is a very distinctive property of these golden section numbers and perhaps it is why they are in nature. It can do multiplication by addition.

MELVYN BRAGG: The fact that it appears in many, many places, does it suggest some sort of platonic attribute, a divine form behind all this?

JACKIE STEDALL: That is too fanciful for me. I can't go there. It is not the sort of thing I can speculate about. Can I turn the question, or the conversation around because I would actually like to ask a question of these two experts, since we have them here, which is when the Fibonacci sequence was rediscovered, as it were, because Fibonacci's book, the text, wasn't published until the nineteenth century in Italy. Until then there would have been early manuscript copies but no printed editions. So where did people learn about these numbers or were they rediscovered independently by Lucas and others?

RON KNOTT: It is just a very small problem. The main thing is, as you said, the book is about arithmetic that we learn in primary schools now, and the numbers certainly went across Europe and everywhere, so it was quite influential.

MARCUS DU SAUTOY: I guess Lucas probably.

JACKIE STEDALL: But where did Lucas find it or did he rediscover for himself?

RON KNOTT: I think it is a French book and I tried to find a copy of the book and I can't.

MARCUS DU SAUTOY: Well again, Lucas. Lucas's numbers which are built in a similar way of course. The point is because they crop up in so many places there are loads. I think the other interesting place we must mention is music. Architecture you can see the way things are being built, boxes put together, you can see the Fibonacci sequence. But I think the interesting thing is that people like Bartok and Debussy who are threading it, and I think again deliberately, you see these numbers in those bars, that are building up the piece of music. And again it is the idea of starting with something simple, which a piece of music generally does, and developing themes and they are very naturally drawn to the Fibonacci sequence as a structure within which to write. I was doing some work with a composer called Dorothy Carr from New Zealand and she has a piece which just has the Fibonacci sequence as its skeleton, a cello piece, and she loves it because she sees the way it builds on the two things that have gone before, builds to create the next piece. A student of mine yesterday told me even a band in America called Tool used the Fibonacci sequence in music. It is a nice structure again because of its aesthetic growth and climax, I think.

MELVYN BRAGG: Do you think, Jackie Stedall, that more discoveries are going to be made about and through the Fibonacci sequence, that it is going to yield entrances to other areas?

JACKIE STEDALL: Undoubtedly. We certainly haven't come to the end of all that can be known about it or through it and, as Marcus said, there are open problems, there are still problems there.

MARCUS DU SAUTOY: Yes, I am trying to prove that my numbers are basically like Fibonacci numbers but I can't do it.

MELVYN BRAGG: Your numbers being what?

MARCUS DU SAUTOY: Numbers which count groups, symmetries, something completely unrelated but some of the theorems I have proved are showing that the structure of these numbers are very similar to the ones that Fibonacci used, so for a modern mathematician this style of mathematics is really important.

RON KNOTT: The Fibonacci Association in America has a journal. Every two years they have an international conference. I have been to them for a few years now and it is quite interesting to see still the development of new ideas in here. I was talking to a firm in California who are using the shapes of these sea shells with the Fibonacci, with the golden section spirals. They have taken the central one of these and made it into a rotor and it turns out to be 30 per cent more efficient than any known rotor. They have patented it for a few years. Its design is based on nature which seems to have many applications.

MARCUS DU SAUTOY: They have even found their way into popular culture because anyone who has read Dan Brown's *Da Vinci Code*, the first code you have to crack is a Fibonacci number, so I think they are really in the public imagination. What better advertisement do you want to show how important these numbers are.

JACKIE STEDALL: And there is now an English translation at last of the *Libra Abaci*, so anybody can read this for themselves and all of the other wonderful things that are in the book.

MELVYN BRAGG: Well, thank you all very much. Thank you for guiding me through that. I was fascinated. I just hope I can remember it.

TRANSMITTED: 29.11.2007

J.S. Mill

The nineteenth-century philosopher John Stuart Mill believed that 'the true philosopher is the marriage of poetry and logic'. He was one of the first thinkers to argue that a social theory must engage with ideas of culture and the internal life. He used Wordsworth to inform his social theory, he was a proto-feminist, and his treatise *On Liberty* is one of the sacred texts of liberalism.

J.S. Mill believed that action was the natural articulation of thought. He battled throughout his life for social reform and individual freedom, and was hugely influential in the extension of the vote. Few modern discussions on race, feminism, birth control, the state and human rights have not been influenced by Mill's theories.

How did Mill's utilitarian background shape his political ideas? Why did he think Romantic literature was significant to the rational structure of society? On what grounds did he argue for women's equality? And how did his notions of the individual become so central to modern social theory?

With me to discuss J.S. Mill are A.C. Grayling, Professor of Philosophy at Birkbeck College, University of London; Janet Radcliffe Richards, Reader in Boethius at the University College, London; and Alan Ryan, Professor of Politics at Oxford University.

Anthony Grayling, can you give us an idea of Mill's significance as a philosophical and political thinker?

A.C. GRAYLING: He is certainly the major British philosopher of the nineteenth century and the impact he has had on subsequent debate in all the different fields that you have just mentioned has been very considerable. You find him mentioned, cited in technical philosophical discussions in the theory of perception logic, the

535

philosophy of mathematics, not always with approval, but he is there anyway. He is certainly a very large figure in political philosophy and social philosophy. His classic *On Liberty* is a much read, much cited, much discussed book. It is a short book, a very interesting and eloquent book, very rich in topics for discussion and has been the centre of an industry, really. His influence has been enormous.

MELVYN BRAGG: When you say industry, can you elaborate that just a little?

A.C. GRAYLING: When you open the essay *On Liberty* and read the first paragraph or so and he says in it: 'I have got a very simple thesis to argue and that is that society has no right to coerce an individual other than to prevent that individual from harming others', and you might think that is a pretty straightforward thing and a worthy line too. Then it turns out immediately to have all sorts of inner, rich complexities and they have been the basis for a lot of scholarly discussion since.

MELVYN BRAGG: He was born in 1806 and was writing to the end of his life in 1873. What were the big themes of British politics at that time? What was his context?

A.C. GRAYLING: When he was born in 1806 of course the UK was at war with France and it was going through tremendous change socially and economically. It was the earliest phases of the industrial revolution. The agricultural revolution had already happened, so it was a pullulating age.

One of the important things happening was the attempt at reform let by Bentham and John Stuart Mill's father James Mill. They were the inheritors of a tradition in the eighteenth century mainly led by Dissenters who were trying to get more social justice, reform of parliament, rights for the working people, all of which had been stymied in the 1790s because of the French Revolution. And so the effort at social reform that had to reinvent itself in the early decades of the nineteenth century and John Stuart Mill was an inheritor of that.

MELVYN BRAGG: So he was riding on the back of this great wave of nationalism, industrialisation, inequality, the woman question, and he, as it were, surfed that in his work as well as going deeper in other areas.

A.C. GRAYLING: It was not just happening all around him. The people who were direct influences on him – his own father, Bentham, Ricardo, who was a big friend of his father's – were themselves at the very centre of these endeavours. After the Great Reform Bill of 1832, which extended the franchise, Mill became disillusioned by the process of reform which had been going on in the previous decades. He felt it necessary to settle down and rethink how this reform process was going to be best conducted. A lot of his best work was done later on political economy and in politics. The essay *On Liberty* and his work on Utilitarianism stems from the rethinking that he did of his legacy from Bentham and his father.

MELVYN BRAGG: Janet Radcliffe Richards, Mill was influenced by Utilitarian thinking, particularly by Jeremy Bentham, who was his godfather. Can you give us the basis of Utilitarianism and how it influenced him?

JANET RADCLIFFE RICHARDS: The essence of Utilitarianism is it gets you out of a lot of traditional ways of thinking about ethics. It has nothing to do with revealed religious ethics and it is not supposed to have anything to do with simply appealing to your intuitions about what is right and wrong. Bentham had the idea that ethics could be turned into a science where you could calculate what the right thing to do was. His idea was that you should be trying to produce happiness, which was the really important thing.

If you regarded yourself as trying to produce happiness then you had to understand the workings of the world and the workings of people in order to try to calculate the best way to produce the best outcome. It wasn't a matter of sitting with pre-existing rules in the assumption that, say, God knew how to bring about the best outcome, we actually had to do the science to work out what the best outcome was. Now there was, of course, an intuition at the root of all that which was the idea that happiness was the important thing to go for.

MELVYN BRAGG: How was it different from Hedonism?

JANET RADCLIFFE RICHARDS: It wasn't in a way, except that it contained the idea that every person's happiness counted as much as everyone else's.

MELVYN BRAGG: As I understand it, Bentham's idea of happiness was quantitative, wasn't it?

JANET RADCLIFFE RICHARDS: Are you now drawing a contrast with Mill?

MELVYN BRAGG: Yes.

JANET RADCLIFFE RICHARDS: Mill was pushing to a different kind of idea of the sort of happiness we should be aiming for. It is often said that Bentham's happiness was that of a contented pig and it is better to be a discontented human being than a contented pig, or that it is better to be a discontented Socrates than a contented fool. Mill was committed to producing the best outcome but he went for what he called 'the higher pleasures' which he thought were not just those of contented pigs. It was better to have discontent.

MELVYN BRAGG: So he made a hierarchy of pleasures?

JANET RADCLIFFE RICHARDS: Yes, he did, except that his view of the hierarchy of pleasures was that if you had experience of all of them you would go for these higher ones. This essentially means that if you had had experience of them, they would make you happier.

MELVYN BRAGG: Bentham was also interested in penal reform and the abolition of capital punishment and other great social issues. Did Mill pick up those views from him?

JANET RADCLIFFE RICHARDS: He certainly picked up the general idea of the approach to social reform and the like, but interestingly he was different on capital punishment. Mill was in favour of capital punishment but on a rather curious ground. The Utilitarian idea of punishment is that you shouldn't do harm to the person being punished just in itself because suffering is always bad. So the only justification you have for punishment is preventing worse kinds of harm. Mill had the idea that penal servitude for life, which was the alternative to capital punishment, was in fact much worse than being killed. On the other hand, people were more afraid of being killed than they were of penal servitude for life. So you actually caused less harm but at the same time deterred people more effectively with capital punishment than you did with penal servitude.

MELVYN BRAGG: Alan Ryan, Mill's father, James Mill, as I have said, was a friend and colleague of Bentham. Can you tell us what impact Bentham's ideas had on J.S. Mill's upbringing and this fabled and most singular education he gave his son?

ALAN RYAN: Mill's autobiography is Mill's own record of that education and he tells the reader that the only thing the reader is to pay any attention to about this autobiography is that it is a record of an education. It is actually in Mill's view a record of two educations, the first of which he got from his father and the second of which he got from Harriet Taylor later in life. Mill was immensely clever. People who try to calculate IQ on flimsy evidence reckon he had an IQ of 192, which is pretty high, and everybody who encountered him thought he was immensely clever. His father told him that he wasn't, persuaded him that his abilities were rather below average, and so he set about educating the boy.

This included learning Greek at the age of three, and learning how to read English by reading Greek. He could read Latin fluently by nine, he was reading Plato and Demosthenes at the age of ten, learnt logic and economics between twelve and fourteen and, as everybody said, by the age of sixteen he had an advantage of about a quarter of a century on any of his contemporaries. A lot of people thought it was bad for him, even at the time. People like Leslie Stephen said it was a pity he never learnt to play cricket. Given that he said rather unhappily in an early draft of the autobiography that he didn't actually learn how to tie his shoelaces until he was twelve, learning cricket might have been a bit difficult too. He did go to France when he was fourteen and learnt to fence and to dance, so some of the graces of life came his way.

MELVYN BRAGG: Why did his father impose that educational experiment in such a draconian fashion on this little boy? It does seem that the boy was a laboratory because the boy also had to teach his eight siblings and he was punished if they didn't answer his father's questions. It is a strange business. What is going on there? What is the purpose of it?

ALAN RYAN: It is half strange and half not. Quite a lot of Mill's contemporaries were tremendously well read by a very, very early age. Mill didn't in fact get much further in a literary direction than Macaulay did. A lot of children learnt a great deal, particularly of a literary kind, very quickly, but Mill's father was obsessed with education. This is Mill's father's side of the whole Bentham story. If what you are obsessed by is calculating the consequences of people's behaviour then one of the things you very much want is for everybody to be good at calculating consequences and you also want to know how to get people to have the right kind of aspirations and the right kind of wishes so that you can organise society in such a way that they become happy.

So there is a natural alliance between Utilitarians and the early educational theories of the nineteenth century. The people who disliked it because they thought it was too calculating and that it didn't give enough scope to the emotions included, for example, Dickens, who mocks the whole thing in his picture of Mr Gradgrind in *Hard Times*. So Bentham and James Mill in a sense were experimenting with little John Stuart but at the same time they wanted him to grow up and become a leader of advanced opinion and to push the whole reforming movement forwards.

MELVYN BRAGG: At sixteen or seventeen he already seems to have been quite a leader of opinion. As an agnostic he couldn't go to Oxford or Cambridge and so he joined his father, who worked for the East India Company, and worked for his father. At the same time he begins to write for magazines and journals. What preoccupations do we gather from his written work at that time?

ALAN RYAN: Not really very much because he is still essentially writing under the influence of his father and Bentham, so it is pretty much early simple pieces on economics and on social reform. He doesn't really begin to find his own voice until ten years later, after the nervous breakdown and when he becomes much more interested in what was happening in France and really begins to strike out on his own. What he calls his youthful propagandism he pretty much dismisses. Much of it was taken up with helping Bentham and helping his father and he himself had a very strong sense that he was really their creation.

MELVYN BRAGG: Anthony Grayling, Alan Ryan referred to the nervous breakdown when he was about twenty. Can you describe that and tell us what effect it had on his thinking?

A.C. GRAYLING: It is an interesting episode in his life because it seems not to have been much noticed by other people. It was a very internal event and the crisis of it lasted for about six months. He managed to survive that period by reading – I think it was Marmontel wasn't it? He became conscious of the fact that in life the sentiments were very important. He read a passage in which somebody's father dies, if I remember – it is a long time since I read it – and he burst into tears when he read this passage, and there is a rather Freudian connection here between that episode and his relationship with his own father. But afterwards he read Wordsworth and felt this tremendous liberating influence of Wordsworth's poetry on him and the great importance of the feelings, the emotions and the fact that they had to be wedded to the life of the mind burst in upon him and had a great effect on him. It changed his whole attitude towards the kind of work he did later.

MELVYN BRAGG: Can you elaborate on what he got from Wordsworth?

A.C. GRAYLING: I think it was the sense that there is beauty to be found in the world to which one can respond emotionally and not rationally. That there is this whole other dimension to experience that one can admit, one can allow it in and it can feed into the rational side of one's life as well as informing it as to what is really important. It had been argued often enough by people beforehand that reason by itself – this is a point that David Hume made a century before – reason by itself couldn't tell you which things to choose and value, which direction to go in in life or in some particular circumstance and that the engagement of your emotions was very important in that process.

And by the way, it is interesting mentioning Hume there, Hume also had a nervous breakdown when he was about twenty and in fact this is a very common feature of the lives of intellectuals that in early adulthood some sort of crisis of this kind happens and it happens in this transforming way. Certainly it did for Mill.

MELVYN BRAGG: Janet, Mill believed that the inner life of individuals should be linked with society in a public role. How radical was this idea, do you think, and what effect did Harriet Taylor have on his inner life?

JANET RADCLIFFE RICHARDS: Harriet Taylor had an enormous effect in showing him emotions, having very strong emotions herself, and he addressed his reasoning to link this with the public life. But one of the problems that he had to face was the extent to which you could develop the individual whilst still having the kind of social constraints which you needed for any functioning society. One of the interesting things about Mill is that he doesn't cover up any of these conflicts – he really wrestles with them. So his feeling about the individual is that what is good for the individual, is to develop as fully as he can, as fully as an individual.

He is very worried about the sort of pressures that society can impose on you and stifle your thinking. It isn't an external individual bullying you into something, it is something much more subtle that social pressures put on you. He is aware that social pressures are necessary for any functioning society but still he is trying to work out how that society can best liberate the individual at the same time.

MELVYN BRAGG: Can we link it to Harriet Taylor and say something not mentioned so far about his autobiography, which is that he doesn't mention his mother in it at all. He meets Harriet Taylor, who is already married to John Taylor, and they have a relationship which we understand is chaste and respectable. This is so as not to hurt the feelings and social standing of John Taylor. Only two years after John Taylor dies do they marry, and then it seems to be a marriage of true minds. He said she helped him, he gave her enormous credit for the work he did very soon after he met her. So did that union further drive the idea of discovering a new way to think through feeling?

JANET RADCLIFFE RICHARDS: There seems to be no doubt at all that it did, though of course he was the one with the expertise to push it into an intellectually structured form. It is interesting that he comments in his work on women how early it is in life that a boy starts to feel superior to his mother. So I presume that it is later in life that he got a sense of what women were capable of, that he fully realised quite how oppressed his mother had been with all these children.

ALAN RYAN: He clearly felt two things which in a way were a bit unkind to both of his parents. He thought that his mother had been turned into a drudge, that she had no intellectual interest, that she became incapable of sharing feelings with her children. He suppressed various passages of an early draft of the autobiography in which he said that he lacked the kind of love that he could have had from a mother who had enough sense of her own existence. Even he must have thought that reflected pretty badly on his father who, after all, was the person who turned his mother into a drudge.

And the thing about Harriet I think is that Harriet had a very strong sense that people had to live their own lives and the whole push of *On Liberty* is an argument in favour of autonomy, in favour of people saying, I have a life of my own to live, the thoughts I steer by must be my thoughts, they must be thoughts I have critically examined. I have got to work with these. It's a curious mixture of what he picks up from Wordsworth and how that pushes back against Bentham and his father because he has this two-level picture of ethics and of what moral philosophy is meant to be about. One level that he always associates with Bentham and his father is the matter-of-fact question – how do you make society work in a successful, economical, functioning fashion so that people are made happy to the extent that social arrangements can do it?

You then ask yourself the question – what would it be like for me to be truly, fully, really happy with my existence? And that, he thinks, is where the poets and other imaginative writers come in. So the intellect is doing the calculating, Bentham-like end of the story, the imagination is doing the non-calculating, receptive part of the story and that comes in with the arrival of the Romantic poets in his life. What is wonderful about it is that it is Harriet Taylor who injects a strong dose of will power into the whole thing. Instead of Mill just elevating the imagination and the receptive side of his life which he is happy to have got, there is also the responsibility to take control of it on your own behalf. *On Liberty* is a fascinating piece of work because it is very much a story about finding what is the best thing that you can do and doing it.

MELVYN BRAGG: We must remember that at this time he was working for the East India Company and in that sense he is a part-time writer, but he is beginning to produce big works. In 1843 he published *A System of Logic*. How important, how useful is that still now?

A.C. GRAYLING: We have got to say at this juncture that we are sitting here in the presence of one of the world's leading authorities on Mill, which is Alan, and Alan has written very interestingly on this subject and on the importance of the *System of Logic* for the whole of his thought. The view that Alan makes in his book which is called *Inductivism* is the idea that the method of enquiry and of proof in the natural sciences and therefore in relation to questions about improvement to society in general are all of a piece. So the *System of Logic* is a crucial piece of work for understanding the whole of Mill's thought.

In itself it is of relatively less importance in the history of technical philosophy because it came just before logic underwent a revolution at the hands of Frege and Russell later on, so that in technical respects it doesn't stand out as an enduring work. Its contribution is to discussion in the philosophy of science and especially on the notion of causation which is in effect the same thing as induction for Mill. He thought that inductive influences relied on the uniformity of nature and that nature is uniform in its actions because it is a causal network.

In that respect that point remains part of the discussion in philosophy now because causation is such an important topic. It is fragments like that that endure. But for an understanding of his work I think you really do have to go to *A System of Logic* and read it because it informs very much else of what he had to say.

MELVYN BRAGG: Janet, can I ask you when Mill and Harriet Taylor finally got married in 1851 they discovered they had TB – his seemed to be worse than hers, although she died before him. Did that act as a spur to him? He began writing feverishly, more books came out and in particular he began to work on *On Liberty*, the great book.

JANET RADCLIFFE RICHARDS: He was obviously trying to influence the world in a significant way and that was when he got very much involved in the politics that were going on at the time with the extension of the franchise and with the issues of women. He was certainly strongly motivated and inspired by the connection with Harriet Taylor. He was dealing at that time with the lead up to the Second Reform Act, so he was concerned about the extension of the franchise into the working class and also he wanted to extend the franchise to women. He wanted to achieve equality for women in other respects as well.

MELVYN BRAGG: How would you say that *On Liberty* illustrated his radicalism? Is that a fair question?

ALAN RYAN: It's an extremely fair question, but the trouble is that it just is the sacred text of a certain kind of radical individualism.

MELVYN BRAGG: Well, I am asking you in the gentlest possible fashion to unravel that. We would be delighted if you did so, instead of actually trying to duck, if it is a fair enough question.

ALAN RYAN: No, no. The trouble is it is too good a question.

MELVYN BRAGG: Flattery will get you nowhere, I am afraid.

ALAN RYAN: It is too good a question for the following reason: Mill assumes that democracy in a broad sense is the tide that is coming in and when I say 'broad sense' what I mean is that Mill thinks that what is characteristic of nineteenth-century society, and what is increasingly characteristic of it, is that it is governed by public opinion. So the actual technical form of the constitution is almost less important than the fact that all governments now are dominated by public opinion. The rise of democracy begins as a good radical movement because it resists the tyranny of kings and aristocrats and bishops and whoever but it brings with it a great danger and the great danger is that we shall all internalise public opinion in our own minds.

Instead of asking ourselves what is true, what is false, what we should do, what should we not do, we simply will get into the frame of mind of wanting to think like everybody else. This is a view that Mill shares with people you wouldn't expect him to share it with, for example Nietzsche. He gets it partly from Alexis de Tocqueville, who is frightened by America because of the American tendency for public opinion to override everything.

The radicalism of *On Liberty* is that it won't give up on the forward momentum of the movement towards democracy but it absolutely turns round and says if it is to be a real democracy and every person takes part in governing themselves and the world, it has got to have this individualist counter-pressure so that each person really sees themselves as having a life of their own.

MELVYN BRAGG: There, you see. It is answerable. You have just answered it.

A.C. GRAYLING: There is a very important chronology there to the point that Alan has just described. This is a somewhat unsung aspect of Mill and that is that he believed that the kind of self-creating progressive individual realising a rich and flourishing life of achievement was the kind of individual you could only have in a certain state of society with a certain degree of development of institutions. So for example when you read Mill on the colonies and on the barbarians and the people to whom the British Empire was carrying civilisation, he has a slightly different idea there that such faith wouldn't be . . .

MELVYN BRAGG: It is more than a slightly different idea. It is a disappointing conclusion he reaches on that, Anthony. You can protect your hero for just so long, but Mill thinks that the colonies have got to grow up to deserve democracy, he thinks they are like children and therefore until they really grow up they can't have it. But how are they going to grow up if they keep being patronised all the time? He is not the Holy Ghost.

A.C. GRAYLING: There you are, you very eloquently state both the view and the problem with the view, so I was just trying to alert people to the fact that there is this subtext that is going on. I can see Alan is bursting to get in here.

ALAN RYAN: That is absolutely true. When you find Mill talking about societies in which we can see the human race, as it were, in its infancy, one begins to twitch. There are two things to be said on the other side. One thing is that Mill is, I believe, the first writer in English who comes up with the idea of black Athena because in a spectacular controversy with Carlyle in 1850 Mill points out that so far from all blacks being designed by nature to be slaves, which is what Carlyle was cheerfully arguing, the Greeks, said Mill, had learnt their civilisation from Nilotic peoples who, as Mill says, from the sculptures and surviving records we can see to have been negroes.

So Mill's notions of the infancy of races wasn't actually racist, it was about different societies being at different places on a road towards self-government. In the case of India, Mill's notion was that you should simply hand over the government of India step by step to Indian native administrators. He was asked by the House of Lords a rather serious question. They said: 'if we educate the natives into this administration, how then will we preserve our government?' And Mill says: 'I would not think it proper that we would preserve it one instant longer than was necessary.' They were deeply shocked. The idea you had an empire in order to stop having an empire was not a very nineteenth-century thought.

A.C. GRAYLING: He wasn't a racist and he wasn't an imperialist of the bad kind. What underlies all this, and indeed goes right the way back to Bentham and James Mill's ideas about his education, was this notion of the perfectibility of man. The fact that individuals could progress, they could grow, they could school themselves into becoming something better. Some of his commentators have pointed out that he has a point when he says that the kind of liberty of the individual that he envisages in *On Liberty* really is something that would be most cherishable and best practised by somebody who was in that kind of setting.

MELVYN BRAGG: Can I turn to Janet Radcliffe Richards again? Harriet died in 1858 and he has still quite a bit of his life left. He said his life was over but he began a huge spurt of writing, some of which was published after his death. Let's focus on the extension of the franchise because that covered various areas. Women are only one of the areas that he is discussing. He became quite briefly but effectively and dramatically a member of parliament. What sort of opposition did he meet?

JANET RADCLIFFE RICHARDS: He was meeting opposition even from liberal people who were afraid of being swamped by the uneducated majority. It is an interesting aspect of Mill, it is another of these ways in which he is aware of a tension between two things that he is committed to but he doesn't fudge it. One of them is the idea that nobody can be a reliable representative of somebody else's interests. So he thinks that everybody ought to be able to speak for themselves and to that extent is keen on the idea of universal suffrage. But he also thinks that if you are not educated you can't understand enough about the facts to know how to bring about the things you are trying to achieve.

He was therefore seriously worried about the idea of all these uneducated, uninformed people having adequate weight. He suggested a version of an idea which was around at the time which was of weighted voting, that some people's votes should be worth more than others. But unlike the other people at the time he was not saying it should be the rich and landed that should have the extra votes but the educated who should have the extra votes. So he was trying to balance two things, one that nobody can speak for anybody else's interests reliably and the other than you have to be careful about education. It's a version of the aberration with the colonies to a certain extent. He did think that people who were living on poor relief and who were not contributing to society should not have the vote.

MELVYN BRAGG: Can I move on to *The Subjection of Women* in 1869? How sensibly could his views be described as feminist?

A.C. GRAYLING: I think they can, yes. The situation of women at the time was that if a woman got married she in effect became a chattel of her husband's, her property became her husband's property. If her husband beat her up she could be forced by law to go back to him and service conjugal interests. If the marriage broke down the father automatically had custody of the children. All these things meant that the situation of women at the time was appalling.

He had been made very conscious of this by Harriet Taylor, and just by looking about him, and for that reason he was passionately interested in liberating that half of humankind whose subjection was depriving the world of half its talents and half its possibilities. He believed that women should be able to work, he believed they should have the vote on the same terms as men and he was persuaded by Harriet Taylor's own experience of married life and attitudes towards the disabilities that women suffered under, that this was a profound injustice in society that really had to be remedied.

JANET RADCLIFFE RICHARDS: He was particularly concerned with the legal position of women. One of the interesting contrasts with later kinds of feminism is that he didn't go in for speculations about what the sexes were actually like by nature. He was completely agnostic about that. He thought that women were men's equals but his arguments didn't in any way depend on that. And he was particularly opposed to the arguments of the people who said that it was natural for women to be in the position they were in and, roughly speaking, he said that if something is natural, if something is what women are going to do anyway, there is no point in all these laws to stop them doing other things. You wouldn't need them. What women by nature cannot do, he said, it is quite superfluous to forbid them from doing.

He also said as regards keeping women under subjection of men in marriage, this is said to be the nature of women, but if you look at the structure of the laws you would think that this was the last thing they wanted to do, because so much effort is put into keeping them out of everything else. He was against arguments based on nature anyway. He said that the naturalism argument which – this is in a different essay – the naturalism argument only comes up when the native promptings of the mind have nothing to oppose them but reason. So he said we can't depend on ideas about the natural. His argument was therefore not that he was claiming that all men were brutal to women or they all treated them like slaves, but he did say that legally speaking they were in the same position as slaves.

It was interesting in that his arguments about the subjection of women were not large systematic theories like the other parts of the work he has been discussing. They were all arguments addressed to people whom he thought had certain ideas already and he was saying if you are going to follow these things through consistently you must recognise that the whole position of women is a complete anomaly. He said now that negro slavery has been abolished there are no slaves except the mistress of every house. This was not about how men treated women but it was about how the law treated them.

MELVYN BRAGG: We started with the idea of Utilitarianism, the greatest happiness for the greatest number, and this extraordinary education to which he was subjected. Do you think that his development as a philosopher, political thinker, thinker on social matters followed from that or did the breakdown throw him in a completely different direction?

A.C. GRAYLING: Do you know, I think it did follow. Let's go right back to the autobiography, which I think Alan has very convincingly in some of his writing shown not to be an autobiography but one of his polemical works, really, because he was trying to persuade his readers of a certain view of the nature of education and the development of the human individual. One thing that is very significant about it is this: the picture of James Mill standing over the young John Stuart Mill with a cane in his hand and forcing him to accept certain facts and so on is just wrong.

What James Mill did was to oblige John Stuart to think for himself and to such an extent indeed that sometimes when John Stuart Mill was puzzled about something and he couldn't get an answer from his father, his father said you go and work it out for yourself And it is that that remains a very living thing in John Stuart Mill later. This idea that the individual has responsibilities to himself or herself as a free agent, a self-creating agent. This, it seems to me, is a direct result of that part of his tutelage when he was a boy and you can't help but think that that at least was a rather positive aspect of it.

MELVYN BRAGG: Janet, you spoke of the influence he had in the area of women's enfranchisement. Do you see that driving straight on from then into the twentieth century?

JANET RADCLIFFE RICHARDS: Curiously not, because I think what went wrong with feminism in the twentieth century was they forgot the Mill element. Mill was, as I have said, agnostic about the differences between men and women and indeed would have been entirely agnostic about the details of the kind of arrangements that would be best for them. He did in fact think that women would choose different directions from men, and in the twentieth century this agnosticism got dropped rather as feminism slipped back into a lot of the arguments that Mill had refuted, saying that you cannot make a direct inference from the characteristics of men and women to the arrangements that there should be. A lot of feminists went back to saying we must insist that the differences between men and women are entirely socially determined because, unless we do that, if we say that they are natural, then we are stuck with the traditional set-up. Now anybody who had read Mill couldn't make that mistake. In fact, Mill is a very good introduction to political thinking because if you take people through Mill's arguments they so much like Mill's conclusions, which are very liberal, that they will accept the arguments that lead to them. Then you can use those very carefully constructed arguments to show that some of the things that are currently believed are wrong.

A.C. GRAYLING: That's a Machiavellian use of Mill.

JANET RADCLIFFE RICHARDS: It is a Machiavellian use of Mill, but it is very effective.

ALAN RYAN: The other thing I think, to end on a slightly lighter note about this, is that Mill was quite good at winning arguments by not making them at all. In *Representative Government*, for example, there is this immensely elaborate discussion of plural voting, an enormously elaborate discussion of proportional representation. The discussion of extending the franchise to women is one sentence. It points out that there is no more reason to exclude women from the vote than there would be to exclude men who happened to have red hair!

TRANSMITTED: 18.5.2006

The Divine Right of Kings

I n *Macbeth*, Malcolm describes the magic healing properties of the king:

> How he solicits heaven,
> Himself best knows; but strangely-visited people,
> All swoln and ulcerous, pitiful to the eye,
> The mere despair of surgery he cures;
> Hanging a golden lamp about their necks,
> Put on with holy prayers . . .

The idea that a monarch could heal with his touch flowed from the idea that a king was sacred, appointed by God and above the judgement of earthly powers. This is called the divine right of kings and it entered so powerfully into British culture during the seventeenth century that it shaped the pomp and circumstance of Stuart monarchs, imbued the writing of Shakespeare, provoked the political thinking of Milton and Locke and helped regicide about a century and a half before the French Revolution.

With me to discuss the divine right of kings are Justin Champion, Professor of the History of Early Modern Ideas at Royal Holloway College, University of London; Clare Jackson, Lecturer and Director of Studies in History at Trinity Hall, Cambridge; and Tom Healy, Professor of Renaissance Studies at Birkbeck College, University of London.

Justin Champion, the idea of the ruler as a God can be traced back a long way, but it became particularly important in Europe during and after the Reformation in the sixteenth century. Can you explain why it emerged so and became so powerful at that particular time?

JUSTIN CHAMPION: I think if we go back to the pre-Reformation period, the idea of divine right monarchy or divine right government is commonplace. It's an assumption, the basic tool for thinking about politics and obligations and perhaps even sovereignty. It's a theocratic argument, so it's driven in one sense by Catholic theology. With the Reformation the fracturing of that carapace of Catholic theology means if you are a Protestant country you need to think of ways of justifying the authority in your own nation. And the monarchy is the ready-made way to do that.

We can see it, for example, in the frontispiece of the Great Bible of 1540. Henry VIII represents himself as being whispered in the ear by God, the *verbum dei* is striking him on the head. It's a descending theory of government that allows a Protestant community to have direct access to God without going through the papacy. So it's sort of counterintuitive. The divine right monarchy one would think is a traditional Catholic viewpoint, but it's re-invented in a much more profound way by Protestant culture.

MELVYN BRAGG: The idea of a person being divinely inspired, being divinely given the gift to rule, had that been around the discussions in medieval and earlier times in Europe? Let's stick to Christian Europe for this discussion.

JUSTIN CHAMPION: Absolutely. In the earlier period one wants to know where authority comes from and there are really two ways of thinking about this. Either political authority ascends from the body of the people, from the community, and there are all sorts of classical traditions for thinking about that. But the dominant ideology is a descending theory of government. Government comes from God and inevitably in the medieval period there is a conflict between the sources for that voice of God – is it the papacy, which is the dominant form, or is it a civil government?

We can think of the political theory in the pre-Reformation period, perhaps all the way back to the ninth century, as being theocratic but also being a contest between civil authority, a regnum and sacred authority, a sacerdotum. So it's priest versus king. And a lot of those debates are, for example, focused on arguments about the coronation. When a king is anointed does that create a sacred authority? If it does, is it the Church that's creating the channel of grace or not? And there are a lot of very technical debates about precisely how authority is divine and how the king himself gets that authority.

MELVYN BRAGG: So even before the Reformation we have two camps. They're not what they become after the Reformation, as it were king versus pope, but there are two camps. There always seem to have been two views about this – the theocratic view and the anti-theocratic view, earthly powers and heavenly powers.

JUSTIN CHAMPION: Absolutely, and thinkers like Marsilius of Padua and William of Ockham want to recognise that secular authority has to be the root cause of sovereignty, although they don't use that word within a state. Where does obligation come from? Do we obey a king or an institution because it's created by God or because we've in some sense consented to it? So I think there are those two tensions all of the way through. That's theory, we've always got to remember this is practice as well. In any parish or in any community there will be powerful men who are not only princes and magistrates but are priests. So the conflict is one that's not only fought in the mind, it's fought out in real life, if you like.

MELVYN BRAGG: Tom Healy, just to play around with the time before the Reformation, does St Augustine – who was so influential in the Middle Ages and beyond as a theologian and as a philosopher and as a man whose ideas were followed – had he planted any ideas in this area which were taken up and were influential in the shaping of what we're talking about?

TOM HEALY: Indeed. You drew attention to this constant tension between the secular and the sacred and this is really at the heart of Augustine's most important work, his *City of God, Civitate Dei*. In that Augustine marks out two cities – the city of men and the city of God – and he suggests that human activity should be directed at the city of God. And this is ultimately, of course, to the afterlife, to where we go after we die and to some extent this means that we should not take too active a view about the conditions that we live under now, that we should be obedient. But it also supports the idea that effectively God is looking after our interests, he's directing us towards the city of God.

MELVYN BRAGG: Is there any sense in Augustine that he is talking about the place of the ruler in all of this?

TOM HEALY: Yes, because what happens within Augustine is that the city of God is not just a spiritual domain, it's also something that can be created on the earth. He feels that the city of men is fundamentally chaotic, it's tumultuous, it's filled with self-interest, whereas the city of God is interested in higher pursuits. So he posits an earthly life presided over by a ruler or a government who has divine authority and to which we fundamentally give up our rights. We agree to be governed by them. And this is a healthy form of government, a healthy form of existence, against that type of chaotic self-interested life that classical antiquity had experienced.

So he provides a powerful argument for this model through God to the monarch and then down to people. But importantly for the Renaissance, I think, Augustine also contains within his thought the very kernel that will affect a questioning of divine right and divine authority. Because what's he's anxious about is, if in the tumultuous concerns of the city of men, if excess takes place, if you have a figure who seems to be following his own appetites, is he really a godly ruler? Although there might be a claim to divine authority, in fact that might be a false claim. This haunts the Renaissance, particularly in the post-Reformation period: that although the king should and can claim divine authority, the individual monarchs might actually either be self-deceiving or deceiving their people. And so they are treacherous to God and satanic in that model.

MELVYN BRAGG: Again we have the duality. Divinity is one thing but absolutism and excess is another thing. Can I just fast forward a thousand years – I'm sorry about this – to Erasmus and bring us to the year before Luther pinned the notes to the door of the church in Wittenberg. Erasmus wrote *The Education of a Christian Prince* that came out in 1516 and he is a thinker, theologian, Dutch humanist. Can you tell us the place he occupied in this argument?

TOM HEALY: Erasmus takes up on this model that the true monarch
is a Christian monarch, someone who follows the teaching of the
Bible. He takes the idea, the classical idea, of the philosopher prince
and he says that a Christian ruler is also a philosophical ruler. In
this model of a moderate, he seeks justice and the best for his people
through moderation in his own life. And he becomes a type of ideal
model for his people. So again the excesses of appetite are put under
control and that creates a health in himself and, as a result, a healthy
nation. This is the model that God wishes, this points us towards true
government which is ultimately interested in our afterlife, pointing
us in the direction of heaven. This model is also against excessive
tyranny and Erasmus creates this ideal of what the true prince, the
true monarch, who is divinely ordained, should reflect. And then
he creates this dilemma – if a monarch is seen to be acting excessively,
can he legitimately claim divinity?

MELVYN BRAGG: 1517 marks the beginning of the Reformation.
At the end of that century, in 1597, James VI of Scotland, soon to be
James I of England, published two books, *Basilikon Doron* and *The
True Law of Free Monarchies*, in which he declared that kings even
by God Himself are called God. He was a very accomplished theologian, a fine linguist who said he'd read everything of theological
value in every European language. It's a big move forward. Can you
give us the gist of his arguments? Clare Jackson.

CLARE JACKSON: Yes. Who better to speak about the divine
right of kings than a monarch who thinks he's divinely ordained
himself? If we're interested in studying political ideas in the context in
which they're written I think the view of kingship from the throne
commands a unique fascination and relevance. And, as you say, James
publishes two major works in the 1590s while he's still King
James VI of Scotland – *The True Law of Free Monarchies*, which is more of
a theoretical work, and the *Basilikon Doron*, which is more of a manual of
kingship, a sort of *Speculum Principis, Handbook of Princes* genre.

   To understand where James is coming from ideologically we need to
go back a little into Scottish history to understand where his ideological
make-up is formed. He's born in 1566, he's crowned when he's only
thirteen months old in 1567 following the forcible deposition of his

mother Mary Queen of Scots and her forced abdication orchestrated by a group of Protestant nobles. These include George Buchanan, who thereafter assumes responsibility for James's education. Through Buchanan's writing we get an idea of the kind of intellectual experiences and theories to which James was exposed as a young child.

Buchanan also writes two major works on kingship, the *De Jure Regni apud Scotos*, which is published in 1579, probably written in the 1560s, and a *History of Scotland*. They're radically de-sacralised, they're very secular theories, they draw a lot on Ciceronian and Stoic ideas. Basically they argue that a monarch is there to serve the people, that there's a contract between ruler and ruled that's affirmed by the coronation oath and that if by any chance a ruler breaks that contract with the people then the subjects have a right and a duty to remove that monarch. Buchanan tends to see a monarch in the same way as one would see a doctor, with responsibility for the health of the body politic, and if the body politic becomes diseased one changes one's doctor. So this is the theory that's put forward to James. It's a very incendiary doctrine of tyrannicide, that subjects have the duty to depose a monarch and even kill them.

And his *History of Scotland* outlines exactly for James how this had operated right back through ancient Scottish constitutionalism. One sees a series of monarchs who, if they've gone down the path of tyranny, a virtuous citizenry has risen up and removed them. So once James achieves his majority and once he begins to rule Scotland as an adult king from the 1580s onwards, which also coincides with Buchanan's death, his intellectual project becomes one of legitimating or re-legitimating his own kingship, and rehabilitating the Scottish monarch with some of the dignity that had suffered at the hands of Mary Queen of Scots. And that expresses itself most fully in the two works *The True Law of Free Monarchies* and *Basilikon Doron*. They're both very short, they're both very readable, they're quite terse in their construction. I think there's probably four strands to *The True Law of Free Monarchies*.

MELVYN BRAGG: We'll have to move forward. Can you crack on a bit?

CLARE JACKSON: Yes. Four brief points : that monarchy is divinely ordained; that kings are accountable to God alone; that hereditary succession governs the monarchy and that subjects have no right of resistance. Those are the four points.

MELVYN BRAGG: When he came to England in 1603 he brought these ideas with him and eventually in 1611 they had a major effect on the new translation of the Bible. It was King James's Bible, it wasn't God's. So did the fact that he was on the throne of England as well as Scotland and Wales change the game in Europe, with James being so powerful?

CLARE JACKSON: I think the dynamics of the debate are slightly different. In Scotland his most prominent intellectual enemies had been the Presbyterian Church, who advanced a theocratic theory of kingship. In England there are other Puritans out there, the hotter sorts of Protestants, but they're not advancing the same kind of pretentions with the same amount of weight behind them as James had experienced in Scotland. James begins to turn his weight on the traditional enemies for divine right monarchs – the claims of the papacy – and he's quickly met by the Gunpowder Plot. He then imposes an oath of allegiance over all of his subjects. I think historians are still divided about whether or not the divine theory that James is proposing is primarily just a theory of obligation negatively advanced against the papacy or whether it's actually something more positive, a theory of sovereignty that claims for him all sorts of absolutist powers.

MELVYN BRAGG: As I understand it, Justin Champion, he was being supported by other thinkers at the time. There's the Dutch Protestant living in London called Hadrian Saravia, and he also wrote about the divine right of kings – could you tell us what he said?

JUSTIN CHAMPION: Saravia, a man who moved from Leiden to Lambeth in the cause of his career, is emblematic of the intertwined politics between religion and secular politics. Saravia is a churchman, he's hostile to all of the Protestant theories of resistance that Clare has talked about and he wants to authorise divine authority within the British state. One of the things we can see from his writings is that this theory – I think we should probably talk about an instinct rather than a theory – is incredibly bibliocentric. Romans 13 – 'obey the powers that be' – various statements in Proverbs – 'you shall obey God, my son, and the King'. The white noise, if you like, of political discourse comes from scripture. What theorists like Saravia and others are trying to do is make a connection between the way people live their lives, their religious expectations and convictions and beliefs, and the way political authority is constructed. So the strands that go in to create this ideology are not simply propositional and theoretical, they are social, they're much more part of the routine lives of everyday people.

MELVYN BRAGG: How is this being received, Justin? Is this an argument among a very few people or is it going through bishops, is it going through the priests, is it going to the country, is the country saying yes?

JUSTIN CHAMPION: I think especially after the accession of James I and the threat of the Gunpowder Plot, which becomes a great set piece for authorising allegiance and oaths of obligation, we can see . . .

MELVYN BRAGG: Gunpowder Plot sounds rather charming on Bonfire Night. It was, as it were, a terrorist attack which very nearly blew up parliament.

JUSTIN CHAMPION: Indeed, it was a huge plot and it gave a massive platform for the production of all sorts of political literature from great set pieces to tiny little pamphlets and more importantly sermons. Every week, every Sunday, and more often if you were a hot Protestant, you would get these sort of arguments preached and believed. So I think we've always got to recognise that the divine right theory of monarchy or of kingship is a basic instinct for a lot of the community.

Certainly on the continent Roman Catholic theories are incredibly hostile. So we have good modern Roman Catholics defending the papacy and old-fashioned English Protestants defending an institution of monarchy. It's a very odd period.

MELVYN BRAGG: Tom Healy, it comes into drama, spectacularly. Christopher Marlowe, *Edward II*, the first time an English king has been killed on stage, and then we have Shakespeare, *Richard II*. Out of those two can you draw us a few conclusions as to what those two playwrights and the literary world at that time were saying about the divine right?

TOM HEALY: At one level they question when it becomes legitimate to overthrow a monarch and indeed whether a monarch can or should be overthrown. Both plays deal with kings who are presented at least in the early part of the play to the audience as giving in to excessive appetite, particularly Edward II. He's made out to be too much under the control of his lover Gaveston, the relationship being homosexual itself causes disquiet among his barons. And similarly in *Richard II*, Richard is presented as a weak and often seen as an effeminate king, a figure who's incapable of ruling authoritatively and again who exceeds his apparent mandate.

But what both plays also do as they progress is to have an audience come back to start questioning this. Is the view of these figures as being really excessive borne out by what happens throughout the play? Is it not that we see those who oppose them actually creating a view of them in this way and that their authority is more absolute or God-given and unquestioned? And particularly in *Richard II*, there is a very serious issue that arises because Richard, in effect, tries to depose himself. He's forced to by Bolingbroke. Technically he resigns the crown, he's not actually forced off the throne.

But then in a very long speech and scene he questions whether this can actually be done. Given that his authority comes from God, whether he can actually give up the crown, whether there isn't something that is invested in him directly. And the play, I think, ultimately suggests that there is a wide acceptance within the public that authority does ultimately emerge from God Himself, that there is a view that this action in deposing Richard is going to have a very unfortunate legacy, it will lead to the Hundred Years War. The other issue that comes back is whether this is actually coming from God. God Himself is chastising the nation for whatever sinful, unhealthy practices it may be engaging with and therefore ultimately all of this stems from God rather than from man.

MELVYN BRAGG: It's ambiguous. Can we just take it a little bit further, Clare Jackson? In *Macbeth* we have regicide. In *Macbeth* we have the idea that the killing of a king leads to despair and the death of Macbeth and his wife. In *Hamlet* one of the reasons we are given to understand that Hamlet is prevented from or doesn't kill Claudius is because Claudius is a king and this would not only be murder, it would be an offence against God. So it's something that the playwrights have battened on to. Do you think they've battened on to it because it's such a good dramatic idea or because this is what they see as – to take up Justin's word – the instinct of the times?

CLARE JACKSON: To pick up on Justin's point, I think a lot of the ways in which divine right monarchy manifests itself can be seen in more cultural, symbolic ways. *Macbeth* is a very good example. One way of looking at *Macbeth* is to look at the relationship between a divinely ordained monarch, such as James conceives himself to be, the monarch who's watching the play – he saw the first performance – and the use of the sisters, the witches. If James, as he very prominently does, regards himself as the Lord's anointed on earth, then he's going to be the biggest enemy the Devil can have, either in England or Scotland. And James himself takes very seriously his responsibility as a divinely ordained monarch to eliminate those elements within society, i.e., witches, who represent the diabolical element.

So that scene where Macbeth goes to seek the witches' or the sisters' supernatural powers to see ahead and have their sense of prophecy would have been deeply shocking to a monarch like James who writes on demonology, who takes his own responsibility for eliminating witchcraft very seriously. James himself has presided over witchcraft trials in Scotland in an attempt to eliminate those agents of the devil. It is very interesting about *Macbeth* as well that Shakespeare does always provide alternative, more rational explanations for some of the more unintelligible of the witches' prophecies, things like the camouflaged army that marches to Dunsinane, or Macduff's unusual caesarean birth. I think the audience would have been just obliged to adjudicate between the supernatural and the rational. But it is all an indication of the way in which the divine right of kings is reinforced in these other spheres.

MELVYN BRAGG: Would it be true to say, Justin, in the context of this conversation, that the idea of divine right was a very telling factor in the eventual regicide, in the eventual public trial of and execution of an anointed king, of Charles I in 1649, an extraordinary action in the middle of the seventeenth century?

JUSTIN CHAMPION: Absolutely. I mean one of the problems is those normal Whig narratives about the execution of Charles I. They say it is some sort of strategic political battle between king and parliament. I think to capture the true horror of that moment in contemporary terms it's equivalent to the planes going into the Twin Towers. It fractured all of the cultural certainties of that period around Europe. If we believe and live in a society where everything is ordained, every hierarchy, every part of social structure, every bit of life within the family, within the Church, is given by God, any deviation from that is blasphemy. Now Charles I himself, an odd man I suspect, a very odd man, who wanted to use his majesty and his sacral authority but unfortunately didn't actually like most of his people, finds himself manoeuvred into a position where he has to claim this anointed quality.

I mean, if I give you one perhaps trivial example. Kings are therapeutic, they're anointed by God, they can cure, they can do miracles, and the great miracle in the Stuart period is the royal touch against scrofula, a sort of version of tuberculosis, very unpleasant. Kings traditionally, way back into the medieval period, could cure by touching. Charles I thought this was wonderful, it represented his divine authority, but he didn't actually like doing it because you had to touch infected, grubby people. So from the late 1620s, while proclaiming his divinity, he issued series after series of proclamations banning these events. Well, of course, once the civil conflict had broken out in the 1640s, all of his advisors say you've got to touch as many people as possible, and we can see in those encounters between divine monarch and ordinary suffering citizen the power of this theory, I think, the power of that instinct.

MELVYN BRAGG: Tom Healy, you want to come in?

TOM HEALY: What happens, I think, is that people become convinced that Charles is fundamentally rather like Satan, that Satan, who was God's first lieutenant in heaven and became the greatest traitor, is in effect now similar to the monarch of England. Charles is satanic in this way, that he who should have been rightly ruling in God's authority has become a traitor to God and that sparks off a wave of what should be done, that ultimately leads to his execution.

MELVYN BRAGG: But Charles – the execution – this is the end of the king, the end of a structure that had been going for as far as most people were concerned for ever. It immediately started a cult of Charles as a saint and martyr in the subsequent Protestant society run by Cromwell. Everything is driven out and we have *Eikon Basilike*, which you'll tell us about and tell us how important it was.

CLARE JACKSON: I think there's a big swing away from what Tom was saying. Suddenly Charles moves from being Satan personified to acquiring this saintly status, the image of a martyr. Within a week a volume of his meditations, known as *Eikon Basilike*, is published with a very dramatic frontispiece which shows a kneeling Charles lit by divine rays with a crown of thorns, very much an imitation of Christ. And a lot of those parallels between Christ's crucifixion and Charles's regicide are exploited by authors.

MELVYN BRAGG: And *Eikon Basilike* sold enormously?

CLARE JACKSON: It's an enormous bestseller and a lot of more courageous writers in the 1650s start exploiting those parallels. Both Christ and Charles had been God's representative on earth, both had been deemed to be above human censure, both had been deemed never to be able to suffer in this way and yet both had suffered at the hands of false witnesses. And they'd each been put to death in a very public manner. You could even begin to abbreviate Charles, as was often done in early modern typography, with CH, and that could also stand for Christ at the same time.

And poignantly the New Testament lesson for 30 January, the date that Charles had actually been executed, was the twenty-seventh chapter of Matthew's Gospel, which discusses Christ's trial and crucifixion. And once the Restoration occurs in 1660, 30 January becomes a fast day in the Book of Common Prayer until 1859. Even in the Alternative Service Book of 1980, Charles is reintroduced in the minor festivals. There's obviously no way of having a canonisation

process in the Anglican Church, but that's about as close as you can
get to it.

MELVYN BRAGG: But immediately what happens, Justin
Champion, is what you said at the very beginning of the programme
– the two-headed nature of the argument comes up again because
Milton writes *Iconclastes*, attacking *Eikon Basilike* and dismantling it.

JUSTIN CHAMPION: There's a long tradition of republican attacks
on *Eikon Basilike*. Clare's pointed out that this is an enormous bestseller, it's reprinted throughout the seventeenth, eighteenth and even
nineteenth centuries. And Milton's tradition is one that says this is
idolatry, and not only that, it's probably plagiarised from Sidney's
poems. Charles didn't even write it. That's something that comes out
in the 1690s, when the whole republican experiment is remembered
and redesigned. *Eikon Basilike*, Charles's text, has a perdurability of
influence that is embodied in the image of the frontispiece. And that
again manifests itself in social practice.

All of the rumours and folklore about the healing power of
Charles's blood, for example, or the little angels that you would get
when you were touched by him, persists through this period into
the eighteenth century. So we get the invention of a miraculous
monarchy. The irony again is at the very moment when his head's
chopped off, he invents an incredibly powerful persistent tradition.

MELVYN BRAGG: Let's just go little further with Milton here,
Tom Healy. Is there – can you tell us the references in *Paradise Lost*
to Charles I?

TOM HEALY: What Milton suggests is that monarchs, our earthly
monarchs, and Charles particularly, can be fundamentally diabolical.
That when Satan is thrown out of heaven and lands in hell, one of
the first things he starts doing is building his city of Pandemonium.
Which has a lot of similarities to Charles's court. There is a strong
presumption that those who support Charles and create this image
are of this diabolical camp. This great fracturing point in English
society is a fight using rather similar tools and similar ideas but
opposed to one another.

So to Milton's mind this type of earthly monarchy goes back to this idea of excess. One way that we can recognise the falsity of the monarchy, Milton is saying, is that it is unstable and excessive, it is involved in the city of man rather than the city of God. It is not what Erasmus, in *The Education of a Christian Prince*, tries to outline as a Christian prince should do, with his sense of moderation. So Charles and the Stuart monarchy in its absolutism is made out to be excessive, given over to its own appetites, not interested in the health of the nation.

MELVYN BRAGG: And yet in 1660 Charles II comes back and the fact that he comes back seems to be a resurrection of the idea of divine right. He loves to touch for King's Evil, 100,000 people turn up, it's a great event. We haven't much evidence for whether it worked or not, I don't say that sarcastically, but we don't have a great deal of evidence. But can I come to you on another point here, Clare Jackson? We've got the Restoration, not only of the Stuart monarchy but of the idea of divine right, and at the same time we have a person such as Locke beginning a very clear attack on that. Can you tell us what Locke said?

CLARE JACKSON: Locke is very directly reacting to these ideas. The first of the two treatises that's published in 1689 is very directly against a work called *Patriarcha*, published by Sir Robert Filmer. In the Restoration, as you say, the cult of divine monarchy flourishes as it's never flourished before. Robert Filmer's *Patriarcha* is published in 1680. Filmer had died in 1653, he didn't get permission to publish *Patriarcha* during the Civil War because it was seen as more royalist than the king – it was too extreme. And the reason that Locke chooses it as the target for the two treatises is because he says this is the current divinity of the times.

What Filmer does is draw a very direct parallel. He moves away from a traditional mode of arguing for divine right monarchy, of using primarily scriptural texts, to move on to much more naturalistic territory. He says Genesis gives us the evidence that kings are the fathers of their people. In Genesis it's totally fallacious to say that people are born free, everybody's born in subjection, everybody's born into families and the obedience that people owe to their fathers is exactly the same as is owed to their kings. Locke very deliberately collapses the distinction between absolute and arbitrary power that James had worked so hard to reinforce at the beginning of the seventeenth century.

In *Basilikon Doron* James had told his heir that the only way you'll understand what a king is, is to know what a tyrant is and you need to keep those two in a mutual antithesis. And Locke immediately collapses it and says this is absolute arbitrary power, it's fallacious to say that people are born in subjection, actually men are born free, they have inalienable rights, government is a construct, kings are appointed for particular offices and, if they fail, then individuals have a right of resistance. And that argument really begins to move the whole debate away from particular texts of scripture on to a much more naturalistic utilitarian basis.

JUSTIN CHAMPION: It's quite interesting though, Clare, isn't it? that many of the conceptual arguments that Locke puts together as an antidote to divine right monarchy can actually be seen being rehearsed earlier in those Catholic theorists who are opposed to Protestant divine right theories. So we've got again a counterintuitive importation of continental ideas that have already existed.

CLARE JACKSON: I think what one therefore sees is the interplay of practice and politics. I think the reason that the Catholic arguments can be discredited at the beginning of the century is because of things like the Gunpowder Plot and then they come back on to the stage again in the late 1680s.

MELVYN BRAGG: So we've brought in Locke just a little, but we have introduced him into conversation. Is the literature still tackling this idea in any significant way, Tom?

TOM HEALY: Yes. Marvell, who similarly has this equation between arbitrary power and popery and writes a tract on it, also writes a striking poem called 'Last Instructions To A Painter' in which he marks out the excesses which are taking place in court, and particularly sexual excesses, as being instrumental in the failure of the English state to defend itself in the Dutch wars. This excess coming from the monarchy and from the top is really responsible for the failure of the nation, the nation is rendered vulnerable.

And there's an astonishingly striking image at the heart of this where England, naked and dishevelled, having been battered around by all these evil kings, counsellors and so forth, comes to the monarch in the dead of night and seeks for succour, for help. England is in the shape of a naked woman. She comes penitent to the king asking to be restored. And the king rapes her. But what is most unsettling about this is that Marvell suggests that the king finds her very distressed condition the fact which causes his arousal. This is the most telling instance that the monarch is really working against the state itself, or against the spirit, against the whole nation. The monarch is actually finding the collapse of the nation in its unhealthy and its distressed state attractive to commit rapine on. This satanic image is really very, very powerful and very distasteful, as it's supposed to be.

MELVYN BRAGG: Was the accession of James II, with his Catholicism, followed by the Glorious Revolution when William of Orange came in and refused to have anything to do with this, did that kill divine right or had ideas already driven it out?

JUSTIN CHAMPION: That's a very tricky question. I mean, the theological premises of society persist right the way through the eighteenth and perhaps into the nineteenth century. The confessional basis of political citizenship is there until 1828. If you're a Catholic you can't be a good citizen. Clearly by the end of the seventeenth century the Church of England is pretty much disestablished, so that the sacred dimensions of the monarchy are also undercut. We need to remember that the rise of science is key here and even if we took something like the royal touch, from the 1660s physicians from the Royal Society start asking questions – how does the royal touch work? Well, perhaps there are natural causes. So it demystifies, disenchants monarchy.

MELVYN BRAGG: And the royal touch is the outward manifestation of the inner divinity . . .

CLARE JACKSON: And William of Orange won't have anything to do with this either.

MELVYN BRAGG: Finally, Clare, do you see the Glorious Revolution and William of Orange as bringing divine right to an effective end?

CLARE JACKSON: No. I think what's very interesting about the way in which resistance to James II occurs is that the emphasis on non-resistance is very important. Everyone's very keen to distance themselves from any notion that James II actually abdicated. None of us really resisted him. I think retrospectively the divine right of kings does acquire this dignity. It did save England from descending into some sort of popish network of inquisitorial jurisdictions. It did save us all being in some sort of Presbyterian theocracy. And also it identifies probably a non-utilitarian attachment to government that Burke picks up in the late eighteenth century, that you can't just judge governments purely on how good they are. There has to be a more emotive affection. I think that does reside through the eighteenth and into the nineteenth centuries.

JUSTIN CHAMPION: I think one of the other things we should perhaps emphasise is that the republican tradition also continues in the seventeenth and into the eighteenth century, but it's a republicanism that takes the institution of a virtuous monarchy at its core. That sounds very counterintuitive and paradoxical. But even republicans recognise in the eighteenth century in England a Protestant monarchy is the best bulwark against continental popery.

TRANSMITTED: 11.10.2007

AFTERWORD

All radio programmes are made by teams: the technical staff, the production unit and the necessary support system of the channel.

Radio 4 seems uniquely blessed in all departments. As a channel it has a place in its listeners' hearts, minds and lives which is, for some, one aspect of their identity – 'a Radio 4 listener'. You are sure that it is something they would march for, even those unaccustomed to public marching. Certainly every single listener seems its strongest guardian.

I mentioned the Controllers in the Introduction. They shared and helped inspire a remarkable dedication to the quality and integrity of their channel. There is a very old-fashioned Reithian atmosphere of public service in the studios and on the air.

Many researchers have come and moved on. Some have become producers of *In Our Time*. To avoid a list as long as your arm, I hope I will be forgiven if I pick out those who have produced the programme since it began in 1998. They make up a remarkably able and committed group. They take on often difficult subjects week after week and put them into shape for me to read and then discuss with them. They win the confidence of the contributors, I am sure, by their doggedness in telephone conversations and have no hesitation at all in landing me often enough with overload on the Friday evenings on which I receive the package of information for the following Thursday's adventure, sometimes, for them as for me, into previously uncharted terrain. When I discuss points with them it can be exhilarating, it can be tough, it is always concerned at once to clarify the subject in hand and make sure we don't simplify it. The programme is pure pleasure and paradise for an autodidact whose only regret is that in the more testing subject areas he finds that his memory after the programme will not retain some or even much of what made the programme intriguing.

Olivia Seligman was the first producer and a presiding presence for ten years afterwards. The others were Ariane Koek, Charlie Taylor, Alice Feinstein, Sarah Peters. Natasha Moir, Elaine Lester and, currently, James Cook, who has also been most helpful in the preparation of this book. I have a lot to thank him for.

I especially want to thank Ingrid Muir (Broadcast Assistant), who has been with the programme from the beginning. Somehow she also manages to do the same job for *Start The Week*. She does this by a conscientious devotion to her work and to the programmes which exemplifies what is best about those who work for the BBC. And she's a joy!

When the programme began many people did not give it more than six months. A programme in the same slot as perennial faithfuls like *Start The Week* and *Desert Island Discs*, to be monopolised by academics only a few with much or even any experience of broadcasting? Anyway, it seems to have worked. The programme holds its own with all the other two-minutes-past-nine-o'clockers and in some areas the figures compare very well. As of the end of April 2009, the figures are:

The morning version attracts 1.8 million listeners

The half-hour evening repeat attracts 317,000 listeners

Web figures are 97,000 weekly

The podcast reaches 80,000 weekly

Audio streams from listening to the archive are 36,500 weekly

The newsletter is taken by just over 34,000 weekly

On the podcasts – of which *In Our Time* was among the first the BBC tried – we've had 5.7 million cumulative downloads (July 2007–March 2009) from the entire world (including 2.8 million from the UK only).

I owe all the above information to Herakles Koumoullos (Producer, Radio 4 Interactive), who has championed us on the playing fields of new technology at every opportunity.

I believe that many of us want to scan the universe of knowledge, be party to the founding conversations and discoveries of our world, understand the depth and variety of contemporary work in the Sciences, in the

Social Sciences, in other disciplines and in the Arts and Humanities. To be able to have an overview of universal knowledge was never possible but until a few centuries ago it seemed within reach of a few great minds. Now it is out of the question. What I want *In Our Time* to do, and what all of us who make and appear in the programme try to achieve, is somehow, over the years, to bring to the table once a week in a small studio in Central London, the span and complexity, the grandeur and diversity of our world, through guides, whose life study it is.

CONTRIBUTORS

a *The Calendar*

Robert Poole, Reader in History, St Martin's College, Lancaster

Kristen Lippincott, Deputy Director, the National Maritime Museum, Greenwich

Peter Watson, Research Associate, the McDonald Institute for Archaeological Research, University of Cambridge

b *The Field of the Cloth of Gold*

John Guy, Fellow of Clare College, University of Cambridge

Steven Gunn, Fellow and Tutor in History, Merton College, University of Oxford

Penny Roberts, Senior Lecturer in History, University of Warwick

c *The Origins of Mathematics*

Ian Stewart, Professor of Mathematics and Gresham Professor of Geometry, University of Warwick

Margaret Wertheim, science writer and journalist

John D. Barrow, Professor of Applied Mathematics and Theoretical Physics, University of Cambridge

d *Witchcraft*

Alison Rowlands, Senior Lecturer in European History, University of Essex

Lyndal Roper, Fellow and Tutor in History, Balliol College, University of Oxford

577

Malcolm Gaskill, Fellow and Director of Studies in History, Churchill College, University of Cambridge

e *Socrates*

David Sedley, Laurence Professor of Ancient Philosophy, University of Cambridge
Angie Hobbs, Associate Professor of Philosophy, University of Warwick
Paul Millet, Senior Lecturer in Classics, University of Cambridge

f *Cryptography*

Simon Singh, science writer
Lisa Jardine, Professor of Renaissance Studies at Queen Mary College, University of London
Professor Fred Piper, Director of the Department of Information Security at Royal Holloway College, University of London.

g *Antimatter*

Ruth Gregory, Professor of Mathematics and Physics at the University of Durham
Frank Close, Professor of Physics, Exeter College, University of Oxford
Val Gibson, Reader in High Energy Physics, University of Cambridge.

h *Darwin: programme* 1

Jim Moore, biographer of Darwin
Steve Jones, Professor of Genetics at University College, University of London
David Norman, Fellow and Reader in Vertebrate Paleobiology, Christ's College, University of Cambridge
Colin Higgins, Assistant College Librarian, Christ's College, University of Cambridge

i *Darwin: programme* 2

David Norman, Fellow and Reader in Vertebrate Paleobiology, Christ's College, University of Cambridge

Steve Jones, Professor of Genetics, University College, University of London

Jim Moore, biographer of Darwin

Jenny Clack, Professor and Curator of Vertebrate Paleology, Zoology Museum, Cambridge

j *Darwin: programme* 3

Jim Moore, biographer of Darwin

Jim Secord, Director, the Darwin Correspondence Project

Sandy Knapp, botanist, the Natural History Museum and Botanical Secretary of the Linnaean Society

Steve Jones, Professor of Genetics, University College, University of London

Johannes Vogel, the Natural History Museum

Judith Magee, Librarian, the Natural History Museum

k *Darwin: programme* 4

Jim Moore, biographer of Darwin

Steve Jones, Professor of Genetics, University College, University of London

Nick Biddle, Garden Curator, Down House

Alison Pearn, Assistant Director, the Darwin Correspondence Project

l *Agincourt*

Anne Curry, Professor of Medieval History, Southampton University

John Watts, Fellow and Tutor in Modern History at Corpus Christi College, University of Oxford

Michael Jones, medieval historian and writer

m *Plate Tectonics*

Joe Cann, Senior Fellow, School of Earth and Environment, University of Leeds

Lynne Frostick, Director of the Hull Environment Research Institute

Richard Corfield, Visiting Senior Lecturer in Earth Sciences, the Open University

n *Kierkegaard*

John Lippitt, Professor of Ethics and Philosophy of Religion, University of Hertfordshire

Clare Carlisle, Lecturer in Philosophy, University of Liverpool

Jonathan Ree, Visiting Professor, Roehampton University and the Royal College of Art.

o *Tea*

Huw Bowen, Senior Lecturer in Economic and Social History, University of Leicester

James Walvin, Professor of History, University of York

Amanda Vickery, Reader in History at Royal Holloway College, University of London.

p *The Peasants' Revolt*

Caroline Barron, Professorial Research Fellow, Royal Holloway College, University of London

Alastair Dunn, teacher of History at Oakham School

Miri Rubin, Professor of Early Modern History, Queen Mary College, University of London

q *Black Holes*

Sir Martin Rees, Astronomer Royal, Professor of Physics and Astronomy, University of Cambridge

Jocelyn Bell Burnell, Professor of Physics, the Open University

Martin Ward, Director of the X-Ray Astronomy Group, University of Leicester, consultant at the European Space Agency

r *Avicenna*

Peter Adamson, Reader in Philosophy at King's College, University of London

Amira Bennison, Senior Lecturer in Middle Eastern and Islamic Studies, University of Cambridge

Nader El-Bizri, Affiliated Lecturer in the History and Philosophy of Science, University of Cambridge.

s *The Origins of Life*

Richard Dawkins, Charles Simonyi Professor of Public Understanding of Science, University of Oxford

Richard Corfield, Visiting Senior Lecturer at the Centre for Earth, Planetary, Space and Astronomical Research, the Open University

Linda Partridge, Biology and Bio-technology Research Council Professor at University College, University of London

t *The Siege of Constantinople*

Roger Crowley, author and historian

Judith Herrin, Professor of Late Antique and Byzantine Studies, King's College, University of London

Colin Imber, former Reader in Turkish at Manchester University

u *Alchemy*

Lauren Kassell, Lecturer in the History and Philosophy of Science, University of Cambridge,

Stephen Pumfrey, Senior Lecturer in the History of Science, University of Lancaster

Peter Forshaw, Lecturer in Renaissance Philosophies, Birkbeck College, University of London

v *Shakespeare's Language*

Frank Kermode, Julian Clarence Levi Professor Emeritus in the Humanities, Columbia University

Michael Bogdanov, theatre and film director

Germaine Greer, Professor of English and Comparative Studies, University of Warwick

w *Angels*

Valery Rees, Renaissance Scholar, the School of Economic Science
Martin Palmer, theologian and Director of the International Consultancy on Religion, Education and Culture
John Haldane, Professor of Philosophy, St Andrews University

x *The Fibonacci Sequence*

Jackie Stedall, Junior Research Fellow in History of Mathematics, Queen's College, University of Oxford
Ron Knott, Visiting Fellow, Department of Mathematics, University of Surrey
Marcus du Sautoy, Professor of Mathematics, Wadham College, University of Oxford

y *J.S. Mill*

A.C. Grayling, Professor of Philosophy, Birkbeck College, University of London
Janet Radcliffe Richards, Reader in Boethius, University College, University of London
Alan Ryan, Professor of Politics, University of Oxford

z *The Divine Right of Kings*

Justin Champion, Professor of the History of Early Modern Ideas, Royal Holloway College, University of London
Clare Jackson, Lecturer and Director of Studies in History, Trinity Hall, University of Cambridge
Tom Healy, Professor of Renaissance Studies, Birkbeck College, University of London

The contributors' positions and academic titles are correct at the transmission date of each programme.

PICTURE ACKNOWLEDGEMENTS

INDEX